OCR GCSE HISTORY

EXPLAINING THE MODE...

D1757763

POWER

- 'Power, Monarchy & Democracy' thematic study
- 'The English Reformation' depth study
- 'Castles' study of the historic environment

BEN WALSH
HANNAH DALTON
PAUL SHUTER

DYNAMIC LEARNING

HODDER EDUCATION
AN HACHETTE UK COMPANY

This resource is endorsed by OCR for use with specification OCR GCSE (9–1) in History A (Explaining the Modern World) (J410). In order to gain OCR endorsement, this resource has undergone an independent quality check. Any references to assessment and/or assessment preparation are the publisher's interpretation of the specification requirements and are not endorsed by OCR. OCR recommends that a range of teaching and learning resources are used in preparing learners for assessment. OCR has not paid for the production of this resource, nor does OCR receive any royalties from its sale. For more information about the endorsement process, please visit the OCR website, www.ocr.org.uk.

Every effort has been made to trace all copyright holders, but if any have been inadvertently overlooked, the Publishers will be pleased to make the necessary arrangements at the first opportunity.

Note: The wording and sentence structure of some written sources have been adapted and simplified to make them accessible to all pupils, while faithfully preserving the sense of the original.

Although every effort has been made to ensure that website addresses are correct at time of going to press, Hodder Education cannot be held responsible for the content of any website mentioned in this book. It is sometimes possible to find a relocated web page by typing in the address of the home page for a website in the URL window of your browser.

Hachette UK's policy is to use papers that are natural, renewable and recyclable products and made from wood grown in sustainable forests. The logging and manufacturing processes are expected to conform to the environmental regulations of the country of origin.

Orders: please contact Bookpoint Ltd, 130 Milton Park, Abingdon, Oxon OX14 4SE. Telephone: (44) 01235 827720. Fax: (44) 01235 400454. Email education@bookpoint.co.uk Lines are open from 9 a.m. to 5 p.m., Monday to Saturday, with a 24-hour message answering service. You can also order through our website: www.hoddereducation.co.uk

ISBN: 978 1 4718 6286 1

© Ben Walsh, Hannah Dalton, Paul Shuter 2016

First published in 2016 by
Hodder Education,
An Hachette UK Company
Carmelite House
50 Victoria Embankment
London EC4Y 0DZ

www.hoddereducation.co.uk

Impression number   10 9 8 7 6 5 4 3 2 1

Year   2020 2019 2018 2017 2016

Cover photo © Steve Eason/Hulton Archive/Getty Images

Illustrations by Peter Lubach and Ron Dixon

Typeset by White-Thomson Publishing Ltd

Printed in Italy

A catalogue record for this title is available from the British Library.

Contents

Prologue: The historian's mind-set

How historians work

If you think that history means reading a lot of information from a textbook and then memorising it all, you are wrong. If you try to learn history in this way, you will probably end up feeling a bit like the picture above!

Even historians get overwhelmed by the amount of historical information to be found in books, archives and other sources. They use a range of techniques to help them make sense of it all.

Focus

No historian can study every aspect of a period of history. To make the subject manageable, historians focus on particular areas. This book does the same – each of the studies focuses on selected parts of the story. In doing so we miss out other historical information, such as science and technology or the economy.

Ask questions

Historians are investigators rather than just collectors of information. They search for new information about the past in order to tackle important questions.

Historians have different interests. They do not all investigate the same questions. So when studying the Norman Conquest, for example, Historian A may be most interested in why the Normans succeeded in conquering England, while Historian B may concentrate on how big an impact the Norman Conquest had. A bit like two different builders, they use the same or similar materials but they ask different questions and tell different stories.

You will follow the same sort of process when preparing for your history exam. You need to learn the content of the specification, but you also need to practise *using this content* to answer important questions. The text in this book, as well as the Key Questions and Focus Tasks for each topic, are designed to help you think in this way.

Select

Another vital technique that historians use is selection. From all the material they study, historians must select just the parts that are relevant and useful to answer a question.

Selection is hard for a historian, but it may be even harder for you under the time pressure of an exam. You have learnt a lot of history facts and you want to show the examiner how much you know – but this is the wrong way of thinking. To begin with, you risk running out of time. Even more serious, you may end up not answering the question clearly because you have included things that are not relevant or helpful. Compare this process to a wardrobe full of clothes. You never wake up in the morning and put on every item of clothing you own! You choose what to wear depending on different factors:

- the weather
- what you will be doing that day (going to school, a wedding, a Saturday job, a sports match).

Selecting information carefully will make your writing more focused and relevant. Thinking carefully about each fact as you select what is relevant and reject what is not will also help you remember the information.

Organise

Once historians have selected the relevant information, they then have to choose what order to present it in to create a coherent argument. You must do the same. If you are responding to the question 'Why did some women get the vote in 1918?', you need to do more than simply list all the reasons. You must build an argument that shows what you think is the most important reason. Listing all the events that led up to some women being given the vote in 1918 does not necessarily explain *why* they were given it. You need to link the events to the outcomes.

Fine tune

But don't stop there. Even the most skilled historians make mistakes when they write and you might, too. When you have finished writing, re-read your text and fine tune it to make it as clear and accurate as possible. When you are about to go out, what is the last thing you do before you leave the house? Check your hair? Check your makeup? That is fine tuning. It is a history skill too, and could make a real difference to how much an examiner enjoys reading what you write.

So remember:

- focus
- ask questions
- select
- organise
- fine tune.

Keep these points in mind as you work through your course. Good luck!

Features of this book

Focus

In every topic there is a Focus box. This sets out the main events and developments that will be covered. It also highlights the issues and questions that we will help you think about and develop your views on.

Key questions

These are the questions that take a really big view of a topic. These questions will help you to prepare for the big questions at the end of your exam.

Factfile

Factfiles are more or less what they say – files full of facts! These give you important background information to a story, without interrupting the narrative too much.

Focus task

Focus Tasks are the main tasks for really making sure you understand what you are studying. They will never ask you to just write something out, take notes or show basic comprehension. These tasks challenge you to show that you know relevant historical information and can use that information to develop an argument.

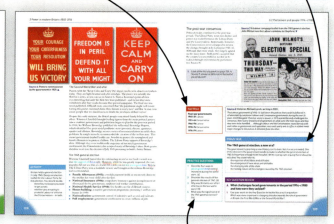

The big picture

At the start of each topic in Part 1, we summarise the big picture – in fact, since the whole thematic study is a big picture we probably should have called it 'the really big picture'! This feature sums up the big questions that historians ask about this period and their thinking about those questions. We hope that it will help you keep an overview of the period in your head and that it will be a useful revision tool.

Practice questions

These questions come at the end of major sections. They are designed to help you think about the kinds of questions you may come across in your exam. We do not know the exact questions you will be asked, but we know the *style* of question. Usually we have shown you the marks that might be available to give you a sense of how much time to spend on it. The question types are explained in the Assessment Focus sections.

Profile

Profiles are essentially factfiles about people, summarising the key facts about a historical figure.

Margin questions

These are designed to keep you on track. They usually focus on a source or a section of text to make sure you have fully understood the important points in there.

Activity

Activities help you think through a particular issue, usually as a building block towards a Focus Task.

Assessment focus

This section takes you through the types of questions in the exam paper, how they are assessed and possible ways to answer them.

Glossary and Key Terms

Glossary terms are highlighted LIKE THIS and defined in the glossary on page 240. Key Terms are listed at the end of each chapter.

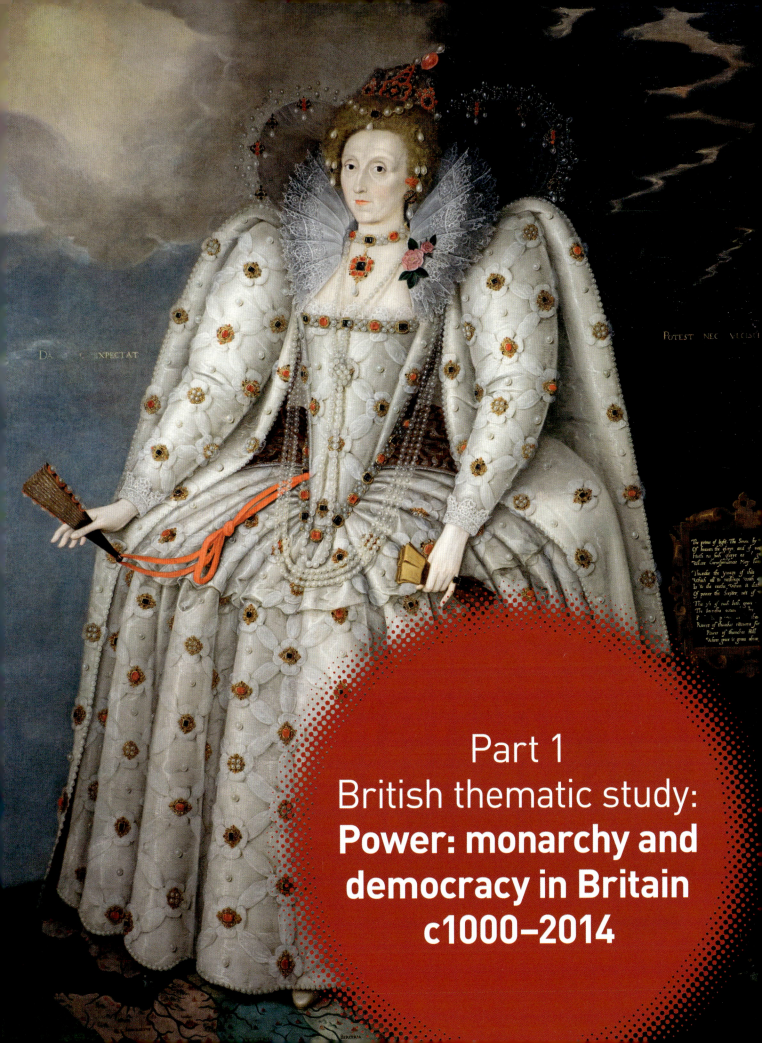

Part 1
British thematic study:
Power: monarchy and democracy in Britain c1000–2014

Introduction to the thematic study

The big picture: Power, monarchy and democracy c1000–2014

This part of the course covers the story of power – how Britain evolved from a monarchy (ruled by a king or queen) to a democracy (ruled by an elected parliament) over a period of a thousand years. It was a slow process and this is a big story! Along the way, you will meet kings, queens, nobles, bishops, members of parliament and a lot of ordinary men and women who helped change the way Britain is governed. Each chapter in this part covers a particular period in British history: medieval, early modern and modern. In each period we will focus on the following information:

Who held power.	**Why** they were so powerful at this time: their claim to power, how they gained it and how they kept hold of it.	How they **used their power**.	**What challenges** they faced in governing Britain and **how successful** they were.	**What factors, events or developments** were important in moving power from one group to another.

The key players

For most of the period 1000–2014, the key players in the story of power are the nobles (also referred to as the barons or the aristocracy) and the monarchs. People like this, who have some say in politics – even if they are only consulted about issues rather than being the decision-makers – can be described as the Political Nation. The number of people in the Political Nation has increased over time. In the modern period it also started to include a wider range of social groups. In the nineteenth and twentieth centuries, in particular, ordinary people began to have a greater say in how the country was run.

The medieval period (c1000–c1485): might is right

From around 1000 to 1485, the question of who ruled Britain was basically decided by military power and wealth (which really meant how much land someone owned). The monarch was usually the 'top noble'. That is, he came from the same social class as the barons or nobles – he was simply the strongest or the wealthiest among them.

The throne usually passed from a king to his son. However, medieval monarchs always faced the prospect of being overthrown. Some kings lost their crown in this period because they were not strong enough or politically clever enough to hold on to it. From Anglo-Saxon times to the end of the Wars of the Roses in 1485, the real claim to leadership was based on whether the ruler was strong enough to defeat his enemies.

The early modern period (c1485–c1800): divine right

After 1485, first the Tudors and then the Stuarts ruled Britain. The period immediately before this had seen a great deal of unrest, with noble families fighting each other over their claims to the throne. The Tudors tried to prevent this happening again by making the king or queen superior to the nobility. They claimed that the monarch had been appointed by God, so their right to the throne could not be challenged. The Stuarts developed this idea further and it became known as 'divine right'. Throughout this period, the nobles found it difficult to protest against the behaviour of the monarch. However, some of the Stuart monarchs failed to understand that divine right had to be balanced by co-operation and compromise. By the end of the early modern period, the power of the monarchy was in decline and parliament was becoming the most important force in British politics.

The modern period (c1800–2014): parliamentary democracy

By 1800, Britain was ruled by parliament, but it was still not a democracy. Parliament was dominated by the landowning aristocracy, and most people in Britain did not have the right to elect who represented them in parliament. Over time, other groups in society campaigned for and won the right to vote. Historians interpret these developments in different ways. Some say that parliament gradually made the country more democratic. Others argue that the people of Britain had to fight for their democratic rights and that these were forced unwillingly from the ruling classes. Either way, by the early twentieth century Britain was a democracy, with all men and women over the age of 21 able to vote (the voting age was lowered to 18 in 1969).

Problems and solutions

Running a country is easier when things are going well. Power is most likely to change hands in times of trouble. In each of the periods covered in this book, the rulers faced similar problems: war against foreign enemies, internal rivals or opposition; financial crises; and religious disagreements. If they dealt successfully with these problems they kept power; if they did not, they lost it. To ensure success, they had to raise taxes efficiently and fairly to avoid the people rebelling and spend the money wisely so they did not bankrupt the country. They had to make laws, then make sure that the whole country understood and obeyed these laws.

To achieve any of these things, rulers needed to surround themselves with people they trusted, who were loyal and could help govern effectively. Keeping this group of advisers happy was vital in maintaining power.

The successes

For much of Britain's history, the rulers got this right. Great medieval kings such as Henry II and Edward I were not only powerful, they also worked effectively with their barons. The Tudors managed to control England through a combination of force and co-operation with the great nobles. Stuart kings such as James I and Charles II also successfully kept the nobility happy. In the modern period, Britain moved towards an increasingly democratic system with relatively little violence, especially compared with other countries.

The disasters

However, not all rulers were successful. King John's leadership resulted in civil war. Later, during the Wars of the Roses, the monarchy collapsed for significant periods. The Stuart king Charles I led the country to another civil war, which ended with his execution, and his son James II was overthrown in a revolution. Lack of government action on poverty and unemployment in the years after the First World War brought real fears of a revolution in Britain, particularly in the 1930s.

SUCCESS   FAILURE

1.1 Anglo-Saxon kingship c1000–66

FOCUS

Our story of power starts 1,000 years ago in Anglo-Saxon England. In this topic, you will investigate how the country was ruled at this time. In particular, you will look at kingship – the role of the king, the power of the king and what made him successful or not.

This topic also sets up some starting-points for the big story: how a king was chosen and who else held power. One of your aims will be to compare later developments and see how power has changed.

The big picture

Power in Anglo-Saxon England

We start every topic with a summary like this – a 'big picture' overview that summarises the main points of the topic, followed by some key questions that direct your reading.

How was the king chosen?

In Anglo-Saxon England, the king was chosen by the Witan. This was a council of the richest and most important nobles (the earls) and churchmen (bishops). The king was normally the richest and most powerful of the nobles. By the 1000s, this was usually the Earl of Wessex (see Factfile), who was the biggest landowner in England. This meant that the king usually came from the ruling family of Wessex. However, there were often challenges for the throne, and kingship did not pass automatically from father to son – a brother or uncle might also inherit it.

What was the king's role?

The king's most important job was to defend the kingdom. He had the wealth to raise and pay for armies. It was also his job to protect and nurture the Church, to make laws and to ensure that everyone obeyed them. There were many able rulers in Anglo-Saxon times, but a weak ruler could cause instability in the kingdom.

What changed in this period?

In the early 1000s, Anglo-Saxon England was attacked and eventually overwhelmed by the Vikings, and in 1016 the Danish leader Cnut became king of England. However, several features of the Anglo-Saxon system of government remained in place, and many Anglo-Saxon nobles rose to even greater power under Cnut. After Cnut's death the Witan chose another king from the family of Wessex. By 1066, the Anglo-Saxons were still very much in charge of England.

How was the Anglo-Saxon state run?

Anglo-Saxon England worked on the idea of give and take. The king gave land and influential jobs to important nobles and churchmen. In return, they helped him govern the country. These men:

- advised the king through the Witan
- encouraged ordinary people to be loyal to the king
- spread information about new laws, taxes or other measures
- provided the king with troops when needed
- kept control in their own areas.

Lesser nobles (thegns) carried out the day-to-day business of government, such as collecting taxes and running law courts.

KEY QUESTIONS

Each topic presents you with lots of detailed information about events, developments and people. However, you are really interested in the *big ideas* in the story of power. These ideas are much more important than the detail when it comes to your exam. The detail will help you support your argument, but it is important to develop an understanding of the big picture. The Key Questions that start each topic are designed to help you with this.

A How did the different features of Anglo-Saxon government relate to each other?

Look at the features of Anglo-Saxon government listed below. Make a card for each feature. Add notes, definitions or details to each card as you work through the topic.

- advice
- king
- Witan
- athelings
- law
- fighting
- defending
- churchmen and women
- taxes
- earls
- thegns
- administration
- peasants

B How did Anglo-Saxon kingship work?

Copy the table below. Look at the qualifications for kingship in the Anglo-Saxon period in column 1. As you read the topic, find evidence of this qualification being imortant and record your findings in column 2. You will use column 3 to review your findings at the end of the topic.

Qualification	Evidence of this qualification being important	Relative importance – rank from most (1) to least (6)
glorious ancestors		
strong legal claim		
support of Witan and nobles		
able to protect country		
support of Church		
military power		

The real point of the research stage is to prepare you for some serious thinking. Here is the kind of question you might be asked:
Anglo-Saxon kingship was based only on military power. How far do you agree?
The question is guiding you to one aspect of Anglo-Saxon kingship: military power. However, you need to consider how important military power was and whether other factors were more or less important.

FACTFILE

A map showing Anglo-Saxon England c1000.

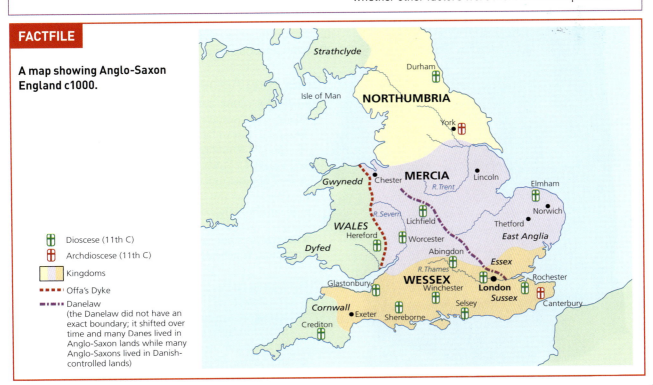

Key:
- Dioscese (11th C)
- Archdioscese (11th C)
- Kingdoms
- Offa's Dyke
- Danelaw (the Danelaw did not have an exact boundary; it shifted over time and many Danes lived in Anglo-Saxon lands while many Anglo-Saxons lived in Danish-controlled lands)

The rise of Wessex

The Anglo-Saxons were not one people. Angles and Saxons came to Britain as MIGRANTS, mainly from what are now Germany, Denmark and the Netherlands. They first invaded in around AD430, then settled in waves up to the 600s. Over time they settled and mixed with each other into the people that we call the Anglo-Saxons, or just Saxons. They did not use that name themselves. They established small, family-based communities around England, and they usually obeyed the AUTHORITY of an elected chief. Loyalty to this lord was an important feature of Anglo-Saxon society.

Some local groups gradually joined together under a common ruler, so that by AD800 there were numerous Anglo-Saxon 'kingdoms' in Britain. The four most powerful were WESSEX, East Anglia, Mercia and Northumbria. Throughout the 800s these kingdoms came under attack from the VIKINGS – formidable warriors and sailors from Denmark and Norway. In the constant wars between the Vikings and the Saxons, the kingdom of Wessex emerged as the most powerful Anglo-Saxon kingdom.

Saxon heroes

Alfred the Great (AD849–99) was the king of Wessex. He used the efficient administration of his kingdom to collect TAXES, raise armies and build a navy. He fought off the Viking invaders, but even this Saxon hero could not get rid of them completely. An uneasy peace was eventually established between Alfred and the Vikings, and they settled in northern and eastern England. This area became known as the DANELAW because many of the Vikings were from Denmark.

Athelstan (cAD894–939) united the various Saxon and Viking kingdoms by force of arms and became the first king of England. Athelstan's successors consolidated his power.

Eadgar (AD959–75) was a lawmaker rather than a conqueror. He set out laws on a wide range of issues, including theft and murder, protection of the Church and how markets and merchants should be regulated. Eadgar used his laws to unite England under his rule.

Enter King Aethelred

Aethelred (cAD968–1016) became king in AD978. He was probably very proud of his heroic ancestors Alfred and Athelstan. Just to be descended from them guaranteed that people would treat him with respect. Aethelred was ruler of a powerful kingdom with an advanced system of government and a rich cultural and SPIRITUAL life. But it was also a troubled kingdom, and these problems only increased in the years after 1000.

◄ **Source 1** A statue of Alfred the Great, which stands in his capital, Winchester.

1 Look at Source 1. What can it tell us about Alfred the Great?
2 Aethelred had capable and greatly respected ancestors such as Alfred and Athelstan. How did this help him as a ruler?
3 In what ways might having glorious ancestors have been a burden to him?

Source 2 King Athelstan presenting a book at the shrine of St Cuthbert. Books were written and illustrated by hand using expensive materials. They were very precious and cost more than a small farm. This is said to be the earliest surviving picture of an English monarch. ▼

What kind of kingdom was Aethelred's England?

By today's standards, England had a small and scattered population in the year 1000. Historians estimate that about 2.5 million people lived there, the majority of them in farmsteads and small settlements not even big enough to be called villages.

Towns and trade

About ten per cent of the population lived in towns, and this number was growing. This tells us something about Anglo-Saxon society. Businesses and workshops cannot easily be moved, and they need political stability to prosper. Towns rely on trade, which requires clear laws and a reliable system of money. Aethelred's kingdom had these things. In fact, England was famous for its efficient administration, its legal system and its coinage. Coins were minted under royal control and made from silver imported from Germany. This also suggests that trade was both efficient and prosperous – England must have given Germany something in exchange for the silver.

The Church

The Church was also flourishing by the time Aethelred came to the throne. For hundreds of years, kings and noblemen had given the Church gifts of land and money. There were important Church communities in London, York, Rochester, Canterbury and Winchester – each centred on a great church or MINSTER built with wealth donated by the king.

At a local level, most of the NOBLES provided money for churches to be built on their lands. This was not only an expression of religious faith, however. Having his 'own' church was an important status symbol for a nobleman, and a reminder to the local population of who was in charge. The church hosted community events as well as religious services, and new laws or taxes would be announced there. Building a church was often the first step towards establishing what we now think of as a typical English village.

As well as looking after the spiritual needs of the population, the Church was a source of learning, art and culture. Because many CHURCHMEN could read and write, the Church also handled many administrative roles. To work in this way, the Church must be protected by a strong and stable state. Anglo-Saxon kings developed a close relationship with the Church, partly to make people think of them as both royal and holy. In return, the Church told the ordinary people how great and generous the king was. The Church could have a great influence on the reputation of a king, as it was the churchmen who wrote down the history of a period. Many historians believe that while Alfred the Great was an effective king, it was Bishop Asser's biography that made him a real legend.

4   Look at Source 2. Why is Athelstan giving the Church such a precious gift?
5   Does this help historians to understand how important the Church was?
6   If we were trying to compare this image to a modern-day action, would it be more appropriate to say:
   –   This is like Athelstan posing for a selfie.
   –   This is like a rich businessman sponsoring a football club.

How was Anglo-Saxon England governed?

The evidence of the coins, the growth of towns and the Church all indicate that Anglo-Saxon England had an efficient system of government. This system was based on give and take.

The royal princes (sons and other relatives of the king, together known as ATHELINGS), the most important nobles (the EARLS) and the churchmen (BISHOPS) advised the king in a council known as the WITAN. These men led the armies and ruled the SHIRES (similar to modern counties) on behalf of the king. In return, they received land, wealth and status.

The next level in society was made up of the king's officials. The LESSER NOBLES, or THEGNS, carried out administrative roles such as bailiffs, estate managers or tax collectors. Shires were divided into districts called HUNDREDS. Each hundred had its own law courts and was responsible for finding and equipping a hundred troops when the king required an army. Although very few Anglo-Saxon peasants would ever see the king, they would be familiar with the officials who ruled on his behalf. At church services, the priest would tell the people about any new laws or rules, and the thegn would punish anyone who broke them.

◀ **Source 3** A coin from the reign of Aethelred, c1000 (front and back).

Source 4 An image from an old English book, showing the king and Witan passing judgement on a criminal. ▲

1 Look at Source 3. Aethelred is shown dressed in the style of Roman emperors. Why would this image be on a coin?

2 How can we tell that Christianity was an important part of Anglo-Saxon kingship?

3 The Anglo-Saxon Church was not just a religious organisation. Use the text to explain how and why this is true.

4 Historians have limited sources of information for this period, but most believe that England was fairly strong and stable in c1000. What evidence might lead them to this conclusion?

5 Study Source 4 closely.
   a What makes it so easy to tell who the king is in this source?
   b Who are the other figures shown?
   c What does the source suggest about the relationship between the king and the Witan?

A kingdom at peace?

So far we have developed a picture of a stable, peaceful and well-governed kingdom. However, as you can see from the Factfile map on page 11, this description only really applied to parts of England. There were rival kingdoms in Wales in the west and Scotland in the north, but the real threat to Aethelred's England came from the Vikings of Norway and Denmark. Aethelred's predecessors had fought battles with Viking raiders and invaders almost constantly since the AD790s. The raiders had settled in northern and eastern England (an area called the Danelaw), but by about AD950 Aethelred's father Eadgar had won back this territory.

A period of peace followed, but by AD980 Viking raiders from Denmark were again attacking the coasts of England. In AD991, Earl Brythnoth and his army were defeated by a Viking force at the Battle of Maldon, in Essex. The young King Aethelred consulted the Witan and they decided to pay off the Vikings with 10,000 pounds, a payment known as DANEGELD. The Vikings had used ports in Normandy as bases for their raids on England, so Aethelred made a TREATY with the Norman rulers in which they each agreed not to help the other's enemies. However, in AD994 the Vikings returned and had to be paid off again. This time the cost was 22,000 pounds. The raids continued through the AD990s and happened again in 1000–02.

Aethelred's problems

Aethelred was in a difficult position. He was king of England but the Viking raids highlighted the fact that most of his support still came from the old kingdom of Wessex. To extend his support from the powerful nobles of the midlands and the north, Aethelred gave them important positions in government. However, in many parts of the country the local lords felt that the king could not protect them from the Vikings.

The historian John Blair has argued that Aethelred did not manage these significant relationships very well. He trusted the wrong people and found it difficult to command the loyalty of others. As a result, the king made some bad decisions. For example, in 1002 he issued an order that all Danes living among the English should be killed. The nobles who were supposed to carry out this order ruled over many people of Danish origin and were unwilling to commit the slaughter. Many refused to do so. When some of them did, the act provoked revenge raids by the Vikings.

Viking raids continued for the next 11 years. Finally, in 1013 a full-scale invasion led by the king of Denmark, Sweyn Forkbeard, forced Aethelred to flee into EXILE in Normandy.

Aethelred the Unready?

Anglo-Saxon kings valued their reputations and wanted to be spoken of well after they died. Aethelred would have been appalled to know that he became known as 'Aethelred the Unready'. However, we should be careful about being too critical of Aethelred. To begin with, 'unready' is a mistranslation of an Old English word, *unraed*, which means 'badly advised'. Historians point out that the Witan advised the king to pay Danegeld to the Vikings when they began their attacks, and that many of Aethelred's predecessors had done the same. Some historians also argue that the scale and effectiveness of the Viking attacks – greater than those faced by any previous king – would have made it very difficult for any ruler to resist. Another fact suggesting that Aethelred was not a bad king is that when Sweyn died in 1014, the leading nobles in England refused to accept his son Cnut as their king. Instead they asked Aethelred to come back and lead them. Aethelred returned to battle Cnut for the throne, but he died in April 1016 and by October that year Cnut had conquered the country.

6 Make a list of the problems Aethelred faced during his time as king.
7 Do you think these problems would have been difficult for any leader to solve, or was Aethelred to blame for his own failures as king?
8 How does the story of Aethelred help you to understand why Anglo-Saxon kings gave money to the Church and sponsored poets and singers?

ACTIVITY

Do an internet search on Aethelred. You will see many sites that are critical of him. Make a case for his defence, using the information in this section and additional research if you have time.

PRACTICE QUESTIONS

1 Describe the Viking attacks on Anglo-Saxon England in the 1000s. (4)
2 How significant were the Viking attacks on England in the 1000s? (14)

The end of Anglo-Saxon England?

England under Cnut

Cnut executed several of Aethelred's leading supporters and gave their lands to his own loyal followers. However, most of the Anglo-Saxon nobles were allowed to keep their lands and status, and by marrying Aethelred's widow Cnut sent a clear signal that he wanted to be accepted by the Anglo-Saxon earls and thegns. In fact, Cnut had proved himself to be a great warrior king, and the Anglo-Saxons both respected this and feared that he was too strong for them to challenge anyway.

Cnut was king of Denmark and Norway as well as England, and he was often away in his other kingdoms. To help keep England stable in his absences, he divided the country into four great EARLDOMS (see the Factfile map on page 11). Northumbria and East Anglia were given to loyal Danes to rule. Mercia was given to the Anglo-Saxon Earl Siward. Wessex – the richest and most powerful earldom – went to the Anglo-Saxon Earl Godwin. Little is known about Godwin's background but he seems to have been a clever and farsighted man. He declared his loyalty to Cnut early in the king's reign and remained a capable and loyal servant, even marrying Cnut's sister. Cnut ruled over a relatively peaceful and stable England until his death in 1035.

From 1035 to 1042, there was a period of turmoil in England as the Witan tried to decide who should be the next ruler. There were four claims to the throne. Aethelred had two sons, Alfred and Edward, living in exile in Normandy. Cnut also had two sons, Harthacnut and Harold. Alfred was murdered by Godwin's men in 1036, so the following year the Witan appointed Cnut's son Harold as king. However, he died in 1039 so the Witan moved on to Harthacnut. On Harthacnut's death in 1040, the throne finally passed to Edward.

Edward the Confessor

The king who became known as Edward the Confessor was not a mighty warrior like some of his ancestors. He was a deeply religious man who was responsible for the building of some great churches, including Westminster Abbey.

Throughout Edward's reign, Anglo-Saxon England remained wealthy and well-governed. Two important developments in this period were the emergence of the position of 'shire reeve' (SHERIFF) and the use of WRITS:

- Sheriffs were usually thegns, but they had more responsibility than the thegns. In Edward's reign they began to take over all the main day-to-day functions of government, such as collecting taxes, running the law courts and making sure that other thegns in the area knew about new laws.
- Edward kept in touch with his sheriffs by sending them information in a new type of document, called a writ. Writs could contain instructions or simply provide information.

> 1 Is it surprising that the Anglo-Saxon nobles accepted Cnut?
> 2 Do you think Cnut ruled wisely? What makes you think this?
> 3 Explain why Godwin has a reputation as a clever man.

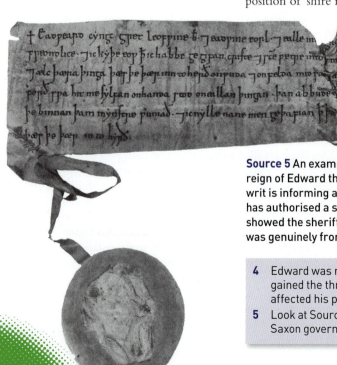

Source 5 An example of a writ from the reign of Edward the Confessor. This writ is informing a sheriff that the king has authorised a sale of land. The seal showed the sheriff that the document was genuinely from the king. ▲

> 4 Edward was not the Witan's first choice to be king of England and he gained the throne as a result of a period of turmoil. How might this have affected his position?
> 5 Look at Source 5. Explain how this type of document helped make Anglo-Saxon government efficient.

The Godwins

Edward may not have had to deal with invading Vikings, but his reign was not without challenges. England was divided into four earldoms and each of the ruling earls was very powerful, so it was vital for Edward to keep their loyalty if he wanted to rule successfully.

His greatest troubles came from Godwin in Wessex. Godwin had supported Edward's claim to the throne (although some historians think this was because he believed Edward would be a weak king whom he could dominate) and Edward married Godwin's daughter. However, the two men never saw eye to eye. To begin with, Edward could not forgive Godwin for ordering the murder of his brother. Edward had grown up in Normandy and when he became king he appointed many of his Norman friends to key positions. For example, he appointed Robert of Jumièges as ARCHBISHOP of Canterbury. Godwin and many other Anglo-Saxon nobles resented this.

The dislike between Edward and Godwin reached a climax in 1051. Godwin raised troops ready to fight the king, but Edward called on the earls of Mercia and Northumbria and they rallied their armies to support him. Godwin backed down and went into exile with his sons. However, the following year he returned at the head of a large fleet, ready to challenge Edward once again. The people of London and the thegns of much of south-east England sided with Godwin, and this time it was Edward who was forced to back down. He removed Jumièges and several other Norman officials. Edward was still king, but Godwin was effectively the ruler of England.

Godwin died in 1053. His son Harold Godwinson took over Wessex and another son, Tostig, became earl of Northumbria in 1055. This gave the Godwin family a great deal of power and influence – much more than Edward had. It did not help Edward that the Anglo-Saxon nobles respected and admired Harold and Tostig, especially after they fought a successful campaign against the Welsh king Gruffydd in 1063.

By 1064, the only power Edward had left was in choosing who would succeed him as king. He had no sons and no obvious heir. Most Anglo-Saxon nobles favoured Harold Godwinson – he was the richest and most powerful man in the country.

6 What enabled Edward to force Godwin to back down in 1051?
7 Why did Godwin triumph the following year?

Source 6 A sixteenth-century interpretation of Edward the Confessor. ▼

8 Compare Source 1 on page 12 with Source 6. These two sources show us how Alfred and Edward are remembered.
   a What qualities of each king are emphasised?
   b Which qualities were most highly prized in Anglo-Saxon England?

KEY QUESTION REVIEW

Remember – the key to success in a thematic study is not to learn lots of facts, details and events for their own sake, but to understand the big ideas to prepare for the different kind of questions you might get asked. These tasks help you do that.

A How did the different features of Anglo-Saxon government relate to each other?

1 You have been making cards to sum up different features of Anglo-Saxon society (see page 11). Use your completed cards to create a large diagram showing who did what in Anglo-Saxon England. For example, you might connect the king, Witan and advice. Use thicker lines to make really important connections and add notes on why this was so important. Take a photo of your finished chart so you can use it later for revision.

B How did Anglo-Saxon kingship work?

2 You have been gathering evidence in a table like this. Complete column 3 based on the evidence you have assembled.

Qualification	Evidence of this qualification being important	Relative importance – rank from most (1) to least (6)
glorious ancestors		
strong legal claim		
support of Witan and nobles		
able to protect country		
support of Church		
military power		

3 Use your completed table to write an essay answering this question: *Anglo-Saxon kingship was based only on military power. How far do you agree?* It can be hard to know how to get started on these big questions. Use the following table to help you.

Question	What you have to do	Ten-second answer	How to develop the ten-second answer
How did Anglo-Saxon kingship work?	Explain that military power was important but that it depended on other things.	The king's first job was to defend the country, so military power was vital. But military power depended on other things, such as the support of the Witan and nobles (who supplied troops) and support of the Church.	Build a paragraph on each aspect. In each paragraph explain how this factor made the military power possible.

ACTIVITY

For each of the following statements, say how much you agree with it on a scale of 1 (strongly agree) to 5 (strongly disagree). Use the information and sources on pages 12–17 to support your judgement.

'Anglo-Saxon England was stable and peaceful.'

'The Anglo-Saxon state had more strengths than weaknesses.'

'The Church was only important as a religious organisation.'

'Aethelred did not do anything wrong, he just faced overwhelming opposition.'

'Kings supported the Church because of their faith.'

'Cnut was a clever ruler.'

'Edward the Confessor was a strong king.'

PRACTICE QUESTIONS

1 Describe the Anglo-Saxon system of government. (4)
2 Explain why the Church was important in Anglo-Saxon England. (8)
3 Explain how Anglo-Saxon kings were chosen. (8)
4 Aethelred should be called 'Aethelred the Unlucky' rather than 'Aethelred the Unready'. Do you agree? (14)

1.2 The Norman Conquest and its impact

FOCUS

In Topic 1.1, you saw how Anglo-Saxon England was one of the richest states in Europe; it had an efficient system of government; it was relatively stable and united, especially compared with other parts of Europe at this time. Then along came the Normans and swept away the Anglo-Saxon rulers. How did this happen? Why were the Anglo-Saxons unable to resist Norman power? According to the historian David Carpenter, it was because Anglo-Saxon England was 'too successful for its own good'!

In this topic, you will examine the events of the Norman Conquest and see how this process happened. You will look at:
● how Normandy was able to defeat and then conquer an older, larger and wealthier state
● how Norman rule worked and how it changed Anglo-Saxon England.

The big picture

The Norman Conquest and its impact

Why did the Normans invade England?
England was a rich prize. It was the wealthiest state in Europe at the time. The Norman leader, Duke William, also believed he had a strong legal claim to the English throne and that the Saxon king Harold Godwinson had taken it illegally.

Why did the Norman invasion succeed?
Anglo-Saxon England was a strong kingdom with a powerful army, but in military terms the Normans were even stronger. Duke William was an able leader and his supporters were fiercely loyal to him. William was also lucky. The weather favoured him when he invaded across the Channel. At the same time his rival Harold was distracted by a Viking attack in northern England. Harold also made some mistakes.

How did the Normans gain control of England?
When Harold was killed, the Anglo-Saxons had no leader to rally round. Within a few months the leading nobles and bishops had surrendered to William. At first he allowed them to keep their lands, but rebellions soon broke out that were ruthlessly crushed. The Normans built a network of castles and William appointed loyal barons and churchmen to look after land on his behalf. The whole country was controlled by 11 men!

How far did the Norman Conquest change England?
The Norman Conquest brought change at the top of society. Virtually all Anglo-Saxon lords and thegns lost their land. The Normans changed the landscape with castles and new cathedrals and churches. They brought their own language, customs, clothing, food and many other aspects of their culture. However, the systems of law, administration and coinage remained. The majority of the population continued to speak English and carried on with their traditional farming way of life.

How and why did power change hands in this period?
Anglo-Saxon kings could be challenged by any noble who could raise enough troops and support. The Norman Conquest reinforced the idea that the throne could be won by force of arms. In this period, the personalities changed but power still lay in military strength.

KEY QUESTIONS

A Why were the Normans successful?

The table below lists several factors behind the Normans' success. Copy the table and look for evidence of each factor at work in 1066 or in the decade after as you read the topic. Record this evidence in column 2. At the end of the topic, use column 3 to rank the factors.

Factor affecting Norman success	Evidence of this factor at work	Importance (rank from most to least)
luck		
a strong legal claim		
effective leadership		
loyal support		
the Church		
military power		
mistakes		
Anglo-Saxon wealth		
Anglo-Saxon administration		
brutal suppression		
other		

The real point of the research stage is to prepare you for some serious thinking. Here is the kind of question you might be asked:
The Norman Conquest was successful because the Normans were brutal. How far do you agree?

The question is guiding you to one factor: brutality. However, you need to consider how important brutality was in the success of the Norman Conquest and whether other factors were more or less important. Your completed table and your judgement should mean you are ready to tackle this question.

B How far did the Norman Conquest change England?

The table below lists some features of Norman England. Copy the table and, as you work through the topic, look for evidence of change or continuity from Anglo-Saxon England. Add more rows if you need them.

Feature of Anglo-Saxon England	Evidence of change	Evidence of continuity
the Church		
land ownership		
government, law and administration		
life for ordinary people		
other		

As you read through the topic, think about the following question. You will answer it at the end.
The Normans did not really bring any changes to England, they simply took over what was already there. How far do you agree with this view?

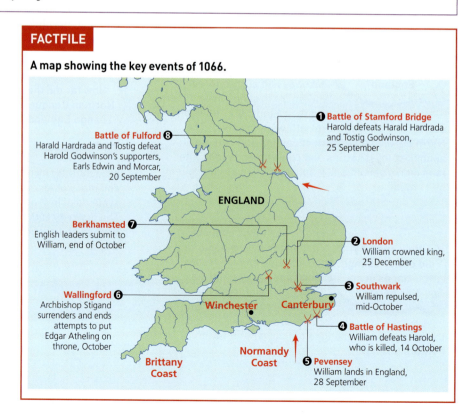

FACTFILE

A map showing the key events of 1066.

❶ **Battle of Stamford Bridge** Harold defeats Harald Hardrada and Tostig Godwinson, 25 September

❽ **Battle of Fulford** Harald Hardrada and Tostig defeat Harold Godwinson's supporters, Earls Edwin and Morcar, 20 September

ENGLAND

❼ **Berkhamsted** English leaders submit to William, end of October

❷ **London** William crowned king, 25 December

❻ **Wallingford** Archbishop Stigand surrenders and ends attempts to put Edgar Atheling on throne, October

❸ **Southwark** William repulsed, mid-October

Winchester **Canterbury**

❹ **Battle of Hastings** William defeats Harold, who is killed, 14 October

Normandy Coast

❺ **Pevensey** William lands in England, 28 September

Brittany Coast

The Norman invasion of 1066

January 1066: Harold Godwinson becomes king

When Edward the Confessor died in January 1066, Harold Godwinson became king. According to the ANGLO-SAXON CHRONICLE it was a simple succession (see Source 1). Edward's great-nephew, Edgar Atheling, had a better legal claim to the throne than Harold, but he was only 15 years old and few Anglo-Saxon nobles preferred him as king. The Witan wanted a strong leader who could defend and run the country, and Harold Godwinson was the richest and most powerful man in England. He was a proven war leader. In 1065 he had even exiled his own brother, Tostig, for ruling badly and upsetting the thegns. Harold had England united behind him.

William of Normandy claims the throne

Across the English Channel sat William, Duke of Normandy. England was extremely wealthy – the richest country in Europe – and William saw it as a tempting prize. He claimed that Edward the Confessor, who had strong links to Normandy and was distantly related to William, had promised him the English throne in 1051. He also claimed that Harold Godwinson had pledged loyalty to him in 1064. This was true, but Harold argued that this oath of loyalty was forced out of him while he was being held hostage by William after a shipwreck. To boost his claim still further, William won the support of the POPE, which allowed him to claim that God was on his side.

> **Source 1** An extract from the *Anglo-Saxon Chronicle*, published soon after 1066.
>
> *Harold Godwinson succeeded to the throne of England in 1066, just as King Edward had granted it to him and as he had been chosen for the position.*

Source 2 A scene from the Bayeux Tapestry, showing Harold promising loyalty to William of Normandy. ▼

1 Study Sources 1–3. What does each source say about William's or Harold's claim to the throne?

2 Explain the differences between the three sources and suggest reasons for these differences.

> **Source 3** Norman writer William of Jumièges, writing c1070.
>
> *Edward king of the English sent his Archbishop of Canterbury to appoint him heir to the kingdom. But he also, at a later date, sent to him Harold, the greatest of the earls in the land, to swear loyalty to the duke concerning the crown.*

War in the north and in the south

The Witan dismissed William's claim and supported Harold. However, in the brutal world of the eleventh century, the disagreement over the succession was certain to be decided by war rather than by legal justifications, family ties or papal support. Throughout 1066, William built up his forces and by August of that year he was ready to invade England. Harold prepared to fight off this threat but was dealt a massive blow when a Viking fleet from Norway landed in northern England to claim the throne for the Norwegian king, Harald Hardrada. Harald was descended from King Cnut and was supported by Tostig, Harold's exiled brother. Tostig persuaded the northern thegns to support the Viking attack.

The Vikings defeated one English army, then made camp at Stamford Bridge, near York. Harold Godwinson marched his forces north at lightning speed and took them by surprise there, killing both Hardrada and Tostig. The victorious Harold then hurried back to fight William of Normandy, who had just reached the south coast. Harold recruited a new army of foot soldiers in London and met William near Hastings on 14 October 1066. After a savage battle, with heavy casualties on both sides, the Normans triumphed and Harold Godwinson was killed.

Why was the Norman invasion in 1066 successful?

So, the Norman invasion succeeded, but why? Was it simply bad luck – Harold having to fight two enemies in a short space of time? Were the Normans the superior force on the day of the Battle of Hastings? Or was there something else about the Norman war machine that secured William's victory?

Source 4 A scene from the Bayeux Tapestry, showing the fighting at the Battle of Hastings. ▼

1 Study Source 4. The Bayeux Tapestry is a biased source as it was commissioned by William of Normandy's brother. Does this mean it is of no use to historians?
2 How far does Source 4 support what David Carpenter says in Source 5?

Source 5 Historian David Carpenter, writing in 2004.

Hastings was a killing match and the Normans had more effective means of killing: horsemen, and also archers. The lack of English archers is one of the puzzles of the battle. Only one English bowman is shown on the tapestry, the consequence perhaps of the haste with which the army had been assembled. By contrast the shields and bodies of the English bristle with Norman arrows.

Anglo-Saxon forces

In England, warfare was typically small-scale – usually to defend borders or retaliate against raids. The English had no archers. Troops were made up of:

- **housecarls:** HOUSECARLS were professional soldiers who fought on foot, usually thegns who were loyal to Harold.
- **the fyrd:** The FYRD were ordinary men called up for service. They were not fully trained or equipped as professional warriors, but that did not mean they were poor soldiers.

Norman forces

In France, warfare centred on capturing castles or moving swiftly through territory, taking control of it. Norman forces were well equipped for this kind of warfare and included:

- **knights:** KNIGHTS were nobles who fought on horseback. Their horses were weapons in their own right and the riders were skilled with swords and axes.
- **foot soldiers:** Like the fyrd, these were men called up for service to their lord. They usually carried spears and swords or knives and shields.
- **archers:** These were skilled specialists, armed with bows and arrows, who were useful in all types of warfare.

A map showing the revolts against William, 1066–75.

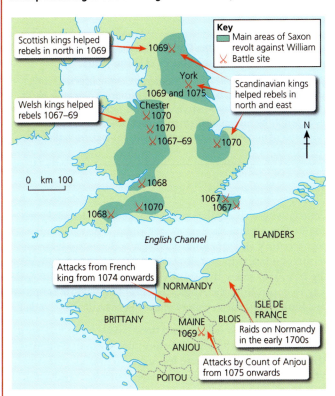

Scottish kings helped rebels in north in 1069

1069

Key
- Main areas of Saxon revolt against William
- Battle site

York
1069 and 1075

Scandinavian kings helped rebels in north and east

Chester
1070

Welsh kings helped rebels 1067–69

1070
1067–69
1070

N

0 km 100

1068

1067
1067

1070
1068

English Channel

FLANDERS

Attacks from French king from 1074 onwards

NORMANDY

ISLE DE FRANCE

BRITTANY

MAINE
1069

BLOIS

Raids on Normandy in the early 1700s

ANJOU

Attacks by Count of Anjou from 1075 onwards

POITOU

Some historians believe that while the English military system was impressive, the Norman one was even more formidable:

- Harold and his closest advisers were a tight-knit group, but William's closest lieutenants were his half-brothers and so were even more loyal to their lord. In contrast, Harold and his own brother Tostig were feuding (although he was on better terms with his other brothers).
- Harold had many well-equipped soldiers. The Normans had about the same number, but they were even better equipped.
- The Norman war machine was more flexible. William had foot soldiers, horsemen *and* archers so they could change tactics more easily than the English, who were mainly foot soldiers. English tactics had not changed much for a century.

One of the most significant factors was the experience that the Norman KNIGHTS and troops had in fighting. William of Normandy had been battling for his dukedom since he was a boy. The great lords of France were constantly at war, besieging castles as well as fighting openly. The duke of Normandy had to guard his territory against the king of France. England, meanwhile, had been relatively stable, without any serious civil war or invasion since 1016. So while Harold and the English thegns were no strangers to warfare, William and the Normans were even more experienced.

The differences between the two sides can be seen clearly in the approaches taken by Harold and William. Harold was a strong leader, as his victory against Harald Hardrada demonstrated, but by turning his forces around and marching straight back south to do battle with the Normans he risked overstretching his resources. In contrast, William refused to strike inland immediately after he landed in England. Instead he stayed near the coast, secured his supply lines to Normandy and rested his troops while waiting for Harold to come to him. This turned out to be a wise decision.

William takes the throne

Winning the Battle of Hastings did not automatically make William king of England. The Archbishop of Canterbury, Stigand, tried to rally support among the thegns for Edgar Atheling and William had to fight his way from Hastings to London to deal with this challenge. He destroyed the town of Dover, fought Anglo-Saxon forces at Canterbury and by December 1066 had set up camp just outside London. However, English forces had been greatly weakened and the thegns decided to support William's claim to the throne.

Ten weeks after his victory at Hastings – on Christmas Day, 1066 – William was crowned as king of England. But this still did not mean that he controlled the country. There were around 10,000 Normans trying to control 2 million Anglo-Saxons, most of whom were hostile to their conquerors. This hostility soon turned into rebellion. There were serious revolts against Norman rule every year between 1067 and 1075 (see the Factfile), all over the country. So how did the Normans survive and indeed thrive in England?

ACTIVITY

Create a diagram like this to record key points from the text about each method of control. Then add lines and explanations to show how these strategies connect with each other.

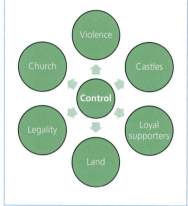

How did the Normans take control of England?

Military efficiency and ruthless violence

The Factfile on page 23 shows the many rebellions that broke out against Norman rule. Several of them were serious, but they never represented a truly united effort to overthrow the Normans. Firstly, there was no obvious leader to rally round in the way that Alfred the Great had rallied the English against the Vikings (see page 12). There was also no obvious place, such as a royal fortress, for the rebels to join forces and make a stand. Years of stability had left the English unprepared for a fight (see Source 6) and the Normans were able to deal with each rebellion as it occurred. They inflicted tens of thousands of casualties and carried out many atrocities against ordinary civilians.

At first William chose to show mercy to those who opposed him, in keeping with the Norman ideal of CHIVALRY. After the Battle of Hastings, English nobles who surrendered were not executed. In fact, William was much more merciful than the Anglo-Saxons or Vikings had traditionally been to those they defeated in battle. When the people of Exeter rose up against him, William crushed the revolt but accepted their surrender without issuing any punishment. However, as the revolts continued William began to deal more harshly with the rebels. The most serious threat came in 1069, when the northern English earls joined forces with the king of Scotland and a Viking fleet to oppose William. This time William showed no mercy – he drove off the rebel forces and sent his forces through northern England, burning homes, barns and other buildings and slaughtering animals. This event became known as the HARRYING OF THE NORTH (see Source 7).

> **Source 6** Orderic Vitalis, an English monk and chronicler, writing in the 1120s. He was of mixed parentage, so he was able to see both sides of the issue. He is one of the best sources available to historians studying this period.
>
> *In spite of their courage and their love of fighting, the English could only put up a weak defence against their enemies.*

> **Source 7** Part of a speech given by William the Conqueror shortly before he died in 1087. It was recorded by Orderic Vitalis (see Source 6) in the 1120s.
>
> *I attacked the English of the northern shires like a lion. I ordered their houses and corn, with all their implements and belongings, to be burnt without exception and large herds of cattle and beasts of burden to be destroyed wherever they were found. It was there that I took revenge on masses of people by subjecting them to a cruel famine; and by doing so – alas! – I became the murderer of many thousands, both young and old, from that fine race of people.*

1 How and why did William's attitude towards his enemies change?
2 Why was the English defence against the Normans weak?

Castles

Castles originated in France, where rival rulers often attacked and invaded each other's lands and there were few natural barriers to stop them. The castle emerged as the best way to protect territory and repel invaders. A few dozen soldiers in a castle could control the surrounding area and slow down invaders even if they were outnumbered. The Normans knew that swiftly establishing a series of castles in England would be key to controlling the Anglo-Saxons. The BAYEUX TAPESTRY shows how the Normans built a castle at Pevensey almost as soon as they landed.

By contrast the English had no castles to help defend their land – there had been no need for them in the relatively peaceful period before the Norman Conquest. There were some fortified houses, but these were too small to provide effective resistance. English towns were large and usually un-walled (another result of Anglo-Saxon prosperity). It would have required a huge number of soldiers to defend them effectively. If the Normans had been forced to besiege a series of

FACTFILE

The early phase of castle building and the Marcher lordships.

The earls of Chester, Shrewsbury and Hereford were almost independent rulers known as 'marcher lords'. Their job was to make sure there was no threat to William from Wales.

Key
- Marcher lordship
- Castle

The Bishop of Durham was given the same role in the north. His job was to stop any threat from Scotland.

N

0   km   100

Source 9 An artist's impression of how Pickering Castle in Yorkshire might have looked soon after 1066. ▼

English castles, one by one, it would have slowed the progress of the conquest and might have eventually worn down the invaders. Without them, the English had few defences.

The first Norman castles were simple buildings with ditches and wooden fences. They could be built fairly quickly, and local peasants would have been forced to construct the mottes (huge mounds of earth) and put up the defences. Back in 1066, these castles would have been a blot on the landscape, surrounded by felled trees and churned-up land. For the English it must have felt like they were being forced to build their own prisons. Each castle and the surrounding area could be defended by a small number of Norman knights, and the buildings would have stood as a constant reminder of who was now in charge.

As the Normans secured their hold in each area, they forced local people to reinforce the temporary castles to make them stronger. During the next 30 years, they built around 500 new castles (the Factfile shows the location of just some of them). William paid for this programme of castle building with a massive tax on the Church, forcing the great monasteries and cathedrals to pay for military service just like any other landholder.

> **Source 8** Historian David Carpenter, writing in 2004.
>
> *Cavalry and castles were integral to the intensely competitive military and political environment in France, where small principalities – Anjou, Maine, Brittany, Normandy, the French kingdom – were engaged in constant fast-moving warfare across great plains and open frontiers. England was very different. Since Cnut's accession in 1016 it had suffered neither invasion nor civil war. Harold had triumphed in Wales, but this was not cavalry territory. There had been no need to develop either cavalry or castles. The English state had been too successful for its own good.*

1 'William used land ownership as a weapon of conquest.' Explain how far you agree with this statement.

PRACTICE QUESTIONS

1 Describe two examples of Norman military tactics. (4)
2 Explain why the Normans were able to hold on to England after 1066 despite English resistance. (8)

A network of loyal supporters … and land

William had a close band of supporters – people he trusted and who were personally loyal to him. The inner circle was made up of William's family and closest friends, but the key to loyalty beyond this group was land. William took land away from English thegns and gave it to his loyal Norman BARONS. They then sub-divided these lands to reward *their* followers, and so on. In return for land William got loyalty. This system is sometimes known as FEUDALISM after the Latin term *feodum*, which means 'a piece of land'. However, historians today do not use the word very much and certainly nobody at the time would have used it.

You can see from the Factfile on page 25 that these loyal Normans were the key to consolidating control of England. Each area of land was controlled by a baron and his knights with their network of castles.

It says a lot about this system that after 1075 William was away fighting in France for most of the time yet Norman control in England was not seriously threatened again. As well as his barons, William had a loyal group of churchmen who helped him to administer England. Lanfranc, his Archbishop of Canterbury, effectively ran England in William's absence.

Making use of the law (legality) and Anglo-Saxon administration

In the years after the Norman Conquest, virtually all the English thegns lost their land. This change came about partly because of the widespread violence of the rebellions. However, in the process William emphasised that he was not 'seizing' England, he was simply taking up his rightful inheritance from Edward the Confessor.

Look back at Sources 2 and 3 on page 21. At face value, they explain William's claim to the throne. However, these sources were produced *after* William had come to power, so why did the Normans bother writing such accounts? They wanted to emphasise that William was acting legally. This claim to legality helped the new king in another way – he was able to persuade officials in the royal government and the sheriffs in the shires to carry out his orders on the grounds that he was now their legal master. As we have seen, the English system of government was extremely efficient in keeping law and order, raising taxes, gathering armies and carrying out royal commands through the use of writs. William now used the strength of this system to his own advantage (see Source 10). As time passed, English sheriffs and other officials were replaced by Normans, or by people who worked faithfully for Norman lords, so the process of administration became faster and easier.

Source 10 Historian Geoffrey Hindle, writing in 2006.

The shire court lies behind the success of the Norman settlement. A Norman who had been granted land by the king needed only to present himself with a sealed writ. If it was agreed to be authentic by the sheriff and other officials of the court it was accepted. The local officials had to inform the newcomer of all the lands he now owned and even help him take possession of them.

2 Look at how the Normans used the English system of government in the years after 1066. Is this an example of the Anglo-Saxon state being 'too successful for its own good'?

A new English Church

The Church in Anglo-Saxon England had been wealthy and influential. In fact, it played a key role in the Anglo-Saxon state, supporting the king and giving the English people a strong sense of identity. William also set about turning this strength to his own advantage. He got rid of the Anglo-Saxon bishops and abbots presiding over the major monasteries, and replaced them with Normans. By 1070, only three of the country's 15 bishops were English. Many churches were renamed and dedicated to different saints from those that the English people had traditionally honoured.

The Normans set about a widespread church-building programme. Over the next 50 years every single English cathedral, and most of the main abbey churches, were destroyed and rebuilt in the Norman style. These new churches were a way for the Normans to thank God for their victory, but they also helped chip away at traditional English culture and traditions.

Source 11 An image of William the Conqueror from an English chronicle produced c1250. ▼

3 Source 11 is not really trying to show what William looked like. Look at the detail and decide what features are being emphasised.
4 Study Source 12. Why do you think the Normans bothered to leave the outline of the old Cathedral?

◀ **Source 12** An aerial photograph of Winchester Cathedral. The outlines to the left of the cathedral show the layout of the old Saxon cathedral that was knocked down and replaced with this one.

Source 13 An extract from the *Anglo-Saxon Chronicle* referring to the *Domesday Book*.

[King William] sent his men over all England into every shire and had them find out how many hides [sections of land] there were in the shire, or what land and cattle the king himself had in the country or what dues he ought to have in the 12 months from the shire. He also recorded how much land his archbishops had and his bishops and his abbots and his earls how much each man who was a landholder in England had in land or livestock and how much money it was worth.

1 Look at Source 13. Before you read any further, ask yourself what questions might be answered by studying a document that records information about land ownership.

How was England changed by the Norman Conquest?

One problem for historians is that there are relatively few records dating from this period. However, on the topic of how England changed after the Norman Conquest we have one spectacular resource – the DOMESDAY BOOK – which records exactly who owned what in England in 1086.

The DOMESDAY SURVEY was carried out for practical reasons. In the 20 years after the Norman invasion almost all land in England had been seized, transferred, subdivided or sold off. Disputes over land ownership inevitably arose because land meant wealth and power. William commissioned the survey to find out exactly who had owned what in 1066 and what had changed in the two decades that followed. He used the efficient Anglo-Saxon network of scribes, officials, local courts and sheriffs to carry out the survey, and every community had to answer 20 questions set by the Domesday Commissioners. The survey was a staggering achievement, taking testimony from thousands of landowners and even peasants across the country. It was completed in less than a year.

All this information was written up in the *Domesday Book* – a source that has survived to give us valuable insight into how Norman rule changed England.

What had happened to the English nobility?

It is not clear whether William set out with the intention of wiping out the English aristocracy. Certainly in the months after the Norman invasion many thegns pledged loyalty to William and were allowed to keep their lands. However, that situation changed rapidly, probably because William wanted to reward his Norman followers by giving them English land, but also because of the rebellions against Norman rule.

The *Domesday Book* gives us a clear picture of the destruction of the English noble class. It shows that by 1086 only four major English lords survived. More than 4,000 thegns had lost their lands and had been replaced by around 200 barons who were loyal to William. The king and his ten most senior knights kept a quarter of all land for themselves. Many Anglo-Saxon lords had been killed at Hastings or in the rebellions. Many thegns had also lost their lives. Others found themselves working as tenants for Norman lords.

What had happened to ordinary people?

It is harder to know how the Norman Conquest affected people further down the social scale. Life probably became harder for many peasants. The new Norman lords wanted to recover the money they had spent in the conquest, so rents probably rose. The new landlords also imposed new conditions on their tenants. The *Domesday Book* often mentions individual freemen with the phrase 'he is now a VILLEIN' (a SERF – someone owned by the lord). After the conquest, the number of serfs rose sharply and the number of freemen declined. In Cambridgeshire, for example, the number of freemen fell from 900 to 177.

The Norman yoke?

These changes, along with the dispossession of the thegns, the changes to the Church and the way William used the Anglo-Saxon legal and administrative system to control the country, gave rise to the idea of the 'Norman yoke' on the shoulders of the English people. (A yoke is the harness worn by an ox pulling a plough; it is a heavy burden.) However, most historians express doubt that Norman rule was significantly harsher on ordinary people than Anglo-Saxon rule had been. For example, the Normans abolished slavery, under pressure from the Church. This actually cost William financially, so it was probably done for moral reasons – the king had already abolished slavery in Normandy.

Source 14 Historian Marc Morris, writing in 2012.

There is still a widespread assumption that the Normans are 'them' and the English are 'us'. The Normans are the villains of the story, introducing bad things like feudalism and the class system. The notion persists that pre-Conquest England had been freer, more liberal with representative institutions and better rights for women. But almost all of this is a myth ... the Normans come across as arrogant, warlike, pleased with themselves and holier than thou. But the English are no better with their binge drinking, slavery and political murders. Whoever these people are they are not us. They are our forebears from 1000 years ago.

Source 15 The Great Seal of William the Conqueror. ▼

ACTIVITY

Study Source 15 carefully. Make sure you examine both sides of the seal. Write a commentary to go with this seal to explain to museum visitors what they can see. You will need to:

- compare it with the coin of the Anglo-Saxon king Aethelred on page 14
- explain the main message of each side of the coin and the details that make up the message (for example, why the king is shown on a horse).

Present the commentary as written work or a slideshow.

KEY QUESTION REVIEW

A Why were the Normans successful?

1 You have been gathering evidence about a range of factors (see page 20). Complete your table by ranking the factors. Then use your table to complete one of these tasks:

Either: A TV company wants you to make a 30-minute documentary to explain the Norman success from 1066 to 1087. Prepare a plan for the documentary. You will need to include all the elements in your table but it is up to you how long you give to each element and what you include in each section. Make a plan for how to divide up the time. You could produce a written piece of work or a storyboard.

Or: Answer this essay question:
The Norman Conquest was successful because the Normans were brutal. How far do you agree?

B How far did the Norman Conquest change England?

2 Review your table of change and continuity from page 20. Use your work to answer one of these questions:

a 'The Normans did not really bring any changes to England; they simply took over what was already there.' How far do you agree with this view?

b How far did the Norman Conquest change England after 1066?

PRACTICE QUESTIONS

1 Describe two examples of the effects of the Norman Conquest. (4)
2 Explain why the Norman invasion was successful in 1066. (8)
3 How significant was the Norman Conquest for England? (14)

1.3

A constant struggle for power: who ruled in the medieval period?

FOCUS

There were still challenges for political power in England after the Norman Conquest, but most of these were internal struggles rather than threats from abroad. In this topic, you will examine five case studies describing struggles for power across the medieval period. In each case you will consider:
- what the struggle reveals about power in the medieval period
- what changes resulted from the conflict.

The big picture

Power in the medieval period

How powerful was the king?

Even the most powerful monarchs could not rule alone. They relied on the loyalty of the nobles and there was always the chance they might be deposed by someone who could command more power and support. How a ruler gained or lost support determined how successful they were – and sometimes whether they kept their throne at all.

How powerful was the Church?

The Church was a key ally – or potential enemy – for every ruler. It was a wealthy and powerful institution, and it had enormous moral influence because people believed in God unquestioningly. Churchmen were greatly respected as God's servants. With the support of the Church, a monarch was less likely to be challenged because it seemed that they had been chosen by God. However, monarchs also wanted to control the Church's wealth and this sometimes led to conflict. The most famous example was the clash between Henry II and the Archbishop of Canterbury, Thomas Becket.

How powerful were the barons?

The barons were a king's greatest asset – they fought alongside him, provided troops, ran the government in the far reaches of the kingdom and collected taxes on the king's behalf. However, the barons were also a potential threat. Many of them were extremely wealthy and powerful. A king had to make sure he kept the barons happy in order to ensure their loyalty, but he also had to assert his authority when necessary to avoid seeming weak. Not all the monarchs of the medieval period managed to get this balance right.

Why did parliament emerge?

By the late 1200s, a new force was beginning to emerge – parliament. Members of parliament were usually lesser nobles and wealthy merchants from the towns. They were not as rich and powerful as the barons but they still played an important role in government. Throughout the medieval period, governing the kingdom became increasingly expensive. A king's personal wealth was no longer enough to run the country and fight wars. To raise the money he needed, a king had to tax his people. In return, the people began to demand a say in how the country was run.

KEY QUESTIONS

A Why did monarchs clash with their subjects in the period c1100–c1485?

When studying the medieval period, historians are interested in why monarchs came into conflict with their subjects and how the balance of power changed over time.

The table below shows some of the main causes of tension in the medieval period. Copy the table and then record examples in column 2 as you work through the topic.

Causes of tension	Examples	Rating
powerful churchmen		
weak monarchs		
money		
powerful barons		
religion		
war		
other		

At the end of the topic you will rank the factors listed according to how significant they were in causing tension.

B How did the balance of power between monarchs and subjects change in the period c1100–c1485?

This chart features the main rulers you will come across in this topic. At the moment the chart shows all kings equally strong, at 100 per cent. As you read about each king, decide how powerful he is and record it on a copy of the chart. As you work through the case studies, you might want to go back and change the strength of previous kings. At the end you will have a graph showing the relative power of these medieval monarchs.

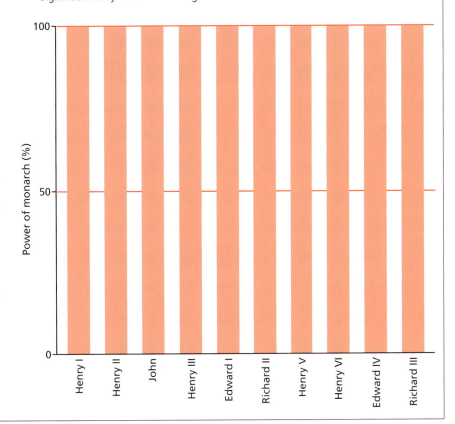

Case study 1: **Henry II and the Church**

Source 1 An image of King Henry II (on the left), who ruled from 1154 to 1189, and his son Richard I (the Lionheart), who ruled from 1189 to 1199. Images like this were not meant to be accurate portraits. These were produced for a chronicle of English history written by the churchman Matthew Paris in the 1250s. ▼

1 Look closely at Source 1. Do you think the image suggests that the king is protecting the Church, controlling it – or both? Make sure you can explain your view.
2 Does Source 1 prove that the Church was important to medieval kings? Explain your answer.

Today we are used to seeing pictures of rulers, politicians, celebrities and others. These people in the public eye try to control the way that such images are used so that people get the 'right' impression of them. Leaders in medieval times were no different – it just took a lot more time to produce a picture of them! Source 1 is a depiction of two powerful warrior kings – Henry II and his son Richard I. Henry was also a great lawmaker who restored order to England after years of civil war. Religious imagery features prominently in the picture, suggesting that both these kings considered the Church to be extremely important.

FACTFILE

Church hierarchy
- The head of the Church was the **pope**. He ruled the Church from Rome, assisted by his most senior officials, the cardinals.
- The pope relied on **archbishops** and **bishops** (based in the great cathedrals) to run the Church in their countries and to make sure the pope's rules were enforced.
- An archbishop was a very senior figure. England had two archbishops – Canterbury and York. The archbishops supervised the bishops.
- Bishops were responsible for the Church in their areas (called **dioceses**). There was another branch to the church – the monastic side. **Monasteries** were run by **abbots** or **abbesses**. The more important abbots and abbesses were similar in status to bishops.
- At the bottom of the hierarchy were **priests** in the churches and **monks** in the monasteries. However, even they had a lot of prestige and status in society.

The importance of the Church

There were many reasons why the Church was so important in medieval times.

The Church was the medieval mass media

The Church helped spread news throughout the country and it played a large role in schools and universities. New laws or taxes were announced during church services. Sermons would usually spell out the virtues of the king and the local baron, and it was churchmen who wrote the history books. Kings would give land to the Church and pay for new religious buildings. In return, they expected CHRONICLERS at those churches to write positive things about them.

The Church owned lots of land and employed many people

According to the *Domesday Book*, by 1087 the Church owned about 25 per cent of all the land in England. Bishops and abbots, in charge of the large abbeys, were effectively the managers of giant corporations. A large proportion of the population worked for the Church, as labourers on the land, TENANT FARMERS, MASONS working on church construction and in many other roles. The Church also cared for the poor and sick.

The Church helped people get to Heaven

In medieval times, almost everyone believed in God – and the Church was the people's link to God. Church leaders could seek God's favour for success in battle or for a good harvest. Above all, churchmen could pray to God to ensure that a person's soul went to Heaven when they died. Religion was a powerful force in medieval England. For example, Pope Alexander II ordered William the Conqueror to build a church to beg God's forgiveness for all the deaths caused by the Conquest. William obeyed and Battle Abbey was built in 1070. Anglo-Saxon and Norman nobles spent huge sums on church-building to praise God.

The Church was the power behind the throne

Almost all the people who wrote official documents and looked after the royal accounts were churchmen. This meant that bishops and abbots were as rich and powerful as the top barons. The Bishop of Durham, for example, had to defend England from a possible Scottish threat, so he had his own armies. When William the Conqueror spent time in his territories overseas, the Archbishop of Canterbury ruled in his place. Henry II appointed his CHANCELLOR (chief minister) Thomas Becket as Archbishop of Canterbury in 1162. Bishops and abbots collected taxes for the king just like the barons. The Church also had its own law courts.

Summary

To get an idea of the importance of the medieval Church in England, you have to imagine the power of an organisation like a giant international bank, or an oil company, or a massive tech company like Google or Facebook – only bigger and more powerful.

Could Church leaders challenge the king?

Throughout the medieval period, clashes arose between the king and the Church. In the 1090s, Archbishop Anselm fought bitterly with William II, claiming that the king was taking too much tax from the Church. He also criticised William for abusing his right to appoint bishops. If there was no bishop in charge of a BISHOPRIC, the king could claim all the rent and other income from that land. William often delayed appointing a new bishop to take advantage of this. As a result of Anselm's complaints, William agreed that the pope would be in charge of appointing new bishops, although he had to consult the king about his choices. However, the most famous conflict between king and Church in the medieval period was that of Henry II and the Archbishop of Canterbury Thomas Becket.

Henry vs Becket

In 1154, Henry II inherited a kingdom in chaos and decline after years of civil war under King Stephen (1135–54). Henry swiftly restored peace and stability to England, bringing the rebellious barons under control and strengthening the power of the law courts. His chancellor, Thomas Becket, played a key role in these successes.

By the 1160s, Henry was trying to increase his control of the Church. Church courts were hearing cases that Henry felt should be tried in the royal courts. He also wanted more influence over the appointment of bishops and abbots so that he could install people loyal to him in these influential positions. When Archbishop Theobald died in 1162, Henry gave Becket the job, believing that he would support the king in his decisions.

Surprise ...

To Henry's disappointment, Becket turned out to be more loyal to the Church than to the king. Becket resisted Henry's demands to have churchmen tried in royal courts if they committed a crime. He also refused to let Henry tax the Church or appoint new bishops and abbots. Becket was an argumentative and difficult man and Henry was notoriously short-tempered. The two soon became bitter enemies and in 1164 Becket was forced to flee to France. The dispute did not end there, though. Both men appealed to the pope, asking for his support. By 1170, Henry and Becket had been persuaded to try and reconcile their differences and Becket returned to England. However, one of his first acts was to EXCOMMUNICATE several powerful churchmen and barons who had supported Henry against him while he was in France. The king was furious when he discovered this, and in his rage is thought to have said, 'Will no one rid me of this turbulent priest?' Thinking they were doing what their king wanted, four knights rode to Canterbury and murdered Becket.

Shock ...

The whole of Europe was outraged at the archbishop's murder. Becket was made a saint and a martyr (someone who had died for God). Henry himself was shocked at what had happened and was left facing some humiliating consequences:

- In 1172, he was forced to make a series of concessions to the pope, known as the Compromise of Avranches.
- He agreed to give up any rights over the Church if the Church objected to them.
- He had to accept Becket's decision to excommunicate some of his advisers.
- He agreed to walk barefoot to Canterbury Cathedral and allowed himself to be whipped by the MONKS of Canterbury Cathedral.

Victory?

This may seem like a victory for the Church, but that is a simplified view. The Church gained an important martyr in Thomas Becket and Canterbury became an internationally important religious site. Henry's own reputation suffered – he was a strong and effective king but he was largely forgotten by history, while Becket became an almost legendary figure. On the other hand, Henry actually strengthened his relations with the Church in the long term, partly because Becket had not been a popular figure during his lifetime. Henry retained the power to appoint bishops (see Source 3) and to collect money from a bishopric when it had no bishop. These were the most important issues as far as Henry was concerned. From 1181 to 1189 he delayed appointing a new Archbishop of York and so collected all the rents and other income himself.

Source 2 An image from a chronicle by the churchman Peter Langtoft, published in the early 1300s. It shows Becket arguing with Henry II. ▼

1 Look at Source 2. Does it suggest that the king and the Church were equally powerful or that one was more powerful than the other? Explain your answer.

2 Discuss with others how far you agree with the following statements:

   a Source 2 is useful because it shows there was a dispute between Becket and Henry II.

   b Source 2 is not useful because it was produced by a churchman.

   c Source 2 is useful because it shows the significance of the argument between Becket and Henry II.

3 What does Source 3 tell you about Henry II?

Source 3 An extract from a letter from Henry II to the electors of Winchester, 1173. Richard of Ilchester was elected.

To the electors of Winchester tasked with choosing a new bishop. I hereby order you to hold a free election but forbid you to elect anyone other than my clerk Richard of Ilchester.

FOCUS TASK

What was the relationship between the king and the Church in the medieval period?

1 Write two paragraphs about the relationship between the king and the Church in medieval times.
   Paragraph 1: Explain why the Church was important to the monarch and the role it played in government and society.
   Paragraph 2: Describe the ways that medieval kings tried to control the Church. Include how and why kings exerted this control, how far the Church allowed this and what happened when there were disagreements.

2 Look again at Source 1 on page 32. Do you think that the image is a fair representation of the relative power of Henry II and the Church? Bear in mind that the image was created more than a hundred years after Henry's death and that it appeared in a book written by a churchman.

3 Look back to Key Questions A and B on page 31 and record your findings for this first case study.

Case study 2: **John and the barons**

You have already seen how important it was to William the Conqueror to be surrounded and supported by loyal barons and bishops. To ensure loyalty, he successfully used a careful balance of both force and reward. It was a good example to set for the medieval kings who followed.

Henry I (1100–35)

Henry I took the throne when his brother, William II (Rufus), was killed in a hunting accident. Another brother, Robert, had a stronger claim but he was away on CRUSADE so Henry seized the opportunity to claim the crown. When Robert returned, Henry captured and imprisoned him. The barons felt that Robert was the rightful heir to the throne and were unhappy about Henry's action. Henry knew he could not force the barons to accept him as king, so he offered a series of concessions designed to win their support. These were set out in his Coronation CHARTER of 1100 (see Source 4).

> **Source 4** Extracts from Henry I's Coronation Charter of 1100.
> * *If any baron or earl of mine shall die, his heirs shall not be forced to purchase their inheritance, but shall retrieve it through force of law and custom.*
> * *Any baron or earl who wishes to betroth his daughter or other women kinsfolk in marriage should consult me first, but I will not stand in the way of any prudent marriage. Any widow who wishes to remarry should consult with me, but I shall abide by the wishes of her close relatives, the other barons and earls. I will not allow her to marry one of my enemies.*
> * *If any of my barons commit a crime, he shall not bind himself to the Crown with a payment as was done in the time of my father and brother, but shall stand for the crime as was custom and law before the time of my father, and make amends as are appropriate. Anyone guilty of treachery or other heinous crime shall make proper amends.*
> * *Those knights who render military service and horses shall not be required to give grain or other farm goods to me.*

1 Read Source 4. What concessions does Henry I make to the barons?
2 What, if anything, does Henry I gain from the charter?

Henry II (1154–89)

Henry II's rule was a good example of balancing force with co-operation. He had to restore royal authority to England after years of civil war and ANARCHY during the reign of King Stephen (1135–54). Many barons had taken the opportunity to seize lands, stop paying taxes, ignore royal officials and build castles without permission.

In the 1150s, Henry seized more than 40 castles from the barons, keeping 30 of them and rewarding loyal barons with the others. In the 1160s, the king forced the barons to provide detailed information about their lands and income. He taxed them on this basis, but he was careful not to over-tax them and cause discontent. Henry II also replaced two-thirds of the local sheriffs with officials of his own choosing.

3 Draw and label a diagram to summarise Henry II's approach to dealing with the barons. You could use a see-saw, a 'carrot and stick' or one of your own ideas.

However, Henry was wise enough to forgive rebellious barons once they accepted his authority. Geoffrey de Mandeville, for example, had his lands seized in 1157 but by the 1160s he had become one of Henry's top judges. The king also consulted his barons on important issues such as changes to the legal system. It is significant that most barons were loyal to Henry during his dispute with Becket.

King John (1199–1216)

Unlike Henry I and Henry II, King John did not grasp the importance of give and take in his relationship with the barons. He was a suspicious man – having rebelled against his own father and brother in the past, he fully expected others to rebel against him. His elder brother, Richard, had spent most of his reign off on crusade or defending his lands in France from the French king, Philip. Richard had sold off many royal lands in England to pay for his wars, and when John inherited the throne he also inherited this costly war with France. However, where Richard had been a great commander and a skilled fighter, John was no more than competent. Where Richard was generous in victory, John was cruel.

When Philip invaded Normandy (the most valuable of the English king's French possessions) John embarked on a disastrous campaign to defend his lands. The barons were not enthusiastic. Very few of them had land in France any more and they felt that this was not their war. They were unwilling to risk their best soldiers and instead only sent small numbers of troops to support John. As a result, Normandy fell to the French king.

John spent the next ten years trying to raise money for a campaign to win back Normandy. He raised 25 per cent more in taxes than Henry I had done and by 1214 had amassed £1.3 million (equivalent to £30 billion today). However, this financial success came at a high political cost.

John fell out with a large proportion of the barons.

Many barons were unhappy about the increased taxes John introduced (although some historians argue that they could afford to pay and that in fact taxes up to this point had been quite low). However, John really got the barons off-side by not consulting them about important decisions and by punishing harshly anyone who stood up to him. For example, he imprisoned Matilda de Braose, claiming that her dead husband owed him money (some sources suggest it was because she talked openly about her belief that John had murdered his nephew Arthur). John demanded £25,000 from her. When she refused to pay, he left her and her son to starve to death. He forced the barons to pay huge sums of money to inherit their estates or to marry (see Source 5 on page 38). He also appointed many sheriffs (including Philip Mark, the infamous Sheriff of Nottingham who features in the tales of Robin Hood) who were not men local to the area. The barons felt that the king did not trust them to carry out the roles that had traditionally belonged to them.

The costs of John's success

John abused the justice system.

Henry II had introduced new courts called assizes. They made the JUSTICE SYSTEM simpler and cheaper. Officials called justices travelled the country and held assizes, meaning that people who wanted justice did not have to travel to London or meet with the king wherever he was. Assizes were popular with many people and John could have built support to help him in his arguments with the barons. However, he became suspicious of his chief justice, Geoffrey fitz Peter, and insisted that all cases be held by judges who were actually with John as he travelled around the country. This proved impossible. In addition, John began to 'sell' justice, judging in favour of nobles who paid him the most money.

John had a major clash with the Church.

In 1205, the Archbishop of Canterbury died. John wanted to appoint his ally John de Gray to the position, but the pope chose Stephen Langton instead. When John refused to accept this decision, the pope placed England under an INTERDICT (effectively excluding England from the Church) and excommunicated the king. Funerals and church services were suspended. This was of great concern to the people of England, who felt that if the pope disapproved of King John then God must, too. The pope also threatened to offer his support to the French king in overthrowing John. This finally convinced John to accept Langton as archbishop in 1213.

1   Compare Source 5 with Source 4 on page 36. What differences do they reveal in the characters of Henry I and John?

Source 5 An order from King John to one of his sheriffs, 1214. Sauer de Mauleon was an ally of John's. Mandeville had failed to pay John £13,000 for permission to marry.

The King to the Sheriff of Southampton, greeting. We order you without delay that you give possession to our beloved and faithful Saer de Mauleon of manors in Petersfield and in Mapledurham with all that was found in them, which belonged to Geoffrey of Mandeville, which we have granted to the said Saer. Witness myself at Reading, 27th day of May.

Source 6 An image of King John, published in a chronicle of English history by the churchman Matthew Paris, c1250. ▼

Magna Carta and the Barons' War

The tension between John and his barons reached a climax in 1215. In January of that year, John met with his opponents to see if a compromise could be reached. However, no agreement could be made and throughout April and May they took up arms against their king. London, Lincoln and Exeter all fell to the rebel barons, and many more barons began to join the rebellion. By June, John was forced to accept the barons' demands. These were set down in a royal charter – MAGNA CARTA – in July 1215.

Magna Carta has become a famous document, marking a turning-point in English political history. In 1215, however, it was seen more as a peace treaty between John and the barons. It contained 61 clauses, most of them demanding an end to specific abuses. However, some clauses established wider reforms:

- Clause 39 stated that people should be tried by jury.
- Clause 40 stated that king was not allowed to 'sell justice' (accept bribes to influence the outcome of a trial).
- Clause 61 stated that a council of 25 barons would be set up to make sure that the king respected the laws and rights set out in the charter.

Magna Carta was important for several reasons. Many kings of the past had worked successfully with their barons, balancing force with compromise, but *Magna Carta* made this relationship a formal contract rather than something that depended on the personality of the ruler. The charter also made the king subject to the law. Such a radical idea had never been necessary before, as kings had understood the need to make concessions to their barons in exchange for support. John's barons felt they had no choice but to force the king to accept these rules.

John overturned *Magna Carta* at the first opportunity, and by autumn 1215 war was raging again. Fighting continued into 1217, but by that time John was dead and his nine-year-old son had become King Henry III.

Magna Carta resurfaced several times in the century that followed. In 1225, Henry III reissued it to show that he accepted the king must abide by the law. It was also reissued in 1265 and 1297, becoming a symbol of the agreement between monarchs and their subjects.

ACTIVITY

1 A copy of *Magna Carta* is on display at the British Library. Write a 150-word caption to go with it to explain what it is and why it is so highly regarded.
2 Look through the rest of this chapter and Chapters 2 and 3 to find examples of *Magna Carta* being referred to in later years. Add these examples to your museum caption.

FOCUS TASK

Comparing medieval monarchs

1 Compare the portrayal of John in Source 6 with the images of Henry II and Richard the Lionheart in Source 1 on page 32. List the similarities and differences. Use the information you have read in this case study to suggest reasons for the differences.
2 Look back to Key Questions A and B on page 31 and draw your conclusions from this second case study.

Case study 3: The emergence of parliament in the thirteenth century

Source 7 A map of England showing where power lay in the thirteenth century. ▼

Source 8 The Chapter House in Westminster Abbey. This was built as a meeting place by Henry III in 1253. ▼

Look at Source 7. At first glance this might look like a bad map of Britain, but in fact this is a political rather than a geographical map. It shows where power lay in the thirteenth century. The rivers are exaggerated in size to show their importance as methods of transport (safer and quicker than travelling by road). There is also a network of castles, cathedrals and abbeys, and whoever controlled these controlled the country. At the start of the thirteenth century, that meant the king. But as time went on this picture began to change.

Now study Source 8. The Chapter House is a magnificent building, designed to impress. An inscription on the floor reads: 'As the rose is the flower of flowers, so this is the house of houses.' Henry III wanted this to be a place where the 'family' of his kingdom could meet, and the barons were important members of this family. When he built the Chapter House, Henry III intended to summon his barons there and tell them what he wanted them to do and how to do it. Within a few years, however, events started to take a different turn and a new political force began to arise in England – PARLIAMENT (see Source 10).

ACTIVITY

Write a caption for Source 7, such as might appear in a history book. Explain the meaning of the source and how historians find it useful, rather than simply describing it.

Source 9 A first day cover published in 2015. First day covers are special envelopes designed to go with commemorative stamps issued by the Royal Mail. This one was to be used with a stamp commemorating *Magna Carta*. ▼

Source 10 An extract from the *Chronicles of the Mayors of London*, 1265.

In January 1265 there came to London, by summons of his lordship the King, all the Bishops, Abbots, Priors, Earls and Barons, of the whole realm, also four men of every city and borough, to hold a parliament in the Chapter-House at Westminster. The king announced he had bound himself to the terms of Magna Carta and that neither he nor his son Edward would attack the Earls of Leicester [Simon de Montfort] or Gloucester, or the citizens of London, or any of those who had sided with them, because of anything done in the time of the past fighting in the realm.

1   Which of Sources 9 and 10 is more useful as evidence that de Montfort was a significant figure in history? You can argue that they are equally useful if that is what you think.

There was no official date for the founding of parliament. We first see the term being used in the 1230s and 1240s during the reign of John's son, Henry III. However, at this time parliament was more of an extended council of barons than the type of organisation that exists today.

Through his reign, Henry III regularly asked his barons for money to pay for his programme of church building and overseas wars. As these costs rose, he began to include lesser nobles and representatives from the towns in his councils. Until the 1250s, relations between Henry and his subjects were relatively stable, but at this point Henry's financial problems began getting out of control. They were made worse by the fact that he had upset many barons by giving his French relatives important jobs and valuable estates.

Once again the cost of war and a failure to consult with the barons led to confrontation. In 1258, a group of barons went to the king and demanded a range of reforms. Throughout the tough negotiations that followed, Simon de Montfort, Earl of Leicester, emerged as the leader of the rebel barons. He forced Henry to accept the PROVISIONS OF OXFORD, which specified that the king must defer to a council of 24 advisers – 12 elected by the barons and 12 chosen by Henry himself. This council was responsible for selecting a PRIVY COUNCIL of 15 men who supervised the appointment of officials, local administration and royal castles. In addition to this, a parliament would meet three times a year to supervise the performance of these councils.

No one had ever tried to exert this kind of control over a king before, and not all the barons approved of such a radical step. In particular, de Montfort was not popular among the wealthiest faction of barons, who were worried that the earl was becoming too powerful. This enabled Henry III to gather some support to stand against de Montfort and soon civil war was raging. De Montfort defeated Henry at the Battle of Lewes in May 1264. The king was effectively kept in prison and the country came under de Montfort's rule.

De Montfort may have been disliked by the great English barons, but he had support from many knights, the GENTRY (the lesser nobles) and the merchants and tradesmen in the towns, especially in London. De Montfort wanted to bring these people (collectively known as the 'Commons') into the political arena, so in 1265 he asked each county and BOROUGH of England to choose two representatives to send to a gathering in London that is often seen as the first parliament. The first thing this parliament discussed when it met in December 1165 was how to limit the power of the king and the great barons. De Montfort reissued *Magna Carta* to demonstrate his belief in the importance of the law.

However, de Montfort's rule was short-lived. Many barons continued to be suspicious of him and within a year war had broken out again. De Montfort was killed at the Battle of Evesham in August 1265, and Henry was reinstated. Significantly, Henry continued to summon parliaments until his death in 1272. At every parliament, the first item of business was to confirm that the king and his subjects all accepted the terms of *Magna Carta*.

ACTIVITY

You may have noticed that there are no headings in this case study so far. Look at the following list of suggested headings for each paragraph. They are not in the right order. Rewrite the list in the correct order, then write a brief summary of the content of each paragraph.

- Civil war
- De Montfort and the first parliament
- Fall of de Montfort
- Early parliaments
- Power in the thirteenth century
- Henry III's Chapter House
- Henry III's problems
- The Provisions of Oxford

Edward I and parliament

Source 11 Historian Marc Morris, writing in 2015.

Edward's lordship was emphatically good. A king who shared the longing of knights for feats of arms, adventure and the pursuit of noble causes – this was a king worth serving for his own sake. Unlike his father, Edward had no need to buy loyalty with lavish grants of land or money. He had friends but not favourites. Edward was no less competent in managing the wider political community. He took care, for example, to involve his greatest magnates in the running of the realm, consulting them in council on matters of importance. He proved able to handle the prickliest of characters, placating them where possible, overruling them when necessary. Thus for example Gilbert de Clare was allowed to lead armies in south Wales and to marry the king's daughter, but given a severe dressing-down when he failed to respect the Crown's authority. ... Smaller landowners, meanwhile, thanks to the development of parliament, were given a greater voice, and in turn became Edward's most consistent allies. For the first time since the Norman Conquest, England had a government that was perceived to be working in the interests of the majority of its subjects.

Source 12 A Royal Proclamation made by Edward I in 1297.

The earl of Hereford and the Earl Marshall have delivered a letter to the king. The letter includes complaints about some of the burdens that the king has placed on his kingdom. The king is well aware of these burdens, such as the taxes that he has often asked of his people. It grieves the king greatly that he has so burdened and exhausted his people. He asks them to be willing to consider his reasons. He has not used the money to buy lands, castles or towns, but on defending himself, his people, and all the realm. The council of barons who met with the king recently in London understood the demands of war. In exchange for the confirmation of the great charter of our liberties and the confirmation of the charter of the forest the barons have agreed a tax to be paid to the king. And let everyone remember how there has been great misery in the past in this realm through words bandied between the lord and his people, and the harm that has resulted from them.

In 1272, Edward I succeeded Henry III. Edward was one of the strongest rulers the country had ever seen (see Source 11). He conquered Wales and built several castles there that still stand today. He was an effective ruler and administrator. Above all, he was a great military commander. Like other effective monarchs, Edward understood that he had to balance force and compromise. For the first 20 years of his reign he summoned parliament regularly – usually twice a year.

As Edward became involved in wars against Wales, Scotland and France, he needed increasing amounts of money. Aware of what had happened in the reigns of Henry II and John, Edward was careful to consult his people. In 1295, he called a parliament that became known as the Model Parliament. This included the great barons and churchmen of course (these were the Lords). Edward invited two knights from each county or shire and he also invited two representatives (burgesses) from the major towns in England. These knights and burgesses were the Commons. A pattern was emerging in which kings used parliament to listen to the concerns of their subjects; in return parliament would give the king the money he needed for wars or other matters. Edward accepted that those who would be affected by the taxes levied to raise that money should have their say in parliament. He even reissued *Magna Carta* in 1297 to show that he would abide by the law.

1 What impression do you get of Edward from Source 11?
2 How far does Source 12 back up this impression?

FOCUS TASK

What changed in the thirteenth century?

1 Copy and complete the table below using the information on pages 36–42.

Statement	Agree or disagree?	Supporting evidence
Kings became less powerful in the thirteenth century.		
By the end of the century parliament was the most powerful force in England.		
The barons were no longer important.		
Magna Carta was still important.		
It was still important to balance force and concessions.		
The fact that Edward I took parliament seriously proves it was important.		

2 Look back to Key Questions A and B on page 31 and draw your conclusions from this third case study.

Factfile: Parliament c1000–c1485

Stage 1: c1000–1215

The barons give the king advice when he asks for it.

- A good king knew he needed the barons' and bishops' support to run the country and to raise taxes or armies, so he invited them to meet him.
- Anglo-Saxon kings did this in the Witan.
- Norman kings did this in their Curia Regis, or Royal Council. Over time, Norman kings began to consult regularly with a smaller group of close advisers, the PRIVY COUNCIL (which met in private).
- So the POLITICAL NATION (the people who have some say in how the country was run) at this time meant kings and barons and bishops.

Stage 2: 1215–64

Kings had to meet with the barons.

- Running the country and fighting wars was becoming too expensive for the king to pay for out of his own wealth. Efforts to raise taxes caused tension between barons and the king, leading to *Magna Carta* in 1215 (see page 39).
- One significant result of *Magna Carta* was that the king had to meet with a council of 25 barons to listen to their advice. This effectively limited his powers. King John rejected this but his son Henry III accepted it. However, Henry also continued to meet with his own close advisers in the Privy Council.
- There was no change to the Political Nation – it was still only the bishops and barons who could advise or supervise the king.

Stage 3: 1264–1337

The Commons are sometimes invited.

- When Simon de Montfort ruled England in 1264–65, he established a parliament that included more than just the nobles in an effort to get more people on his side.
- He sent out a writ to each county ordering them to send two knights to parliament. Large towns were also asked to send two representatives.
- The way the representatives were chosen varied from place to place, but mostly they were selected by rich property owners.
- These people became known as the 'Commons'. They were not ordinary people and certainly not peasants – they were rich property holders. However, the fact that they were not noblemen marked a big change.
- The Political Nation had now grown slightly. De Montfort's rule was short-lived, but after Edward I's Model Parliament in 1285 it was accepted that parliament would include knights and burgesses as well as the great barons and churchmen.

Stage 4: 1337–1485

The Commons becomes more important but power is still held by the king and barons.

- The king did not have to call parliament regularly and most of the time he made decisions with just the help of his close advisers (usually great nobles or bishops) in the Privy Council.
- However, for much of this period England was at war with France. War was funded by taxes, but representatives from the counties and towns had to agree to the taxes before they could be collected.
- The Lords and the Commons met separately. The Commons began to ask the king for certain reforms in exchange for their approval of taxes. Sometimes these reforms were local matters, such as the right to build a new bridge, but sometimes the Commons expressed views on how the country should be run.
- By the end of the Middle Ages parliament, with a HOUSE OF COMMONS and a HOUSE OF LORDS, had been established as a key feature of English government. The Commons did become more important, but they could be called or dismissed according to the king's wishes. They had no 'right' to sit, and ordinary people who worked in towns or in the fields still had no say in government.
- The Political Nation had not expanded and power had not really shifted. It still included the knights and gentry, but the king remained the greatest power in the land, and stability still depended on the relationship between the king and the nobles.

See page 86 for the continuation of this story.

Case study 4: Deposing a king – Richard II

So far in this chapter you have seen:

- kings fighting each other for the throne
- kings struggling for power with barons and the Church
- the emergence of parliament.

In this case study you are going to look at a new twist in the story – barons getting rid of a king.

A boy king

Source 13 A painting that appeared in the *Chronicles* of Jean Froissart. These chronicles were written in the later 1300s, probably the 1380s and 1390s. The chronicles covered events in England and France in the 1300s. The painting shows two scenes. On the left, Wat Tyler is killed in an argument with the mayor of London, with Richard watching from his horse. Richard then goes over to the rebels (on the right) and wins them over. Froissart was a poet and writer and produced written work for both the French and English royal families. ▼

Richard II became king in 1377, at the age of ten. When a child inherited the throne, real power lay with a regent – someone who advised the boy and effectively ruled on the king's behalf until he came of age. The strongest candidate as regent for Richard II was his uncle, John of Gaunt. However, Gaunt was head of the powerful Lancastrian family, and many barons suspected that he secretly wanted to seize the throne for himself. So instead of a single regent, a council of barons was set up to advise the boy king.

King vs peasants

One of the most significant events of Richard's reign was the Peasants' Revolt of 1381, in which a group of rebels protested against the high levels of taxation they were asked to pay to fund the on-going war with France. The burden of taxation had been made worse when half the population of England died in an outbreak of the Black Death in 1349–50. The ranks of the rebels were swelled by men from higher up the social scale who resented the behaviour of many royal officials. In London, more people joined the rebellion, unhappy about the number of foreign merchants trading in the city and about who should be mayor of London.

This unrest simmered and grew, and in the summer of 1381 a large rebel army, led by Wat Tyler, advanced on London. The king and his ministers were besieged in the Tower of London. But at this point the king – still aged only 14 – showed his strength. He met with the rebels, offering concessions and promising to show mercy to those who had opposed him. Shortly after meeting the king Tyler was killed, but the peasants believed Richard's promises and went home. The king then ordered a ruthless suppression of all the rebels, and more than 5,000 people were killed.

King vs barons

Richard's relations with the barons declined in the 1380s when he started promoting men from more humble origins to positions of power, including making Michael de la Pole Earl of Suffolk and chancellor. The barons began to form a party to oppose the king.

In 1386, facing a possible invasion from France, the king asked parliament for money to defend the realm. Led by the earls of Gloucester and Arundel, parliament demanded that the chancellor should be sacked before it would agree to the funds. Richard refused. As the two sides prepared for war, the powerful Lancastrians Henry Bolingbroke and Thomas Mowbray joined the rebel forces. By 1387, Richard had been defeated and the king was forced to execute several of his close allies. De la Pole fled the country.

1 Study Source 13. What impression do you get of Richard II?
2 What can Source 13 tell us about how the king was regarded by his people?

Richard's revenge

Over the next ten years, Richard gradually restored his authority and gained support from some noble families. However, he did not forget what the barons had done, and in 1397 he arrested his leading opponents – Gloucester, Arundel and Warwick – and accused them of plotting against him. Arundel was tried and executed, Gloucester was murdered before his trial and Warwick was imprisoned.

With these three main enemies gone Richard felt more secure, but the Lancaster family still posed a threat and there were rumours that Henry Bolingbroke might make a bid for the throne. Richard exploited a quarrel that had arisen between Bolingbroke and Mowbray to exile them both. When John of Gaunt died the following year, Richard confiscated Bolingbroke's inheritance. He now felt his position at home was secure enough to take his forces on a campaign to Ireland.

This was a mistake. While Richard was away, Bolingbroke returned to England. He convinced powerful allies such as the Percy family of Northumberland to help him win back his lands. When Richard returned from Ireland in July 1399, he was met by superior forces and defeated. The king surrendered to Bolingbroke at Flint Castle in North Wales.

Source 14 A representation showing Richard II (against the orange background) giving up his crown to Henry (on the right against the blue background). It was published in a chronicle in 1470. ▼

Henry claims the throne

With Richard his prisoner, Henry was free to take the throne. However, things had changed since Norman times – the increasing importance of the rule of law meant that a powerful nobleman could not simply seize a kingdom through force of arms. Henry needed to make a case that he had a rightful claim to the throne. So, he first undermined Richard's support by claiming that the king was unfit to rule. Henry then argued that his descent from Edward III through male relatives gave him a stronger claim to the throne than any of his rivals, who were all descended from female relatives.

Official accounts of the time state that Richard II ABDICATED (gave up the throne voluntarily) and allowed Henry to take over, although it is unlikely that this is a true record of events. Henry was crowned Henry IV in October 1399.

3 Describe the scene in Source 14. Then explain some of the features you described – for example the troops on each side, the changing wall hangings, the top of the church tower.
4 Does this approve or disapprove of Henry IV taking the crown? Explain your answer.
5 Images like this were time-consuming and expensive to produce. Why do you think this was created almost 100 years after the events it showed? Was it purely to record what happened or might there be other motives? Explain your answer.

FOCUS TASK

Comparing medieval monarchs

1 So far in this topic you have looked the following rulers: Henry I, Henry II, John, Henry III, Edward I.
   a Which of these rulers do you think was most similar to Richard II? Make a list of events or actions that support your view.
   b Which king do you think was *least* like Richard II? Again, make a list of events or actions to support your view.
2 Look back to Key Questions A and B on page 31 and draw your conclusions from this fourth case study.

Case study 5: **The Wars of the Roses 1455–85**

This is the final twist in our tale of power in the medieval period – a struggle for power between two great noble families. Here is an outline of the main events.

1413 Lancastrian Henry Bolingbroke, who had seized the throne from Richard II, dies. His son becomes Henry V.

1413–22 Henry V is a successful monarch. England is peaceful and orderly and the king wins an important victory against the French at Agincourt in 1415. He dies of dysentery while fighting in France.

1422–37 Henry VI is only nine months old when he becomes king. A council of nobles rules until he is 16. England is relatively stable. There are some disagreements among the nobles but for the most part they put their own interests second to the good of the kingdom.

1437–50 Henry VI rules in his own right. Unfortunately he is a weak and ineffective king who dislikes making decisions. The French win back a lot of the territory that Henry V had taken. Senior nobles try to rule in Henry's name but discontent arises because of poor government and increasing economic problems in England. A violent protest breaks out in 1450.

1450–55 The situation worsens. Two of the most powerful nobles – the Duke of York and the Duke of Somerset – clash as each man thinks he was the right person to be Henry's chief adviser. They fight a battle at St Albans. Somerset is killed.

1455–61 Most nobles understand that civil war would be disastrous and hope that this will be the end of the dispute. They feel a duty to stay loyal to Henry VI. However, by 1459 the Lancaster family is beginning to suspect that the Duke of York plans to depose Henry VI. Each side builds up an army and a series of battles takes place. York is killed but his son, Edward, wins the decisive Battle of Towton. He deposes Henry VI (who flees from England) and makes himself Edward IV.

1461–68 Edward gradually restores peace and stability, with the help of the powerful Earl of Warwick. By 1464, the remaining Lancastrians are defeated and Henry VI is captured before escaping to Scotland. However, Warwick and Edward IV fall out over what to do about war with France and about Edward's marriage (he had secretly married for love, but Warwick had expected him to make a political alliance). Edward has also refused to grant Warwick more power in government.

1469–71 Warwick rebels against Edward and forces him to flee the country. However, Edward gains help from the Duke of Burgundy and returns with an army to defeat and kill Warwick in 1471. Edward orders the murder of Henry VI and his son to remove potential rivals.

1471–83 Edward rules and England becomes relatively stable again.

1483 Edward IV dies and his 13-year-old son becomes Edward V. The young king's reign lasts only three months. His uncle, Richard, seizes the throne and becomes Richard III before Edward V is even crowned. Edward and his younger brother disappear – probably murdered.

1485 Richard III faces opposition from those who believe he has seized the throne illegally. Rebels rally around Henry Tudor, a distant relative of Henry VI. In August 1485, Henry invades England and kills Richard III at the Battle of Bosworth.

FOCUS TASK

How do you interpret the Wars of the Roses?

Historians have long been fascinated by the Wars of the Roses. Over time, the events of this long period of civil war have been reinterpreted in different ways. The main lines of thinking can be summed up as follows.

View 1: 'Monarchy failed. Kings were unable to control the greedy nobles.'

Some historians regarded the Wars of the Roses as a total collapse of the medieval monarchy and the rise of greedy nobles in a period of anarchy. Each noble family fought other families to grab as much land and power as they could for their own gain. In the process, ordinary people faced horror, death and destruction. Only the arrival of the Tudors, with a new style of government that involved greater royal control and less freedom for the nobles, managed to restore stability to England.

View 2: 'Some monarchs failed and many nobles tried to keep the country stable.'

In the 1920s, historians began to change their views on the Wars of the Roses, and they continue to do so. Instead of thinking that the system of monarchy had failed, they argue that it was individual monarchs who failed and that on the whole the nobles had tried to maintain stability and avoid war. These historians argue that many nobles were honourable. They suggest that Tudor rule did not bring about a lot of change – the Tudors were strong monarchs rather than bringing in a new system.

1 Study the outline of events opposite.
   a Choose five events that seem to support the first view above. Explain how they support the view.
   b Now choose five events that support the second view. Explain how they support the view.
   Remember, the same event might support both views, depending on how you interpret it.

PRACTICE QUESTIONS

1 Describe two examples of the work of the Church in medieval England. (4)
2 Explain why kings and barons clashed in the medieval period. (8)
3 What was the significance of *Magna Carta*? (14)
4 'The most significant problem faced by medieval monarchs was war.' How far do you agree with this view? (14)

KEY QUESTION REVIEW

A Why did monarchs clash with their subjects in the period c1100–c1485?

You have been collecting examples of the following causes of tension:
– powerful churchmen   – religion
– weak monarchs   – war
– money   – other.
– powerful barons

1 Rank these causes in terms of their importance in causing tension. Explain your order, giving examples. These examples will be useful in your written work. Think about which you would use if you were answering this question:
Explain why there was so much instability in England in the later 1300s and 1400s. (8)

B How did the balance of power between monarchs and subjects change in the period c1100–c1485?

2 Look back to the chart on page 31. Decide how the power bars should look for each reign. Explain your chart.

1.4 Review: Power c1000–c1485

PERIOD REVIEW TASKS

You have now studied many different examples of power in action from Anglo-Saxon times to the end of the medieval period. In this review, we are interested in patterns and trends across the whole period. You have read 'big picture' overviews for each topic – now it is time for even bigger thinking!

A Claims to the throne

In the medieval period, what gave someone a claim to the throne and how important were the different claims? Were they all equal? Did the importance of different claims change at different times?

1   Look back over your work from this chapter, then copy and complete the table below.

	Examples of this being important or not important	
	c1000–c1100	c1100–c1485
glorious ancestors		
a legal claim		
inheritance		
military power		
support of leading nobles		

2   Draw conclusions. When was each kind of claim most important?

B Conflict and co-operation in the medieval period

A book publisher is looking for a title for a book about the period 1000–1485. There are two options:

3   Draw up two lists from your knowledge of the whole period:
    –   examples of co-operation
    –   examples of conflict.
4   Now decide on the best title and back up your choice with examples.

KEY TERMS

Make sure you know what these terms mean and can use them confidently in your writing.
●   barons
●   *Domesday Book*
●   House of Commons
●   House of Lords
●   *Magna Carta*
●   noble
●   parliament
●   Political Nation

C What were the biggest problems facing monarchs in the medieval period?

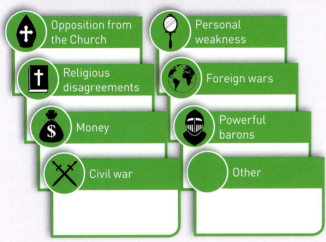

Opposition from the Church

Personal weakness

Religious disagreements

Foreign wars

Money

Powerful barons

Civil war

Other

5 Make a set of cards like this, each big enough to add examples. Then look back over this chapter and complete your cards. You can add extra cards for other problems if you think this list is incomplete.

6 When you have completed your research, decide which factors were most important in causing tension in the Middle Ages. Keep your cards and order of their importance, as you are going to compare them with later periods.

D Who were the most effective rulers in the medieval period?

7 Ideally work with a partner for this one. Make your own copy of the table below, then choose one column each and find as many examples as you can of success or failure.

Key factors in effective rule	Examples of successful monarchs	Examples of unsuccessful monarchs
relations with the Church		
relations with the barons		
success in war		
enough money		
relations with parliament		

8 When you have finished, compare your lists with your partner and see if you can agree on:
– the three *most* effective monarchs in c1000–c1485
– the three *least* effective monarchs in c1000–c1485.

E Which were the most significant events in the medieval period?

Look at the following criteria, used to judge whether each historical events is significant:

? Did it matter to people at the time?

? Did it affect a large number of people?

? Did it affect a small but important group of people?

? Did it cause change and if so how great was the change?

? Was the change long-lasting or short-term?

? Is it still seen as important today, and if so why?

9 Use these criteria to decide the ways in which each of the following events is significant. Write each event on a card, then write your notes on the back of the card: arguments that this event is significant; arguments it is not significant.
a Viking attacks
b *Magna Carta*
c Simon de Montfort's parliament
d Wars of the Roses
You can add other events if you think anything significant is missing.

10 When you have finished, rearrange your cards to put the most significant event (in your opinion) at the top.

The Tudors: why did the monarchy become more powerful in the 1500s?

FOCUS

Under the Tudors, the monarch became much more powerful. Instead of being little more than the most important noble, the Tudors raised the role of king or queen higher than the aristocracy. In this topic, you will examine how they did this and what changed as a result.

The big picture

Power in the Tudor period

> How did the Tudor monarchs increase their power?

The first Tudor king, Henry VII, tried to place the monarch above the nobles. He used royal courts to control the nobility. He also used patronage so the nobles depended on him for important jobs, gifts of land and other privileges.

Henry VIII built on this. He appointed administrators from outside the aristocracy, although he still relied on the great nobles and rewarded loyal allies generously. He was ruthless in crushing his opponents. Henry took royal power to new levels when he made himself Head of the Church of England.

Elizabeth I had to struggle first for survival and then to succeed to the throne. However, once in power she became one of England's most successful rulers. Like her father, she could be ruthless in crushing rebellions. She could also be intimidating and on several occasions she refused to accept the advice of her nobles. However, she tried to be a more approachable monarch than her father. She presented herself as a mother to the kingdom. She controlled the nobles and parliament through charm and persuasion as much as by power and force.

> How did the power of the nobles change?

There was a definite shift in power away from the nobles in this period. Henry VIII's top ministers, Thomas Wolsey and Thomas Cromwell, were not noblemen. The great nobles found that they had to fight for a place at court to have any influence on important decisions or to be granted a high-ranking job or gifts of land. Henry VIII and Elizabeth were clever in fostering rivalry between nobles for these prizes, which kept them divided among themselves yet loyal to their ruler.

Despite this, the nobility remained very important. The great families still ruled large areas of the country on behalf of the monarch. Without them, the kingdom could not be properly run. The Privy Council remained dominated by great lords. They provided armies when monarchs went to war. Henry VIII and Elizabeth both relied on the nobles to persuade parliament to accept laws, taxes and other measures.

> How did parliament change?

Parliament had grown in importance towards the end of the medieval period and this continued under the Tudors. There were two major reasons for this: religion and money. Henry VIII's decision to break with the Catholic Church was a huge step and he needed a wide base of support for his Reformation. He had to appeal to the lesser nobles and the wealthy merchants in the towns – and they were represented in parliament. Both Henry and Elizabeth were short of money. Government had become too expensive for the monarch to pay for it out of their own pocket. In return for being consulted on important issues, parliament agreed to taxes and other measures to create this much-needed wealth.

A How did the balance of power between monarchs and nobles change in the Tudor period?

Make a copy of this swingometer. Throughout this topic, you will be prompted to decide where you would put each of the Tudor monarchs (Henry VII, Henry VIII, Elizabeth I). Be ready to support your judgement with evidence.

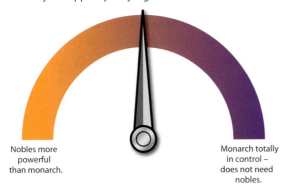

Nobles more powerful than monarch.

Monarch totally in control – does not need nobles.

B How did the power of the nobles change in the Tudor period?

The following list shows some of the powers of the nobility in medieval times. As you work through this topic, look for examples of these powers being reduced, maintained or increased.

a They ruled large areas on behalf of the monarch.
b They raised armies for the monarch.
c They were independent in their area and able to ignore the monarch.
d They rebelled against and deposed weak monarchs.
e They advised the monarch through their private council.
f They performed the most important roles in government.
g They receiving patronage (land or privileges) from the monarch.

C Why did parliament become more important?

The table below lists some of the reasons for the increasing power of parliament in the Tudor period. Copy the table and complete it by looking for examples in the reigns of Henry VIII and Elizabeth.

Reason for growing importance of parliament	Examples in reign of Henry VIII	Examples in reign of Elizabeth I
supporting monarch against enemies		
religion		
finance		
advising the monarch		

Henry VII and the Political Nation

The 'Political Nation' is a term used to describe the people who have a say in government. The Political Nation changes over time. In the Anglo-Saxon period the Witan was the Political Nation. In the reign of King John, it was the barons. Later the Political Nation broadened to include the gentry, as they were invited to parliament and won an increased role in approving taxes. Henry VII transformed the Political Nation still further. He wanted to limit the power of the great nobles:

- Decisions were made in the royal court. Nobles who did not attend court were left out of the big decisions.
- Nobles who misbehaved or who challenged royal authority were disciplined in a special court called the Star Chamber.
- He made clever use of royal PATRONAGE (grants of land or important jobs). Nobles did not want to miss these opportunities so they generally stayed at court near the king. This meant that Henry could keep a watchful eye on them.
- He built up the wealth of the Crown by avoiding expensive wars and by determinedly collecting taxes.
- He promoted able members of the gentry to important posts.

What impression do you get of the balance of power between Henry VII and his nobles? Record this on your swingometer.

Source 1 A contemporary copy of a portrait of Henry VIII produced in 1536 by Hans Holbein. ▼

What kind of ruler was Henry VIII?

Henry VIII continued many of his father's measures to extend the power of the monarchy.

A portrait of power ...

Source 1 is the most famous portrait of Henry VIII – and it is more than just a painting. It is the work of the most famous portrait painter of the time, Hans Holbein, and is a powerful piece of PROPAGANDA. It is designed to show Henry's power, strength and aggression. He is portrayed as a man in charge, certainly not a man to be challenged. Unlike medieval monarchs, he is shown with no royal family crests, no swords, shields or horses, no sceptres or orbs indicating law and justice. Henry VIII was saying that he did not need these symbols. Anyone who saw this painting would have found it impressive but also intimidating.

It cost a fortune to have your portrait painted in the 1530s. Despite this, many nobles tried to show their loyalty and admiration for Henry by having copies made to hang in their houses. In fact, the original was destroyed so we only know about the painting because of the copies.

... or is it?

Interestingly, the painting was created in what was probably the worst year of Henry's reign, 1536. In reality, at this age Henry would have looked a lot older and heavier – and much less healthy. He had been king for 27 years and he still did not have a son to inherit the throne. He had almost died in a jousting accident the previous year, which had raised serious concerns about this lack of an heir. Worst of all, he had recently faced a rebellion known as the Pilgrimage of Grace. This was a protest against him making himself Head of the Church of England and confiscating the lands of the monasteries. It took a lot of time and effort to crush this rebellion (see pages 163–64).

1   Look carefully at Source 1. Try to identify ways in which the artist portrays Henry as:
    a   physically impressive
    b   rich
    c   powerful and intimidating.
2   Compare this portrait with some of the royal seals and other symbols you have seen in this book. In what ways are they similar or different?
3   What can you infer from the fact that so many copies were made for great nobles?

Another portrait of power

Nobles also had their portraits painted for much the same reasons as the king – to project an image of themselves that would impress others. Source 2 is a good example of such a portrait. Henry Howard's story also tells us a lot about the relationship between monarch and nobles in the Tudor period.

Henry Howard was wealthy and powerful. He had military experience. He showed his loyalty to Henry VIII when he helped his father crush the Pilgrimage of Grace in 1536. However, he was also vain and arrogant. In 1546, Howard had his portrait painted. As well as making him look good, the painting is making a statement through the shields on either side, which show family coats of arms. They reveal that Howard was descended from the Plantagenet family, which ruled England from 1154 to 1399. The portrait suggests an ambitious and power-hungry nobleman.

Source 2 A portrait of Henry Howard, Earl of Surrey, painted in 1546. ▶

Source 3 Historian Susan Brigden, writing in 2001.

In the spring of 1521 Buckingham was arrested for treason, tried and condemned by his peers, and executed. For all his wealth and power, Buckingham could not raise support: not from his fellow nobles, who condemned him; nor from his tenants, whom he had oppressed. Loyalty to their lord would not persuade Buckingham's tenants to take up arms in support of his private quarrels, especially not against his sovereign. The ambition and fate of Buckingham, and of his grandson Surrey after him, shows both the potential of the nobility for disruption and the real power of the Tudors to contain them.

4 Compare the portraits in Sources 1 and 2. In what ways are they similar or different? What inferences can you draw from these differences?

5 Imagine you are one of Henry Howard's closest advisers. How could you explain to him that having Source 2 painted might not be a good idea?

6 What impression do you get of the balance of power between nobles and king from the story of Henry Howard?

When this painting was made, Henry VIII was near death. He was in constant pain, suspicious and bad-tempered. He saw in Howard a man who might challenge his own son Edward (still only a boy) as the next king. Despite their wealth and influence, Howard and his father were arrested and imprisoned, and Howard was executed in January 1547. None of the noble families came to his aid. This was a case of history repeating itself. Twenty-six years earlier, when Henry VIII was new to the throne, Howard's grandfather the Duke of Buckingham had attempted to build an alliance of the great nobles of the kingdom and install himself as lord protector. This would have meant that Henry remained king but that the real power would be in Buckingham's hands. Buckingham was charged with TREASON and executed (see Source 3)

> **1** Study the profiles of Wolsey and Cromwell. Do they challenge or support the judgement you reached about the balance of power between crown and nobles based on the story of Henry Howard? Use examples to support what you say.

Henry VIII and his ministers

Just like his father, rather than relying on nobles Henry VIII promoted ordinary men to positions of power because of their abilities. He had two key advisers: Thomas Wolsey and Thomas Cromwell. Both came from humble backgrounds.

PROFILE

Thomas Wolsey (1473–1529)

- Born in 1473, the son of a butcher.
- Excelled at Oxford University then entered the Church and rose through the ranks because of his intelligence and capacity for hard work.
- Became chaplain (personal priest) to several prominent churchmen and nobles, and eventually to Henry VII. Henry recognised his abilities and used him on diplomatic missions.
- Wolsey's real rise began under Henry VIII, who also recognised his abilities. Henry made him Archbishop of York and the pope made him a cardinal. In 1515, Wolsey became Henry's lord chancellor – effectively the king's chief minister.
- He brought in effective reforms to taxation such as the subsidy that spread the burden of taxes more fairly, making the wealthy pay more, and raised more money – around £300,000 per year.
- Wolsey also reformed the justice system, limiting the power of the great nobles through the Star Chamber.
- Wolsey used his position to acquire lands, titles and wealth for himself. He built the beautiful palace at Hampton Court as his home.
- Wolsey fell from power when he was unable to convince the pope to annul Henry VIII's marriage to his first wife, Catherine of Aragon. In 1529, Henry accused Wolsey of treason and had him arrested. Wolsey died before he could face trial.

PROFILE

Thomas Cromwell (1485–1540)

- Born in 1485, the son of a blacksmith.
- Travelled widely as a young man and then became a successful merchant and lawyer.
- Recruited by Wolsey in 1516, who recognised Cromwell's intelligence and abilities.
- Successfully survived Wolsey's fall from power and became a member of parliament (MP) in 1529, where he attracted the attention of Henry VIII. Henry appointed Cromwell to his Privy Council (circle of closest advisers).
- Made Henry VIII's chief minister in 1534 and held numerous other important offices in government. He used these roles to control the leading nobles in a similar way to Wolsey.
- Cromwell ruthlessly carried out Henry VIII's break with the Roman Catholic Church. He oversaw the creation of the Church of England with Henry at its head. He had anyone who opposed this policy, such as Sir Thomas More, imprisoned or executed.
- He also carried out the dissolution of the monasteries in the 1530s, which brought vast wealth to the king.
- In early 1540, Henry VIII made Cromwell Earl of Essex – an incredible rise in status for a man of his background.
- Cromwell fell from power later that year after arranging Henry VIII's marriage to Anne of Cleves. He hoped the marriage would bring a political alliance with France, but it did not.
- Leading nobles turned the king against Cromwell. He was arrested and executed without trial in July 1540.

Henry VIII and parliament

Today, we tend to think of 'parliament' as the government – something that is constantly at work running the country. In Henry VIII's time, however, parliament was only summoned when the king needed something. It was made up of the House of Lords, which represented the bishops and the great nobles (about 50 people), and the House of Commons (300–350 MEMBERS OF PARLIAMENT), which represented the wealthy merchants of the towns and the lesser nobles in the countryside, often known as the GENTRY.

Henry did not sit in parliament himself. He relied on his close allies, such as the Duke of Norfolk, to get what he wanted from the Lords, and he used a combination of co-operation and intimidation to get what he wanted from MPs in the House of Commons.

Throughout the medieval period, monarchs had gradually been forced to accept that they were not above the law, and parliament became increasingly important. Under Henry VIII, parliament became even more significant for several reasons.

War and money

Unlike his father, Henry was eager to go to war and dreamed of regaining English lands in France – possibly even the French throne. He went to war with France in 1513 and again in the 1540s. He also fought battles against the Scots. War was an expensive business and Henry spent huge amounts of money building alliances to raise England's status in Europe. Wolsey and Cromwell were both efficient at raising new taxes and finding other measures of raising money, but taxes in particular had to be approved by parliament. The more Henry needed money, the more important parliament became.

Religion

The greatest challenge of Henry VIII's reign was his clash with the Catholic Church. Henry wanted an ANNULMENT of his marriage to his first wife, Catherine of Aragon. When the pope refused, Henry decided to make himself head of the Church of England so he could make the decision to annul the marriage himself. Even a powerful king like Henry could not take such a drastic step without the support of the people – and this meant persuading parliament.

After much argument and compromise, and some skilful negotiation by Thomas Cromwell, parliament supported Henry. The ACT OF SUPREMACY was passed in 1534, making Henry head of a new and independent Church of England. You will look at this in more detail in Chapter 5. For now, it is important to understand how this act changed the relationship between king and parliament.

As arguments raged over the break with Rome, it became clear that a king could no longer create and impose a new law on his own – he had to get parliament to accept it. This was an important moment in the development of parliament, and it set a pattern for the future. Things did not change overnight – Henry did not suddenly start consulting parliament on every new law – but he did make efforts to seek approval on significant measures. The story of power is often like this. Changes were rarely sudden and dramatic; more often the process of change was subtle and gradual, characterised more by trends than turning-points. Like all historical trends, things can also switch into reverse. The ebb and flow of power between king and parliament continued for another 300 years.

Co-operation

Developments in Henry VIII's time meant that a wider range of people, including lesser nobles, the gentry and wealthy merchants in the towns, started to become part of the Political Nation. They also resulted in a closer collaboration between the monarch and parliament. Parliament helped Henry crush several of his opponents among the great nobles by passing Acts of Attainder. These were acts in which parliament decided that particular people were guilty of treason without the accused having the chance to defend themselves in a court of law.

Throughout his reign Henry often clashed with parliament, but compromises were usually reached. This meant that new laws and taxes met with relatively little opposition from the people because MPs had been involved in the decision-making process. Henry VIII increased his authority by working with parliament and parliament's authority increased through its co-operation with the king.

2 Does the information in this section support or contradict the judgement you reached about the balance of power between king and nobles based on the story of Henry Howard and by studying Wolsey and Cromwell?

Henry VIII and the nobles

You have already seen how even powerful nobles like Henry Howard could be curbed by the king. Henry resisted the power of the nobles in other ways, too. He passed laws restricting the number of RETAINERS that a nobleman could have. Retainers were men in the service of a nobleman who would fight for him if called upon to do so. He also undermined the authority of his nobles by promoting men from humble backgrounds such as Wolsey and Cromwell to positions of power.

Did all this mean that the great nobles lost their power? The answer is almost certainly no. Most historians, such as Susan Brigden (see Source 4), believe that despite the increasing influence of parliament and men from lower social classes, the nobles remained incredibly influential. There were a number of reasons for this.

- **War:** Henry VIII fought several wars during his reign. He could only do so if the nobles were willing to assemble their armies and bring them to fight under Henry's command. For example, when Henry invaded France in 1513, he had an army of 30,000 men. The Earl of Shrewsbury provided 4,400 of those men and was rewarded with a senior command.
- **Security:** During rebellions such as the Pilgrimage of Grace, Henry relied completely on forces commanded by nobles such as the Duke of Norfolk and the Earl of Surrey.
- **Communications:** These were still so poor in England that whether Henry liked it or not, he had to rely on the powerful nobles to represent him and his authority in distant parts of the country.
- **The Privy Council:** The Privy Council was made up of the most powerful and important nobles in the country. These were the king's closest advisers and were given responsibility for key tasks.

The nobles also influenced the king through parliament. Although parliament was made up of both Lords and Commons, it was the Lords who wielded the most influence over matters of government. It is also worth noting that both Wolsey and Cromwell eventually fell from the king's grace, largely because powerful nobles like the Duke of Norfolk persuaded Henry to get rid of them.

Source 4 Historian Susan Brigden, writing in 2001.

Yet if the King sometimes found it difficult to rule with the nobility, he could not rule without them. At the end of his reign, as at the beginning, nobles counselled him, and in their regional strongholds they ruled under the Crown: Lord Derby still held sway in Lancashire; the Earl of Shrewsbury in Derbyshire [and] Shropshire; the Earl of Arundel in Sussex. But there had been changes. New men – Wriothesley, Audley, Seymour, Dudley, Paget, Rich – had partially succeeded the older peers in the Privy Council and were rewarded with lands, titles and provincial commands.

Source 5 A Victorian redrawing of an image of Henry VIII with his Privy Council, probably in the later 1530s. A record of one such meeting on 10 August 1540 records the following people attending: five lords, an archbishop, two bishops, a great admiral and six knights (most of whom were part of Henry's personal staff). ▶

1 Study Sources 4 and 5. Do these sources change your views about the balance of power between the monarch and the nobles in Henry VIII's reign?
2 Taking into account each of the examples you have studied, where would you place Henry VIII on the swingometer? Choose extracts from the written sources to support what you say.

KING HENRY THE EIGHTH, IN COUNCIL.

What kind of ruler was Elizabeth I?

Source 6 A portrait of Elizabeth I from around 1575. This is known as the 'Pelican Portrait' because of the pelican brooch she is wearing. The pelican was associated with motherhood due to the way the bird nurtured its young. ▼

Source 7 A portrait of Elizabeth I painted to mark the defeat of the Spanish Armada in 1588. The Armada can be seen through the windows behind Elizabeth. She is shown with her hand on a globe. ▼

Source 8 A portrait of Elizabeth I from 1592, known as the 'Ditchley Portrait'. This was a gift from one of her nobles, Sir Henry Lee. She is shown standing on a map of England. Her toe is on Sir Henry's lands, Ditchley Park. ▼

Sources 6–8 show three different portraits of Elizabeth I at different times in her reign. Hundreds of other portraits, murals and miniatures that carried images of the queen were painted during her reign. Elizabeth does not seem to age much in the paintings, which gives us a clue that, like the picture of Henry VIII in Source 1, this is propaganda. But is the propaganda message the same? Or does it change between the rule of Henry VIII and Elizabeth I?

FOCUS TASK

How similar were Henry VIII and Elizabeth I as rulers?

1   Consider the portraits of Elizabeth in the same way you considered the portrait of Henry VIII on page 52. What do each of these pictures suggest about the queen and the way she ruled? Look for aspects of the images that represent wealth, power, caring, authority, wisdom, peace.
2   Do the portraits of Elizabeth I suggest that she was a similar ruler to Henry VIII or that she approached things differently? Make sure you can explain your answer. You will refer back to your answers here as you read the next section, to see whether your ideas are supported by the events of her reign.

Elizabeth's challenges

Elizabeth I faced many challenges during her reign – some similar to those her father faced, and others quite different.

> **Source 9** Sir John Harington, a noble and Elizabeth's godson, writing after her death.
>
> *Elizabeth ruled by love rather than by fear. She never feared to rule or command, as she knew her people would willingly follow her from their own love of her. When obedience was ever found lacking she left no doubt as to whose daughter she was.*

Challenge 1: Accession

When she was young, Elizabeth faced great danger. She was a Protestant but her sister, Queen Mary, was a Catholic and the country was still divided over religion. Mary was afraid that Elizabeth might try to seize the throne, so she imprisoned her. However, Elizabeth was clever – she made sure that she never said or did anything that could be seen as a threat to her sister.

When Mary died in 1558, Elizabeth was made queen. The country was in desperate need of stability. Many people were nervous about there being another change in religious policy, and about another woman ruling the country. However, Elizabeth got off to good start. She charmed the crowds at her coronation by waving, smiling and listening to their cheers. In her coronation speech, she reassured the nobles and members of parliament by promising to take notice of good advice and counsel. On the whole she proved true to her word. She did listen to her advisers and consulted with parliament. In fact, she often frustrated her advisers by dithering and delaying over important decisions.

However, Elizabeth was also quite prepared to ignore advice if she thought she was right. Like other monarchs in Europe at this time, she believed she had been appointed by God. She felt that the trials and tribulations she had experienced in her path to the throne were proof that God had chosen her. As a result, although she sought advice on many things, she also believed that her decisions should not be challenged.

Challenge 2: Religion

Although Henry had broken with the Catholic Church in 1534 and established the Protestant Church of England, many religious practices remained the same, including use of the prayer book and the typical pattern of church services. Henry's son, Edward VI, was a committed Protestant and began to introduce changes to religious practices. All decoration was removed from church buildings, and new church services and prayer books were introduced. Many people were unhappy with these changes.

Edward died in 1553, aged only 16. He had chosen the Protestant Lady Jane Grey to succeed him but Jane was swept aside by his sister Mary, who was legally the next in line to the throne. Mary was a devout Catholic and tried to reverse the changes her brother had introduced. Many people were burnt at the stake for refusing to convert from the Protestant faith back to Catholicism. Her treatment of Catholics earned the queen the nickname 'Bloody Mary'.

When Elizabeth came to the throne her biggest challenge was deciding what to do about religion in England. There were sound political reasons for continuing Mary's work in re-establishing the Catholic faith. France and Spain, the two greatest powers in Europe, were both Catholic countries and would regard England as a threat if it reverted to Protestantism. However, there was a lot of support for Protestantism within England. Some extreme Protestants, later known as the PURITANS, wanted radical religious change, but most nobles and gentry hoped for a more moderate form of Protestantism.

Elizabeth also wanted a moderate Protestant faith and she acted quickly to settle the issue. In May 1559, she announced that England was to become a Protestant country again. A new Act of Supremacy was passed, making Elizabeth head of the Church. All public officials had to swear an oath of loyalty and accept her leadership or they would lose their jobs. A new prayer book was issued and it became compulsory to use this book and attend church services.

Elizabeth did not strictly PERSECUTE Catholics and others who objected to the new religious rules. However, recusants (people who refused to go to Church of England services) had to pay fines. Many Catholic families were impoverished by RECUSANCY fines year after year.

Challenge 3: Plots and rebellions

Catholics were viewed with suspicion by the government and were watched carefully as potential traitors or spies for the Catholic powers of France and Spain. These countries were a genuine threat to the safety of England, as demonstrated by the Spanish Armada of 1588, when Spain tried to invade England. The Spanish also helped Irish lords in a rebellion against Elizabeth in the 1590s. Elizabeth and her ministers used the threat of Catholic France and Spain to their advantage. They spread propaganda about the terrible things that Catholics had been doing to Protestants in Europe, including torture. This made people suspicious of Catholics in England. In fact, such paranoia was not completely unfounded. There were numerous Catholic plots to overthrow Elizabeth. The nobleman Sir Francis Walsingham was put in charge of a network of spies who kept a watchful eye on known suspects.

In 1569, Elizabeth faced the most serious rebellion of her reign – the Northern Rebellion. The leading northern nobles, Westmoreland and Northumberland, hatched a plot to put the Catholic Mary, Queen of Scots on the throne in place of Elizabeth. In the event, the rebellion failed and Elizabeth executed 750 people who had been involved. Despite this, she resisted attempts by parliament to bring in harsh laws against all Catholics. Mary was imprisoned until 1586, when Walsingham discovered she had been writing letters to Catholic plotters led by a man named Antony Babington. After this Elizabeth felt she had no choice but to execute her royal cousin.

Challenge 4: Marriage and succession

Henry VIII had married six times in an effort to secure the Tudor dynasty on the throne of England. In contrast, Elizabeth never married. Throughout her reign, however, she came under constant pressure from her closest advisers and parliament to marry. There were several reasons for this:

- The vast majority of leading nobles and MPs were men, and they were simply uncomfortable being ruled by a woman. If Elizabeth married, her husband would become the real leader of the country.
- Elizabeth was a attractive catch! Any English noble would have gained status by marrying her, and by marrying a foreign prince Elizabeth could have secured a strong political alliance with another country.
- It was important that she had an heir to become ruler after her death.

Elizabeth had many offers of marriage from English and foreign nobles. In the 1560s, she seemed close to marrying Robert Dudley, but her advisers in the Privy Council, including William Cecil, disapproved of Dudley and persuaded her against him. She listened to proposals from foreign princes but in the end she decided never to marry. She knew that if she did, her husband would be king and her own influence would decline.

Elizabeth used her status as the 'Virgin Queen' to boost her own authority. A 'personality cult' developed in which all the great nobles had to pretend to be in love with her. She claimed that she could not marry because her true love and devotion lay with her country – in 1599 she talked of how she was married to her people.

Once it was clear the queen was never going to marry, ministers encouraged her to name an heir, but she even refused to do this. This can be seen as a serious failure to do her duty to provide a stable succession to the throne. However, it is also possible to argue that Elizabeth remembered how she had been used by rebels plotting against her sister and would have been worried that opponents might similarly try to overthrow her before her death.

---

1 Look at how Catholics were treated during Elizabeth's reign. Write down five words to describe Elizabeth's approach to dealing with Catholics.

2 Explain how Elizabeth I used the marriage question to her own advantage.

3 Make a list of the ways in which Elizabeth I's style of ruling was like Henry VIII's. Then make a list of ways in which it was different.

4 Do your answers to Question 3 support your views from the Focus Task 2 on page 57?

Elizabeth and her nobles

The nobles continued to be a significant force in Elizabeth's reign. The most important nobles belonged to her Privy Council. She also had a Council of the North and a Council of the Marches (the borderlands with Wales), run by the most powerful nobles in those areas. They advised Elizabeth about policies and they represented her authority, administering justice and collecting taxes. Elizabeth kept the same courts as Henry VIII, including the Star Chamber.

Like her father, Elizabeth also relied on the great nobles in times of war. Many had tenants whom they could call on to fight when needed. Of course, these forces could also be called on to oppose the monarch if the noble lord was so inclined, but the monarch needed them to go to war, defend the country or crush rebellions.

The nobles were extremely ambitious and competed with each other for top posts or grants of land. For most of her reign Elizabeth balanced these rivalries well, although the Cecil family – William Cecil, then his son Robert – were close favourites of the queen. The most serious breakdown in loyalty from a noble supporter came towards the end of Elizabeth's reign. In January 1601, the Earl of Essex rebelled, claiming he was trying to free the queen from the evil influence of the Cecils. However, he had little support and was quickly captured and executed.

Elizabeth and parliament

On the whole, Elizabeth's relations with parliament were good. William Cecil and other members of her Privy Council represented the queen in the House of Lords, and worked with MPs to pass laws and agree taxes. MPs in the Commons were not organised into political parties as they are today, so it was sometimes difficult to manage discussions and debates. Elizabeth relied on privy councillors like Cecil to meet with MPs and explain policies. These men sometimes encouraged MPs to raise questions about policies if they disagreed with Elizabeth or wanted her to reconsider something. For example, in 1563 and 1566, Cecil encouraged MPs to ask Elizabeth to consider marrying. In 1571, MPs asked her to consider Church reform and in 1586 they asked her to consider the fate of Mary, Queen of Scots.

Elizabeth worked with parliament much as Henry VIII had done. The Lords and the Commons were her point of contact with the needs of her people. As in Henry's reign, the fact that MPs could voice their concerns and hear Elizabeth's policies explained meant that they were more likely to accept and approve of them.

Parliament did not meet as often under Elizabeth as it had under Henry (it only met in 18 of her 44 years). However, during this time parliament and the queen had a good working relationship. They expressed similar views on most issues. The majority favoured Elizabeth's moderate stance on religion and supported her policies in defending England from its enemies, particularly Spain. They encouraged her attempts to build up trade and colonies overseas, especially in the Americas.

1 Look carefully at Source 10. Is there any doubt as to who is the most important person in the picture? Explain your answer.
2 What other parts of the picture give clues about power and status in Elizabeth's time?

Source 10 An engraving representing Elizabeth I in parliament. It was published in 1682, 80 years after Elizabeth's death. It represents the hierarchy: the people nearest Elizabeth are the Lords, the people at bottom of the picture are MPs from the House of Commons. ▼

Her Majesty grants you freedom of speech but with due limitation. There can be no good consultation where all freedom to advise and speak freely is banned. However, there will be no sensible conversation if all men may speak as they want, when they want, without respecting their betters. Her Majesty commands me to say that you may say 'Yea' or 'Nay' to bills as you see fit, and with short explanations. But you are not to give long speeches demanding great change to government or religion. No ruler will put up with this.

Source 12 A speech by Elizabeth at the end of her last parliament in 1601. This particular parliament had seen numerous serious arguments between the queen and MPs.

I have always tried to rule in the knowledge that at the end of my life I would be judged by God on how I have ruled. I have always tried to rule for the good of my people. You have had many princes more mighty and wise sitting in this seat before you, yet you will never have one who is more caring or loving. So I ask that you continue with your good advice. And I ask that before you all return to your lands you may kiss my hand.

3 Study Source 11. Explain why it is useful to historians as evidence about Elizabeth's relationship with parliament.
4 Study Source 12. Is this a good example of Elizabeth's charm? Explain your answer.
5 Where would you put Elizabeth on your balance of power swingometer?

However, some MPs openly challenged their queen. In 1571, Walter Strickland tried to get parliament to accept much stricter religious reform than Elizabeth had proposed. In 1593, Peter Wentworth raised the issue of the succession in parliament. As a result, he was imprisoned in the Tower of London until his death three years later. Overall, though, MPs in the House of Commons knew their place. Most of them were cautious about raising controversial issues, or even about making long speeches.

FOCUS TASK

How similar were Henry VIII and Elizabeth I as rulers?

1 You have been making comparisons between Henry and Elizabeth. Review that work using a table like the one below. Does this confirm your view in the Focus Task on page 57?

Key factors in effective rule	Examples of similarities	Examples of differences
good relations with the Church		
good relations with the nobles		
success in war		
enough money		
good relations with parliament		
appropriate style and approach		

2 Extension: Are there any medieval monarchs you think were similar to Henry VIII or Elizabeth I? Use examples to support your answer.

KEY QUESTION REVIEW

A How did the balance of power between monarchs and nobles change in the Tudor period?

1 How did your swingometer move through the Tudor period?

B How did the power of the nobles change in the Tudor period?

2 Which powers changed the most? Which changed the least?
3 Now use your work on Key Questions A and B to answer these practice questions:
   a Describe two ways in which Tudor monarchs controlled the nobles.
   b How far did the power of the nobles decline under the Tudor monarchs?

C Why did parliament become more important?

4 Review your work from Key Question C and use your findings to answer these practice questions:
   a Describe two examples of the role of parliament in the Tudor period.
   b How significant was parliament in the Tudor period?

PRACTICE QUESTIONS

1 How important was religion in helping Henry VIII and Elizabeth I rule? (14)
2 What was the most serious challenge facing monarchs in the Tudor period? (14)

2.2 Revolution and restoration

FOCUS

When Elizabeth I died with no heir, the throne passed to her Scottish cousins the Stuarts. The Stuarts had little in common with the Tudors. They had different ideas about monarchy and religion, and different approaches to ruling. In this topic, you will examine how tensions between the Stuart king Charles I and parliament led to the English Civil War, and investigate the consequences of this.

The big picture

The English Civil War and the Restoration

What were the causes of the English Civil War?

The Tudors had tried to raise the status of the monarchy to be superior to the nobles. James I took this process further. He argued that he was king by 'divine right' – he was appointed by God so he could not be challenged by nobles or parliament and he was not bound by the law. His son Charles believed even more strongly in divine right, but he was not the clever politician that James had been. He relied on a small group of advisers, which left many in the Political Nation feeling excluded from important decisions. Charles introduced unpopular religious reforms and taxes. Opposition to Charles grew and in 1642, the country descended into civil war.

Why was the king executed?

Charles lost the war; he was captured in 1646 and imprisoned. Even so, he was still in a strong position. The people were weary of war, and felt that being ruled by parliament was worse than being ruled by Charles. At the same time, radical new political and religious ideas alarmed many members of the Political Nation. Charles could have negotiated a settlement with virtually no loss of his powers, but he felt that a divinely appointed king should not have to negotiate with his subjects. Instead, he tried to play his enemies off against one another. Charles eventually escaped prison, and this led to the Second Civil War in 1648–49. By this time, his leading opponents in parliament and the army decided the king could not be trusted. Charles was tried and executed in 1649.

How was England ruled without a king?

The monarchy was abolished and so was the House of Lords. England became a republic, ruled by parliament. However, in 1653 Oliver Cromwell was offered the position of lord protector – king in all but name. Britain was deeply divided over the issues of religion and politics. Cromwell had the support of parliament and the army, and the nobles both feared and respected him. For these reasons Cromwell was able to rule the country and keep it fairly stable.

Why was the monarchy restored?

Cromwell died in 1658 and the different factions could not agree on who should succeed him. As army commanders vied with each other to take control, the country nearly fell into civil war again. Eventually, however, all parties agreed that the only acceptable solution was to restore the monarchy. Charles I's son was invited to return to England and take his place as Charles II in 1660.

How did power change hands in this period and why?

The English Civil War changed the nature of politics in the country. Parliament became much more powerful – strong enough to challenge the king. Another new force emerged in politics: the New Model Army. Its commanders did not just fight; they also wanted a say in the running of the country. Even though the monarchy was restored in 1660, the relationship between king and parliament had changed significantly.

KEY QUESTIONS

A What factors caused tension between rulers and subjects in the period 1625–60?

Make a copy of the table below. As you read the topic, add examples (you do not need every example of every area). In columns 3 and 5, use a scale of 1–4, where 1 = minor problem and handled well and 4 = a huge problem and handled disastrously.

Causes of tension	Examples of this tension under Charles	How serious a problem?	Examples of this tension under Cromwell	How serious a problem?
attitude or action of ruler	ship money	3	major-generals	3
attitude or action of Political Nation (including parliament)				
religion				
money				
war				

B How did the balance of power change in the period 1625–60?

Copy this graph and put dots in the relevant colour to mark the high points and low points of power in this period for key groups and individuals: We have suggested how to represent Richard Cromwell. The rest is up to you!

- Charles I
- parliament
- the army
- Oliver Cromwell
- Charles II

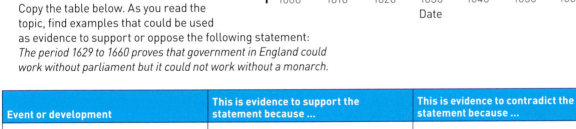

Richard Cromwell becomes lord protector 1658.

Richard Cromwell steps down as lord protector 1659.

C How important was monarchy?

Copy the table below. As you read the topic, find examples that could be used as evidence to support or oppose the following statement:
The period 1629 to 1660 proves that government in England could work without parliament but it could not work without a monarch.

Event or development	This is evidence to support the statement because ...	This is evidence to contradict the statement because ...

63

Source 1 A painting from the Palace of Whitehall, called *The Apotheosis of James I.* ▼

Part 1: The road to civil war

What kind of ruler was Charles I?

Look closely at Source 1, which shows James I, who ruled England from 1603 to 1625. It was commissioned by his son, Charles I. It really tells us more about Charles than it does about his father. The painting shows James being taken up to Heaven by angels, to sit by God's side. The painting is making a clear statement about the God-like status of the king.

The idea that kings were appointed by God is an important development in the story of power. The belief that kings had a 'divine right' to rule became very strong in Britain and Europe in the sixteenth and seventeenth centuries. You have seen how Henry VIII made himself head of the Church and how Elizabeth believed that while she should consult with her advisers, she really only answered to God. After James I became king, he wrote books explaining and justifying his idea of this divine right. He would not tolerate any challenge to the idea that his authority, his right to rule, came from God (see Source 2).

Source 1 A painting from the Palace of Whitehall, called *The Apotheosis of James I.*

James I

> **Source 2** A speech by James I to parliament in 1610, in which he quotes from one of his own books.
>
> *The state of monarchy is the supremest thing upon earth, for kings are not only God's lieutenants upon earth, and sit upon God's throne, but even by God himself kings are called Gods. In the Scriptures kings are called Gods, and so their power can be compared to the divine power. Kings are also compared to fathers of families: for a king is truly the father of his people. And lastly, kings can be compared to the head of a body, if the body is the country that the head rules.*

When Charles I commissioned the painting of his father in 1635, James had been dead a long time. Charles wanted it partly to honour his father but he also wanted to send a clear message to his subjects that he too had a divine right to rule. It might seem that James I and Charles I would be similar rulers because of this, but in fact father and son were very different. James had believed in the divine right of kings, but he also recognised that a successful ruler worked *with* the Political Nation and was willing to compromise (see Source 3). Charles felt that his rule was absolute – no one had the right to challenge him and his word was law. By 1640, this had resulted in a country in crisis.

1. Study Source 1 closely. Make a list of all the ways in which James I is shown as godlike.
2. What impression do you get of James I from Source 2?
3. How is this impression affected by Source 3?
4. Why does this source really tell us more about James's son Charles than it does about James?

> **Source 3** Historian Barry Coward, writing in 1997.
>
> *One of James' greatest qualities was his ability to recognise what was politically possible and what was not. He realised that his dream to unite England and Scotland was not acceptable so he dropped it and remained king of England and king of Scotland separately. His religious policies show the same politically astute mix of idealism and realism. He was often the peacemaker between different religious factions. He learned that it was important for his court to be open to a wide variety of different people and opinions. Under James the court and parliament remained an important point of contact between the king and his most important subjects. As a result, before 1625 political tensions never really erupted into crises in the way that they did soon after his son took the throne.*

Source 4 A portrait of Charles I, representing the fact that he was King of England, Ireland and Scotland. ▼

5 What impression do you get of Charles I from Source 4?

Early divisions: the Petition of Right 1628

Charles's rule as King of England, Ireland and Scotland began in 1625. Within three years he was facing a crisis and his relationship with parliament became bitter and hostile:

- He wanted to raise the wealth and status of the Church. He began by trying to take back all Church land that had been given to nobles in Scotland since 1540. The Scottish nobles were appalled and open rebellion almost broke out before Charles backed down.
- Charles was not a Catholic but he seemed to favour Catholic-style religious ceremonies. He was married to a Catholic French princess and he suspended the recusancy laws that fined people for not attending Protestant services. Charles also increased the power and authority of bishops. After decades of anti-Catholic propaganda throughout the reigns of Elizabeth and James I, Charles's pro-Catholic views were alarming.
- Charles went to war with Spain in 1625. This was an unpopular move with many MPs, who disagreed not only with the cost but also with the way the war was run by Charles's closest adviser, the Duke of Buckingham.

All these concerns resulted in criticism from MPs – and Charles could not stand criticism. When MPs threatened to put Buckingham on trial in 1626, Charles simply dissolved parliament. The following year the king found himself in need of money, but instead of calling parliament to approve a tax, he tried to raise money through a forced loan (in reality a tax rather than a loan). There was widespread discontent at this action and some MPs, landowners and even lords refused to pay. In one court case, five such 'refusers', who became known as the 'Five Knights', were held in prison without trial.

Even with the forced loan Charles was still short of money, and in 1628 he was forced to reconvene parliament. MPs had been appalled at the case of the Five Knights, and the Lords – who usually sided with the king – and the Commons joined together to force Charles to agree to the Petition of Right. This basically meant Charles could not take any steps to raise money without parliament's approval. The Petition of Right did not really heal the divisions, however, and Charles dissolved parliament again in March 1629.

ACTIVITY

Work in pairs. One of you is Charles I, the other is the ghost of his father James I, who has visited him one dark night. How do you think the conversation would go? Would James approve of Charles? Would he warn him of the dangers of exerting his authority like this? How might Charles react? Make sure you can bring real historical examples into this conversation so that it is more than just an imaginative exercise.

Discontent builds: Charles I's 'Personal Rule' 1629–40

After 1629, Charles ruled for 11 years without calling parliament once. This period became known as his 'Personal Rule', and in many respects it was quite successful:

He appointed effective ministers: In 1628, the Duke of Buckingham was assassinated. Charles mourned the loss of his friend, but it allowed him to appoint several men to the Privy Council who had not liked Buckingham but who became the king's loyal allies. These included William Laud, Thomas Wentworth, William Noy and Richard Weston, among others. Charles also appointed bishops to key political roles, including appointing the Bishop of London, William Juxon, as lord treasurer.

He brought in the religious changes he wanted: Under William Laud, churches were decorated and made more beautiful. Church services had more ceremony and ritual. A new Book of Common Prayer was introduced to Scotland in 1637.

The 'Personal Rule'

He doubled his income: Charles found ways of raising money without having to ask parliament. Juxon, Noy and Weston proved quite successful in this area, reviving a number of medieval taxes such as 'knighthood fines', which wealthy landowners had to pay if they did not go to court to receive their knighthood officially. Charles continued to collect customs duties, even though he was supposed to get parliament's agreement to do so. He also collected Ship Money – a tax traditionally levied in times of war on counties near the coast, in order to pay for the navy. Charles extended Ship Money to all counties.

He secured his rule in Ireland: Ireland had technically been under English control for centuries, but this rule was never very secure. Charles appointed Thomas Wentworth to sort this out. Wentworth had been a critic of Charles I in the 1620s, but he honoured his new appointment and ruthlessly used his forces in Ireland to suppress opposition. Wentworth was feared by his Irish enemies and became fiercely loyal to Charles, who rewarded him in 1640 by making him Earl of Strafford.

The rise of ideological opposition

These successes came at a heavy political cost. For the 11 years of the Personal Rule discontent gradually increased, especially among important sections of the Political Nation.

Practical discontent

Most people were unhappy about having to pay more taxes, and some of the wealthiest people in the kingdom were taxed especially heavily. Many priests, local gentry or nobles also disliked the king and Archbishop Laud interfering in how their churches were run. Despite this, no major protests or riots broke out during this period.

Ideological discontent

Ideological discontent was much more serious. A small but highly committed number of people began to oppose Charles for ideological reasons:

- **Religion:** Many Protestants were concerned that Charles would try to make the country Catholic again. There were rumours of a 'Popish plot' against England and Protestantism. The most dedicated of Charles's opponents were the Puritans (see Factfile), who bitterly criticised the religious changes. Hundreds of Puritans were imprisoned or tortured for this opposition (see Source 5).
- **Taxes:** Other opponents believed that Charles did not have the right to raise taxes without the consent of parliament. John Hampden, a landowner and Puritan, refused to pay Ship Money. He did not deny refusing to pay but he argued in court that the tax was illegal. The 12 judges ruled against him but it was clear that several of the king's judges shared Hampden's view. Hampden and others continued to protest against what they saw as illegal taxes.

1 Study Source 5. What impression is it trying to give about Laud? Explain how it does this.
2 What does Source 5 tell you about Puritans at this time?
3 How are Sources 6 and 7 useful to historians studying this period? Is one more useful than the other? Explain your answer.

◀ **Source 5** A woodcut published by Puritans in 1637. The man in the foreground is the Puritan William Prynne, who was arrested several times for criticising Archbishop Laud (next to Prynne). Prynne was branded on his face and had his ears cut off. In this image the ears are on a plate in front of Laud. Publishing a picture like this would have been risky.

The Puritans
● Puritans began to emerge in England in the sixteenth century, notably in the reign of Elizabeth I.
● Puritans wanted to 'purify' the Church of England to free it of all Catholic influences.
● They wanted to get rid of statues, stained-glass windows and other ornaments because they believed this distracted people from worshipping God. Puritans also believed in good manners, cleanliness and behaving in a 'godly' fashion.
● They wanted churches and worshippers to be free from the control of bishops. They believed in simple services based on readings from the Bible and discussion. It was important that people found their own way to God rather than being explicitly directed by the Church.
● Governments regarded the Puritans as troublemakers and were suspicious of them because they rejected the authority of the bishops. The government needed the bishops to control the Church and the Church to control the people. Puritans did not conform (they became known as 'dissenters' or 'nonconformists') and this was seen as a threat.

Source 6 A letter of complaint to the king from Sir Richard Strode, 1637. Strode was a Puritan and a critic of Charles I.

Laws were passed in the reign of Edward I that no tax shall be taken by the king or his heirs without the good will and agreement of the Lords and Commons. In the reign of Edward III another law said that no one shall be forced to make any loans to the king against his will. Yet contrary to these laws and freedoms, one cow worth £4 10 shillings, belonging to me was taken by the local constable and sold for the king's service to raise money for shipping, without the consent of parliament.

Source 7 Sir Edward Coke, in his book *The Institutes*, published in 1642 after his death. Coke was a lawyer and critic of Charles I. He had played a leading role in drawing up the Petition of Right in 1628.

Magna Carta is still in force today as it always has been. No free man is to be held in prison unless some lawful cause be shown. He should be given a trial by jury, or should be entitled to bail or be freed.

● **The law:** Opponents resented the king breaking with the custom of ruling with the consent of the people. He imposed strict censorship and anyone who criticised him could be imprisoned or tortured. Many of his opponents were arrested and held without trial. Sir Edward Coke was an outspoken critic of these methods and became famous for trying to use *Magna Carta* to prevent Charles ruling without the consent of the people (see Source 7).

All these forms of ideological discontent posed a potentially serious problem for Charles because those who opposed him for ideological reasons were prepared to face prison and torture for their beliefs. Despite this, however, Charles's political opponents made little headway and from 1629 to 1638 the country remained fairly stable. But then a major crisis changed all that …

War with Scotland

The crisis came when Charles tried to force Scotland to accept the religious changes he had introduced in England. The Scots refused. In 1638, their leaders set out the National Covenant, rejecting Charles's policies. In response, Charles led an army north in 1639. The Scots also gathered an army. An uneasy stalemate followed, but Charles knew he would need more soldiers to win a battle.

Convinced that the country would support him in this time of crisis, he finally called parliament in order to raise the money he needed. Many MPs did indeed support the king simply because he was the king, but there were more who were angry at the way he had governed over the past 11 years. MPs including John Pym, John Hampden and Oliver St John openly criticised the king, and Puritan MPs announced their support for the Scots. In the face of this opposition, Charles dissolved this 'Short Parliament' after only a month.

Without support, the war against the Scots went badly for Charles, and by October 1640 they had captured Newcastle. In desperation Charles called parliament again, finally willing to compromise to get the money he needed. However, when this new parliament assembled his critics launched a blistering attack on the king and forced major concessions:

- **February 1641:** MPs forced Charles to accept the Triennial Act, which stated that parliament had to meet at least once every three years.
- **May 1641:** Strafford was put on trial and executed. In the same month an act was passed stating that parliament could not be dismissed without the consent of MPs.
- **August 1641:** Ship Money was abolished.

Trust breaks down completely: the slide to civil war

The Grand Remonstrance

These concessions did not satisfy Charles's most radical opponents. In November 1641, Pym and other opposition MPs persuaded parliament to pass the Grand Remonstrance, by a majority of 259 to 148. This document listed over 200 criticisms and demands, including major changes to religious policies and an agreement that parliament should appoint the king's advisers. Charles refused them all.

Rebellion in Ireland

Matters became more serious still when news arrived of a Catholic rebellion in Ireland. Without Strafford and his army, Charles needed to find soldiers from elsewhere. However, the leading opposition MPs feared the king would use this army against them rather than against the Irish. In December 1641, they introduced the Militia Bill, which demanded that any new army should be under the control of parliament, not the king.

Charles tries to arrest five MPs

Charles accused the MPs of treason and in January 1642 he tried to arrest five of them, including Pym and Hampden. He broke the traditional rules by bringing troops into parliament, eliminating all trust between the monarch and parliament. Both sides called on the local gentry in the counties of England to join their militias and encourage their tenants and neighbours to join them. In August 1642, Charles declared war on his own parliament.

Source 8 A report on the rebellion in Ireland in 1641. The majority of the Irish were Catholics and they rose up against Protestant settlers loyal to England. Terrible atrocities were committed and propaganda like this exaggerated them further, which alarmed and angered Protestants in England. ▼

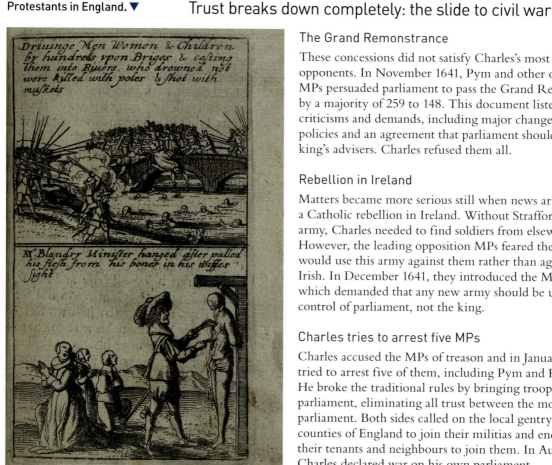

Taking sides: the Political Nation divides

So far we have focused mainly on the opponents of Charles I, investigating why many MPs and members of the House of Lords opposed him. But not everyone was against the king. In fact the country was deeply and bitterly divided, and it was not unusual for members of the same family to be on opposite sides. Even parliament was not united. Some members of the House of Commons and many members of the House of Lords were on the king's side.

Reasons why people sided with parliament	Reasons why people sided with the king
• Charles had tried to rule without parliament. • He was not respecting the law. • His religious views seemed too Catholic.	• The king was appointed by God and challenging him was wrong, even if they disagreed with some of his actions. • Rule by the Puritans and Charles's opponents would be even worse than rule by the king himself. • The king stood for order. Without him society would fall apart.

However, the majority of the population was probably neutral and were keen to avoid war.

> **Source 9** A letter from a gentleman called Thomas Wiseman to his friend Sir John Penington, describing events in early 1642.
>
> *His Majesty yesterday made a gracious speech to the Lord Mayor and city officials. He did as much as he could to satisfy them all. They cried out to his Majesty to maintain the privilege of parliament. He gently replied to them that it was his wish to do so and he would not in the least invade upon them. But they must allow him to distinguish between the parliament and some discontented members in it who have tried by acts of treason to hurt him and to take away the loyalty of his people. Afterwards, returning to Whitehall, the crowd followed him crying: 'Privileges of Parliament!' The good king was somewhat affected and I believe was glad when he was at home. ...*
>
> *What these disorders will produce God only knows, but it is feared they must end in blood. The Puritan groups are too many, both in city and countryside, so that if the king and Parliament should disagree, no man can tell which party would be strongest.*
>
> *On Tuesday his Majesty went to the House of Commons to arrest those that were accused of treason, but they were not there to be found. The House it seems is taking it badly that the king should come to break their privileges. From what I understand, they decided to protect their members and not to deliver them into the hands of the king. They have such support in the city that to take them by force will cost great misery.*

> **Source 10** A petition sent to the king and to parliament from the gentry of Somerset, August 1642.
>
> *We hear conflicting commands issued from the commanders of both sides, to the great terror of us who are ready to obey all commands based on the laws of this kingdom. We ask that his gracious Majesty would please suspend the call for troops for his forces. We ask that the High Court of Parliament would likewise please suspend the carrying out of their order for the militia. We ask that his Majesty and the members of both Houses of Parliament would please assemble again and come to an arrangement according to the law. Or take some other good course to establish the peace and security of this kingdom. And we ask that in the meantime the militia of this county be controlled by the Justices of the Peace of this county according to the laws now in force.*

1 Study Sources 9 and 10. Is it possible to say whether one is more useful than the other to a historian studying this period? Explain your answer.

ACTIVITY

There are many key events described on these pages. We have chosen to illustrate only one – the Irish rebellion in 1641 (Source 8). Was this a good choice? Would you have chosen a picture of a different event if you were the author of this book? If so, make a suggestion using websites such as the British Library and the National Archives.

Part 2: From civil war to revolution to republic 1642–49

The English Civil War was horrific. The fighting was brutal and atrocities were carried out against civilians by both sides. Ordinary people were taxed and taxed again. As armies moved around, people were forced to give up food and horses to provide for the troops. There was widespread LOOTING. In some areas local 'neutralist' forces set themselves up to keep both sides out of their counties. Large areas of England, Scotland and Ireland were devastated by war, starvation and disease. There are no accurate figures but historians estimate that England suffered around 3.7 per cent loss of population (more than in the First World War), Scotland lost around 6 per cent and Ireland a catastrophic 41 per cent.

> **Source 11** A petition from Mary Baker to stop a parliamentary County Committee in Kent taking her husband's money, July 1643. County Committees were set up by parliament to raise money for its war effort.
>
> *In April the parliament's County Committee in Kent seized the estate of Mary's husband in Kent, where his mansion house (about 40 miles from London) and all his land lies, to the value of about £2000. Mary's husband is in very poor health, his whole estate has been seized, and so he cannot pay any extra. Yet a warrant was issued against Mary's husband to pay more tax. In truth Mary's husband is much in debt, and has at this time no means left to maintain himself, and his wife and children.*

Source 12 The front page of a news sheet showing events in the north of England during the war. Scenes like this would have been seen all over England, Scotland and Ireland. ▼

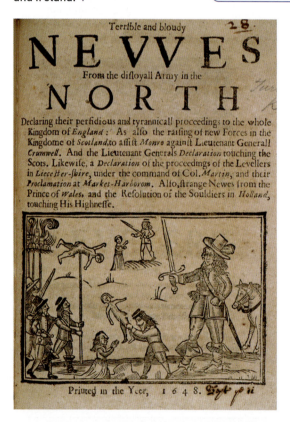

1 Study Sources 11 and 12. Do you think they would make people more likely to support king or parliament, or just to want an end to the war? Explain your answer.

The First Civil War 1642–46

By the summer of 1643 it looked as though Charles had the upper hand, but this changed in September the following year when the Scots joined parliamentary forces to defeat Charles at the Battle of Marston Moor. Despite this, both sides were weakened by internal disagreements and neither could maintain the upper hand.

In 1645, parliament established the New Model Army – a better-organised, well-equipped, well-trained and disciplined fighting force. Many soldiers were Puritans, or sympathetic to Puritan ideas, who had read about the new political and religious ideas that emerged during the war. The troops saw themselves as an army in the service of God against a bad king who was in league with Catholics. The most important of the army's commanders was a fiery Puritan cavalry officer called Oliver Cromwell. The New Model Army inflicted a series of defeats on Charles. In May 1646, the king surrendered to Scottish forces but they handed him over to parliament and he was imprisoned (see Source 13).

Trying to reach a settlement 1646–48

Everyone in the country – ordinary people and the Political Nation – now wanted peace above all else. The big problem for parliamentary leaders was how to reach a settlement with Charles. There was no suggestion at this stage of getting rid of the king or replacing him, but parliament wanted an agreement that would allow it more control over the Church, the army and who the king chose as his advisers.

Between July 1646 and December 1647, parliament put four different proposals to Charles, but he refused them all. Despite the fact that that he was in prison, the king was still in a reasonably strong position for two main reasons, which are outlined opposite.

People wanted to get back to the way things were before the war

After a war, armies usually disbanded and went home. But after Charles's defeat the New Model Army did not do this. People were sick of having to feed, house and pay for troops.

Rule by parliament in the Civil War had turned out to be just as harsh as rule by Charles I.

Many traditionally powerful people had lost status to new men appointed by parliament to the County Committees. They wanted their old status and position back. They also worried about the growing political power of the army.

Most of the Political Nation, and probably the ordinary people too, were alarmed by the emergence of new political and religious groups with radical ideas (see Factfile on page 72). The king represented certainty and stability in a frightening world. The strict control that Charles and Laud had used began to look like a good idea.

Charles's opponents were divided

The Political Presbyterians wanted:
- little or no limit on Charles's power
- a strict religious policy and to crush those who disagreed with it
- to get rid of the New Model Army.

The Political Independents:
- wanted more control over Charles
- wanted more toleration of different religious views
- were generally sympathetic towards the New Model Army.

There was tension between the army and parliament because:
- parliament was behind with its pay
- during the war many army officers and soldiers became more interested in politics.

The army was divided among itself. The ordinary soldiers and officers generally wanted a tougher settlement with the king. Many troops agreed with or supported the Levellers (see Factfile on page 72). The Levellers wanted the vote for all men and much more power for ordinary people. These ideas were too radical for the army commanders and eventually they crushed the Levellers by force. However, the top army commanders were more cautious and were closer to the Political Independents in parliament.

Source 13 The cover of a pamphlet entitled 'The World Turned Upside Down'. It was published in London in 1647 and reprinted in 1649. ▼

THE
World turn'd upfide down:
OR,
A briefe defcription of the ridiculous Fafhions of thefe diftracted Times.
By T.J. a well-willer to King, Parliament and Kingdom.

London : Printed for John Smith. 1647.
Jan: 24

The Second Civil War 1648–49

In this context, Charles could probably have negotiated a favourable settlement. Instead he tried to exploit the divisions among his opponents. He rejected all the proposals presented by parliament. In November 1647, he escaped from prison and formed an alliance with parliament's former allies, the Scots. From March to July 1648 Charles's supporters attacked the New Model Army in parts of southern England and Wales while the Scots attacked from the north.

This Second Civil War was over by August. Charles was recaptured in 1648 and imprisoned on the Isle of Wight (see Source 14 on page 72). Parliament tried once again to negotiate with the king but even now he would not consider compromise. Despite this, the majority of the population still wanted the king restored.

2 Make a list of all of the ways the world has been turned upside down in Source 13.

3 Suggest four events that you think inspired the artist to create Source 13.

4 Do you get the impression that the artist was a supporter of one side or the other?

5 Explain how this source is helpful in understanding why many people were anxious at this time and saw the restoration of the king as the answer.

FACTFILE

Radical groups

During the English Civil War, most of the censorship and other restrictions under Laud were not maintained. There was an outburst of radical new political and religious ideas. Here are some of the new groups that emerged at this time.

The Levellers

- Led by John Lilburne and Richard Overton, the Levellers argued for much greater equality (or levelling) in society.
- They generated huge support in the army and in many towns and cities in particular. Thousands signed petitions or went to demonstrations, and branches were set up all over the country.
- The Levellers believed that government should have the consent of the people. They wanted to make sure parliament met regularly and that there would be frequent elections in which most men could vote, not just those with property.
- The Levellers also wanted all local officials (such as magistrates) to be locally elected, not appointed by the king or parliament.
- They wanted freedom of religion – a person's right to worship in any way they wanted.

The Diggers

- The Diggers or True Levellers were more radical than the Levellers. They basically believed in living in communes with no Church, no government or authority figures at all – the people would police themselves.

The Ranters

- Ranters were more religious than political. They believed that since God made them, and He was without sin, then they too could not sin. This essentially meant they could do what they liked. Accounts of the Ranters describe them getting up to all kinds of mischief, mainly involving sex and drinking.

The Quakers

- Quakers rejected the need for churches, bishops or any other kind of religious authority. They believed that individuals should make decisions according to their own conscience.
- Authority figures regarded the Quakers as particularly dangerous because their ideas challenged the position of traditional figures of authority.

Impact

We do not have much evidence about these groups, and what we have was largely created by people who were hostile to them. They were probably very small in number and their real significance was how they alarmed people at the time. The nobles, gentry and the men who served as MPs genuinely feared that law and order would break down if these groups were allowed to question traditional authority. The radical groups probably increased support for a settlement with the king – not what they would have intended at all!

Source 14 A pamphlet exhorting (urging) all people to be faithful subjects to the king, printed in 1648. At this time Charles was imprisoned on the Isle of Wight. ▼

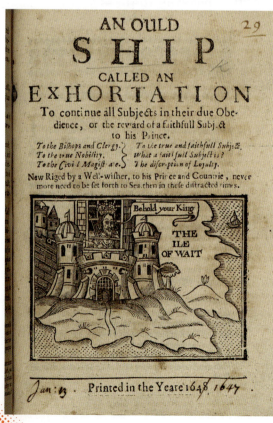

Source 15 The cover page of *Eikon Basilike*, a book that was thought to be Charles's own writings about himself, published soon after his death. Thousands of copies were printed and sold, including miniature copies that were easy to hide. ▼

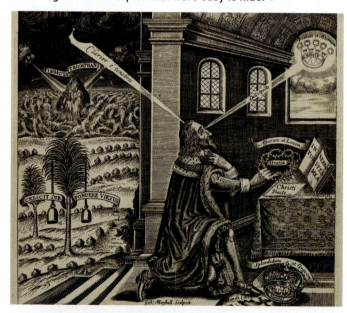

1 Source 14 is sympathetic to the king. How can you tell? Explain your answer
2 Study Source 15. Find three examples of imagery that suggests Charles was holy or saint-like. You can find detailed analyses of this image on the internet.

The trial and execution of Charles: the English Revolution

By January 1649, Charles I was dead and England no longer had a monarch. Such a dramatic turn of events came about because of a small group of MPs and army commanders. The key figure in this revolution was Oliver Cromwell – by now the most respected figure in the army. Throughout 1647 he had favoured a settlement with Charles, but by late 1648 his views had changed. He and the other senior commanders now wanted to put Charles on trial:

- Cromwell felt that Charles could not be trusted to stick to any agreement. If he was restored to power he would behave exactly as before and cause another war.
- Cromwell also believed that God had shown his disapproval of Charles through his defeats. Cromwell was intensely religious and he saw the victories of the New Model Army as proof that the army had God's favour.

Even a powerful figure like Cromwell faced intense opposition. Parliament was opposed to putting the king on trial. So in December 1648, Colonel Thomas Pride threw out a large number of MPs opposed to the measure, leaving behind a 'Rump Parliament' of about 200 MPs (out of over 500). It is not known whether Cromwell ordered this action, but it seems likely.

Once the king was put on trial it was inevitable he would be found guilty. Charles's son (also called Charles) pleaded with Cromwell for his father's life and sent a signed, sealed, blank parchment indicating he would agree to anything to save him. Charles himself refused to recognise the authority of the court and made no attempt to defend himself. Some historians believe that he had already decided that he was on his way to Heaven (see Source 15).

Charles was executed on 30 January 1649. The nation was shocked and terrified – it is difficult for us to imagine today what a traumatic event this was for people at the time (see Source 16). It was also a hugely significant event politically – a reigning monarch had been overthrown and executed, not by barons or nobles but by the commanders of the army with some support from parliament. What is more, he had met this end because he had ruled badly. The idea of divine right had not only been challenged, it had been destroyed. England now had to find a new way to rule itself.

Source 16 Historian Mark Goldie, speaking on a radio programme in 2001.

The execution of Charles I was very unpopular indeed. It was carried out by a small clique within the army. I think they had very good reasons for doing it, the main reason being that Charles I was simply a man you could not do business with. You could never trust anything he said. He would agree to things but his secret letters to his wife or friends made it clear he had no intention of honouring his word. The officers felt that they had no choice other than to remove him, but the country was horrified. Next to executing God it is hard to see what could be more horrifying – after all most people thought of the king as God's representative on earth.

Source 17 A playing card produced in the 1660s. It is claiming that Cromwell was a hypocrite, praying while he had the king murdered. ▼

Oliver seeking God while the K. is murthered by his order.

FOCUS TASK

Why was the king executed in 1649?

Source 17 suggests that Cromwell plotted the murder of Charles I. Your task is to investigate whether there is any evidence to support this view. Study this section on the Civil War and put together two cases:

- evidence that Cromwell planned the death of Charles I
- evidence that Charles brought about his own death through his actions.

You could hold an inquest on this issue and vote as a class.

Part 3: England without a king

The Commonwealth and the Rump Parliament 1649–53

England was now the Commonwealth, ruled by the Rump Parliament. The Rump abolished the monarchy and the House of Lords. These were revolutionary measures. However, most of the time the Rump MPs were very cautious. They feared change and new ideas. They pressured Cromwell to crush the Levellers. They brought back censorship. MPs saw the Church as a key force to regain stability and control. They wanted to make church attendance compulsory and all services to be the same. People would start to know their place again and this would restore respect for authority.

However, Cromwell and the army leaders had not fought a war and executed the king just to return to the old style of worship, in which they were told what to think and how to behave. As Puritans, they wanted more religious toleration (freedom) so people could study the Bible, ask questions, discuss ideas and so come closer to God. This type of thinking terrified the Rump MPs. Eventually, Cromwell lost patience dismissed the Rump in April 1653.

The Barebones Parliament 1653

At this point Cromwell could have made England a dictatorship ruled by the army, but he realised how unpopular this would be. On the other hand he was not prepared to let people elect a new parliament because he feared they would elect many anti-army MPs. Instead he appointed a parliament of 144 men who were generally sympathetic to Cromwell's views. Unfortunately, this 'Barebones Parliament' actually turned out to be so radical that even Cromwell was alarmed! He dismissed the Barebones Parliament in 1653.

Rule by Cromwell: the Protectorate 1653–58

In the next attempt, a new constitution called the Instrument of Government was drawn up by the army. Cromwell became lord protector. Parliament was reformed too. There were 400 MPs and as far as possible their CONSTITUENCIES had similar populations. Parliament would meet regularly. Parliament and the lord protector shared control of the army. Cromwell promised to work with a Council of State of 15 members, only four of whom were from the army. It was a sensible attempt to find a solution that was acceptable to the army and to parliament.

The major-generals

Cromwell wanted political and social stability but he also wanted religious reform. In addition, he wanted what he called 'a reformation of manners', which meant people behaving more like Puritans. He divided England into regions, each ruled by a major-general. The major-generals passed laws to stamp out swearing, adultery, prostitution, drunkenness and gambling. Most famously, they tried to ban Christmas! The rule of the major-generals was deeply unpopular and a failure. The local gentry resented the major-generals because they interfered with their authority as justices and magistrates

The Humble Petition and Advice 1657

In 1657, parliament presented Cromwell with the Humble Petition and Advice. This proposed abolishing the major-generals, a reduction in the army and that parliament should have more power over taxes. It also asked Cromwell to become king. Cromwell recognised how unpopular the major-generals were. To compromise with parliament he accepted almost all the proposals. However, he knew that the army would not want him to accept the Crown, so he refused.

1 Which of these is a fairer statement about Cromwell?
   a He was weak because he could not make up his mind.
   b He was committed to two different causes and they were not compatible.
   Make sure you can explain your answer.

Source 18 A Royalist propaganda print called 'The Royal Oak of Britain'. It was created in 1649 but not officially published until 1660. We do not know how widely it was seen in the 1650s, but its creator was arrested for treason in 1651 and died in prison. ▶

Source 19 Edward Hyde, a Royalist, commenting on Cromwell in a book begun in the 1640s but not published until the 1720s.

Cromwell was guilty of many crimes for which he will be damned and for which hell-fire is prepared. He also had some good qualities, which have caused the memory of some men in all ages to be celebrated. He will be looked upon in future as a brave wicked man.

Source 20 Historian Barry Coward, writing in 2001.

Royalist attempts to start uprisings against Cromwell had little or no support. The traditionalist style of Cromwell's government made his regime respectable and attractive. Cromwell generally did not try to bypass local authority figures and concentrate power in his own hands. Above all, republican government was attractive because it worked. It maintained social order and stability. In the economic disruption which followed the civil wars the system of poor relief was generally effective. From the perspective of most English people, government worked at least as well and in some cases better than at any other time in the century. The wounds opened up by the Civil War began to heal in the 1650s. There was a comforting drift back to normality and stability.

2 What is Source 18 saying about Cromwell? How is the message put across?
3 Do you think Sources 18–20 provide a good summary of Cromwell's career? Explain your answer.

FOCUS TASK

Cromwell's qualities

In this book so far, you have seen some of the qualities of an effective ruler. For example:
- a strong legal claim to the throne
- military success
- successful introduction of laws, taxes, etc.
- ability to exert authority over subjects
- co-operation with and support from subjects
- control of religion/the Church.

On a scale of 1 to 10 (where 10 is the best), how well do you think Cromwell scores in these areas?

Extension: How would you rate Charles I on this scale? Or other rulers you have studied in Chapters 1 and 2?

Part 4: The Restoration

Cromwell died in 1658. He had nominated his son Richard to rule England after him and there were no strong objections to this decision. The Political Nation and the people wanted peace and stability and they did not care who provided it. We know from his letters that Charles I's son was not expecting to be restored to the throne of England even after Cromwell died. Yet within two years, he had been crowned Charles II. How did this happen?

Richard Cromwell did not have his father's personality, ability or drive to run the country.

His father had not involved him in politics so he had little experience and no support in the army or parliament. Richard Cromwell gave up his leadership and retired to his lands in May 1659.

Parliament and the army could not work together.

The Rump Parliament was restored in May 1659, but by October the commander of the army in England, John Lambert, had dismissed the MPs and replaced the Rump with an army-dominated Committee of Public Safety.

The army was divided.

The commander of the army in Scotland, George Monck, refused to accept Lambert's actions and supported parliament. He also had the support of many troops and most of the navy. In December 1659, Lambert backed down and the Rump Parliament was restored a month later.

It was clear that government could not work without a king or a king-like figure.

Oliver Cromwell had been acceptable to both the army and parliament, but no one matched him in drive or stature. The Political Nation feared more conflict. The most obvious solution was to restore the monarchy.

Parliament began to negotiate with Charles I's son.

He accepted the terms parliament offered in the Declaration of Breda. In April 1660, Charles II returned as king, to be greeted by cheering crowds.

RESTORATION

Source 21 A print from a book published in England in 1681. The top image shows Charles II returning. ▼

1 Look at Source 21. Does this image prove that the Restoration of Charles II was popular?

Charles II: back to square one?

From a modern perspective, it is easy to see the 1640s and 1650s as a time of progress for parliament. However, at the time few people viewed parliament as a good thing. Greater powers for parliament had brought civil war, death and destruction. It had unleashed disruptive forces such as the Levellers. Parliament's County Committees and the major-generals had attacked the authority of many members of the Political Nation in their local areas in a way that the king never had. Even many MPs wanted to strengthen the power of the Crown rather than weaken it, so on his restoration Charles II was granted many of the same powers his father had enjoyed.

Charles II controlled the army, not parliament. However, he could VETO any law put forward by parliament and parliament could not pass a new law without the king's approval. Censorship was brought back and mass demonstrations were banned.

On the other hand, some of the limitations that parliament had placed the king's power since 1640 remained. Charles II could never claim Ship Money or other taxes that his father had used. These limitations were confirmed by a new parliament (often called the 'Cavalier Parliament'), which was elected in 1661. So although Charles II did not have to call parliament, he actually did so regularly – almost every year from 1661 to 1679.

On his restoration, Charles faced three major issues.

- **How to treat those who had opposed his father:** Charles effectively agreed in the Declaration of Breda that he would forgive and forget. The Indemnity Act of 1661 pardoned all but a small number who had been involved in the king's death. Charles faced criticism for this act from some of his own supporters but there was probably little else he could do without risking another civil war.
- **How to raise money to pay for the running of the country:** The Crown lost a lot of land and wealth in the 1640s and 1650s. Parliament agreed a new hearth tax (a tax on every fireplace in a house – so houses with more fireplaces paid more tax). This raised a lot of money but not enough, so Charles would still need to ask parliament if he was short of money.
- **What to do about the Church and religious beliefs:** One religious group, the Fifth Monarchists, staged an unsuccessful rebellion in 1661. This led to the introduction of the Clarendon Code. Dissenters (Puritans, Quakers and other groups) were not actively persecuted, but the Code enforced a conformist Anglican (Church of England) Church on the majority of the population:
  - People were fined if they did not attend an Anglican church.
  - Anglican services used the same prayer book and services.
  - The government had a say in the appointment of bishops and in the sermons that were preached every Sunday.
  - Only Anglicans could be educated or hold public offices.

Whigs and Tories

Charles proved a capable ruler, but in the late 1670s and early 1680s there was a growing concern that he was too sympathetic towards Catholics. Two political groups emerged – WHIGS and TORIES. Both sides published petitions and pamphlets, and held demonstrations and public meetings. The Whigs wanted more restrictions on the power of the king and greater powers for parliament. They also wanted to exclude Charles's brother James from the line of succession because he was a Catholic. The Tories opposed the Whigs.

Charles came down hard on the Whigs – several members of the group were executed and their leader went into exile.

By the time Charles II died, therefore, there were already some serious divisions within the country. How well would his brother, now James II, handle them?

2.3 The Glorious Revolution and its consequences

FOCUS

Historians tend to get suspicious when an event in history is given a title that includes the words 'glorious' or 'great'. After all, war and revolution are seldom glorious. In this topic, you will examine the Glorious Revolution of 1688 and see how the events of that year earned this title. You will examine:

- the rule of James II
- the events that led to his overthrow in 1688
- the settlement that followed and its short- and long-term significance.

The big questions historians are interested in about this period are the causes of the Glorious Revolution and how far it changed the balance of power.

The big picture

The Glorious Revolution

What did James II do wrong?

After the Restoration in 1660, Charles II faced many challenges but he proved to be a reasonably effective ruler. He asserted his authority but he also made concessions to the Political Nation to keep them on his side. James II was much less able. He began to favour Catholics by giving them posts in government and relaxing some of the restrictions that parliament had placed on them. James also acted like his father, Charles I, by listening to his close friends and allies and excluding others from the decision-making process.

What was the Glorious Revolution?

James II's actions alarmed some of the more powerful members of the aristocracy. This became more serious when James's Catholic wife gave birth to a son, meaning that the country might one day have a Catholic king. The leading nobles organised a rebellion against James. They invited James's Protestant daughter Mary and her husband William, the ruler of most of the provinces of the Netherlands (of which Holland was the most powerful), to take James's place. James fled to his friend Louis XIV of France. Louis gave him an army to try to win back his throne, and James landed in Ireland to gather support from Irish Catholics. He was defeated in 1689.

The Glorious Revolution was an illegal overthrow of a legitimate monarch, so William and Mary, and their rebel supporters, came up with a version of events that made them seem legal. Laws were set in place to guarantee that a Catholic could never rule England.

How and why did power change hands in this period?

The leading nobles in parliament had overthrown one king and placed another on the throne. William and Mary agreed to a new constitution that limited their powers. From this point on parliament became increasingly powerful, while the monarchy's power declined.

FOCUS TASK

The changing balance of power 1660–88

In previous sections, you have made some comparisons between the power of different individuals or groups. This is the last challenge for the early modern period. Draw your own version of this graph and chart the high points and low points of power in this period for:

- Charles II
- parliament
- James II
- William and Mary.

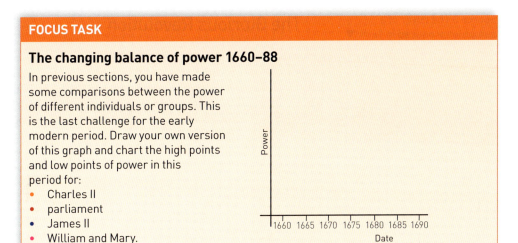

The brief reign of James II

Charles II's reign had enjoyed some success, but there were still tensions when his brother James II came to the throne in 1685. James would need skill and diplomacy to manage them – unfortunately, he lacked both these qualities. He immediately faced a rebellion by the Duke of Monmouth, Charles II's illegitimate son, who felt he had a claim to the throne. James crushed the rebellion, but parliament grew concerned when James kept his large army in case of further trouble. Recent history had shown the dangers of a monarch with a large army at his command.

James's religious policies were the biggest problem for the Political Nation. In the years after the Civil War, James had lived in France and had converted to Catholicism. His wife was Catholic and he remained on friendly terms with King Louis XIV even after Louis revoked tolerance for Huguenots in France in 1685, causing many to flee the country. James began to show signs of restoring England to Catholicism:

- In 1686, he forbade Anglican ministers to preach anti-Catholic sermons.
- In 1687, he began to remove Protestants from government posts, replacing them with Catholic ministers.
- In 1687 and 1688, he published documents called Indulgences, which said that the king had the right to set aside particular laws if he felt it necessary. The laws he had in mind were the Test and Corporation Acts (which barred Catholics from roles such as army officers, justices and MPs) and Habeas Corpus (which said that a person could not be arrested and held without being given a fair trial).
- In 1688, his wife had a son. Until this point James's heir was his Protestant daughter Mary, born before his conversion. Now he had a Catholic son.

Source 1 Historian Mark Goldie, speaking on a radio programme in 2001.

James II was quite unsuited to be king. In fact he was a complete idiot. He attempted to enforce a return to the Catholic Church on a country which was bitterly opposed to anything even remotely connected to the Catholic Church.

1 Think back over your course so far. Is James II the worst ruler you have come across? If **yes**, list the reasons and contrast his actions with one ruler you think was effective. If **no**, state which ruler you think was worse. List reasons why this other ruler was worse than James II.

Source 2 An engraving showing William of Orange landing in Devon with his army in 1688. ▼

'Please invade us!'

Although the Political Nation was reluctant to rebel for fear of plunging the country back into war, many felt there was no choice. Several Protestant nobles and bishops sent a petition to the Dutch prince William of Orange, inviting him to invade England. William was the husband of James II's daughter Mary. As well as upholding his wife's inheritance, William was eager to gain the support of England in his wars against France.

James began to frantically reverse his policies in an attempt to avoid his overthrow, but his opponents were determined to remove him. William landed his forces in Devon in November 1688 and James fled to France.

The Glorious Revolution

Although Mary was officially now ruler of the country, William insisted on – and was given – the full authority of the monarchy. As part of the deal with parliament to put them on the throne, William and Mary had to agree to a new CONSTITUTION (a set of rules for government). This event was called the GLORIOUS REVOLUTION by John Hampden, the grandson of the John Hampden you met on page 68. He was clearly pleased at the way things had turned out – a bad monarch gone, a new and more acceptable monarch in his place. The name stuck. But how much of a 'revolution' was this really?

For many ordinary people in England, the change of monarch would have had little impact. This was not like the Civil War or the Protectorate – there was no fighting and no attempt to change the laws that governed daily life or church services. However, it did bring about changes for the Political Nation (Lords, MPs, gentry) – those who were most closely involved in government. The main consequences are outlined below.

1 Scotland became more independent

Scottish MPs demanded full control of the Church in Scotland. They also insisted on the abolition of bishops and the right to appoint chief ministers in Scotland. William did not want to agree to any of these demands but he knew that some of his strongest support was in Scotland, so in 1690 he conceded to these demands. Scotland became more independent than it had been since the time of Cromwell.

2 Ireland came under Protestant control

James fled to France, where Louis XIV supplied him with troops to win back his throne. James landed in Catholic Ireland, where he knew he could gain more support. After several bloody battles and sieges, William's forces finally defeated James in 1690. William offered the rebels fairly generous terms in the Treaty of Limerick, but his own supporters in Ireland demanded much harsher terms. Ireland was now ruled by a small class of English Protestants and the large Catholic population of Ireland found themselves second-class citizens. In the short term Ireland became stable, but this situation would result in further rebellions in the 1700s and 1800s.

3 Catholics were barred from the throne

To prevent future disagreement or rebellion it was important to agree on exactly what had happened in legal terms:

- The Whigs seized on Hampden's name for the events of 1688 and claimed the 'Glorious Revolution' as a triumph of the people and parliament. They had overthrown a monarch who had failed in his duty to rule with the consent of the people.
- Tories could not accept this. They believed in the principle of the divine right of kings, which meant that overthrowing a king was a sin against God. They did not want James II back but they felt that William should legally be the regent rather than the king.

William and the Whigs refused to accept the lesser status, so eventually it was agreed that James II had abdicated (given up) his throne and parliament had been forced to invite William to take his place. Of course this was not what had actually happened, but it was a version of events that kept everyone happy. Once this was agreed, the BILL OF RIGHTS confirmed that Catholics would be barred from inheriting the throne of England, Scotland and Ireland.

4 The powers of the monarchy were limited ...

William remained an influential ruler, but there were limits placed on his power:

- William and Mary had to swear an oath at their coronation to rule *according to the laws passed in parliament*. This was an important statement – the monarchy accepted that it was not above the law.
- A Bill of Rights was agreed that prevented the monarch from suspending laws or keeping a large army in peacetime.
- The same bill also made sure that parliament would meet at least once a year, and gave MPs the right to free speech while they were in parliament (so they would not be arrested for criticising the monarch).
- William was also given the right to collect important taxes, such as customs, but only for a four-year period. This was a way of guaranteeing that he would continue to work with parliament.

... to a degree!

Despite these limits William was more than just a figurehead. Parliament proposed 20 other measures to be included in the Bill of Rights, which William refused. The king still took the major decisions, such as going to war. He appointed most of the top jobs in the army, the government and the Church. It was not difficult to find allies when they knew they would be rewarded with these sorts of positions.

More importantly, however, most people – nobles, MPs and the rest of the Political Nation – did not want to disagree with the king. The position of monarch was still regarded with awe and reverence by virtually all his subjects. For most, the limits imposed were in case of emergencies such as a monarch ruling badly like Charles I or James II.

5 Religious freedom increased ... for Protestants

In 1689, a Toleration Act was passed. This made it legal for Protestants to belong to churches other than the Church of England. There were still many restrictions on non-Anglicans, however. They were still unable to get a university education or serve in the army or in government.

> **Source 5** Historian Professor John Morrill, writing in 1996.
>
> *The Glorious Revolution was more like one of those occasions in the medieval period when a king was overthrown. It changed the monarch without doing much to the monarchy. The political settlement which followed was a compromise but like Elizabeth's settlement in 1559 it turned out to be long-lasting. The compromise came about because those who were moderately Tory and those who were moderately Whig agreed not to force their ideas down each other's throats. Most importantly, the principle of religious toleration – that you could be a Protestant but not in the Church of England – was accepted. It was grudging and it did not go very far but it was still an important principle.*

> **Source 4** Historian Paul Langford, writing in 1984.
>
> *With some reservations the changes of 1688 can be seen as revolutionary. The Bill of Rights clearly over-rode the inherited rights and powers of the monarch and replaced it with the will of the nation expressed through Parliament. William and Mary, and then Queen Anne, and then the Hanoverians all owed their position to the landowning aristocracy.*

FOCUS TASK

A Glorious *Revolution*? Part 1

We are not going to ask whether you think the Glorious Revolution was glorious, because this cannot be measured with evidence. However, it is possible to consider whether these events deserve the term 'revolution'.

1 Study Sources 4 and 5. How far do they agree or disagree?
2 Think about how the following aspects of politics changed in the Glorious Revolution and give each a mark on a scale of 1 to 10, where 10 means the change was revolutionary:
   a how the ruler was chosen
   b the attitude of the political factions (the Whigs and Tories) towards each other
   c the balance of power between parliament and monarch
   d religion.

Make sure you can explain your decision and back it up with evidence.

How did Britain change after 1688?

You may have had a lively debate about how much change the Glorious Revolution brought about in the short term, but there is no doubt that a lot changed in the years that followed.

War with France

William of Orange was already at war with Louis XIV of France when he became king. He brought Britain into this war, which continued for another 25 years.

The Bank of England

Wars required money, and such a long and large-scale war effort needed a *lot* of money. The BANK OF ENGLAND was set up and investors effectively loaned the country money in return for interest or other benefits. This was the NATIONAL DEBT, which governments still have today.

Source 6 The Royal Charter of the Bank of England, 1694. Set up to raise £1.2 million for the monarchy, the bank also acted as the government's banker and debt manager. Its role today is much broader. ▼

Parliament and the emergence of political parties

Investors lent to the Bank of England because they knew that parliament would raise taxes to pay back the loans and interest. This made parliament more important, and rulers had to get a majority of MPs on their side in order to vote through taxes. As a result, parliament began to meet more and more regularly, and many elections were held.

MPs needed support because being a member of parliament was no longer a part-time job. MPs tended to group into parties – at first the Whigs and the Tories. Rulers tried to work with the leaders of the parties to try to get taxes and other measures they wanted through parliament. Instead of rulers appointing advisers, they began to appoint ministers from particular parties in return for their help in pushing the required measures through parliament.

Government developed into a system of parliamentary monarchy, with ministers, rather than the monarch, doing much of the business of running the country. This was especially true in the reign of Queen Anne (1702–14), as she was often pregnant or unwell and therefore unable to rule directly. This reliance on ministers increased during the 1700s under the Georgian kings.

This marked the beginning of the system of government we have today, although it was not democratic by today's standards. Ministers and MPs were almost all from the landowning aristocracy or gentry classes.

A new royal family

Mary died in 1694 and William died in 1702. They had no children so Mary's younger sister Anne inherited the throne. Anne had 14 children, but none of them survived into adulthood. There were still members of the Stuart family with a claim to the throne, but Catholics were banned from the line of inheritance. As early as 1701, parliament had passed the Act of Settlement, offering the crown to the ruling family of Hanover in Germany. So when Anne died in 1714, the Hanoverians took over (also known as the Georgians as the next four kings were all called George).

England and Scotland: the Act of Union 1707

Scotland suffered a massive economic disaster in the early 1700s. In return for financial investment from England, the Scottish parliament agreed to dissolve itself, and England and Scotland were united in the Act of Union of 1707. Not all Scots accepted this, especially once George I became king in 1714. In 1715, there was an uprising in Scotland by supporters of the Stuarts (known as Jacobites). This rebellion, and another in 1745, were both crushed.

The triumph of the British aristocracy

The Glorious Revolution laid the foundations for the landowning aristocracy to become the dominant force in Britain for the next 200 years. This was remarkable given that only 40 years earlier the House of Lords had been abolished and many nobles had fled into exile. As a result of Queen Anne's health problems and pregnancies, and the fact that the Georgian kings were often absent and were unfamiliar with Britain, aristocrats took on the key roles in government, and the aristocracy came to dominate parliament.

Source 7 Parliament in the 1790s, showing the prime minister speaking to MPs. The man in the big chair is the Speaker of the House, who makes sure MPs follow the rules. ▶

1. Look closely at the MPs shown in the painting in Source 7. What can you tell about them from their appearance, clothing, hair, etc.?
2. Use a search engine to find a modern picture of parliament. How much change can you see?

PRACTICE QUESTIONS

1. Describe the problems between James II and parliament in the 1680s. (4)
2. Explain why James II was overthrown in 1688. (8)
3. What was the significance of the Restoration in 1660? (14)

FOCUS TASK

A Glorious *Revolution*? Part 2

Make a table like the one below and complete it to analyse the changes described on these two pages.

Changes after 1688	How significant a change? (on a scale of 1 to 5)	Connection to Glorious Revolution: Direct result? Indirect result? No connection at all?

2.4 Review: Power c1000–c1800

PERIOD REVIEW TASK

In this chapter, you have studied different examples of power in action through the early modern period. You are now going to at those developments in a wider context – seeing how this part of the story compares with medieval times.

A Claims to the throne

1 In the early modern period, what gave rulers a claim to the throne and how was that different from in the medieval period?

2 On page 48 you considered what gave people a claim to the throne in medieval times. Look back at that work to fill out column 2 in a copy of the table below. We have added an extra row, so you might need to think hard about that for the medieval period.

3 Using your work from Chapter 2, add examples from the early modern period. You do not have to include every example you can find. Remember, you are looking for the big picture!

Basis of claim	Examples from c1000–c1485 of this being ...		Examples from c1485–c1700 of this being ...		Observations (e.g. more important at particular times)
	important	not important	important	not important	
glorious ancestors					
a legal claim					
inheritance					
military power					
support of leading nobles					
religion					

B Conflict and co-operation in the medieval and early modern periods

4 A book publisher is looking for a title for a book about the period 1000–1688. There are two possible titles. Which title would you recommend? Make your own copy of the table below and fill it in before you decide.

Power and Monarchy c1000 – c1688 A Period of Co-operation

Power and Monarchy c1000 – c1688 A Period of Conflict

Examples of conflict		Examples of co-operation	
c1000–c1485	c1485–c1700	c1000–c1485	c1485–c1700

C What were the biggest problems facing monarchs in the medieval and early modern periods?

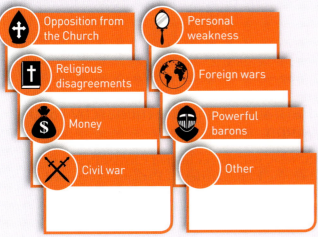

Opposition from the Church

Personal weakness

Religious disagreements

Foreign wars

Money

Powerful barons

Civil war

Other

5 Make another set of cards like these – big enough to add examples from the early modern period in each space. Then look back over this chapter to complete it.

6 When you have completed your research, put the factors in order of importance in causing tensions in the early modern period. Record your order.

7 Compare your rank with what you had for the medieval period. Has the order changed? If so, in what way and why?

D Who were the most effective rulers in the period c1000–c1700?

8 On page 49 you completed a table to assess the effectiveness of medieval rulers. Now add some examples of early modern rulers. You do not have to cover them all, but make sure you have a range of examples.

9 From your extended table choose:
   a the two most effective monarchs of the period c1000–c1700
   b the two least effective monarchs of the period c1000–c1700.
   Be ready to explain why you consider them successful or unsuccessful.

E What were the most significant events in the period c1000–c1800?

10 On page 49 there are some criteria for evaluating significance. Use those criteria to evaluate the following events. Make a set of cards and write notes on the back of each card: arguments that this event is significant; arguments this is not significant.

Henry VIII's break with the Catholic Church	execution of Charles I
Elizabeth I's religious settlement	Cromwell becoming lord protector
increasing importance of parliament in Tudor period	the Restoration
the Civil War	the Glorious Revolution

11 When you have completed this task, add the cards from the medieval period. Now decide which you think are the six most significant events of the period c1000–c1700.

KEY TERMS

Make sure you know what these terms mean and can use them confidently in your writing.
- Act of Supremacy
- Glorious Revolution
- members of parliament
- Puritans
- Tories
- treason
- veto
- Whigs

PRACTICE QUESTIONS

The final question will cover two periods. For example:
1 Did monarchs rely more on conflict or on co-operation with their subjects in the period c1000–c1800? (24)
2 'Monarchs were more powerful than their subjects in c1000–c1800.' How far do you agree with this view? (24)
3 Was war the most serious problem rulers faced in the period c1000–c1800? Explain your answer. (24)
4 'In the period c1000–c1800 the main cause of tension between rulers and their subjects was taxation.' How far do you agree with this view? (24)

Factfile: Parliament c1485–c1800

Parliament and the Tudor monarchs 1485–1603

In some respects, parliament did not change under the Tudors – the main decisions were still made by the monarch and the Privy Council. The key changes were in parliament's authority and value.

- Parliament only met when summoned by the monarch, usually when money was needed or an important law had to be passed.
- Parliament's structure and membership stayed the same.
- The Speaker was in charge of the House of Commons. He made sure that MPs obeyed the rules.
- MPs sat in the House of Commons and represented the counties or large towns. There was no standard way of choosing MPs.
- The *types* of people in the Political Nation changed. The population was growing and becoming more prosperous so more people were eligible to choose an MP. In Henry VII's parliament there were an estimated 250–300 MPs. By the end of Henry VIII's reign it was 343. By the end of Elizabeth's reign it was 462.
- During the Tudor period the Commons also gained important privileges:
  - Freedom of speech: MPs in parliament had the right to speak freely about matters of state.
  - Freedom from arrest: MPs could not be arrested while they were sitting in parliaments.
  - The Speaker had the right to speak to the monarch when he needed to.
- Henry VII used Acts of Attainder to reduce the power of the nobles. These acts accused an individual (usually of treason) and parliament voted him guilty or not.
- In Henry VIII's reign, parliament became even more important because of his constant need to raise taxes. The break from Rome also required the acceptance of the people. This partnership increased parliament's prestige, and it became accepted that it would be consulted about important changes.
- Elizabeth did not call parliament as often as Henry VIII had done. However, she did consult it on important measures.

Parliament and the Stuart monarchs 1603–48

Parliament in the Stuart period worked on the same principles as it had under the Tudors.

- The main decisions were still taken by the monarch and the Privy Council.
- Parliament was still made up of the House of Lords and the House of Commons. MPs were still chosen in the same way and their numbers were similar. The House of Commons rose to just over 500 members.

Parliament overthrows the monarchy 1649–60

England saw some momentous changes in this period, and parliament was at the centre of them.

- Parliament and Charles I went to war in 1642. The period of conflict ended with Charles's execution in 1649. The House of Lords was abolished and England became a republic.
- The Political Nation changed. The monarchy was gone. The great nobles lost some of their influence. The key change was the emergence of the army commanders, especially Oliver Cromwell.

Parliament and the monarchy 1660–c1800

In 1660, parliament invited Charles I's son to become King Charles II. Parliament retained the same structure as before – Lords and Commons. However, some things had changed.

- The powers of the king were limited.
- Charles initially relied on his Privy Council, but parliament started to become more powerful. In theory the monarch could still summon or dismiss parliament, but in reality it began to sit most of the time.
- Over time the Privy Council became less important and the monarch's Council of Ministers became more important. This eventually became the Cabinet.
- The Political Nation was starting to change. The great nobles began to dominate both the Lords and the Commons. In 1688, parliament DEPOSED James II and invited his daughter Mary and her husband William to become monarch.
- The Glorious Revolution increased the power of parliament (Lords and Commons) still further:
  - William and Mary had to swear an oath to rule according to the laws passed in parliament – the monarchy accepted that it was not above the law.
  - A Bill of Rights prevented the monarch from suspending laws or keeping a large army in peacetime. It also confirmed that parliament would meet at least once every year.
  - William was allowed to collect important taxes but only for a four-year period. This guaranteed that he would continue to work with parliament.
- In 1707, the Scottish and English parliaments joined. In 1800, the Act of Union incorporated the Irish parliament as well. Parliament now ruled the United Kingdom of Great Britain.
- Throughout the 1700s, parliament gradually became the main power in the land and the monarch much less important.

See page 122 for the conclusion to this story.

3.1 The struggle for the vote: parliament and people c1800–1918

FOCUS

Throughout the nineteenth century, major changes took place in British society. This led to a century-long struggle for political change. In this topic, you will examine the changing relationship between parliament and the people through the nineteenth and early twentieth centuries, and how different groups succeeded in winning the right to vote.

The big picture

Parliament and people c1800–1918

Who had the right to rule?

By the mid-1700s, the monarch's power was in decline and the country was being run by parliament. However, parliament was dominated by the landowning aristocracy. They sat in the House of Lords, which was the senior house. The leading ministers were always lords, and they could override anything the elected House of Commons wanted to do. The right to rule England was to own (a lot of) land and to be very wealthy! The most powerful politicians came from noble families that had been running Britain for centuries.

Despite this, a key change had taken place: the idea of divine right was no longer accepted. Britain was ruled by parliament and in order to do this it had to have the consent of the people, even if this was only a small proportion of the people. They could show their approval or disapproval of parliament and MPs in elections. To some extent, parliament had to listen to the views of the population.

Who had the right to vote?

In 1800, very few people could vote. This began to change as Britain itself began to change. The population expanded rapidly. Industry overtook farming as the most important sector of the economy and by 1851 more people lived in the towns than in the countryside. Parliament no longer seemed to represent the interests of the majority of the population. More and more people began to demand the vote. Parliament was slow to respond to these pressures, but through a series of measures more sections of society gained the right to vote.

How did working men and women win the right to vote?

By the later 1800s and early 1900s, many working-class men and women still toiled in poor conditions. They felt that the existing political parties did not really represent them in government. This led to the development of a mass labour movement, led by trade unions, and eventually of a new political party, the Labour Party. At the same time, another excluded group – women – also campaigned for the vote. Campaigners tried a range of methods to persuade parliament to give them the vote and they eventually succeeded in 1918.

KEY QUESTIONS

A How did the balance of power change in the period c1800–1918?

Draw your own version of the graph below and chart the high and low points of power in this period for:

- the landed aristocracy
- the middle classes
- working-class men
- women.

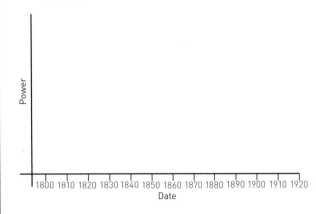

B Was force (or the threat of force) more effective than peaceful methods in bringing about change in the period c1800–1918?

Work in pairs or small groups. Draw up lists of events and developments that could be used to support each idea in the table below.

Key changes in this period	Evidence that this was brought about by force or threat of force	Evidence that this was brought about by other methods
Reform Act 1832		
Reform Act 1867		
Reform Act 1884		
emergence of trade union movement and Labour Party		
Representation of the People Act 1918		

---

1 If you were a reformer wanting change in 1800, which aspects of the system would you change first? Make sure you can explain your answer.

Source 1 An aerial photograph of Old Sarum in Wiltshire as it looks today. The area had no voters but two MPs! ▼

1800 to the Great Reform Act

The political system in 1800

In 1800, there were 658 MPs in the House of Commons. MPs represented CONSTITUENCIES (or 'seats'). Oxford and Cambridge universities each had two MPs. The remaining constituencies were either county or BOROUGH seats. Today, the electoral system in 1800 seems strange in several ways:

- Constituencies were different sizes with different populations. County seats varied from 23,000 voters in Yorkshire to 800 in Rutland. The most notorious constituency was the borough of Old Sarum, which had no voters at all but which still had two MPs (chosen by whoever owned the land).

- Constituencies had different rules about who was allowed to vote. Usually only land- or property-owners could vote. A common rule for the right to vote was owning property worth more than 40 shillings, but in some boroughs anyone who paid rates (local taxes) could vote.

- Big towns and cities were not represented. Many constituencies sent MPs to parliament because they *had been* important places in medieval or Tudor times. Some growing industrial towns, such as Manchester (which had a population of 80,000) had no MPs at all.

- There was no secret ballot, where people put their vote in a box. Voting was done by a show of hands. This meant that people could be intimidated into voting for the candidate their landlord wanted.

- Corruption was a problem. Voters might sell their vote for money, so wealthy men could effectively 'buy' constituencies where there were only a few voters. These were known as 'rotten boroughs'.

Source 2 A cartoon by the artist James Gilray, published in 1795. Gilray was a savage critic of the political system. In this cartoon he is showing how England is full of people attending meetings complaining about the existing system. The most prominent meeting at the front is being held by the English Radical speaker John Gale Jones at Copenhagen Fields in London. There are other interesting details such as 'Real Democratic Gin' on the barrel in the left-hand corner. The table in the front is labelled 'Equality & no Sedition Bill' (a sedition bill meant banning political demonstrations). In the meeting on the left one of the men on the platform is holding a petition saying 'Rights of Citizens'. ▶

2 Study Source 2. What are the people in the crowd demanding?

3 Is the artist sympathetic or hostile to the speaker and his followers? Explain your answer.

Although the House of Commons was made up of elected representatives, the House of Lords was not. It comprised mainly landowners and Anglican bishops. The House of Lords could veto (stop) any measures passed by the House of Commons. The monarch could also veto them.

The French Revolution

There was plenty of corruption and hypocrisy in the British political system, but most criticism was directed at individual MPs. Few people challenged the system itself. Two revolutions in the wider world helped turn a spotlight on the British political system. In 1776, Britain's American colonies rebelled and declared their independence. Then, in 1789, a serious revolution broke out in France. King Louis XVI was overthrown and a revolutionary government took the place of the monarchy. At first the British government was sympathetic to the revolutionaries, but it grew alarmed as events turned more radical and violent.

The philosopher and writer Edmund Burke published a book called *Reflections on the Revolution in France* in 1790, which criticised the revolution and praised the British system. Burke said that in Britain the main interest groups and the people who worked for them (the aristocracy, farmers, bankers and new industrialists) were represented, even though it was not always a perfectly accurate representation. In 1791, the radical writer Thomas Paine published a furious attack on this view in *The Rights of Man*. Paine argued that the British system was corrupt and only represented the privileged landowning aristocracy. He called for more people to have the right to vote. Paine's book sold 200,000 copies in two years. It was banned by the government.

ACTIVITY

1 Imagine that you work for the company that is publishing *The Rights of Man*. Write a brief blurb for the back cover of the book. Remember, you do not have much space so you will have to be selective. Focus on:
   a what Paine attacks in his book
   b what he thinks should be done.

2 Extension: Go online and see how your summary compares to published editions.

Source 3 Historian Eric Evans, writing in 1997.

People without the vote could and did hold strong opinions. In many constituencies they were able to communicate these views in public meetings or simple conversations to those who did have the vote and to their MPs. In larger constituencies it was practically impossible to 'buy' influence with voters so an election was a genuine test of public opinion. Although landowners were a large majority in parliament, it was possible for others to become MPs. There were plenty of doctors, lawyers and retired army officers in the House of Commons. Though a long way from being democratic (an idea which almost all MPs hated) parliament was more representative than the stereotype of rotten boroughs suggests. And it was one of, if not the most democratic system of government existing in the world at that time.

Why was there no revolution in Britain by 1800?

Historians are still debating this issue, but there are several possible explanations:

- The French Revolution became increasingly violent. Many of those who had initially been sympathetic to the revolutionaries changed their minds.
- The aristocracy was determined to stamp out revolution. This became easier when Britain went to war with revolutionary France in 1792–1815. The government banned radical publications. In 1794, it suspended the Habeas Corpus Act. This meant that people could be imprisoned without trial.
- In 1799, the government passed the Combination Acts, which made it illegal for workers to join together to campaign for better wages or conditions.
- Traditional respect for authority remained strong. In 1800, most people were still agricultural workers. They lived in small villages, went to church every Sunday and knew their neighbours well. They respected local authority figures such as the local gentry (the squire), the local magistrate (often the squire himself) and the vicar.
- Although the British system was not democratic, some historians have argued it was just democratic enough to stave off revolution (see Source 3 on page 89).

Despite these factors, Britain was changing.

FOCUS TASK

How democratic was Britain in 1800?

1 Study the features of the British system in 1800 and create two lists:
   a ways in which Britain *was not* democratic compared with today
   b ways in which at least *some* people were represented in Britain.
2 Prepare a one-minute speech summarising your views on the following statement: 'The fact that Britain did not have a revolution before 1800 proved that the system of government was fair.'
3 Extension: As a class, debate this view: 'Historians should not criticise people and societies in the past because they are not like today. That is not their job.'

Source 4 Maps of Sheffield in 1736 and 1823. Sheffield was the centre of the metal industry. To give you an idea of the scale of growth, the first map is shown in the top right corner of the second map. ▼

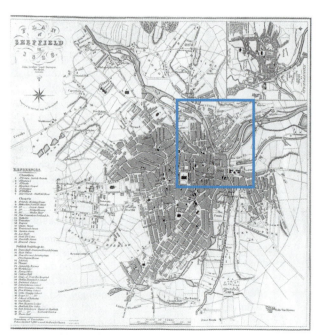

1 Most historians agree that the rapid growth of towns undermined traditional authority. Why do you think this might be?

Source 5 A table showing the population of Britain's main towns 1750–1851.

	1750	1801	1851
London	675,000	959,000	2,800,000
Bristol	45,000	64,000	154,000
Birmingham	24,000	74,000	296,000
Liverpool	22,000	80,000	444,000
Manchester	18,000	90,000	338,000
Leeds	16,000	53,000	207,000
Sheffield	12,000	31,000	185,000

Campaign for reform 1812–20

People in towns worked in factories and workshops. Middle-class people worked in areas like banking and insurance, or they ran businesses. Many began to question whether the landowning MPs in parliament really represented them.

The Radicals

A new breed of political reformers emerged, known as the Radicals. One leading Radical was William Cobbett, who published a magazine called *The Political Register*, which often criticised parliament and social inequalities. Another famous Radical was John Cartwright, who founded the Hampden Club in 1812. It was named after the Civil War rebel John Hampden (see page 68). Cartwright believed that all men should have the vote. Many working-people in the industrial regions founded their own Hampden Clubs and produced pamphlets and petitions calling for reform.

Urbanisation helped the Radicals. It was easier for people to meet and discuss new ideas in the towns. The movement was also helped by economic factors. Britain had been at war with France for 23 years (1792–1815). War had boosted industries such as iron and textiles, but there was an economic slump when the war ended. Economic hardship boosted the movement. In 1816, thousands of people came to meetings at Spa Fields in London to hear the Radical leader Henry Hunt speak. In 1817, over 700 petitions were submitted to parliament calling for electoral reform.

Government responses

The Tories had been in power since 1784. Their leader, Lord Liverpool, was completely opposed to reform:

- His response to economic hardship was to introduce the Corn Laws, which put a tariff (an import tax) on imported food. This protected the profits of the landowners but it made food more expensive for most people.
- His response to protest meetings was to introduce the so-called 'Gagging Laws', which restricted public meetings and free speech.
- Even more drastically, in 1819 a huge protest meeting was held at St Peter's Fields in Manchester. Local militia charged into the crowd, killing 11 and injuring 400 more in the panic that followed. The event was sarcastically called 'Peterloo', after the British military victory of Waterloo in 1815 (although government troops were not involved).
- In 1819, Liverpool's government introduced the Six Acts. These limited public meetings further, put new restrictions on what newspaper were allowed to publish, increased the taxes on newspapers (which hit Radical publications hard) and extended the powers of the government to search private properties. Arrests of Radical campaigners increased dramatically.

The government's use of force proved effective. The majority of Radical campaigners were committed to protest by legal means anyway and when the economy began to improve in the 1820s, support for Radical protest began to fade.

ACTIVITY

When you look up a topic on Wikipedia, the first paragraph is usually a short summary of the whole article. Write a summary paragraph for a Wikipedia article titled 'The Radical reform movement in Britain 1812–20'.

The Great Reform Act 1832

Political unions

The Radical campaign had not achieved electoral reform, but it had got people talking about the issues. Although they feared the Radicals, many middle-class people agreed that the electoral system was out of date. In 1830, the Birmingham banker Thomas Attwood founded the Birmingham Political Union (BPU). Attwood believed that middle-class industrialists and businessmen (people like him) should have the vote and be able to become MPs. They would represent industry better in parliament than existing MPs, and if industry prospered then workers would also prosper. Attwood also felt that the best way to put pressure on the government was for the middle and working classes to form an alliance. The BPU meetings regularly drew audiences of between 50,000 and 100,000 and other political unions quickly emerged in industrial towns. In London, Francis Place formed the National Political Union. Place had been a Radical campaigner but he now realised that people like him would have to work with middle-class activists like Attwood to achieve reform. Many other former Radicals joined the campaign.

◀ **Source 6** A cartoon called 'The New Reform Coach', published in 1832. The driver of the coach is Whig leader Earl Grey and the passenger is the king.

Source 7 A cartoon published in 1831. The cartoon was widely published in newspapers and pamphlets and even printed on a silk handkerchief! ▲

1 Study Sources 6 and 7. Which one is pro-reform and which one is anti-reform? Explain how you know.

2 Both sources are very biased. Explain why this makes them useful to historians studying this issue.

A new government

The reform cause seemed stronger when the Whig Party won the election of 1830. The Whig prime minister, Earl Grey, finally managed to get the House of Commons to pass a new Reform Bill through the House of Commons in July 1831. This bill not radical measure, but the House of Lords still rejected it.

The passing of the Great Reform Act

There was furious reaction across the country. Riots broke out in Nottingham, Derby and Bristol, and troops were sent in to crush the rioters. The unions had organised large political meetings throughout 1831 and there was clearly great support for the bill among the middle and working classes. Violent revolution did seem a real possibility. In May 1832, another Reform Bill was passed through the Commons. This time Grey asked the king to create many new Whig lords so that it would pass through the House of Lords. At first the king refused and the Tory leader, the war hero the Duke of Wellington, to form a new government, but Wellington refused. The king and the House of Lords backed down and reluctantly accepted the Reform Bill. It was formally passed as the Parliamentary Reform Act in June 1832.

The impact of the Great Reform Act

Although the act is often referred to as the 'Great' Reform Act, it was actually a relatively small change. Earl Grey had no intention of significantly changing the electoral system. He wanted to secure the existing system by giving the vote to some of the middle classes and continuing to exclude the majority of the population. The main changes were as follows:

- 143 seats were taken away from boroughs and distributed among the large industrial towns.
- Only people paying at least £10 per year in rates could vote in boroughs. In Birmingham, for example, only 4,000 men could vote out of a population of 144,000.
- Across the country the proportion of men who could vote rose from 11 per cent to 18 per cent in 1832.

Many other aspects of the system did not change:

- The majority of MPs were still landowners because they were the only ones who could afford to do the job. Very few middle- or working-class men could afford to give up working and become MPs.
- There was still no secret ballot, so the intimidation and corruption continued.

Some historians argue that the passing of the act was important because it brought the middle classes into the Political Nation and because a revolution had been avoided. Parliament had shown that it could reform itself, even if the reform was small in scale and only achieved as a result of enormous effort and pressure.

FOCUS TASK

Why did the reform campaign succeed in 1832 when it had failed in 1812–20?

1. Copy the table below and complete it to record the importance of various factors in the reform movement at different times.

2. Work in pairs or small groups to agree on the three most important differences.

3. Prepare a one-minute speech summarising your views on the following statement:
   The fact that Britain did not have a revolution in 1832 proved that the system of government was fair.

	Tories	Whigs	Working classes	Middle classes	Urbanisation	Population growth	Industrial change	Economic depression
Importance 1812–20								
Importance 1820–32								

1832 to the development of the Labour Party

Many working-class activists felt betrayed by the 1832 Reform Act. They had not expected to get the vote, but they had hoped the new parliament would pass LEGISLATION to improve their lives. What they got was very disappointing. For example, in 1834 the government passed the Poor Law Amendment Act, which brought in the harsh system of workhouses for the unemployed.

Chartism

Many working people believed that they would have to force change in the political system before their lives would improve. The movement that emerged from this discontent and determination for change was Chartism. Chartism was really a collection of working-class movements that centred on the six points, or principles, of the People's Charter:

- universal SUFFRAGE
- no property qualification to become an MP
- annual parliaments
- equal representation
- payment for MPs
- secret ballot.

Source 8 A photograph of the Chartist meeting at Kennington Common 1848. This is the first known photo of a political meeting in Britain. ▼

We do not know the exact scale of support for Chartism, but it was certainly large. In 1839, the Chartists presented a petition to parliament with 1.2 million signatures. In 1842, another petition was presented, demanding change. Both were rejected. The Chartists made one last attempt to get parliament to accept their charter. In 1848, the Chartists planned a huge meeting at Kennington Common in London (see Source 8). A third petition, containing over 1.5 million signatures, was presented to parliament. Once again it was rejected.

The achievements of Chartism

Opponents of Chartism argued that the working classes were not ready to be given the responsibility of the vote. Support for Chartism faded after 1848, and for many years the movement was regarded as a failure. More recently, however, historians have seen Chartism in a different light:

- The Chartists were up against a powerful and united opposition. The only way they could have brought about change was through violent revolution. It was an achievement in itself to run a dignified and organised protest movement that was legal and peaceful.
- Many Chartists also helped to achieve other reforms, such as the end of the Corn Laws and improved conditions in factories.
- Chartism provided many activists with experience of political campaigning and organisation that proved important over the next 20–30 years, particularly trade unions.

New Model Unions

In the 1850s a new type of union, known as a New Model Union, emerged. The best-known was the Amalgamated Society of Engineers (ASE), led by Robert Applegarth. The ASE charged quite high membership fees (an unskilled worker would not have been able to afford it) and had full-time officials. It paid benefits to its members when they were ill or out of work. The ASE, like other New Model Unions, avoided strikes and preferred to negotiate with employers to solve disputes. Membership rose steadily, and by 1874 around 1 million men belonged to New Model Unions.

1 Write two captions for Source 8 as they might have appeared in a pro-Chartist and anti-Chartist newspaper in 1848.

FOCUS TASK

Did Chartism fail?

Prepare a one-minute speech summarising your views on the following statement:

The fact that the Charter was never accepted proves that Chartism was a failure.

Source 9 A membership certificate for the Amalgamated Society of Engineers (ASE). ▼

Source 10 A cartoon from *Punch* magazine, 1867. Conservative prime minister Benjamin Disraeli is pulling the pint of beer. The man behind Disraeli is the Conservative leader Lord Derby. The inspector looking through the window is Liberal MP William Gladstone. The caption read: 'No half measures this time Ben.' ▼

2 Look carefully at Source 9. What does the ASE union believe in?

3 How would the message of this source help politicians who wanted to give the vote to more working-class men?

4 What is the cartoon saying about the 1867 Reform Act?

5 What is it saying about the 1832 Reform Act?

Working men get the vote 1867 and 1884

Organisations like the ASE convinced many MPs that the vote could safely be extended to 'respectable' working-class men. In the 1850s, the Whigs merged with other groups to form the Liberal Party, which proposed that the vote should be extended. This was rejected, but support was growing.

In 1864, the Radical MP John Bright formed the Reform Union. The following year several trade unions, including the ASE, created an organisation called the Reform League. These two groups collaborated closely. Large and occasionally violent meetings took place. The Liberals (who had evolved from the Whigs and politicians with similar views) and the Conservatives (who had evolved from the Tories) all now accepted the need for reform. In fact, a rivalry developed between leading Liberal William Gladstone and the Tory prime minister, Benjamin Disraeli, over which party would achieve reform and take credit for it.

In the end it was the Tories who passed the Second Reform Act, in 1867. This was a much more radical measure than the act of 1832 (see Factfile). Seventeen years later, Gladstone, by then prime minister himself, passed the Third Reform Act, which meant the majority of men could vote.

FACTFILE

The 1867 and 1884 Reform Acts
1867
- Passed by the Tories under Disraeli.
- Another 45 small constituencies lost their MPs and these seats were given to the towns and counties with large populations.
- In the boroughs, all men who owned or rented a house could vote (this was mainly the better-off working classes).
- In the counties, men who owned or leased land could vote.
- The act doubled the size of the electorate from 20 per cent to 40 per cent of the male population. Those without the vote were mostly agricultural labourers and unskilled industrial workers.

1884
- Passed by the Liberals under Gladstone.
- Gave the vote to the respectable householder in the countryside (the equivalent of the men who had gained the vote in towns in 1867).
- Gave yet more seats to the big towns and cities.
- The electorate rose from 3 to 5 million.
- For the first time, constituencies represented fairly similar populations (around one MP to 50,000 constituents).

Trade unions and the emergence of the Labour Party

After the Reform Acts of 1867 and 1884, Britain was certainly more democratic, but even so 40 per cent of men and 100 per cent of women still had no right to vote. For the poorest in society Britain was still a harsh place to live – long hours, low pay, and appalling conditions for many. Of course, they had no way to change their situation because they could not vote.

New Unions

In the 1870s and 1880s, these people began to form what became known as New Unions. They represented workers such as dockers, farm labourers or women working in small sweatshops. In five years, membership of New Unions more than doubled to nearly 2 million. A body called the Trades Union Congress (TUC) was formed in 1868. By the 1890s, it represented almost all the trade unions.

Challenges

The New Unions and their members faced serious challenges. A serious of court cases in the 1890s restricted the rights of unions to picket or take other actions against employers. In 1900, workers on the Taff Vale railway in South Wales went on strike. The courts ordered the union to pay compensation for the losses to the company caused by the strike. This ruling made things very difficult for the trade unions, because it meant their members could no longer go on strike.

The emergence of the Labour Party

At this time, numerous groups and individuals were trying to build up support for a political party to represent working-class people. In 1893, these groups came together as the Independent Labour Party (ILP). In 1899, the ILP persuaded the Trades Union Congress to back the idea of a workers' party. The TUC had previously preferred to focus on wages and conditions rather than politics, but the Taff Vale judgement of 1900 persuaded them. A new party was set up, the Labour Representation Committee. The LRC won two seats in the 1901 election. By 1903, it represented 8 million trade unionists. In the 1906 election, the LRC won 29 seats, and in 1910, 42 LRC candidates were elected.

Welfare reform and the Parliament Act 1911

Labour was a small party compared with the Liberals and the Conservatives. However, it still had an impact because the Liberals in particular were concerned that many working-class people would desert them and support Labour. This was a significant factor behind the welfare reforms passed by the Liberals between 1906 and 1911, which included Old Age Pensions (1908) and National Insurance (1911), which paid benefits to workers when they were ill or unemployed.

When the House of Lords blocked the People's Budget, the Liberals passed the Parliament Act in 1911. This effectively meant that the House of Lords could no longer block a measure approved by the House of Commons. This was a major development in the overall story of power in Britain.

PRACTICE QUESTIONS

1 Describe the actions of working-class movements in the 1800s. (4)
2 What was the significance of the 1832 Parliamentary Reform Act? (8)

FOCUS TASK

Was Labour a serious force in British politics by the early 1900s?

Look at Sources 11–14. They are all biased, but this makes them very useful. They can tell us a lot about:

- the people who created them
- what those people were concerned about
- what they were trying to achieve
- how they tried to achieve it.

Analyse each source carefully and then decide whether you think it shows that Labour was an important force by the early 1900s.

Source 11 Proposals to help the unemployed, published by the Labour Party in 1907.

Unemployment is a national scandal. Over one million ordinary men and women battle daily with the threat of starving. Neither Liberals nor Conservatives care. We call for the following measures to be made law immediately:

- *Where a workman has registered as unemployed, it shall be the duty of the local unemployment authority to provide work for him, or to provide funds to feed and clothe that person and those depending on him.*
- *Unemployment authorities shall keep a register of unemployed workers and, as far as possible, offer them work which is best suited to each individual.*
- *Unemployment authorities should be able to help an unemployed person and any of his dependants to move to another area for work.*

Source 12 An extract from a secret report by Winston Churchill, a member of the Liberal government, in 1908. The Cabinet is the group of senior ministers who run the government.

CONFIDENTIAL – FOR THE CABINET ONLY

Only a rascal is permanently without a job. But large numbers are unemployed for short periods. Some employers take advantage of this situation. They keep a larger number of workers than they need hanging around their gates. A system like this smashes households like egg-shells. The worker feels helpless and often turns to drink. If we do not address this issue then the working man will no longer support us.

Source 13 A Tory poster from the 1910 election. At this time the Conservatives regarded socialism and the Labour Party as the same thing. ▼

Source 14 A poster published by the Labour Party in 1911. ▼

Votes for women

So far in this topic all the campaigning has been about votes for men. Women were heavily involved in campaigning, but it was not until the second half of the 1800s that the campaign for female suffrage (giving women the vote) really got going.

When parliament passed the Reform Act in 1867, the MP John Stuart Mill put forward a proposal for some women to be given the vote as well, but it was rejected. This established a pattern of determined campaigning and equally solid resistance that lasted until 1918. Supporters and opponents of female suffrage stated their cases in the press, at public meetings and, of course, in parliament.

Some of the arguments in favour of votes for women	Some of the arguments against votes for women
• Women should be able to vote for the MPs who passed laws because the laws affected men and women. • Women could already vote in local elections so this showed they could be trusted with the vote. • Women took part in many election campaigns. • Women paid the same taxes as men.	• If women did get the vote then it would still only be wealthier women. • The majority of women were either not interested in the vote or actively opposed votes for women. • Women would develop their careers and neglect their families if they got the vote. • Women did not fight in wars. They should not have a say in whether their country should go to war.

Rather like the working-class movements, the campaign for women's suffrage encompassed a wide range of different groups from all over the country and included different sections of society. Many of the early suffrage campaigners were well-educated middle-class women, frustrated because they were denied opportunities to work in areas such as medicine or the law. However, there was also a strong working-class women's suffrage movement in the industrial towns of northern England.

The NUWSS (Suffragists)

In 1897, these different groups came together under one banner – the National Union of Women Suffrage Societies (NUWSS). They were usually known as the Suffragists and were led by Millicent Fawcett. The NUWSS had over 500 local branches around the country, around 50,000 fee-paying members and many volunteers. Fawcett and other Suffragists wrote thousands of letters to MPs. They organised rallies and marches. They went to meetings held by all the political parties and asked questions about women's suffrage. Everybody knew who Fawcett was and what her movement wanted because the NUWSS effectively promoted their agenda in newspapers.

It is estimated that when the Liberals came to power in 1906, about 400 MPs supported the idea of giving the vote to some women. In 1913, the NUWSS ran a campaign that included more than 400 meetings around the country. By 1914, Fawcett was exploring a possible alliance with the Labour Party, using the NUWSS's publicity machine to promote Labour candidates against Liberals in elections. Historian Sandra Holton believes that the prime minister, Herbert Asquith, was so worried by this that he was considering giving some women the vote by 1914.

Between 1906 and 1913, new laws to give women the vote were proposed on six occasions and met with a variety of responses:

● Sometimes opposition MPs defeated the measure (1906).
● Sometimes parliament did not have enough time to turn the measure into law (1908).
● Sometimes the measure was abandoned because there was an election (1910).
● It came closest in 1913, but a technical hitch stopped the proposal being passed.

Source 15 A poster published by the NUWSS. It was first published in 1909 and re-published regularly until 1913. The tree is shown growing from an acorn in 1867. This was the first time MPs were asked to consider female suffrage. It has now become a mighty oak with many branches. ▼

1 What does Source 15 reveal about the NUWSS in terms of the size of the movement, its organisation and its skill in publicising its agenda?
2 Source 15 is an NUWSS publication. Is it still useful to historians?

The WSPU (Suffragettes)

The NUWSS was not the only women's suffrage organisation. In 1903, Emmeline Pankhurst formed a new organisation – the Women's Social and Political Union (WSPU). Pankhurst and her daughters dominated the movement. They believed the NUWSS campaign was getting nowhere, and that the campaign for women's suffrage should be much more militant (forceful). The *Daily Mail* newspaper called the new organisation the Suffragettes. They used a variety of methods to promote their agenda:

- **Protests:** They disrupted political meetings, especially when government ministers were speaking. The Suffragette Edith New chained herself to the railings of Downing Street. In 1908, Emmeline Pankhurst and her daughter Christabel led an attempt to barge into the House of Commons.
- **Prison and hunger strike:** They deliberately set out to get arrested to draw attention to their campaign. Once in prison, Suffragettes went on hunger strike. At first they were force fed, but when the government realised this was earning them sympathy, it passed a law allowing Suffragettes on hunger strike to be released, but they were imprisoned again when they recovered. Suffragettes called this the 'Cat and Mouse Act'.
- **Increasing militancy:** Suffragette actions became more extreme: smashing windows, attacking politicians and even committing arson. The most publicised event of all came in June 1913 at the Derby horse race. The Suffragette Emily Davison stepped out in front of the king's horse. The horse was brought down and Emily was killed.

Impact

The Suffragettes achieved sensational publicity and made it impossible to ignore the campaign for female suffrage. Their courage won them sympathy as individuals, but the increasing violence of their actions, especially after 1911, alienated support for their cause. Many left the WSPU and transferred to the Suffragists.

The WSPU had always been a minority organisation anyway. At its peak it had about 2,000 members (compared with the NUWSS's 50,000). By 1914 the WSPU had become an even smaller movement. Many suffragettes were in prison and Christabel Pankhurst was co-ordinating the campaign from exile in Paris.

The Suffragettes damaged their own cause because they gave their opponents a reason for rejecting women's suffrage. If MPs gave in to violence on this matter, then other groups would also turn to violence to get their way. From 1911 onwards, each time the issue was raised in parliament there was an increasing majority *opposed to* women's suffrage.

Source 16 A still image from a newsreel in 1913, showing a church burned by Suffragettes. ▶

3 What kind of impact would Source 16 have had on most audiences?

4 The Suffragettes are much better known than the Suffragists. Explain why.

Did women get the vote because of war work?

When the First World War broke out in 1914, almost everyone in Britain threw themselves into the war effort. Women played a vital role in this, particularly in filling in for male workers who were away fighting:

- Around 800,000 women worked in heavy industries such as the coal industry.
- They made up the majority of workers in the vital munitions factories.
- Government departments took on 200,000 female clerks.
- Women worked in the Women's Land Army doing farming jobs.
- They served in the armed forces as nurses, drivers and wireless operators.

In January 1918, the government passed the Representation of the People Act. This was partly in recognition of the contribution of Britain's men in the war – the act gave the vote to all British men over the age of 21. However, it also granted some women the vote.

There was a lot of argument about the detail of this act. Some women were upset that suffrage would not be extended to all women, but Suffragist leader Millicent Fawcett accepted this as an important first step. In the end, the act was passed easily in the Commons by 385 votes to 55. It faced more opposition in the House of Lords, notably from Lord Curzon, the president of the Anti-suffrage League (who said that the act would be the 'ruin of the country'). Despite this opposition, the bill passed by 134 votes to 71. Women voted in their first elections in December 1918.

Source 17 An extract from a speech by ex-prime minister Herbert Asquith in 1917. Asquith had been one of the chief opponents of women's suffrage before the war.

Some years ago I used the expression 'Let the women work out their own salvation.' Well, Sir, they had worked it out during the war. How could we have carried on the war without them? Wherever we turn we see them doing work which three years ago we would have regarded as being exclusively 'men's work'. When the war is over the question will then arise about women's labour and their function in the new order of things. I would find it impossible to withhold from women the power and the right of making their voices directly heard.

1 Study Source 18. What is the message of the source?
2 What does Source 18 reveal about the work of the Suffragists during the war?

Source 18 The front cover of the magazine *Votes for Women*, 26 November 1915. The figure at the desk represents the government. ▼

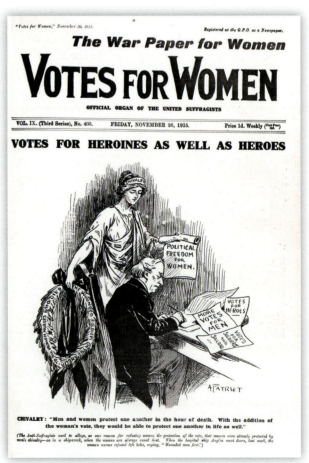

FOCUS TASK

Why did some women get the vote in 1918?

Here are two views expressed on this question in 1918:

Women got the vote because of war work.
(Former prime minister Herbert Asquith)

Women got the vote as a result of 50 years of campaigning. The war work was the last piece of the jigsaw to fit into place.
(Suffragist leader Millicent Fawcett)

1 Which view do you support? Work in stages:
Make three cards:
- Suffragist campaigning
- Suffragette campaigning
- War work

On each card, write notes explaining how it helped to achieve the vote for women.
Take one card away. Explain whether women could have got the vote without that factor.

2 Now try answering this practice question:
Why did women get the vote in 1918?

KEY QUESTION REVIEW

Are you a Liberal/Whig historian or a Marxist historian?

How do you interpret the changes to parliament and power that you have investigated in this topic?

Whig/Liberal narrative
- The story of British political history is one of steady progress.
- The aristocracy were the guardians of the people, looking after their best interests and keeping order.
- As groups in society became ready – the middle classes, then the working classes, then the women – parliament brought these people into the system when they judged that the time was right.

Marxist narrative
- The story of British political history is one of class conflict.
- The aristocracy did their utmost to hold on to power, using every tool they had to keep it.
- Only well-organised and determined pressure, including the possibility of violent revolution, forced the aristocracy to give way.
- Once the middle classes gained power, they allied with the aristocracy so the working classes had to continue to struggle to get the vote.

1 Look back over this topic and find events or developments that you think could support each narrative. Some events or developments might support both views, depending on how you interpret them.
2 When you have completed your research, decide which viewpoint you find more convincing and write an account of your events so it reflects that narrative.
  Do not write more than 300 words.
3 The Whig narrative is not generally taken seriously by historians these days. Why do you think this is? Does this fact change your own view?
4 Extension: Would you change your mind about which narrative is more convincing if you started the story in an earlier period (medieval, Tudor or early modern)?

PRACTICE QUESTIONS

1 Describe the electoral system in 1800. (4)
2 Why was the electoral system being criticised in the early 1800s? (8)
3 Which was more important: the 1867 Reform Act or the 1884 Reform Act? (8)
4 How significant were working-class movements in the period c1840 to the early 1900s? (14)

3.2 Parliament and people 1914–c1980

FOCUS

By the early twentieth century, Britain was not a full democracy but it was much more democratic than it had ever been. As a result, the relationship between parliament and the people developed as well. Governments became much more involved in the lives of the general population. This process began in the early 1900s and developed enormously during the two world wars. In this topic, you will examine:

● the impact of war on the relationship between government and people
● how governments became more involved in areas such as health and welfare
● how political parties adapted to this relationship.

The big picture

Parliament and people 1914–c1980

Should governments stay out of ordinary life?

Throughout most of the history of Britain, people believed that they were better off if the government stayed out of their lives. Governments ought to handle big issues like wars or the economy. Looking after the sick and others in need was the responsibility of family, neighbours, local officials or the Church. By the early 1900s, however, this attitude was changing and governments were beginning to pass measures on welfare and similar areas. This process accelerated when the First World War broke out in 1914. The war required a huge effort by everyone in Britain and it needed strong government control to co-ordinate it.

How did the two world wars change government?

During the world wars, a consensus emerged about the relationship between government and people. Many people believed that increasing government control made life better for the majority of the population. After the First World War, however, governments seemed to do less to help people. There were high levels of unemployment and poverty, and this caused resentment. After the Second World War the people of Britain voted for a Labour government, which promised a welfare state that would look after its people.

How and why did power change hands in this period?

Politicians of all parties agreed that governments should be heavily involved in the lives of the people in areas such as the economy, health, education and welfare. This consensus lasted from the end of the Second World War in 1945 until the late 1970s. People accepted a much greater level of control over their daily lives in return.

KEY QUESTIONS

A What challenges did governments face in the period 1914–c1980 and how were they tackled?

Make a copy of the table below and fill it in as you read this topic. Note how governments reacted to challenges in both wartime and peacetime and how this affected the relationship between parliament and the people.

Challenges	Government response	Effect on relationship between parliament and people
Wartime		
enough men and women for armed forces		
producing equipment needed for war effort		
feeding people		
morale and support		
defending the country		
Peacetime		
recognising the sacrifices people made		
unemployment and poverty		
faith in parliament and the political system		

1   The aim of Sources 1 and 2 was to get people involved in the war effort. Select three details from each source and explain how these details help the poster achieve its aim.
2   Sources 1 and 2 are both examples of propaganda. Does that mean we should dismiss them as evidence about the war effort in each of the world wars? Explain your answer.

Source 1 A government poster from the First World War. ▼

How did war affect the relationship between government and the people?

The First World War was the first example of what historians now call a 'total war'. A total war involves or affects the whole of society – not just the armed forces. Previous wars had been distanced from everyday life for most people, fought far away by small professional armies. Ordinary people only knew about the fighting from newspapers or from soldiers who had taken part.

In the two world wars, this situation changed. War touched almost everybody's life in one way or another, whether they were soldiers or civilians, men or women, adults or children. Both wars brought changes to everyday life. Government control of news, information and even movement changed the way people lived. So did the demands of the war effort and the actions of the enemy. War brought about important changes in the role of women in society. Above all, the world wars changed the nature of the 'deal' between rulers and ruled.

Sources 1 and 2 give a flavour of the atmosphere in Britain during the world wars. They are propaganda posters. The main message of each poster is to suggest that every person in Britain was completely involved in the war effort. They were designed to make people not involved in the war effort feel guilty.

◄**Source 2** A government poster from the Second World War. The term 'combined operations' usually referred to actions involving different branches of the military (such as the army working with the navy to land an invasion force).

Government control in the world wars

Conscription and war work in the First World War

At the start of the First World War, the government tried to get the soldiers it needed from volunteers. The recruitment campaign was highly successful to begin with. Half a million men signed up in the first month alone. By 1916, over 2 million had enlisted. Despite this, the army was still short of troops. There were other problems too. The volunteer system was inefficient. For example, so many miners joined the army that production levels fell dramatically and some miners had to be sent home. Volunteering also meant that not all groups shared the burden of war. The factors eventually led the government to introduce CONSCRIPTION in 1916 – forcing men up to a certain age to join the army.

This was a difficult decision. Fifty MPs, including leading Liberals, voted against it in parliament. On the other hand, there was a system of appeals, where people could ask for exemption from miltary service. The most famous appeals came from those who opposed the war for religious or political reasons. These people became known as 'conscientious objectors', or 'conchies'. Many were not believed. Some conchies were sent to prison, where they were often badly treated. Others went to the front lines, where the war was being fought, and worked in hospitals or as stretcher-bearers. Only about 5 per cent of appeals were from conchies. The majority were from men who had businesses to run or children to care for. Many of these were given temporary exemptions to give them time to make arrangements.

The government controlled civilian workers as well as troops. It took control of the coal industry and set up its own munitions factories. There were clashes with trade unions as the government tried to stop workers moving from where they were needed to better-paid jobs. There were many strikes. The government usually backed down and workers' wages rose throughout the war. Unfortunately, so did the cost of goods, so many workers were no better off. Unions also clashed over plans to introduce female workers because they would be paid less and would undercut male workers. The government agreed that women would be paid the same as men, but that they would not be kept on after the war ended.

> **1** Make a list of the ways in which government control of people's lives increased in the First World War.

Conscription and war work in the Second World War

The government learnt important lessons from the First World War. In the Second World War a coalition government was formed, involving ministers from the Conservative, Liberal and Labour parties. Conscription began in 1938, before the war even began.

The Second World War was a different type of war for Britain. Large armies did not fight on battlefields, but huge levels of industrial production were needed. The trade unions were heavily involved in the war effort. Many of the Labour ministers in Winston Churchill's wartime government came from a trade union background, including Ernest Bevin – the minister of labour. One of the most large-scale examples of co-operation between government and trade unions was the conscription of men as young as 16 into the coal mines. Although the trade unions fully supported the war effort, they also stood up for the rights, working conditions and pay of their members. Wages were controlled, but this time so were prices.

By the middle of 1941, over half the population was employed by the government. However, there was still a shortage of workers and many women were conscripted into the war effort in late 1941. Eight times as many women were involved in war work in the Second World War as in the First World War. Women from all sections of society worked, whereas in the First World War they had been mostly young, working-class women. Governments and employers introduced flexible working schemes and childcare facilities to help women juggle work and family.

> **2** Make a list of the ways in which government control of people's lives increased in the Second World War.

Propaganda and censorship

Governments also controlled information in the two world wars. In both wars, journalists had to submit articles to be approved by the censors before they could be published. In the First World War the *Tribune* newspaper was closed down because it published anti-war articles. In 1941, the *Daily Worker* was closed down for suggesting that industry bosses were benefiting from the war while workers made all the sacrifices. However, the latest research by historians suggests that local newspapers were not as closely controlled as national ones, and they usually provided the public with a great deal of information.

Books and films were also censored in both wars. By the Second World War, the BBC had been created. Although it was not government-owned, it effectively censored itself and played a key role in informing the public and keeping up morale.

It is difficult to measure the effects of propaganda. Just because propaganda was circulated that does not mean that people believed it. However, most historians think that British propaganda was generally very effective in both world wars. The German leader Adolf Hitler admired the work of the British newspaper owner Lord Northcliffe in the First World War, which suggests that it was reasonably effective. In the Second World War the media turned the British prime minister into an almost legendary figure.

Source 3 A propaganda game aimed at children in the First World War. ▶

3 Study Sources 3 and 4. What similarities and differences do they reveal about propaganda in the First and Second World Wars?

4 Look at Source 4. What does it suggest about the views of the government towards the population? Do any of these terms seem appropriate: trust, respect, patronising, concerned, optimistic.

Source 4 Extracts from a British government document called 'The Programme for Film Propaganda', produced in January 1940.

Film propaganda should come under one of three themes:
- *What Britain is fighting for: British ideas and institutions. Ideals such as freedom, and institutions such as parliamentary government.*
- *How Britain fights: the extent of our war effort.*
- *The need for sacrifice if the fight is to be won.*

The film, being a popular medium, must be good entertainment if it is to be good propaganda. Film propaganda will be most effective when it is not recognisable as propaganda. The government's involvement should not normally be announced. The influence brought to bear by the Ministry on the producers of feature films must be kept secret.

Food and rationing

In both wars, feeding the country was a serious concern. The main threat was German U-boat (submarine) attacks on ships bringing vital supplies to Britain from the United States and Canada. In 1917, the government estimated that Britain had only six weeks' supply of wheat remaining. In the Second World War, prime minister Winston Churchill declared that the U-boat threat was the only thing that really frightened him!

In the First World War, compulsory rationing was not introduced until 1918. But long before then the government had worked with local councils and other organisations to increase food production, including ploughing up playing fields and planting crops in them. In the Second World War, rationing was introduced at the start and it covered items such as fuel and clothing as well as food. There was a flourishing black market of luxury goods for those who could afford them, but the majority of the population followed the rules. Most historians believe that the rationing system was relatively fair and that the health of the population actually improved as a result of rationing in both wars.

Home defence

In the First World War, defence concerns mainly focused on the possibility of German ships attacking coastal areas and raids from the air. In the Second World War, however, there was a real concern that Britain might face a full German invasion. In both wars, the government took control of many coastal areas. People were banned from these areas, partly for their own safety as the government built fortifications and planted mines.

Another way in which the government increased control was through identity papers. There was widespread fear of spies and SABOTEURS. People were urged not to talk about their work or spread news from their relatives fighting abroad in case this information fell into enemy hands. Both wars saw German air raids on British towns and cities, although these were much more extensive in the Second World War. The government recruited Air Raid Precautions (ARP) wardens who enforced blackouts, so no lights could be seen. The government also provided thousands of air-raid shelters and organised the evacuation of hundreds of thousands of children from the cities to the countryside.

FOCUS TASK

Government control in the world wars: similarities and differences

Copy the table below and complete it using the information in the section you have just read.

Types of government control	Examples from the First World War	Examples from the Second World War	Ways in which they were similar or different

War, parliament and the people

The process of mobilising for war was more difficult to manage in the First World War because it had never been done before. In the Second World War the process was quicker and more efficient. This was particularly impressive because, as a democracy, Britain's war effort depended on the British people supporting it. There were protests about hardships and about the efficiency of the government, but on the whole the population backed the government in these difficult times. They did this out of patriotism (loyalty to their country), fear of the enemy (especially Nazi Germany in the Second World War) and because of the agreement between parliament and the people that loyalty would be rewarded.

The bargain between parliament and people

One of the reasons why people accepted government control during the wars was that there was a general feeling that government involvement – up to a point – made things better for the majority of the population.

The First World War and after

Throughout the nineteenth century, most people felt that governments should not interfere in the lives of ordinary people. It was the responsibility of individual people to look after themselves. By the early 1900s, this attitude was changing and the government brought in welfare reforms, including measures to protect children, pensions and National Insurance. So when war broke out in 1914 people were more ready to accept government control of other aspects of their lives and work. As the war progressed, it became clear that even more government control was needed.

In return for their support and sacrifice in the war, parliament recognised that all people should have a say in government and be rewarded for their efforts. The first sign that this agreement would be honoured was the 1918 Representation of the People Act, which gave the vote to all men over 21, and to some women. The remaining women gained the vote in 1928.

However, the path to rewarding the people was not always easy. In 1918 the prime minister, David Lloyd George, made a speech in which he said: 'What is our task? To make Britain a fit country for heroes to live in.' But throughout the 1920s and 1930s this proved difficult to implement. There was high unemployment in many areas of Britain. For most of the period there was a Conservative government, which clashed with trade unions. There were many strikes, including the massive General Strike of May 1926. The government introduced some measures to help, but anyone claiming such help had to take a means test to reveal how much money they really had in case they were trying to cheat the system. To many it felt like the workers who fought in the war were no longer needed or valued. The working classes in Britain's industrial areas were left feeling particularly bitter and betrayed.

Source 5 A photograph of the Jarrow March in 1936. Jarrow's shipyards closed in the 1930s, leading workers to march 480 km to London. Parliament refused to meet the marchers and they were monitored closely by the Police Special Branch, which feared they were political agitators. The woman at the front in this picture is the Labour MP Ellen Wilkinson. ▶

1 How might the Labour Party make use of a photograph like Source 5 in an election campaign?

107

Source 6 Posters commissioned by the government in 1939. ▲

The Second World War and after

Posters with the 'Keep Calm and Carry On' slogan can be seen almost everywhere today. They are light-hearted and a bit nostalgic. The poster was actually the third in a series, as you can see in Source 6. From a historian's point of view it is interesting that only the first two were published – and in fact they were withdrawn after four weeks because they proved unpopular. The final one was never published. Officials were concerned that 'the population might well resent having this poster crammed down their throats at every turn' and that 'it may even annoy people that we should seem to doubt the steadiness of their nerves'.

Despite this early mistrust, the British people soon stood firmly behind the war effort. Winston Churchill brought leading figures from the main political parties into a coalition government and politicians began to plan for the post-war period. In 1944, Sir William Beveridge published the influential Beveridge Report, which identified five great social problems: want (poverty), disease, ignorance, squalor and idleness. Beveridge set out a series of recommendations to tackle these problems. In simple terms he recommended the creation of the welfare state. This meant government-funded health care, benefits to protect the unemployed and family allowances to protect children. The Labour Party supported Beveridge's ideas. Although they were traditionally suspicious of too much government involvement, the Conservatives also accepted many of Beveridge's ideas. Both parties therefore went into the election of July 1945 promising to build a better Britain.

The 1945 general election

Winston Churchill hoped that his outstanding record as war leader would win him the support of the people. However, while he was greatly respected, the vast majority did not see him as a leader for a new era and for a new peacetime Britain. The Labour Party won a landslide victory and brought in the reforms Beveridge had recommended:

- **Family Allowances (1945):** a weekly payment (with no means test) direct to the mother for every child after the first.
- **National Insurance (1946):** compulsory insurance against unemployment or illness paid for by government, employer and worker contributions.
- **National Health Service (1948):** free health care for all British citizens.
- **House-building:** a massive government programme promising 1 million new homes by 1950.
- **Nationalisation:** government control of industries such as coal and railways.
- **Full employment:** government involvement to create millions of jobs.

ACTIVITY

Britain held a general election in July 1945. Design an election leaflet for the Labour Party for this election. You should decide:
- three key messages you want to get across
- whether you are going to promote Labour or criticise the Conservatives – or both.

The post-war consensus

Political rivalry continued in the post-war period. The Liberal Party went into decline and power was traded between the Labour Party and the Conservatives. Importantly, however, the Conservatives never attempted to reverse the changes brought in by Labour in 1945–51. Although they were rivals, they largely agreed on the main issues. Both parties accepted that the country's main problems needed to be tackled through intervention by parliament (see Source 8).

1 Look at the Activity panel on page 108. Is Source 7 similar to or different from the leaflet you produced?

Source 7 A Labour campaign leaflet from the 1945 general election. John Wilmot was the Labour candidate for Deptford. ▼

FACTFILE

Post-war governments
1945–51 Labour
1951–64 Conservative
1964–70 Labour
1970–74 Conservative
1974–79 Labour

Source 8 Historian Michael Lynch, writing in 2001.

The Labour government of 1945–51 laid down the policies that would be followed in all essentials by successive Labour and Conservative governments during the next 35 years. Until Margaret Thatcher came to power in 1979 and deliberately challenged this consensus, there was a broad level of agreement on what were the main issues and how they were to be handled. ... Although Labour and the Conservatives rowed fiercely with each other as government and opposition, once each party was in office it seldom made major changes to the policies it inherited from the other.

FOCUS TASK

The 1945 general election: a new era?

The government is planning a new History curriculum, but it is very crowded. One of the decisions the government needs to make is whether the general election of 1945 is important enough to be included. Write a paragraph arguing that it *should* be included. You could refer to:
- the rejection of old ideas and attitudes
- the emergence of new ideas and attitudes
- the changing role of the state
- the lasting nature of the changes caused by the 1945 election.

PRACTICE QUESTIONS

1 Describe four ways in which government control increased during the world wars. (4)
2 Describe the results of the general election of 1945. (4)
3 Why was Britain's war effort effective in the two world wars? (8)
4 What was the significance of the 1945 general election? (14)

KEY QUESTION REVIEW

A **What challenges faced governments in the period 1914–c1980 and how were they tackled?**

1 Use your work on the Key Question to tackle this practice question:
Which was more important in changing attitudes towards the role of government in Britain: the First World War or the Second World War?

3.3 Challenges to parliament and British democracy c1980–2014

FOCUS

The period 1945 to the later 1970s is often known as the 'post-war consensus'. There was a general agreement that government action was essential in tackling key issues like the economy, health and welfare. But since 1979 this consensus has been increasingly challenged and the powers of parliament reduced. In this topic, you will examine the various challenges and their impact.

The big picture

Challenges to parliament and British democracy c1980–2014

How did politicians change the role of government?

Conservative prime minister Margaret Thatcher attacked the post-war consensus. She questioned whether it really was the job of parliament to deal with major social and economic problems. She believed that individuals, communities and businesses should tackle their own problems. Labour prime minister Tony Blair also believed that parliament could not solve all Britain's problems, but should instead work with businesses and other groups. Both prime ministers tended to bypass parliament and even their own parties. They used the media to talk directly to the population, more like US presidents than traditional British prime ministers.

Who challenged the power of parliament?

Many groups felt that parliament did not understand or care about their views and would not listen to them. Organisations such as CND and the National Union of Mineworkers challenged the power of parliament in the 1980s.

The regions of the UK (Scotland, Wales and Northern Ireland) demanded greater powers to govern themselves, and this resulted in a devolution of power from 1999 onwards. New parliaments were set up in Belfast, Cardiff and Edinburgh.

Another challenge came from membership of the European Union. Many aspects of law (such as human rights) were decided in the European court, which could overrule British courts. Certain aspects of the economy and areas such as business regulations were also heavily influenced by the EU.

How did voters react?

By the early twenty-first century, many groups were disillusioned with parliament. They felt that MPs, civil servants, journalists and wealthy business people were part of a cosy club who looked after each other and did not really represent ordinary people. Fewer and fewer people turned out to vote at elections, and radical political parties began to gain support. In 2010, Britain ended up with a coalition government because no single party could gain the majority of support from the British people.

KEY QUESTION

How serious were the challenges facing parliament and British democracy c1980–2014?

Make a copy of the table below and fill it out as you read the information. At the end of the topic, rank the seriousness of each challenge on a scale of 1 to 10, where 10 is the most serious.

Challenge	Challenge to parliament? (Explain how)	Challenge to democracy? (Explain how)	Seriousness on a scale of 1–10
Thatcher			
Blair			
CND			
miners			
devolution			
disengagement			

Source 1 Margaret Thatcher, in a speech at the Conservative Party Conference, 1968.

There are dangers in consensus: it could be an attempt to satisfy people holding no particular views about anything. It seems to me more important to have a philosophy and policy which, because they are good, appeal to a sufficient majority.

Challenges from politicians: Margaret Thatcher

Thatcher's beliefs

By the 1970s, Britain was facing severe social and economic problems. Margaret Thatcher, the new leader of the Conservative Party, believed that the post-war consensus was not just failing to tackle Britain's problems, it was actually causing them. She felt that government had become too involved in the lives of the people, which was wasteful and inefficient. Thatcher claimed that welfare had undermined people's sense of responsibility and their drive to better themselves. She also believed that too much state involvement and regulation had harmed businesses.

Thatcher won the general election in 1979 and set out to dismantle the consensus. It was a risky strategy and many people – some even in her own party – were unsure about her decisions. However, most people changed their minds about Thatcher's leadership after the Falklands War in 1982. When Argentina invaded the British territory of the Falkland Islands, she overruled her military commanders and sent forces to take it back. The British victory secured her position and she went on to dominate British politics in the 1980s. She was dynamic, forceful and radical, but this began to alienate many of her own MPs.

Thatcher's fall from power

Thatcher's fall from power was dramatic. She was effectively forced out by her own party. One key reason was the Poll Tax that she introduced in 1990. Instead of rates being paid on a property, the Poll Tax (officially called the Community Charge) made individuals pay the same, regardless of how much money they had. Many people considered this unfair and it was very unpopular.

Sometimes it works when people in power press ahead with their decisions despite objections, but it can also spell disaster (as it did with King John and James II, for example). Thatcher insisted on keeping the Poll Tax and this led to massive demonstrations and full-scale riots (shown on the cover of this book). Many Conservatives began to doubt her judgement. She clashed with many of her own ministers on other issues, including Britain's relationship with Europe. The foreign secretary, Geoffrey Howe, resigned and made a highly critical speech about Thatcher. Soon afterwards another minister, Michael Heseltine, challenged her to a leadership contest. Although she defeated Heseltine, so many of her own MPs had not voted for her and she decided to resign.

Changing policies

Thatcher is one of the most controversial prime ministers in British history – adored by her supporters and hated by her critics. However, historians tend to agree that her policies changed Britain dramatically:

- She clashed with the trade unions and severely weakened their power.
- She drastically cut back public spending in almost all areas, including health, welfare and education.
- She privatised (sold to private investors) major industries and utilities, including the railways and the telephone system, which had always been owned and run by the state.
- She stopped state subsidies (support payments) to industries that were no longer making any money, such as coal mining.
- She reduced income tax and corporation tax on businesses so that individuals and businesses could keep more of their own money.

Thatcher also reduced the power of local government. She fought a bitter battle with the Labour council in Liverpool in 1982 and abolished the Labour-dominated Greater London Council in 1983. In fact, this was one of several areas where her policies were inconsistent. She claimed that she wanted to free people from too much government interference, but the powers she took away from local councils were taken up by the central government. In some respects, therefore, Thatcher actually increased the power of the state.

Although she had a reputation as someone who said what she thought without worrying who she offended, Thatcher still worked closely with public-relations experts. These people helped her create the 'right' public image. She was the first prime minister to adopt a more 'presidential' style of leadership. She was also prepared to attack anyone who criticised her. Famously, she clashed with the BBC several times over how it reported her policies.

Source 2 Journalist Charlie Beckett, writing soon after Thatcher's death in 2013. He worked for the BBC for most of the time Thatcher was in power.

Margaret Thatcher was the dominant figure in British politics in the 1980s. What she represented continues to shape Westminster policy, practice and party strategy up to the present day. But she was also a break-through figure in terms of political communications. She took political presentation and media relations into the modern age of spin. And yet she was also remarkably untypical in that she dealt with (un)popularity in a manner that few contemporary politicians would dare. As Prime Minister she was divisive in an age when most party leaders are desperate to appeal beyond their base and to avoid being seen as ideological.

In many practical ways she was a political PR pioneer. I remember a serious discussion in the BBC newsroom in the mid-80s about whether we should cover political PR stunts because they weren't 'real news events'. It was a pointless debate by then as Mrs Thatcher's Conservative Party had already turned elections into a procession of calf-cuddling photo opportunities, poster launches and TV broadcasts.

She was also central to the creation of 'presidential' style politics. Leaders like Wilson were media-obsessed and nurtured a cult of personality with props like pipes and raincoats. But it was Mrs Thatcher who understood how to convert that into the domination of cabinet government and to identify her own will with that of the nation.

Source 3 A Conservative election poster from 1978. ▼

1. Explain the thinking behind Source 3. Who is it meant to appeal to and why?
2. Would a historian find Source 3 more or less useful than a Labour poster as a source about Thatcher? Explain your answer.

Challenges from politicians: Tony Blair

Although Margaret Thatcher fell from power in 1990, the Conservatives did not. It was not until 1997 that the Labour Party, under the leadership of Tony Blair, took control of government again. Blair was young and dynamic. He renamed the Labour Party 'New Labour' and introduced some radical changes to traditional Labour policies. Once in power, he made no attempt to undo the changes that Thatcher had brought about:

- He rejected the idea that the government should run industries.
- He worked hard to win over businesses, particularly the big banks.
- He involved private companies in issues such as health and education.
- He increased the power of the central government in education, for example by introducing academy schools, which were run directly by the Department of Education rather than by local councils.
- He kept many of the restrictions on trade unions introduced by the Conservative government.
- He ordered Labour candidates to avoid using the term 'socialism'.

Blair took a great deal of care over his public image. He was a good speaker and he made extensive use of press advisers, known as spin doctors. Like Thatcher, Blair found working closely with his own party and with parliament tiresome. He saw himself more as a manager of a big corporation than an elected prime minister. He often announced new policies in the media before they had been discussed in parliament. In this way, Blair too was acting more like an American president than a typical prime minister.

Blair was popular with the people and won three elections, but members of his own party began to criticise his approach and his policies. MPs of all parties disliked the fact that he appointed many of his supporters to the House of Lords (more in three years than the Conservatives had appointed in 18 years). Blair also made himself unpopular by involving Britain in the US-led invasion of Iraq in 2003. In 2007, he was effectively forced to stand down as prime minister.

ACTIVITY

Study Source 4. Is the cartoonist's opinion of Thatcher and Blair valid? Use a table like the one below to analyse the source.

Points being made about Thatcher and Blair	How the cartoonist makes these points	Evidence from the text that supports or contradicts points

Source 4 A cartoon published in *The Times* newspaper, December 1997. ▼

Challenges from pressure groups in the 1980s

Since its earliest days, parliament has been influenced by pressure groups. In the medieval period, barons, the Church and even ordinary peasants could present petitions to parliament, asking it to take action on particular issues. In the early modern period, parliament faced pressure from religious pressure groups such as the Puritans. In the modern period, parliament faced pressure from men and women demanding the vote. In the 1980s, Margaret Thatcher's style of leadership – seeking confrontation rather than compromise – encouraged opponents to exert pressure on parliament by non-parliamentary methods. They pressed for measures on issues including the economy, health care, international relations, the European Union and the environment.

Campaign for Nuclear Disarmament

The Campaign for Nuclear Disarmament (CND) began in Britain in the 1950s. Its main aim was simple – to remove nuclear weapons from British soil. From 1957 to 1963, CND campaigned actively and gained a great deal of support from well-known figures, particularly in universities, the media and the entertainment industry. Its activity declined in the 1960s but CND resurged in the 1980s. This was mainly due to Cold War tensions between the USSR and the USA, which made the threat of nuclear war very real. The British government allowed the USA to place nuclear missiles on British soil.

Hundreds of thousands of people joined CND, from all sections of society. There were Labour and Conservative activists, trade unionists, ex-servicemen and women and members of the newly emerging environmental movement. Women and young people were particularly drawn to the movement. In 1981, 250,000 CND supporters gathered for a rally in London. In October 1983, CND organised what may have been the largest ever public meeting – an estimated 300,000 people. It also set up long-term protest camps at Molesworth and Greenham Common. The Greenham Common women's camp was active from 1982 to 2000.

CND raised some serious issues for parliament. At its height, it had an extremely large membership and it may have had the support of up to 30 per cent of the population. The organisation posed some awkward questions. Should a country have nuclear weapons simply because other nations did? Did parliament have the right to allow a foreign power to put nuclear weapons in Britain, making Britain a target for its own enemies? Did politicians have the right to make decisions about whether the country should own or use such lethal weapons or should it be decided by a referendum? MPs and the security forces were afraid that foreign enemies, especially from the USSR, could have infiltrated the CND movement in Britain.

Source 5 A CND demonstration. ▲

Like other pressure groups, CND was not attached to any political party (although it had more support from Labour than the Conservatives). It appealed to the population directly and seemed to have no broader political agenda than the single issue of removing nuclear weapons from Britain. In the end, CND did not achieve disarmament, but it did raise public awareness of the issue and dramatically influenced public opinion. Throughout the 1990s, countries around the world signed treaties limiting nuclear weapons, although it is impossible to say how far this came about due to the actions of CND.

> **Source 6** An extract about the history of CND from the CND website.
>
> *The Conservative government under Margaret Thatcher became alarmed. Michael Heseltine was made Minister of Defence in January 1983. A very important part of his brief was to counter CND's influence. Not only was a well-funded anti-CND propaganda unit set up by the Government but the Intelligence Service (MI5) began to spy on CND activists: bugging their telephones and even infiltrating an agent into the London office. At the same time several organisations opposed to CND and its policies became very active. Some played a legitimate part – for instance by providing speakers to debate in schools against Youth CND and publishing reasoned arguments in opposition to CND. Others had a less reputable role: disrupting meetings, publishing personal attacks. The connections between these organisations and the government and the exact sources of their funding were never quite clear.*

1 Does Source 6 prove that CND was an important and effective campaigning group? Explain your answer.

The National Union of Mineworkers and the Miners' Strike 1984–85

There was a long history of hostility between the miners and the Conservative Party, dating back to the 1920s. Mine owners tried to keep wages and costs as low as possible, while unions tried to raise wages and improve conditions, especially safety. There were many strikes and on most occasions the government sided with the mine owners. In the Second World War, the government took control of the mines and later nationalised them, bringing them under the control of the state-run National Coal Board (NCB).

By the 1970s, the coal industry was losing money. There was strong competition from overseas and governments had not invested in new equipment for the mines, so they were inefficient. Margaret Thatcher appointed Neil MacGregor as head of the NCB and told him to close all the mines that were no longer making money. This move was bitterly opposed by the miners. They argued that the industry could make money if government invested in it. They also pointed out that thousands of mining communities would be devastated if the mines were closed. The leader of the National Union of Mineworkers (NUM), Arthur Scargill, called a strike. This lasted for a year and resulted in many violent clashes between police and miners.

There was a great deal of public sympathy for the miners over the effect the mine closures would have on their lives and communities. However, most people also agreed that the government could not keep providing support to an industry that was losing money. The government had prepared for the possibility of a strike, and had gathered stockpiles of coal to keep the power stations running.

To this day the strike has left a legacy of anger and division.

Criticisms of the miners	Criticisms of the government
• There was a lot of violence. Many police officers were injured in outbreaks of violence. • Scargill was accused of trying to overthrow a democratically elected prime minister. • Scargill refused to hold a democratic ballot to see whether the majority of miners supported the strike. As a result many miners refused to follow Scargill. A rival miners' union (the Union of Democratic Mineworkers) was set up. • Workers from other industries, such as the power workers, refused to go out on strike in support of the miners.	• Many believed that Thatcher deliberately provoked the conflict with the miners to make an example of them and damage the power of the unions. • Some people claim that Thatcher encouraged the police to be aggressive towards the miners. Many miners believed that the police acted illegally by stopping miners going to demonstrations and claim they were excessively violent. • Mining communities were devastated, causing decades of hardship and social problems. More could have been done to save the industry.

Source 7 A cartoon published in *The Evening Standard* newspaper, January 1985. ▶

> **2** Study Source 7 closely. Does it support or attack Arthur Scargill? Make sure you can explain your decision.

Greenpeace

Greenpeace was an environmental pressure group founded in Canada in 1971. It focused on carrying out high-profile direct action protests to highlight environmental issues. Across the world, Greenpeace campaigned against the Japanese government's policies on whaling, for example. It also highlighted the dumping of toxic waste by large companies.

In the UK, one of the main targets of Greenpeace was the British Nuclear Fuels Limited (BNFL) reprocessing plant at Sellafield. Greenpeace kept up a constant campaign in the media to highlight what it saw as the waste and danger of the plant. In 1983, four Greenpeace divers tried to block a discharge pipe at the plant, claiming it was releasing more than 10 million litres of radioactive water into the sea every day. As a result, Greenpeace was fined £50,000 and BNFL was granted a permanent injunction against the organisation. BNFL was later found guilty of the discharge.

Apart from the obvious environmental point, Greenpeace was also challenging the government and accusing it of being in league with big businesses like BNFL at the expense of the environment and of the health of local people. Greenpeace was an embarrassment to the government throughout the 1980s, although the Sellafield plant is still operating.

Source 8 A photograph on the Greenpeace website, posted in 2008. The caption was 'Back in 1999, Greenpeace was protesting about plutonium shipments destined for the Mox plant at Sellafield. Now the plant may have to close.' The plant was still open in 2015. ▼

Challenges from the regions of the UK

From the 1980s onwards, parliament faced another challenge: demands from the various regions of the United Kingdom for greater control of their own affairs.

Northern Ireland

Northern Ireland had been created in 1922. It was part of the United Kingdom, but until 1972 it had its own parliament. It was a deeply divided community, scarred by conflicts dating back centuries. From 1969 to 1996, the province faced extreme violence between people who wanted to stay part of the UK (Unionists) and those who wanted independence (Nationalists). About 3,000 people died in these clashes and thousands more were injured. However, in 1998 the UK government and the representatives of the main communities in Ireland reached an agreement that ended the violence. Part of this deal was the establishment of an Assembly to represent the different groups that made up the population of Northern Ireland.

There was no revival of the conflict, so in this sense the Assembly was successful, but the parties struggled to work together and the Assembly was suspended in 2002–06. The Northern Ireland Assembly now controls law and order, social and health, policy, environment, transport and education in the province, removing these powers from parliament in London.

Scotland

Throughout the 1980s and early 1990s, Scotland elected very few Conservative MPs. However, since the Conservatives won the general elections country-wide, most Scots lived ended up living under a government they did not support. A campaign for Scottish independence began to develop. When Tony Blair came to power in 1997, he had already agreed to a referendum on the issue of DEVOLUTION. A majority of Scots voted in favour and a new Scottish parliament was created. This parliament had wide-ranging powers over health, education, transport and many other areas. It could even raise some taxes.

The Scottish parliament has generally been seen as a success, but it has created new challenges. The most successful party in the new parliament has been the Scottish National Party, which wants *full* independence from the United Kingdom. A referendum in 2014 was defeated 55 per cent to 45 per cent, but debate still rages.

Source 9 A cartoon published in *The Glasgow Herald* in 1999. Whitehall mandarins are senior civil servants in London. At this time the Scottish parliament had announced plans to scrap tuition fees for students going to university in Scotland. A mandarin is a senior civil servant. The term goes back to Ancient China. ▼

"Damn Jocks...give them Devolution and they think they run the country."

Wales

The devolution of power to Wales followed a similar pattern to that in Scotland. A referendum was held in 1997 and most Welsh people voted in favour. By 2007, Wales had a fully functioning assembly in Cardiff, with control over education, health, law and order and most other aspects of ordinary life.

The three assemblies do not have control over defence, immigration, the currency and many aspects of economic policy and taxation. These powers are still held by parliament in London.

1 According to Source 9, what is the Scottish parliament doing?
2 According to the source, how do civil servants in London feel about the Scottish parliament?
3 Do you think this source is more useful for understanding attitudes to devolution in London or attitudes in Scotland? Explain your answer.

Challenges from the electorate and the challenge of coalition government

As you have seen, Britain's journey to becoming a parliamentary democracy has been a long and sometimes difficult one. And the problems are far from over. In the early 2000s a new challenge emerged – disillusion with parliamentary politics.

Disengagement

In the early 2000s, the Hansard Society began a yearly survey of how the public felt about parliament, political parties and politics in general. The trends revealed by these surveys have been worrying:

- Only around 50 per cent of the population is certain to vote in a general election. This was under 20 per cent for people aged 18–24.
- Fewer than 50 per cent of people say they are interested in politics.
- Only 24 per cent of the population thinks the parliamentary system works well.
- The proportion of voters who think parliament is essential fell from 85 per cent in 2010 to 61 per cent in 2015.
- Only 32 per cent of voters think that getting involved in politics makes any difference to their lives.
- The public's perception of MPs, civil servants and other officials is overwhelmingly negative (see Source 10).

> **Source 10** An extract from the 2015 'Audit of Political Engagement'.
>
> *Overall the public has a fairly bleak view of standards in public life. Few think that the standard of conduct of people in public life is high, there is a belief that standards have got worse in recent years, and there is a lack of confidence in the authorities to uphold standards and uncover and punish wrongdoing. Just 18% of the public think that the standards of conduct of public office holders are high; twice as many (36%) believe, on the contrary, that standards are low. Thirty-five percent believe that standards of conduct have declined compared with a few years ago, and just 15% think that they have improved at least 'a little'. Over half the public (56%) are not confident that the authorities are committed to upholding standards in public life; with just under four in 10 people (38%) disagreeing.*

Professional politicians

Politicians and historians are still debating the reasons for this problem. As Source 10 shows, many people think that MPs and other officials do a poor job and look out for themselves rather than the public. Another factor has been the rise of 'professional politicians'. Until the 1980s most politicians had careers in industry, the law, trade unions, journalism and many other areas before they became MPs. From the 1980s, however, the main political parties became much more centralised. They controlled which candidates stood for which constituencies (often the candidate was not local). This meant that increasing numbers of MPs had no career outside politics. They began as party officials, often worked as researchers or assistants to MPs, and then stood as MPs themselves.

The European Union

One other factor changing the perception of parliament has been the European Union (EU). As part of the EU, some aspects of British life and work are beyond the control of parliament. Critics of the EU say this makes parliament more irrelevant.

A key part of EU policy is free movement of people, which has brought large numbers of migrants to Britain, mainly from EU member states in eastern Europe. Supporters of immigration argue that migrants improve Britain's economy, but critics argue that they compete with British people for jobs and benefits such as housing, which causes tensions.

New parties

These factors have given rise to new more radical parties, particularly the United Kingdom Independence Party (UKIP), which opposed British membership of the EU and sought restrictions on immigration. UKIP increased its support dramatically in the 2010s and most observers believed that this reflected people's disillusionment with the main political parties.

Source 11 An extract from a report by the Institute for Government, May 2011. The Institute is an independent charity that campaigns to make government more efficient.

Overall results of a poll in April 2011 show that people are more put off by the idea of coalition government this year than they were when polled on the eve of the May 2010 general election. Then, 55% said it would be a 'bad thing' for no party to win an overall majority, today that number is 63%.

Two thirds of people (68%) also felt the country was weaker being run by a coalition rather than a single party. Only 24% said it was stronger. Nearly three quarters (73%) of all polled said that government was more indecisive, 80% said government was more confused and 57% said government was less responsive to the public.

ACTIVITY

Work in pairs. One of you is in favour of changing Britain's voting system. The other is against such a move. Draw up a list of reasons why you hold your particular view. You should consider:

- the advantages or disadvantages of the existing system
- the advantages or disadvantages of the alternative systems.

PRACTICE QUESTIONS

1   Describe *two* examples of challenges to the power of parliament in the period 1979–90. (4)
2   Explain why there was a lot of disillusionment with politics and politicians in Britain by the early 2000s. (8)
3   How significant a challenge to government were pressure groups in the 1980s? (14)

One result of this disillusionment was a 'hung parliament' in the 2010 election. The existing Labour government failed to win a majority, but the Conservatives also failed to gain the support of enough voters. The result was a coalition government in which the Conservatives worked with the Liberal Democrats.

Coalition government

In practice, the coalition worked better than many people expected. Each party had to compromise, but they also had the chance to propose policies that were important to them. For example, the Liberal Democrats wanted to change the electoral system so that seats in parliament would be proportional (based on each party's share of the vote). This was put to a referendum in 2011 but the public rejected the change. This may have been because the proposed change would be more likely to result in coalition governments in the future, which many people are uneasy about. Source 11 reports research undertaken at the time of this referendum.

The 2015 general election

Most commentators expected another hung parliament after the 2015 election. Opinion polls suggested that no party really had strong support from the population. UKIP was taking support from the Conservatives while the Scottish National Party was taking support from Labour, which held most seats in Scotland.

However, Britain's 'first past the post' electoral system means that a party can gain large numbers of votes nationally but because they do not do well in individual constituencies they can end up with few or no seats (see Source 12). To the surprise of politicians and commentators, the Conservatives won an outright majority in the 2015 election and the experiment in coalition government was over.

Source 12 A table showing the number of seats and share of votes in the 2015 general election.

	Millions of votes	Percentage of vote	Seats won (i.e. number of MPs)	MPs if allocated by share of vote
Conservative	11.3	36.9	331	240
Labour	9.3	30.4	232	198
Scottish National Party	1.4	4.7	56	30
Liberal Democrats	2.4	7.9	8	51
UKIP	3.9	12.6	1	82

KEY QUESTION REVIEW

A   How serious were the challenges facing parliament and British democracy c1980–2014?

1   Use your work on the key question to answer this practice question:
'Despite all the challenges to parliament and government between 1980 and 2014, the British people never lost faith in democracy.' How far do you agree with this view?

3.4 Review: Power c1485–2014

PERIOD REVIEW TASKS

In this chapter, you have studied different examples of power in action through the modern period. You are now going to pull the early modern and modern periods together and get a bigger picture.

A Claims to power

From the early modern period to the modern period, the claim to power changes like this:

a Power in the hands of the monarch because he or she is appointed by God.

b Power in the hands of the Political Nation because they know what is best for the country and its people.

c Power in hands of a democratically elected parliament because the party with the most seats has the support of most of the population.

1 Make a copy of the timeline below and decide when you think stages a, b and c begin and end. You may decide that there is some overlap.

2 Add key events to your timeline that you think are important in moving Britain from one stage to the next.

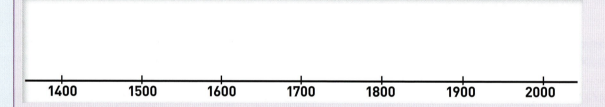

| 1400 | 1500 | 1600 | 1700 | 1800 | 1900 | 2000 |

B Who was in power and where did power lie?

3 Look at the statements in the table below, which describe power in the early modern period. Copy and complete the table to explain how far these are true in the modern period.

In the early modern period	In the modern period this is less true/more true/ changes at different times	Evidence to support judgement
Succession from one monarch to the next was a key factor in keeping peace and stability.		
Personality of the monarch was very important.		
It was important to be successful in war.		
Ruler needed to be able to get measures (laws, taxes, etc.) accepted by parliament.		
Control of religion/the Church was important.		
Power was concentrated with a relatively small group of rich and powerful people.		
Neither monarchs nor parliament had to concern themselves about what the majority of the population thought.		
Monarchs were far more powerful and important than parliament.		

C What were the biggest problems facing rulers and governments in the early modern and modern periods?

4 Create a table like this – big enough to add examples from each period on either side. Then look back over Chapters 2 and 3 to complete it.

5 When you have finished your research, decide whether the factors are in the right order of importance in causing tensions in the each period. If not, number them in the order you think most appropriate.

Examples from early modern period	Problems facing rulers and governments	Examples from modern period
	conflict with own subjects	
	defending the people of the country	
	getting the approval and support of the population	
	improving the welfare of the population	
	managing the economy	
	raising money through taxes	
	religion	
	ruler not having the right personal qualities	
	tackling social problems	
	war against foreign enemies	

6 Compare your rank orders with the order you had for the medieval period. Has the order changed? If so in what way and why?

D What were the most significant events in the period?

7 On page 49 there are some criteria for evaluating significance. Use the same criteria to evaluate the following events from the period 1800–2014. You can add other events if you think anything significant has been omitted.

- Reform Acts of 1832, 1867 and 1884
- foundation of Labour Party
- First World War
- Second World War
- general election 1945
- election of Thatcher
- election of Blair
- Miners' Strike
- devolution
- general election 2010

PRACTICE QUESTIONS

The final question on your paper will be a big question that covers two periods. For the early modern and modern periods possible questions might be:

1 'Britain became much more democratic in the period c1485–2014.' How far do you agree? (24)

2 'For most of the period c1485–2014, monarchs were more powerful than their subjects.' How far do you agree with this view? (24)

3 Was war the most serious problem which faced rulers in the period c1485–2014? Explain your answer. (24)

4 'In the period c1485–2014 the balance of power shifted decisively towards the majority of the population.' How far do you agree? (24)

KEY TERMS

Make sure you know what these terms mean and can use them confidently in your writing.
- devolution
- legislation
- suffrage

Factfile: Parliament c1800–2014

Parliament and the people 1800–32

Parliament continued to be the main power in Britain, dominated by the landowning aristocracy.

- Most senior ministers were members of the House of Lords.
- There were 658 MPs in the House of Commons, most of them also wealthy landowners. There were some exceptions – lawyers, industrialists and some political radicals – but they were a minority.
- Parliament was not a democratic system as we know it today:
  - Constituencies were different sizes with different population levels.
  - Usually only land or property owners could vote, although in some places paying local taxes gave people the right to vote.
  - Many of the growing industrial towns, such as Manchester, had no MPs at all, while other areas that were no longer very important did have MPs.
  - Votes were taken by a show of hands – there was no secret ballot. This led to people being intimidated into voting a particular way.

Reform of parliament and a growing Political Nation 1832–1969

As a result of hard campaigning – and in the face of severe opposition – more reforms were gradually won in the twentieth and twenty-first centuries.

- 1832 Reform Act:
  - Increased the electorate to include much of the new middle classes. Across the country the proportion of men who could vote rose from 11 per cent to 18 per cent in 1832.
  - 143 seats were taken away from small boroughs and distributed among the large industrial towns. Only people paying at least £10 per year in rates could vote in boroughs – this meant people with property (mostly the middle classes).
  - The majority of MPs were still landowners because they were the only ones who could afford to do the job.
  - There was still no secret ballot, so intimidation and corruption continued.

- 1867 Reform Act:
  - Passed by the Tories under Disraeli.
  - Another 45 small constituencies lost their MPs and these seats were given to the big towns and counties with large populations.
  - In the boroughs, all men who owned or rented a house could vote (this was mainly the better-off working classes).
  - In the counties, men who owned or leased land could vote.
  - The act doubled the size of the electorate from 20 per cent to 40 per cent of the male population. Those without the vote were mostly agricultural labourers and unskilled industrial workers.

- 1872 Secret Ballot Act: Voting was carried out by secret ballot, which cut down on corruption and intimidation.

- 1884 Reform Act:
  - Passed by the Liberals under Gladstone.
  - Gave the vote to respectable householders in the countryside (the equivalent of the men who had gained the vote in towns in 1867).
  - Gave yet more seats to the big towns and cities.
  - The electorate rose from 3 to 5 million.
  - For the first time, constituencies represented fairly similar populations (around one MP to 50,000 constituents).

- 1911 Parliament Act and payment of MPs:
  - After a clash between the House of Commons and the House of Lords over welfare reform, the government passed the Parliament Act. This removed the power of the House of Lords to block measures that had been passed by the Commons.
  - Payment for MPs was also introduced, so people who were not wealthy could afford to become MPs.

- 1918 Representation of the People Act:
  - Gave the vote to all men over the age of 21.
  - The vote was also given to women over the age of 30 if they were a property owner or married to a registered voter.

- 1928 Representation of the People Act: Gave the vote to all women over the age of 21.

- Representation of the People Act 1969: Gave the vote to all men and women aged 18 or over.

ASSESSMENT FOCUS

How the thematic study will be assessed

The thematic study will be examined in Paper 2. It is worth 25 per cent of the overall marks for the GCSE. There will be four questions, which test the first two assessment objectives:

- AO1: knowledge and understanding
- AO2: explanation and analysis.

The questions could be on any part of the content, but that *does not* mean you have to try to remember every event! Above all, the paper is assessing your ability to think and work like a historian. In the introduction, you looked at how historians work (page 4). There we set out some steps that historians take:

1 focus
2 ask questions
3 select
4 organise
5 fine tune.

If you have tackled all the Key Question Review tasks you will be fine. In fact, our advice is not to take lots of notes and try to remember them. Revise your work from the Focus Tasks and Key Question Review tasks. That will prepare you more effectively.

Question 1

Question 1 will usually ask you to describe an event or development in the story of Power c1000–2014. It is a simple knowledge question, probably requiring a description of two examples of a type of event. For example:

> **Describe two examples of how Charles I tried to rule without parliament in the years 1629–40. (4 marks)**

Aim of the question

There are no tricks to this question. It is simply testing your knowledge. There will not be anything obscure. The examiner wants to see that you can describe important events accurately without simply writing down everything you know.

Advice

Select: The question asks you to select two examples of what Charles did during the period of Personal Rule in 1629–40 to try to avoid working with parliament. Do not 'over-answer'. There are many examples, but the question requires *two*. Selecting just two is part of the task. You will not gain anything by selecting more examples. In fact you may lose marks. The examiner is looking for a description of what Charles did to avoid working with parliament, so you do not need to go into detail about how parliament reacted, for example.

Organise: The important thing is to use your knowledge in a relevant way. In this question a good way to organise your answer might be: 'Charles wanted to achieve X, so he did Y.'

Fine tune: Make sure that your spellings and dates are correct. Make sure that your answer is clear – in the pressure of an exam it is easy to accidentally say something you do not mean to say.

Example answer

> Charles I quarrelled with parliament in 1628 and then ruled without calling it from 1629–40. He tried many different ways to rule without parliament.
>
> One example was Ship Money. Charles was short of money most of the time and usually monarchs called parliament to ask for taxes to be raised. Charles tried to get round this by making all counties pay Ship Money. Ship Money was meant to help the king defend the coast and maintain the navy. Originally only counties on the coast had paid it. By making all counties pay it Charles was able to raise a lot of money. He also caused controversy – for example, John Hampden refused to pay Ship Money and it became a famous court case. Another example was knighthood fines. Overall Charles doubled his income.

Comments

This answer has lots of good points. It would definitely get two marks – possibly even three.

The opening statement is good. It is not absolutely essential, but it is a nice example of fine tuning – it shows that the candidate understands the answer.

The description of Ship Money is very thorough. If we were being really mean we might say it is too good – there is a lot of detail about Ship Money, and the answer also goes on to mention the Hampden court case. That bit is not really needed.

The knighthood fines are a relevant and sensible choice, but this example is clearly under-developed.

To improve this answer: remove some of the detail on Ship Money and explain that knighthood fines meant fines for landowners who did not come to court to be knighted, as an ancient law laid down.

Practice

There are plenty of practice questions at the end of every topic. Go back and try a couple of the four-mark 'Describe...' questions.

General advice on Questions 2–4

Questions 2–4 ask you to do more than simply describe. You have to explain things and reach judgements. You have to answer the question and explain why you think what you think. A useful way to think about Questions 2, 3 and 4 is to assess your answers yourself. Examiners use mark schemes but you don't need anything that complicated. Think of it like an Olympic medal ceremony. Read some of your practice answers and ask yourself which of these medals your answer deserves.

GOLD
(up to 100% of marks)

SILVER
(up to 60% of marks)

BRONZE
(up to 25% of marks)

Bronze: You describe something you know (which is good) but it is not really relevant to the question (which is a shame). Or you assert something (which is good) but you provide no supporting evidence (which is a shame).

Silver: You describe relevant events or developments (which is good) but you do not connect them to the question or explain why they are important in answering the question (which is a shame).

Gold: You make it really clear what you think the answer to the question is. You support your answer with at least one event or development and you explain how that event or development supports your answer.

Even a Gold answer can be improved by ensuring you have:
- a clear conclusion that rounds off your argument
- a balanced answer that shows you understand that there might be more than one view about the question or explains how the different elements are connected
- supporting evidence: using relevant knowledge and a good range of examples to support each point you make.

Question 2

Question 2 will usually be an 'explain' question. This might ask you to explain *why* something happened, or to explain *what* the effects of something were, or it might ask you to explain *how* something happened. For example:

> ***Explain why medieval rulers sometimes clashed with their barons or bishops. (8 marks)***

Advice

Select: It is sensible to think in terms of at least two reasons, or effects, or whatever the question is asking for. This will show the examiner what you know without spending too much time on the question.

Organise: The important thing is to use your knowledge in a relevant way. In this question a good way to organise your answer might be: 'One reason kings and barons clashed was A. In DATE King B brought in C. The king was trying to D. However, this upset E because F. This led to clashes like G.'

Fine tune: Do all the usual checking, but when answering an 'explain' question it can also be a good idea to say which of your reasons you think is more important.

Example answer

> Medieval rulers clashed with their barons and bishops for many different reasons. When King John took the throne in 1199 he was short of money. John simply brought in new taxes without asking the barons. Many of his barons rebelled against him in 1215. He was forced to accept the terms of Magna Carta, which said that John was not above the law and had to obey it. He was also watched over by a council of 25 barons.
>
> In the 1380s, Richard II appointed his close friends to important jobs. For example, he made Michael de la Pole Earl of Suffolk and chancellor – effectively his chief minister. The barons rebelled and Richard was defeated in 1387.

Practice

There are plenty of practice questions at the end of every topic. Go back and try a couple of the eight-mark 'Explain...' questions.

The aim of the question

This type of question is designed to stretch you a bit further. When examiners ask you to explain they want you to show that you know the events but also that you can explain why those events were important in affecting people or making something happen. In a 'describe' question you might say: 'Kings wanted taxes.' In an 'explain' question you might say: 'Kings wanted taxes so sometimes raised them without the barons' approval, which caused tension.'

Comments

This answer has some good points but also some weaknesses. It is probably a silver medal.

The opening is promising, but it goes on to simply *describe* problems rather than explaining them. The knowledge is good but there is no real explanation.

It shows a common mistake – it lists events that are connected to the question, but the student thinks it is obvious how and why these points are relevant and so gives no explanation. Examiners cannot award the marks because the student has not 'explained why'.

To improve this answer: Explain why John was short of money. Explain why the barons disliked his actions. Explain why they thought *Magna Carta* would tackle the problem. Similarly, explain why Richard II's actions upset the barons – how Richard was going against the normal way of doing things.

Question 3

Question 3 will usually be about how *significant* or *important* something was. It can come in a number of forms. For example:

- How significant a change was X?
- How important was X in causing Y?
- How significant was X in how Y worked?

This is probably the most important type of question for you to practise. If you can master this, then you will master all the techniques needed for the other question types. Here is an example:

The aim of the question
This question is asking you to assess the ways in which military power was important to Anglo-Saxon kings, and whether it was more or less important – or worked alongside – other factors.

> *How significant was military power to Anglo-Saxon kings? (14 marks)*

Advice

Select: You need to select facts, events and developments which show that military power was important. You also need to select facts, events and dates that show how other factors, like the Church or the Witan, were important too.

Organise: A possible way to tackle this question is to put together three paragraphs. Military power is the focus of the question so it should get a paragraph to itself. Then you can explain how important other factors were in one further paragraph. Then write a concluding paragraph.

Fine tune: Do all the usual checking, but here it is worth making sure you have said what you think about the question. In questions like this, a conclusion usually means saying something like:

- Military power was the most important factor because ... *or*
- Military power was important but X was more important because ... *or*
- Military power and other factors cannot really be separated out because ...

Example answer

Comments
This answer is definitely Gold. It would probably score 12 out of the 14 marks. The opening is clear and the student follows up on that opening very effectively.

One paragraph explains why military power mattered – it was the king's job and the lands had to be defended. The next paragraph explains how other factors were important. The conclusion is really helpful.

This answer does not need a lot of improvement. However, it could be improved with a little more detail in the first paragraph. For instance, examples of important military victories by either Harold or Alfred would support the general statements.

> Military power was a very important factor in Anglo-Saxon kingship. However, it was not the only factor that was important.
>
> Military power was very important. The Anglo-Saxon king was a warrior-king. His main job was to lead his warriors and defend his lands. He might have to defend them from other Anglo-Saxon rivals, like Harold Godwinson did against his brother Tostig, or he might have to defend them against Viking invaders the way Alfred the Great had done.
>
> However, other factors were important as well. An effective king needed to have the support of the Witan – the great nobles of the kingdom. The Church was also important. It helped to run the government and it kept people loyal to the king. Another really important factor was the Anglo-Saxon system of administration. The king could send out instructions called writs to his local sheriffs and this meant that he could control what was happening in his lands. This system also made it much easier to collect taxes. Anglo-Saxon England was one of the wealthiest states in Europe in the 1000s.
>
> So on balance, military power was important but it was only one factor in Anglo-Saxon kingship. Without the loyalty of the great nobles and the taxation system to pay for the armies the king would not have had any military power.

Practice

There are plenty of practice questions at the end of every topic. Go back and try a couple of the 14-mark 'How significant...' questions.

The aim of the question

This is a thematic study that encourages you to see the big picture over hundreds of years. So this question is testing how far you have this overview.

You need to reach your own judgement as to whether or not the support of the people really affected the way a monarch or a government ran the country. You do *not* need to write a summary of the history of the period. The aim of this question is to get you to give an answer to the question and support it with a few examples from each period.

Comments

This outline answer has the potential to get a Gold (between 19 and 24 marks). It puts forward a balanced argument, using evidence on both sides of the argument from both periods. It also gives a sensible conclusion.

It would probably come in at the bottom of the mark range for Gold (19 marks) because it does not really use a wide range of examples to support the points being made. There are several ways it could be improved.

- *In the 'yes' paragraph it could have added an example like the Pilgrimage of Grace, where clearly a lot of people opposed Henry VIII but he crushed them anyway.*

- *There is a good point in the 'no' paragraph about Elizabeth and Henry having to listen to their people. The student could have given a few examples of how both monarchs worked with parliament.*

- *In the 'no' paragraph there is a mention of the majority – it would have been good to point out that in the early modern period monarchs needed the support of at least some of the important people, whereas by the twentieth century, governments needed the support of the majority of the whole population.*

- *It would have been nice to have had some twentieth-century examples*

For some Keys to success tips, see page 188.

Question 4

Question 4 will usually be a big overview question. It will ask you to compare two eras – medieval and early modern *or* early modern and modern. It will give you a statement and ask you how far you agree with it. For example:

> *'In the early modern and modern periods monarchs and governments did not need the support of the people they ruled over.' How far do you agree with this statement? (24 marks)*

Advice

Select: Selection is extremely important in this question. You *do not* need to cover the whole early modern and modern periods in your answer. The fact that there are 24 marks does not mean you have to *write* a lot. It means you have to *think* a lot! Select examples that support the view in the statement *and* examples that oppose it. Do this for the early modern *and* the modern period. So think in terms of four examples.

Organise: A good way to tackle this question might be to put together an introduction, two paragraphs (the 'yes' paragraph and the 'no' paragraph) and then a conclusion.

Fine tune: Do all the usual checking, but here it is worth making sure you have said what you think about the question. In questions like this, a conclusion usually means:

- you agree *or* you disagree *or*
- the statement is true at some points in time but not in others.

Example answer

The statement is partially true but it depends on the period you are looking at. It is more true for the early modern period and the earlier part of the modern period, but from the later nineteenth century onwards it is less and less true.

In the early modern period, monarchs and governments could certainly rule without the support of the people. To begin with, none of the monarchs was elected, so in that sense they did not need the support of the people they ruled. There was nothing anyone could do to oppose a monarch unless they rebelled. Perhaps the most extreme example of a monarch ruling without support was Charles I. From 1629 to 1640 he ruled without once summoning parliament. He used taxes like Ship Money and knighthood fines to raise the money he needed. But even in the modern period governments ruled without the support of the majority of the people. In the early 1800s very few people were able to vote. Big industrial towns like Manchester had no MPs at all. Rich men could buy and sell parliamentary constituencies. It was not until 1832 that parliament gave more people the vote and not until 1884 that most working-class men could vote. And only men could vote – not women.

On the other hand, there are many ways that the statement is wrong. To begin with, Charles I was eventually overthrown by parliament and executed in 1649. And even powerful monarchs like Henry VIII and Elizabeth had to listen to their people. In the modern period, parliament was gradually forced to become more democratic. There were Reform Acts in 1832, 1867 and 1884, which gradually gave the majority of men the vote. Parliament granted the 1832 Reform Act because it feared there would be a revolution if it did not accept reform. Later Reform Acts were passed by the different political parties because they thought the reforms would win them votes. By 1928, all men and women could vote.

On balance the statement is more wrong than it is right. Even in the early modern period, when monarchs did not have to worry about elections, they still had to have the support of at least some of their people, like the nobles or parliament. By the modern period it was virtually impossible to rule without the support of the majority of the people. Apart from anything else a government could not get elected.

Practice

First of all, have a go at this question using our structure. Do not use our example though. Pick others from Chapters 2 and 3 – for example from the reigns of Henry VIII and Elizabeth I or from the world wars. There are practice questions at the end of Chapters 2 and 3. Try a couple of the 24-mark 'period comparison' questions.

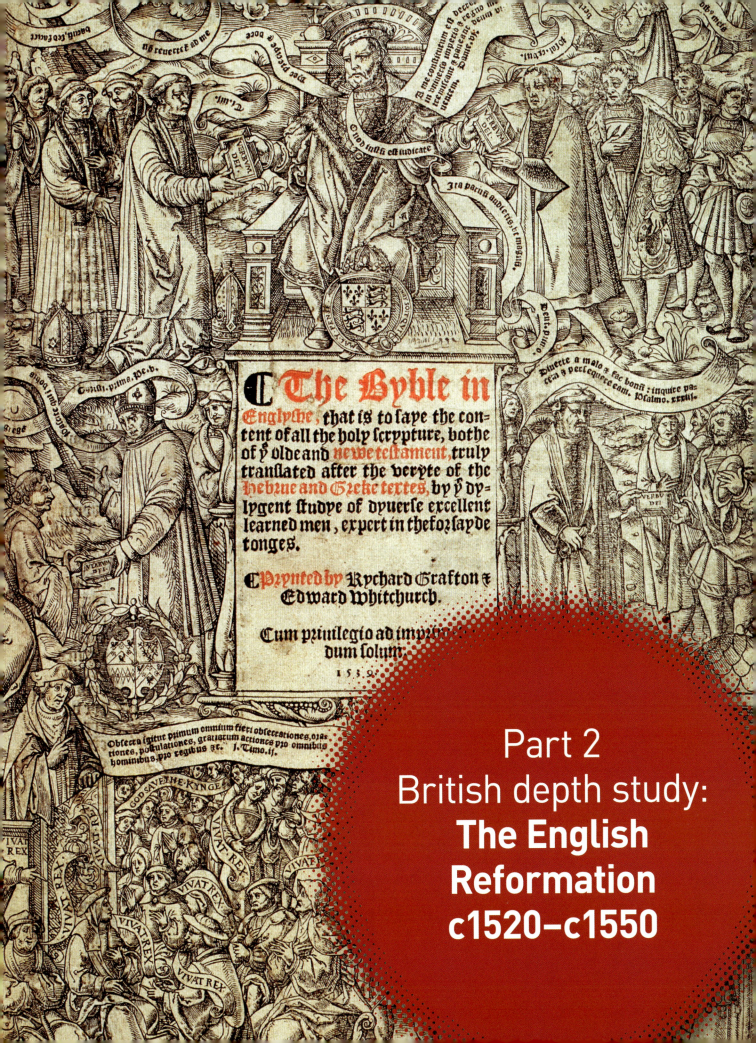

Part 2
British depth study:
The English Reformation c1520–c1550

Introduction to the depth study

In this part of the book you will be studying the English REFORMATION.

What was the Reformation?

In simple terms, the Reformation was a religious change. Up to 1534, England belonged to the Roman Catholic Church. Its leader was the pope in Rome. However, in 1534, King Henry VIII broke with the Catholic Church. England remained a Christian country but now it was PROTESTANT, with Henry himself as head of the new Church of England.

Why study the Reformation?

The Reformation was a hugely significant event in British history. It shook the foundations of the Catholic Church in England. That may not sound like a big thing today, but in the 1500s it meant changing an institution that was a thousand years old and was a huge part of everyone's daily life.

- The Church was people's link to God.
- The Church was the centre of the social life of the country.
- The Church provided work for a large proportion of the population.
- The Church provided care for the sick and it looked after the poor and the old.
- The church building was people's gateway to Heaven. It looked heavenly, it sounded heavenly (rich people paid for hymns to be sung) and it even smelt heavenly (because of burning incense).

To understand the scale of change, imagine a government today abolishing the National Health Service, ending all welfare payments, then closing the schools, art galleries, cinemas and pubs. Imagine the government then comes into your home and tells you what posters to put on your walls, what music you can listen to and who you can be friends with. The Reformation was similarly dramatic and overwhelming for people in the sixteenth century.

The focus of the study

The effects of the Reformation can still be seen in many parts of England, in the form of ruined abbeys or churches that once sparkled with decoration but are now plain and whitewashed. It affected the language and culture of England. As you have seen in the thematic study, it also had a huge political impact, making parliament far more important. This depth study does not focus on politics, though, it focuses on people – how they felt about the Reformation and the changes it brought to their lives.

Instead of the broad overview of a long period you developed in your study of power, you are going to look at *a short period of time* in detail here – just 30 years. You are going to try and understand the people who caused the Reformation, those who opposed it and those who were most affected by it. To do this, you will look at a wide range of historical sources that these people created. Official documents, personal letters and diaries, propaganda publications, prayer books, even church financial accounts, all help us to build a picture of the time and the people involved.

The big questions

Although we are looking at a small timescale and focusing on individuals and communities, this depth study still investigates some big questions:

- Why was the English Church so powerful in the 1520s?
- What did the reformers change and why did they want to change it?
- How did people in England react to the Reformation?

Assessment

You will be assessed using two main question types:

- The first will ask you to 'explain' something. This question is designed to test your knowledge and your ability to explain an aspect of the period, such as why the Church was wealthy, or why some people wanted to reform the Church.
- The second type will focus on one of the big issues. You will be given three sources and asked whether they convince you that a particular view is correct. You will need to show your understanding of the sources, as well as your ability to use them to support a viewpoint.

4.1 The role and importance of the Church in the 1500s

What is William Melton worried about?

Source 1 An extract from William Melton's *Exhortation*, 1510.

Everywhere throughout town and countryside there exists a crop of oafish and boorish priests, some of whom are engaged on ignoble and servile tasks, while others abandon themselves to tavern hunting, swilling and drunkenness. Some cannot get along without their wenches; others pursue their amusements in dice and gambling and other such trifling all day long. There are some who waste their time in hunting and hawking. ... This is inevitable, for since they are all completely ignorant of good literature, how can they obtain improvement or enjoy reading and study?

We must avoid and keep far from ourselves that grasping, deadly plague of avarice for which practically every priest is accused and held in disrepute before the people, when it is said that we are greedy for rich promotions ... and spend little or nothing on works of piety.

In 1510, the chancellor of York (an official who helped the archbishop with legal cases) William Melton wrote his *Exhortation*. Source 1 shows what he said about the English Church. On the face of it, this source suggests that in the early 1500s the Church was not a popular organisation. In fact, you could INFER that there was widespread criticism of the Church from his words 'practically every priest is accused'. However, it is important to understand why William Melton was writing this. Melton made his career in the Church. He was also a deeply religious man who wanted to strengthen the Catholic Church in England.

Melton was clearly outraged at the priests' behaviour and wanted the CLERGY to undertake more reading and learning. However, he represents only a small group of PIOUS, educated members of the gentry who felt a personal duty to reform the Church. They called for changes to ensure the Catholic Church remained part of the fabric of society. In fact there is little evidence to suggest that the majority of the population of England agreed with William Melton.

FACTFILE

The structure of the Catholic Church in England at the beginning of the sixteenth century.

The pope (Bishop of Rome): God's representative on Earth.

Secular clergy

Regular clergy

Cardinals: very senior churchmen who elected the pope.

Archbishops: the senior churchmen in each country.

Bishops: regional leaders of the Church.

Parish priests: ministered to local congregations.

Enclosed monastic orders: devoted their lives to worship and had hardly any contact with the community.

Open monastic orders: worked within society, providing medical aid, charity and teaching.

The power of the Church

In 1520, the Roman Catholic Church was a very powerful force in England:

- Its annual earnings were an estimated £400,000, compared with £40,000 for the income from the royal lands.
- The vast majority of the population went to weekly or more regular services.
- There were 45,000 clergy. The majority of these were parish priests who led the services.
- The Church had its own system of law courts and privileges.
- It was part of a massive international Church under the authority of the pope in Rome.

Hierarchy

All Catholics (collectively known as CHRISTENDOM) had to accept the pope as head of the Church, with supreme authority over all religious matters. The pope had his own court, through which he ruled the most important people in Christendom and made sure they did what he wanted them to do.

1 Look at Source 2. Why might this idea of a 'Chain of Being' appeal to ordinary people?
2 Some versions of this image created subdivisions so that kings, aristocracy, merchants, etc. were shown in a hierarchy too. Why might kings have supported this vision of a 'chain'?

Source 2 A sketch entitled *The Great Chain of Being*, drawn by a Franciscan monk in 1579. ▼

Church and monarch

In England, the Church played an important political role. Churchmen were the most highly educated men in the country, so they were often government ministers. Bishops and abbots sat in the House of Lords and helped govern the country. This created strong links between the monarch and the Church. Some of Henry VIII's closest advisors were also churchmen. Thomas Wolsey was Henry's chief minister for 15 years as well as holding many Church titles, including Archbishop of York and cardinal, while in the king's service.

The Church also boosted the monarch's authority through concepts such as the 'Great Chain of Being' (see Source 2). This showed society as a hierarchy, with everyone knowing their place. This suggested that God would punish those who rebelled against their king (treason) or who questioned the authority of the Church (HERESY). In this way, the Church played a fundamental role in maintaining control throughout the kingdom.

Donations

The Church taught that worship of God should be beautiful. This led wealthy people to give money to rebuild and decorate churches and chapels across the country. Many churches in East Anglia were sumptuously rebuilt in the fifteenth century due to the donations of wealthy cloth merchants. These people hoped that their contribution would ensure their souls did not linger too long in purgatory.

People were also encouraged to leave money to the Church in their wills, and special prayers might be said for those who had done so (see Sources 3 and 4). Some wealthier people left money to found a CHANTRY, where a priest would celebrate masses for the soul of its founder. Chantry priests celebrated thousands of private masses for the souls of the dead. The Church also offered services called INDULGENCES, where members of the congregation could pay for extra prayers to be said to help speed the soul of a loved one to Heaven.

Historians have discovered that many ordinary people donated personal items, such as bed linen and wedding rings, to the Church. This was partly because they wanted to be remembered after their deaths. Every year the names of people who had made such donations would be read out in the 'requiem for the dead' ceremony, so their friends and family would be reminded of them.

> **Source 3** The will of Thomas Foldyngton, June 1530.
>
> 1 *In return for land Thomas' daughter, Joan, will keep a candle burning in front of an image of the Virgin Mary and pay 4d during the first week of Lent.*
> 2 *His best goods to be given to the priest at Barholm who will pray for his soul.*
> 3 *He leaves some barley to pay for tithes that had been forgotten.*
> 4 *He leaves the church at Barholm 2s and a blue cloth to cover the sacrament.*
> 5 *He leaves 3s and 4d to the convent of the abbey in Bourne to pray for his soul.*
> 6 *He leaves 3s and 4d to the Church of Stow.*
> 7 *He leaves 5s to each of the four orders of monks in Stamford to sing for his soul.*

> **Source 4** An extract from a book called *The Church of Our Fathers* by D. Rock, detailing parish traditions from centuries past, written in 1903.
>
> *The souls of Simon Chapman and Juliann his wife, of whose goods was given whole vestments for a priest of cloth of gold lined with green thread, and a chalice silver and gilt. Also for the souls of Stephen Gerard and Margery his wife of whose goods was given a good new masse book.*

Source 5 A painted stone Jesus in the chantry chapel at St John the Baptist Church, Burford. Chantry chapels were private chapels in churches to perform masses for the dead. The original chapel dates from the fourteenth century. ▼

3 Study Sources 3 and 4. What kinds of items did people leave to the Church?
4 Why do you think the Chapmans (Source 4) left their church clothes for the priest and a new silver chalice?
5 Why do you think Thomas Foldyngton (Source 3) made the Church a central part of his will?
6 Do Sources 3–5 convince you that people only attended church because they were afraid of dying?

Figure 6 A plan of a typical parish church. ▼

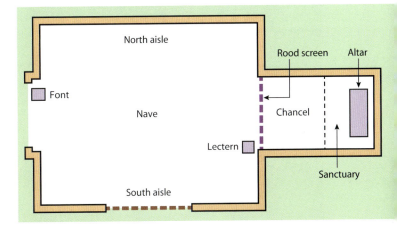

7 Look at Figure 6 and Source 7. Why do you think some people criticised the use of rood screens in churches?

Source 7 The Skidmore rood screen in Lichfield Cathedral in Staffordshire. These screens were erected to separate the congregation from the chancel, which was where the priest carried out ceremonies such as the Eucharist and the choir sang hymns. ▼

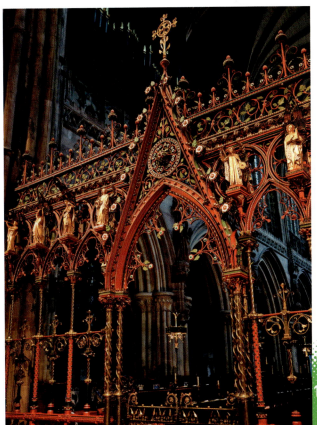

Source 8 A painting showing the Day of Judgment, in the church at Wenhaston in Suffolk, c1480. ▼

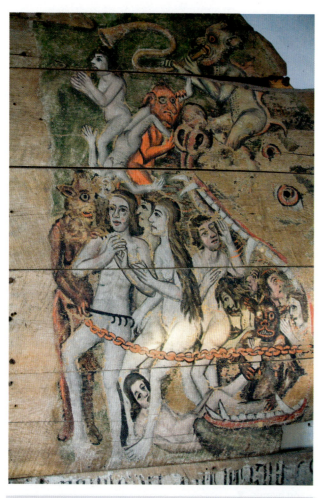

1 Describe the scene in Source 8 to a person who cannot see it. Explain what you can see, but also describe the emotions the picture tries to evoke.
2 Explain why an image like this would have had a powerful impact on people at the time.

Tithes

Parishioners also had to pay 10 per cent of their earnings to the Church (a TITHE). Tithes could be paid in money or in goods. As peasant farmers had very little money, they almost always paid in seeds or harvested grain and animals. Churchmen collected this tax and it went to the local parish church.

The Church and the people

Priests

The majority of English people would never see the pope, or his cardinals or archbishops. For most communities the Church was represented by their local parish priest or monk. Only formally appointed priests were allowed to conduct church services. The Bible and the prayer book were written in Latin, so only priests and the most educated people could read them.

The unique status of the clergy as God's representatives in the community was highlighted by the elaborate VESTMENTS (robes) they wore for church services. It was also shown by their vow of CELIBACY – they could never marry, because they had dedicated their lives to the service of God.

Priests came from a range of social backgrounds and ordinary priests of small parishes were often no more wealthy than their parishioners. However, they were usually better educated than most people in their parish. The process of ORDINATION (becoming a priest) promoted the idea that priests were elevated above the ordinary villagers.

Performance

The church service (known as MASS) was a solemn performance. Barriers called ROOD SCREENS separated the priest from the congregation when he performed significant parts of the ceremony at the ALTAR (see Figure 6 and Source 7). For example, during the Mass, the priest would 'reveal' the bread and wine (the HOST and the CHALICE) by raising it so the people could see it. At the ring of a bell, this bread and wine would be miraculously changed into the body and blood of Jesus – a process known as TRANSUBSTANTIATION. The congregation joined in some parts of the service by reciting prayers in Latin, kneeling to pray and standing when the Gospel was read. The whole experience of mass was theatrical and appealed to the senses – the priest's colourful vestments, the ringing bell, the smell of incense burning and the sprinkling of holy water.

Certainty

Part of the Church's appeal was that it provided people with certainty. For the majority of people, life was short. Most were farmers whose lives were dominated by the seasons of the year. Disease, death and worries about a bad harvest were a part of everyday life. In this uncertain world, religious beliefs brought comfort and helped people understand events. The priest emphasised how God controlled nature, so pleasing God was a way to ensure a good harvest.

The priest educated people about HEAVEN AND HELL. He promised that if they lived a good life, by following Christ's teaching, they would go to Heaven when they died. Church walls showed vivid images of the beauties of Heaven and the horrors of Hell (see Source 8). The Church also taught there was a place called PURGATORY on the way to Heaven or Hell. After death, those left behind could pray for a loved one's soul so it did not spend too long in purgatory.

Submission

The desire to get to Heaven gave the Church enormous power over ordinary people. Living a good Christian life meant attending regular services and submitting to the authority of the Church. If their souls were to be saved, people had to confess their sins to the priest and show their faith in God. They also had to believe in the SACRAMENTS – special ceremonies whereby God's goodness was revealed.

Culture

Churches were iconic buildings, usually the most lavishly decorated building in a village or town, and provided large open spaces for community gatherings (see Source 9). The stained-glass windows and ornate wood carvings were made by specialist craftsmen. Some of the finest art and music of the era was created for and celebrated in the churches.

> **Source 9** Roger Martyn, a village church warden, describing his parish church in Long Melford, Suffolk, c1560.
>
> *On St James's eve there was a bonfire, and a tub of ale and bread then given to the poor, and … on Midsummer eve, on the eve of St Peter and St Paul, when they had the like drinkings, and on St Thomas's eve, on which, if it fell not on the fish day, they had some long pies of mutton, and pease cods, set out upon boards, with … bread and ale. And in all these bonfires, some of the friends and more civil poor neighbours were called in, and sat at the board with my grandfather, who had at the lighting of the bonfires wax tapers with balls of wax, yellow and green.*

> 3   Look at Source 9. Why do you think Roger Martyn remembered these feast days so fondly?
>
> 4   Could this source provide evidence of the Church's power over the everyday life of ordinary people? How?

Festivals, folklore and saints

Villagers gathered at church to celebrate holy days and seasonal festivals with dancing and drinking. Among the favourites were Candlemas, Shrove Tuesday, Ash Wednesday and Easter Sunday. Evidence suggests that ordinary people were particularly keen on the feast of Corpus Christi in June, when crowds lined the streets to catch a glimpse of the host. Some festivals were unique to particular parishes. Others, such as May Day, were celebrated everywhere.

The Church incorporated local traditions and folklore. One example is the cult of Saint Walstan, who was said to have performed miracles and helped the poor. Walstan's shrine in Norfolk was a focus for annual pilgrimage for three centuries, right up until the Reformation. People from all walks of life attended his shrine and said prayers for him (see Source 10). At a more local level, the people

of a parish usually felt intense loyalty to the saint whose church they belonged to, not unlike loyalty to a football team or working in a large factory. The Church was therefore associated with belonging to a community, celebration (adding colour and fun to daily life) and comfort (bringing reassurance in the face of problems or death). These things made it an incredibly important part of every villager's life.

> **Source 10** This short prayer to Saint Walstan of Bawburgh demonstrates the importance of pilgrimage to ordinary people.
>
> *You knight of Christ, Walston holy,*
> *Our cry to thee meekly we pray;*
> *Shield us from mischief, sorrow and folly,*
> *Engendring and renewing from day to day,*
> *Replenishd with misery, Job doth truly say,*
> *And bring us to health blessed with [Jesus's] right hand*
> *Him to love and know in everlasting land.*

> 5   Read Source 10. What did people expect to happen to them if they prayed to the shrine of St Walstan?

Faith and fear

So the Church was clearly central to almost every aspect of people's everyday lives. It is sometimes hard for a person in Britain today to understand this fully. Even many regular churchgoers do not have the same faith that someone would have had in the sixteenth century. They would have seen the will of God in the weather, the harvests, illness, family. They would have seen their daily work as a prayer to God and in return they would hope for His blessing.

Most people never questioned this. To do so would have been to question the whole basis of their life and to risk their soul. Questioning it would have put their own and their family's welfare at risk. There were harsh punishments for heresy, usually torture and execution. In Henry VII's reign 24 heretics were burned. Henry VIII burned 81. The family of a heretic would also be shunned.

People and priests

Of course this did not mean people lived in terror of the Church and their priests. There are plenty of records of people in parishes complaining when they thought their own particular priest was not very good, but usually this was a complaint about the quality of individual priests rather than against the Church. In fact, historians such as Eamon Duffy and J. J. Scarisbrick have argued that most complaints reflect the fact that people had high expectations of their priests and they usually complained when priests did not come up to scratch.

Source 11 Historian Peter Marshall, writing in 2012.

It is easy enough to find examples of priests who failed to say services properly or who demanded too much in their tithes or were even sexually immoral, but it can be tempting to give too much attention to the juicy cases. Complaints by parishioners often complained that their own priests 'did not behave as other vicars do'. In other words the bad behaviour of a few did not necessarily reflect on the standing of the clergy as a whole.

1 Do you think Source 12 supports what historian Peter Marshall in saying in Source 11? Explain your answer.

ACTIVITY

Imagine you have heard rumours that Henry VIII wants to introduce some major changes to the Church in England – possibly even to break away from the pope altogether. Write a short report advising him on why this might be both risky and difficult.

Source 12 An extract from the records of a court case, 1531.

On Palm Sunday John Vasye, parson of Lytchett Maltravers in Dorset, was listening to confessions when a number of parishioners burst in, threw Vesye out of the church, and took from him both his chalice and his keys. Afterwards the parishioners, without authority assigned another priest to sing in the same church, without license or permission of the local squire.

FOCUS TASK

How popular was the English Church?

You should now have a completed concept map showing the power of the Church in the 1520s. From the evidence you have selected, how far do you agree with the viewpoint expressed by the historian Eamon Duffy below? Use evidence from your concept map to support your answer.

Late medieval Catholicism exerted an enormously diverse and vigorous hold over the imagination and the loyalty of the people. … Traditional religion had about it no particular marks of exhaustion or decay.

PRACTICE QUESTIONS

1 Explain why the Church was so wealthy. (10)
2 Explain why the Church played such an important role in communities in c1520. (10)
3 Why was the Church so powerful in England? (10)
4 'The Church was popular in England in c1520.' Using the sources in this topic as evidence, how far do you agree with this view? (20)

TOPIC SUMMARY

The role and importance of the Church

1 The Roman Catholic Church was a massive international organisation under the authority of the pope in Rome.
2 The English Church was part of this Catholic Church and was a very powerful force in England. It was extremely wealthy and its leaders helped run the country.
3 Priests represented the Church to most ordinary people. They were set apart by their education, their vestments and their celibate lifestyle.
4 Churches were highly decorated and were often the grandest building in a village. Mass was a performance to delight all the senses.
5 The Church had great hold over people's lives. The teachings of the Church showed people how to get to Heaven, avoid Hell and not spend too long in purgatory by living a good Christian life – going to services, believing the right things and submitting to authority.
6 The Church encouraged ordinary people to obey their superiors, who were all linked together in the 'Great Chain of Being'.
7 Rents, tithes, legacies and donations helped make the Church very wealthy.
8 Christian festivals brought colour and fun to people's daily lives.
9 Although the Church had its critics, in the 1520s it remained very popular among the ordinary people of England.

4.2 Critics of the Church

FOCUS TASK

What did the reformers want?

This topic includes many sources made or written by the reformers. Copy the table below and use it to record and analyse what they say. Add as many rows as you need.

Source	What kind of person are they (e.g. priest, lawyer, craftsman) and what nationality?	What is their criticism of the Church?	What do they want to happen instead?
1			
2			
3			

Early English reformers

The Lollards

Criticism of the Church was not a new thing. In the late 1300s there had been calls for reform from a group known as the LOLLARDS, led by John Wycliffe. They got their name from the word 'lollen', which means to sing in a low voice. Wycliffe suggested that the priesthood and the sacraments were not important aspects of faith. He even questioned transubstantiation – the belief that the communion bread and wine really became the body and blood of Christ during the celebration of the EUCHARIST. Lollards wanted ordinary people to read the Bible.

The movement was suppressed. Under Henry VII, more than 73 people were tried in Church courts for heresy for following the teachings of Wycliffe, and 11 were burned for their beliefs. However, the ideas did not disappear (see Source 3 overleaf).

1 Read Source 1. Why did the Lollards call transubstantiation a 'pretended miracle'?

2 Why do the Lollards dislike idolatry (praying to idols instead of God)?

3 Why do you think Henry VII took the Lollards so seriously?

Source 1 A description of a Lollard petition presented to parliament in 1374. Necromancy was a form of black magic.

[They claimed that] the English priesthood derived from Rome, and pretending to a power superior to angels, is not that priesthood which Christ settled upon his apostles. That the enjoining of celibacy upon the clergy was the occasion of scandalous irregularities. That the pretended miracle of transubstantiation runs the greatest part of Christendom upon idolatry. That exorcism and benedictions pronounced over wine, bread, water, oil, wax, and incense, over the stones for the altar and the church walls, over the holy vestments, the mitre, the cross, and the pilgrim's staff, have more of necromancy than religion in them. ... That pilgrimages, prayers, and offerings made to images and crosses have nothing of charity in them and are near akin to idolatry.

Source 2 From a tract (religious pamphlet) written by Erasmus in 1516.

I strongly disagree with the people who do not want the Bible to be translated into everyday language and be read by the uneducated. Did Christ teach such complex doctrines that only a handful of theologians can understand them? … I want the lowliest woman to read the Gospels and Paul's letters. I want them to be translated into every language so that, not only will the Scots and Irish be able to read them, but even the Turk and Saracen. I would like to hear a farmer sing scripture as he ploughs, a weaver keep time to his moving shuttle by humming the Bible.

1 Why was it considered heresy for tracts like Source 2 to be published?

Source 4 Martin Luther, writing about his views on Christian faith, 1520.

One man builds a chapel, another donates this, still another one that. However, they refuse to face the true issue, that is, they will not give their inmost self to God and thus become his kingdom. They perform many outward works which glitter very nicely, but inwardly they remain full of malice, anger, hatred, pride, impatience, unchastity, etc. It is against them that Christ spoke when he was asked when the kingdom of God was coming, 'The kingdom of God does not come with outward signs or appearances; for behold, the kingdom of God is within you'.

2 Read Source 4. What are the 'outward works' Luther refers to?
3 What is it about the Catholic Church that Luther rejects?
4 What does Luther want people to focus on?

Source 3 Thomas Topley, a Suffolk friar, writing in 1528. Topley was introduced to the ideas of the Lollards by Richard Foxe, a curate (junior priest).

I found a certain book called Wycliffe's Wicket. When I read it I felt a great troubling of my mind. When I remembered it afterwards it troubled me more. Nevertheless, I did not agree with it, until I had heard Richard Foxe preach. That was upon St Anthony's day. My mind was still much troubled by this book .

Humanism

In the late 1400s, another dramatic cultural trend – called the RENAISSANCE – was affecting intellectual life in Europe. One aspect of the Renaissance was a movement called HUMANISM, which centred on studying ancient texts.

The most celebrated humanist scholar was Erasmus. He visited England in 1499, where he met with John Colet, the founder of St Paul's School in London. English humanists like Colet believed that individuals could choose a virtuous life. They took a scientific approach to studying the Bible. They studied the scriptures in their earliest form – trying to see what the original said rather than what the Church claimed it said. Colet taught these beliefs at his school. However, there is little evidence that this sort of teaching occurred elsewhere.

The visit inspired Erasmus to publish the New Testament in Greek so people could read the original. However, he knew that most people could not read Greek so he also argued that the Bible should be translated into the language of ordinary people (see Source 2). Erasmus pointed out differences between the teaching and practices of the Catholic Church and the original sources in the Bible. He argued for a religion based less on theatrical ceremonies and more on studying the Bible.

Early European reformers

During the 1520s, a new group of reformers in Europe fiercely attacked Church practices. The most influential of them were Martin Luther from Saxony and Huldrych Zwingli from Zurich. They became known as Protestants, as their Christian beliefs were so radically different from those of the Catholic Church. Many of their criticisms echoed those of earlier reformers. They believed that:

- only faith could make people closer to God, and studying the Bible (not listening to Church leaders) was the only way to improve faith
- every Christian should be able to read the Bible in their own language and not be told what to believe by the Church
- church services should be in the language of the people and should focus on Bible readings
- praying to the Virgin Mary and saints should stop
- purgatory did not exist
- priests did not need to be celibate
- religious authority in a country should be the responsibility of the ruler of that country, not the pope in Rome.

Luther also savagely criticised the Church for some of its practices:

- **The selling of relics:** These were items sold to people as things that had been nearest to Jesus on Earth. For example, wood might be sold as a piece of the cross on which Jesus had been crucified. They were often sold by fraudsters, who took the money for themselves rather than donating it to the Church. RELICS were objects of veneration and believed to have healing powers.
- **The selling of indulgences:** INDULGENCES were prayers for the dead to speed them from purgatory to Heaven.
- **Pilgrimages:** PILGRIMAGES were journeys people made to worship at sites associated with saints (see Source 5).

5 According to Source 5, what does Luther suggest are the main reasons people went on pilgrimages?

6 How might Luther's words threaten the Catholic Church?

7 What sorts of things are being criticised in Source 6?

8 Why are the pope, priests and bishops not welcome in the Kingdom of God?

9 Why is Source 6 useful for historians trying to find out about critics of the Church during the 1520s?

Source 5 Martin Luther, commenting on pilgrimages.

Those who make pilgrimages do so for many reasons, very seldom for legitimate ones. The first reason for making pilgrimages is the most common of all, namely, the curiosity to see and hear strange and unknown things. This levity proceeds from a loathing for and boredom with the worship services, which have been neglected in the pilgrims' own church. Otherwise one would find incomparably better indulgences at home than in all the other places put together. Furthermore, he would be closer to Christ and the saints if he were not so foolish as to prefer sticks and stones to the poor and his neighbours whom he should serve out of love. And he would be closer to Christ also if he were to provide for his own family.

Source 6 *Christ in the Sheep Shed* by Hans Sebald Beham, printed in 1524. It is attacking the Catholic Church. The house represents the kingdom of God. ▼

The pope, priests and bishops trying to break into the Kingdom of God.

Jesus is barring the door to the unworthy pope, bishops and priests.

Ordinary people listening to God's word.

The sheep represent good Christian people everywhere. Jesus is often represented as a shepherd guiding his flock towards God.

1 Look at Source 7. Summarise the basic points being made by Latimer.
2 Would you say the tone of this letter is respectful?
3 Latimer was a chaplain and scholar at Cambridge University. Do you think he really knew nothing of Luther's ideas?
4 Study Source 8. Why would Fish's views have been controversial?
5 Why might some merchants and landowners find these criticisms of the Church attractive?
6 Is this source more useful about priests at this time or about the views of Fish? Explain your answer.
7 Look back at Source 11 on page 134. How far do these sources agree or disagree and why?

How did Reformation ideas develop in England?

Ideas about Church reform reached England from Europe via cloth traders who travelled between Holland and England. In London and other port cities, such as Bristol, Harwich and Portsmouth, Protestant-like preaching began to take place during the 1520s. Reforming ideas were also taken up at England's two universities, Oxford and Cambridge. From there, they began to spread widely. Previously, critics of the Church had been mostly insiders (Church leaders who wanted their priests to rediscover true spirituality and piety). Now, LAYMEN – ordinary people who were not employed by the Church – also took up the call for reform.

Criticisms from laymen

The reformers' ideas became particularly important among the lawyers at the Inns of Court. The Inns of Court were like universities, with many clever and keen young people eager to learn about new ideas. They picked up and spread ideas about Church reform through pamphlets and other publications. One of the most enthusiastic reformers was a lawyer called Simon Fish. He had studied at Oxford before entering Grays Inn in 1525 to train as a lawyer. Not much is recorded about his personal life until 1526, when he is said to have taken part in a Christmas play that mocked Church authorities. Because of this he was forced into exile, where he made contact with others who wanted to reform the Church.

In 1528, Fish published 'A Supplication for Beggars' – a 5,000-word pamphlet that condemned the English priesthood. Fish was a layman, and he wrote his pamphlet for other laymen to read. It was welcomed by merchants and landowners, who were envious of how much land and power the Church and the clergy had. The pamphlet was widely circulated and there were even rumours that Henry VIII read it.

Source 8 An extract from 'A Supplication for Beggars' by Simon Fish, 1528.

Priests are not shepherds but ravenous wolves in sheep's clothing attacking the people. They have begged so cleverly that they have got more than a third of the wealth of the country into their hands; the best manors and lands are theirs.

They have a tenth of all the corn, meadow, pasture, grass, wool, calves, lambs, pigs, geese and chickens. They also take a tenth of every person's wage, a tenth of all the wool, milk, honey, wax, cheese and butter too. They are cruel, unclean, unmerciful and hypocrites.

Criticisms from insiders (clerics)

At the same time, criticism from within the Church was intensifying. One particularly fierce critic was William Tyndale (see Profile opposite). He was a clergyman and he wanted to renew the role of the clergy – demanding educated priests who could preach effectively. Tyndale gained financial support from wealthy London drapers (men who sold fabric and textiles), including Humphrey Monmouth, and he used this money to publish an English translation of the Bible. Tyndale also influenced many young lawyers, such as Simon Fish.

The earliest Protestants were centred on Cambridge University. This was a hotbed of religious radicals who believed that the Church needed to be drastically reformed. They met in the White Horse Inn in Cambridge and exchanged ideas and texts (often ones that were banned). Their leader was Robert Barnes and many key reformers attended his meetings, including Tyndale, Miles Coverdale (who became well known for criticising transubstantiation), Thomas Bilney (who was arrested for criticising the worshipping of statues and images), John Frith (who criticised the belief in purgatory, see Source 9), Hugh Latimer (see Source 7) and Thomas Cranmer (who was eventually burned for his beliefs). They discussed the ideas of Luther and Erasmus, but they were most gripped by an EVANGELICAL belief in JUSTIFICATION BY FAITH ALONE. This was the idea that people were saved by their own faith – they could not 'buy' their way into Heaven.

Source 9 An extract from *The Disputation of Purgatory* by John Frith, 1531. Sir Thomas More was the lord chancellor and a bitter opponent of the reformers.

I give respect to Thomas More for the power and fire of his words. The fire of my words is like water in comparison to it. The fire of his words has alone melted more gold and silver for the profit of the Church than all the goldsmiths' fires within England. And so must we graunt hym that this fire is very hot. But it is a pity that this profit comes from the purses of poor men.

8 Why was it so important to Tyndale and other reformers to publish the Bible in the vernacular (the spoken language of the people)?

9 What do you think the inset image in Source 10 is supposed to represent?

Source 10 The first page of the Gospel of John, from Tyndale's Bible in English, 1526. Three thousand copies of this Bible were published. ▶

The authorities began to take notice of this group. We know from government records that spies were watching and listening and reporting back conversations in the White Horse Inn! Many of the group fled to the continent for safety. This limited their influence beyond Cambridge, but there is still evidence to suggest that reformist ideas were spreading. For example, the will of William Tracy of Gloucestershire began with the instruction that his family should 'bestow no part of my goods for [the] intent, that any man should say or do to help my soul'. This meant he did not want any indulgences or prayers said for his soul. Tracy's will was printed and circulated in London almost immediately, and it appeared in one of Tyndale's pamphlets.

PROFILE

William Tyndale (1494–1536)

- Educated at Oxford, he was ordained as a priest in 1521.
- Influenced by the works of Erasmus and Luther.
- He believed that people should be able to read the Bible in their own language. He spent much of his life in exile for his beliefs.
- Tyndale was most famous for his publication of the first Bible translated into English, in 1526.
- Tyndale's translation was regarded as heretical in England. Despite this his Bibles were still smuggled into the country in bales of cloth, even though being caught with one would mean death.
- In 1530, he wrote *The Practyse of Prelates*, which opposed Cardinal Wolsey and Henry VIII's divorce from Catherine of Aragon because it went against Scripture.
- He was executed in 1536 for his writings. Despite this, two years after his death, Henry VIII published Tyndale's Bible.

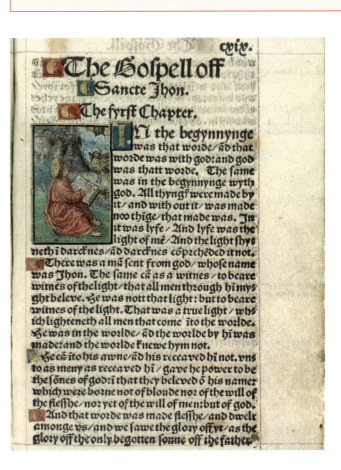

Other criticisms

Many of the reformers' criticisms were about DOCTRINE and detail – not things that would grab the headlines today! However, a few issues did capture the public's interest and help reforming ideas to gain popularity.

Wolsey's power and wealth

As far as the reformers were concerned, one person stood for the excesses of the Church more than any other – Thomas Wolsey. Wolsey had been a humble cleric, who rose through the Church hierarchy to became the Archbishop of York, cardinal and papal legate (representing the pope in England). At the same time, he worked as Henry VIII's lord chancellor, one of the most influential political positions in the country. He used these positions to make himself immensely wealthy. Wolsey built himself the lavish Hampton Court Palace to live in.

> **Source 11** The Venetian ambassador, Giustaniani, writing about Cardinal Wolsey in 1519.
>
> *The cardinal is the first person who rules both the king and the entire kingdom. On the ambassador's first arrival in England he used to say to him, 'His majesty will do so and so', but, by degrees, he began to forget himself and started to say, 'we shall do so and so'. Now he has reached such a height that he says, 'I shall do so and so'.*

Pluralism

Wolsey's career highlighted another, more general problem: PLURALISM (holding positions in more than one parish). This was an accepted part of Church life. For example, in Canterbury in 1521, more than half the clergy held more than one post. However, the reformers believed that it was impossible to serve more than one parish effectively and that because of pluralism, many parish duties were being left to poorly trained CURATES (assistants).

Morals

Reformers also questioned the moral standards of the priests. Priests took a vow of celibacy, but many of them broke this vow. In the parish of St John Zachary in London, for example, a brothel had been set up for the clergy. Alexander Thornton, a Lancashire priest, lived openly with his partner and had a son by her. These were not isolated cases.

The 'benefit of the clergy'

Church courts came under criticism in 1511 after the tragic case of Richard Hunne. Hunne was a London merchant who refused to pay the fee for his son's burial. He was imprisoned, but in December 1514 was found hanged in his cell. A verdict of murder was declared, but officers of the Church courts claimed a special privilege called the 'benefit of the clergy'. This meant that they could not be tried in an ordinary court, only in a Church court, and so they escaped punishment. When word of this spread, the people of London were outraged and support for the reformers' ideas grew.

Despite all these examples of ANTICLERICALISM, it is important to note that those who criticised the Church – even the laymen – were usually devout Christians themselves. To begin with, there were also not many people who openly criticised the Church. Reformist ideas were confined to a few key parts of the country (see Factfile).

Source 12 John Fisher, Bishop of Rochester, writing in 1526. Fisher was one of several bishops commissioned by Wolsey to root out heretics.

These heretics do not speak for the people – let them talk to the people and hear their views. They are like blind men, so they must ask for mercy to be cured. They must accept the ways of the Church if they are to be forgiven. Just as the blind man went to Jesus and had his sight restored, so the heretic must return to the Church to have his spiritual sight restored.

1 Re-read Simon Fish's criticisms of the church in Source 8 on page 138. Now make a list of the ways in which More disagrees with Fish in Source 13.
2 Does Source 13 seem more like a defence of the Church or an attack on Fish? Explain your answer.

Defenders of the Church

In 1521, Wolsey commissioned university THEOLOGIANS to write books attacking Luther's ideas. Luther's works were publicly burned in London in May 1521 and again in 1526. Wolsey and the Archbishop of Canterbury, William Warham, decided it would be better to privately persuade those clergy who had strayed towards Luther's ideas to return to traditional beliefs, rather than publicly denouncing them.

Another strong defender of the Catholic Church was Thomas More. More was a Christian humanist, but he believed that Protestant ideas were heresy. He wrote a point-by-point rebuttal of Simon Fish's 'A Supplication to Beggars' (see Source 13). In October 1529, More replaced Wolsey as CHANCELLOR. He proved he was willing to take much more drastic measures to limit the influence of Protestantism. For example, in February 1530, John Tewkesbury, who had imported and sold books criticising the Church, was burned to death in Kent. In August the following year, the Cambridge scholar Thomas Bilney was executed in Norwich for heresy.

Source 13 Thomas More's response to Simon Fish, 1529.

It is very hard to work out if the views of Fish are mostly lies or simply foolish. The faults of any immoral priest he attributes to all the priests of the realm while he also rebukes those priests who keep their vows because they destroy the realm by turning it into a wilderness because they have not married and produced children.

He aggravates his great crimes by calling the clergy bloodsuckers, drunk on the blood of the holy martyrs and saints; gluttons sucking up the wealth of the country.

Critics get the upper hand at court ...

However, the influence of both Wolsey and More began to decline around this time. Wolsey fell out of favour with Henry VIII after he could not convince the pope to ANNUL the king's marriage to Catherine of Aragon. More took the pope's side over the issue of the annulment, which angered the king.

As these two men fell from power, a new group of Protestant reformers rose to high-ranking positions in government. Thomas Cranmer and Thomas Cromwell in particular were helped into court by the Boleyn family, who supported Luther's teachings. These new men were hostile to the clergy. They were also deeply critical of traditional ideas about purgatory, believing it was simply a way for the Church to gain wealth and lands through indulgences and bequests from anxious Christians. These reformers regarded the pope as a scheming foreign ruler. Their powerful positions in Henry VIII's court allowed them to start convincing him that Church reform was the best thing for England – and for the king.

... while ordinary people get on with their lives

It is difficult for historians to assess how far ideas about Church reform affected the ordinary people of England at this time. Many people would probably not even be aware of them. If they were, they would also have heard of the dreadful fate awaiting heretics, so only the bravest would openly support reform or write down their beliefs. The majority of the population was illiterate, so there are few written records that allow us to infer what they believed.

It is likely that many ordinary people felt that the Church took too much money, and certainly some individual priests came in for criticism. However, the kind of changes that Henry VIII was about to unleash would hardly have been imagined, let alone desired, by the common people of England.

ACTIVITY

In order to get a balanced view, Henry has invited the defenders of the Church to the meeting to make their case. Use your work from pages 132–33 and page 141 to draw up a list of the main points that defenders of the Church would have made. For example:
The Church does not need reforming
Point 1: The clergy ...
Point 2:
Point 3:
Point 4:

FOCUS TASK

Was the English Church in crisis?

1 At the start of this topic you created a table to analyse the reformers' ideas outlined in the sources. Now use your completed table to decide whether you agree or disagree with the following statements:
   a Problems in the Church were everywhere.
   b Bishops and abbots behaved like princes instead of churchmen.
   c The clergy were not interested in wealth.
   d The clergy were well trained.
   e The clergy were well respected.

2 In the 1960s, the historian A. G. Dickens wrote: 'Long before Henry VIII broke with Rome numerous developments were preparing Englishmen for some sort of religious and ecclesiastical change or crisis. Anticlericalism ... had reached a new height by the early years of the sixteenth century.'
   a What evidence is there in this topic to support his view? What evidence is there to oppose it?
   b Look back to the conclusions you drew at the end of Topic 4.1 about the popularity of the Church by the 1520s. Have you changed your opinion in light of this quotation and the information in this topic?

PRACTICE QUESTIONS

1 Explain why the Church was being criticised in the 1520s and 1530s. (10)
2 Explain why some people wanted religious reform in the 1520s and 1530s. (10)
3 Study Sources 5, 6 and 8. How far do they convince you that supporters of Church reform were motivated by political aims rather than religious convictions?

TOPIC SUMMARY

Critics of the Church

1 Since the fourteenth century, there had been a small but established anticlerical movement called Lollardy in England, led by John Wycliffe.
2 In the early 1500s, humanists such as Erasmus and Protestants such as Luther called for people to read the Bible for themselves and used the teachings of the Bible to challenge traditional Church practices.
3 These criticisms began to infiltrate England in the 1520s via cloth traders from Holland.
4 Reformist ideas were picked up by young lawyers in London and scholars at Cambridge University, and spread through pamphlets and sermons.
5 The majority of the country was not clamouring for Church reform. It was only in certain parts of the country, such as London, Bristol, Kent and Essex, that churches were preaching these new 'evangelical' ideas.
6 Many of those reformers who did want change were highly educated and influential people, such as lawyers and clerics.
7 Many of those at court were jealous of Wolsey's influence and wealth. They began to attack the practice of pluralism in order to force him out of office.
8 The humanist Thomas More replaced Wolsey as chancellor, but he too fell from favour. A new group of powerful Protestant reformers were awarded key positions at Henry VIII's court.

4.3 Henry VIII breaks with Rome

FOCUS

Initially, Henry VIII's response to the reformers' ideas was to write a book defending the Church against Protestant attack. Yet fewer than ten years later he had broken with the Catholic Church in Rome and established himself as Supreme Head of the Church in England. In this topic, you will examine:

● how and why Henry changed his mind and broke with Rome
● who opposed him and why.

FOCUS TASK

Why did Henry break with Rome?

Create six cards and write one of the following headings at the top of each card:
1 Need for a legitimate royal heir
2 Henry's religious conscience
3 Henry's desire for more power
4 Henry's need for more money
5 Key individuals at court, e.g. Cromwell or Boleyn
6 Anticlericalism and reformist ideas

As you work through this topic, add notes to each card to explain how the factor contributed to the break with Rome. Use evidence from the sources to indicate the importance of that factor. At the end, you will arrange the cards to show the relationships between these factors and their relative significance.

Source 1 Henry's description of Martin Luther in *Assertion of the Seven Sacraments*, 1521. It is possible that this was actually written by Bishop John Fisher.

What pest so pernicious has ever attacked the flock of Christ? What serpent so poisonous has ever come forth ... twisting Holy Scripture to his own liking against the sacrament of Christ? ... What a wolf of hell is he, seeking to scatter Christ's flock? What a limb of Satan! How rotten is his mind! How execrable his purpose!

Source 2 A painting made shortly after Henry VIII was given the title 'Defender of the Faith' by Pope Leo X. In it, the king holds a text from the Gospel of Mark, Chapter 16: 'Go out in to the world and preach the gospel to every creature.' The text is in one of the fashionable new humanist translations. ▶

1 Look at Sources 1 and 2. What do they suggest about Henry's beliefs and attitudes?
2 Why do you think Henry commissioned this painting of himself?

'Defender of the Faith'

In 1521, Henry VIII wrote a book called *Assertion of the Seven Sacraments* (see Source 1) – a response to Martin Luther's attack on the Catholic Church. Pope Leo X rewarded the king with a new title: 'Defender of the Faith'.

The 'King's Great Matter'

All kings in the medieval and early modern periods were very concerned with ensuring a secure and legal succession after their death. This meant having a healthy, LEGITIMATE son. Henry VIII took this responsibility very seriously.

Henry had been happily married to Catherine of Aragon for over 20 years. The queen fell pregnant six times but only one child, a girl named Mary (born in 1516), survived. By 1525, Catherine was 40 years old and Henry was sure she was no longer capable of bearing him a son. He was deeply troubled by this, and at court the issue became known as the 'King's Great Matter'.

Henry came to the conclusion that he needed a new wife. His eye had already fallen on Anne Boleyn, one of Catherine's ladies-in-waiting, but how could he get rid of Catherine so that he would be free to marry Anne? The Church taught that marriage was a sacred vow, made in the sight of God – and Henry took religion seriously. Divorce did not exist at the time; the only way to end a marriage was to have it annulled, which meant saying it had not been legal the first place. Only the pope could annul a marriage because he was God's representative on Earth. So, working with his advisers, Henry developed an argument for annulment to present to the pope.

Before her marriage to Henry, Catherine had been married to Henry's brother, Arthur, until his death in 1502. It was highly unusual to marry your brother's widow and Henry had needed special DISPENSATION (permission) from the pope to do so. Now he argued that this dispensation should never have been granted. Henry pointed to two passages in the Bible which warned that if a man took his brother's wife 'it was an unclean thing' and 'they shall be childless'. We will never know for sure whether this was just a legal argument or whether the king really did believe that God disapproved of his marriage to Catherine. However, Henry was a religious man and it is possible that his conscience troubled him. He may have started to believe that this was why he and Catherine had never had a son.

By 1526, Henry VIII had ordered Wolsey to launch a campaign to persuade Pope Clement VII to pronounce the king's marriage invalid. Both Henry and Wolsey were sure they would succeed, and Henry even proposed to Anne (see Source 3). Catherine was devastated. She totally opposed the annulment and had no intention of slipping quietly into the background.

Source 3 A letter from Henry VIII to Anne Boleyn, written in the summer of 1527 (when he was still married to Catherine), asking her to be his wife, not just his mistress.

The proofs of your affections are such, the fine poesies of the letters so warmly couched, that they constrain me ever truly to honour, love and serve you, praying that you will continue in this firm and constant purpose. ...

Henceforth my heart shall be dedicated to you alone, greatly desirous that so my body could be as well, as God can bring to pass if it pleaseth Him, whom I entreat once each day for the accomplishment thereof. ...

Written with the hand of that secretary who in heart, body and will is

Your loyal and most ensured servant

Henry aultre A B ne cherse R. [Henry looks for no other]

---

1 Look at Source 3. Why does Henry VIII propose by letter and not in person?
2 Does this source prove that Henry was religious?

PROFILE

Anne Boleyn (1501–36)

- Born 1501, the daughter of the Earl of Wiltshire.
- Brought up at the French court.
- She had an interest in biblical teachings.
- Became one of the most important patrons of the English religious reformers.
- She gave Henry VIII a copy of Simon Fish's 'A Supplication of Beggars'.
- On becoming queen, she made sure many Protestant reformers were appointed as the king's advisers (they became known as the 'Boleyn faction' because they supported Anne and religious reform).
- Accused of adultery and executed in 1536.

The pope's decision

Pope Clement might have granted the annulment but other considerations prevented him. Most significantly, he was at war with France and needed the support of the Habsburg emperor, Charles V, to defend northern Italy. Charles was Catherine of Aragon's nephew and was furious at Henry VIII's treatment of his aunt.

In 1529, the pope allowed Wolsey and another cardinal, Lorenzo Campeggio, to set up a commission in England to investigate whether or not there were grounds for annulment, but he ordered Cardinal Campeggio to waste time and delay making a decision. Eventually the commission announced that it could not decide, so the pope took control and said that only he could settle the outcome. And the pope was in Rome – far away from Henry's influence. Henry refused to accept this, and so the 'King's Great Matter' became a struggle not for an annulment but for control of the Church in England.

The fall of Wolsey

As papal legate (messenger), Wolsey was the pope's representative in England, so Henry blamed Wolsey for this failure. In fact, some historians have suggested that secretly Wolsey was not in favour of the annulment, afraid that it might cause serious religious divisions. Although Wolsey was never a fan of the PAPACY, he felt that reforming ideas were heresy.

Henry himself was becoming increasing influenced by anticlericalism – perhaps by Anne Boleyn, who was a keen supporter of religious reform. The new advisers who rose to power at Henry's court under her influence (known as the 'Boleyn faction') were all Protestants. In 1529, Henry removed Wolsey as chancellor and replaced him with Thomas More, a layman. We should not read too much into this. Henry was not becoming a Protestant reformer – More was probably more ruthless in attacking Protestants than Wolsey had been.

The issue of *praemunire*

Henry summoned parliament. Most MPs probably shared Henry's views – anticlerical but not really committed Protestants. In 1530, under the skilful direction of his new adviser Thomas Cromwell (who was an MP, a privy councillor and a reformer - although he skilfully kept his views to himself), the king accused first Wolsey then the entire clergy of England of PRAEMUNIRE. This was an old medieval law that said people could not support a foreign power (including the pope) over the king in civil matters. By accusing the clergy of *praemunire*, Henry was effectively accusing them of treason.

This was an extraordinary act – and one that shows Henry's desperation. He had no intention of bringing every priest in the country to court, but it allowed him to raise the question of the pope's authority over the king. It also allowed Henry to 'pardon' the clergy for the princely sum of £100,000! Cromwell, probably encouraged by the Boleyns, added words to the pardon which meant priests had to recognise the king as 'singular protector, supreme lord and even, so far as the law of Christ allows, supreme head of the English Church and clergy'. Reluctantly, they accepted.

Meanwhile, other reformers at court, led by Thomas Cranmer, Edward Foxe and Edward Lee (the archbishop of York), were writing up a document called *Collectanea* ('The Collection') which demonstrated that since Anglo-Saxon times, kings had enjoyed spiritual supremacy in their own kingdoms. They argued that Henry could call on any English bishop to announce his annulment. By September 1530, Henry was certain that a break with Rome was justified.

> **Source 4** Bishop John Fisher of Rochester, writing c1530. Fisher was not convinced that the Pardon of the Clergy would be the end of Henry's meddling with the Church.
>
> *What if he should shortly after change his mind, and exercise in deed the supremacy over the church of this realm. Or what if he should in time fall to an infant or a woman that shall still continue and take the same upon them? What shall we then do? Whom shall we sue unto? Or where shall we have remedy?*

3 What is Bishop John Fisher worried about?

The rise of Thomas Cromwell

Thomas More pleaded with Henry not to go ahead, but his influence had waned and Cromwell was now driving events:

- Cromwell and his assistant Thomas Audley proposed cutting off ANNATES (large payments made to the pope by newly appointed bishops). Parliament did not immediately agree to the Act of Annates and Henry himself had to appear before parliament three times to force through the bill. He ordered those who opposed him to literally stand up and be counted!
- Cromwell then drafted the Supplication of the Ordinaries, a bill criticising the abuses of Church courts. The Supplication argued that Church courts interfered with royal laws, which gave Henry a line of attack against the pope.

The day after the Supplication was passed by parliament, More was dismissed as chancellor. Henry was now firmly being led by the Boleyns and Cromwell, who pushed him towards reform of the Church.

Henry published an explanation (printed in English) of the religious reasons why he should be granted an annulment. A host of publicity and propaganda followed (see Source 5). In August 1532 Archbishop Warham died, removing another significant obstacle to reform. He was replaced by Thomas Cranmer. Cranmer had spent the past three years on the continent learning more about Protestantism and campaigning for Henry's divorce.

> **1** Look at Source 5. Why do you think this book was reprinted in England in 1532?

> **Source 6** An extract from the Act in Restraint of Appeals.
>
> *Many old histories and chronicles describe the realm of England as an Empire. It has been accepted by the world as an Empire with one Supreme Head and King ... all the people including the clergy are bound to be obedient to the King.*

> **Source 5** Thomas Berthelet was Henry VIII's royal printer, who wrote many books himself. He printed this thirteenth-century French text, *Disputatio*, to offer a vision of a Church that did not recognise the authority of the pope in Rome. It takes the form of an imaginary conversation between a priest (Clericus) and a knight (Miles).
>
> *Clericus: Many kings and princes have worshipped the Church in the past, now I see that the Church has preyed upon them. The Church takes goods and riches but does not give anything back.*
>
> *Miles: I cannot believe that the clergy would do such an unjust thing.*
>
> *Clericus: Yes, we have all suffered under the Church.*
>
> *Miles: Whatever the Church says in Rome, it is not law to us. Only the king may decide the laws to govern people.*

The final break with Rome

Despite all these developments, Henry VIII still showed no signs of actually *making* the break with Rome. But then Anne Boleyn fell pregnant and Henry was desperate to ensure that the child was born LEGITIMATE. Events began to gather pace:

- In January 1533, Henry and Anne married secretly.
- Cromwell and Audley drafted laws that would make the marriage legal and stop the pope interfering. Again, Henry VIII forced this bill through the House of Commons against considerable resistance, particularly from Sir George Throckmorton, who suggested the Commons give Henry £200,000 to drop the bill. Henry VIII and Cromwell personally interviewed every man who spoke against the marriage to ensure its safe passage through parliament.
- In May 1533, Cranmer announced the annulment of Henry's marriage to Catherine of Aragon. Later that month he declared the king's marriage to Anne Boleyn to be lawful.
- The pope threatened to excommunicate Henry if he did not return to Catherine. This finally forced the king to break with Rome, as he could not risk his heir being declared illegitimate.
- In 1534, the Act of Supremacy made Henry the Supreme Head of the Church in England.

> **2** Look at Source 6. Why do you think this act appealed to Henry VIII?

Source 7 Thomas Audley, in the Journal of the House of Lords. Audley was a talented lawyer who worked closely with Cromwell on early legislation surrounding the annulment. He was promoted to lord chancellor after More's dismissal and pressured parliament into following the king's wishes.

Declining neither to the right nor the left, but with one unified standpoint sincerely prescribing according to the pure Word of God and the gospel.

3 In Source 7, Audley mentions the 'pure word of God and the gospel'. Does this indicate to you whether he is a reformer or not?

4 Why do you think Audley says there ought to be a 'unified standpoint'?

6 Look at Source 9. Does this prove that the break with Rome was popular?

7 How far does Source 9 convince you that Henry and the reformers were anxious about whether people would obey the new religious reforms?

FACTFILE

Key legislation of the Reformation parliament

1530 Clergy accused of *praemunire* (following the pope instead of their king).

1532 First Act of Annates; Supplication of the Ordinaries; Submission of the Clergy.

1533 Annulment of marriage to Catherine of Aragon; Act in Restraint of Appeals to Rome.

1534 Act of Supremacy; Act for First Fruits and Tenths; Act of Succession.

1535 Valor Ecclesiasticus: a survey on the wealth and condition of the Church.

Source 8 A letter from Thomas Cranmer to Thomas Cromwell in 1537, recommending Tyndale's Bible.

And as for the translation, so far as I have read, I like it better than any translation ever made. There may be faults found since no one can do such work perfectly but it can be amended from time to time.

Since it is dedicated to the king and great pains have been taken to set this forth I pray you will show it to the king and obtain a licence so that it may be sold and read to every person, without any danger of proclamation or law against it.

If you continue to take such pains to set forth the word of God as you do, even though you may suffer for it, God will judge you kindly.

Thus, my lord, right heartily fare you well.

At Forde, the ivth day of August.

5 In Source 8, Cranmer is asking for Cromwell's help in getting the king to approve this translation. Does this prove Cromwell was a dedicated Protestant?

Source 9 A woodcut from *Foxe's Book of Martyrs*, published in 1563 to describe the suffering of Protestants in England and Scotland. This image shows Henry VIII becoming Supreme Head of the Church. ▼

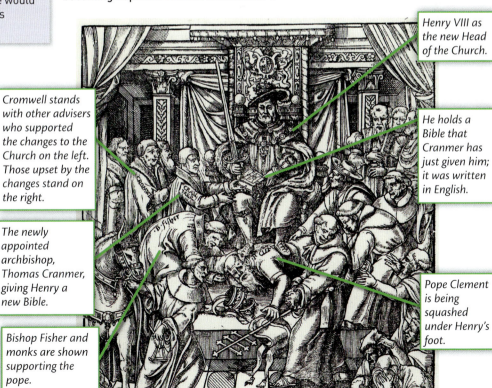

Cromwell stands with other advisers who supported the changes to the Church on the left. Those upset by the changes stand on the right.

The newly appointed archbishop, Thomas Cranmer, giving Henry a new Bible.

Bishop Fisher and monks are shown supporting the pope.

Henry VIII as the new Head of the Church.

He holds a Bible that Cranmer has just given him; it was written in English.

Pope Clement is being squashed under Henry's foot.

Source 10 Historian George Hoskins, writing in 1976.

The despoiling of the Church in the 16th century is one of the great events in English history. Some called it the Great Sacrilege. I call it the Great Plunder. The Tudors had a continuous problem of lack of money. The massive taxation of the 1520s was wasted on wars. Henry had raised an official loan from parliament in 1522 and then refused to pay it back in 1529. But there still remained the vast wealth of the Church to tempt him even though the Church had paid its full share of taxes. Not only Henry, but the nobility also, had their eyes on this wealth.

Henry VIII as Supreme Head of the Church

The Act of Supremacy not only confirmed the king's leadership of the Church, it also gave Henry specific powers over it. He could survey the Church, discipline the clergy, correct the opinions of preachers, supervise Church teachings and put heretics on trial. In their prayers, the people of England must mention him not as the king but as the head of their Church. This meant he was head of the English Church by name, in law, by the clergy's oath and even by popular prayer.

Henry's beliefs

It is important to note that all the Acts of Parliament passed between 1529 and 1534 were about the teachings of the Church. Church reform was a political process driven by Cromwell and the king himself. Most historians agree that although Henry's closest advisers introduced him to new ideas, he remained in complete control of policy. The early Reformation therefore reflects his personality, his ego and his contradictions. Henry was not purposefully striding towards reforming the Church or asserting his supremacy, but once he had that power he rather liked it! It seems that Henry VIII truly believed he was the rightful head of the Church and he expected others to believe it too. However, it probably did not escape his attention that the Church was very wealthy (see Source 10).

Edward Foxe set about publishing TRACTS that explained the difference between royal and ecclesiastical (Church) power for those at court. These tracts argued that national churches had always been subject to the law of their king. For the less educated, a pamphlet was published called 'Little Treatise against the Mutterings of some Papists in Corners', which justified the supremacy based on Bible teachings. This emphasised that Henry was a caring king, so the people of England should show him loyalty.

Opposition to Henry

In the country

The people of England do not seem to have reacted badly to the news of Henry's marriage to Anne Boleyn or the Act of Supremacy. There is no evidence of widespread discontent. This may be because very little changed for the ordinary people in their parishes.

At court

The most fervent opposition to Henry VIII's annulment came from Catherine of Aragon herself. Some nobles, such as Lord Hussey, sympathised with the former queen, but she does not seem to have won anyone over completely to her cause. There is no evidence of letters or contact between Catherine and either Thomas More or John Fisher, the most senior members of court who spoke out against the annulment. These two men met the same fate:

- Bishop John Fisher was arrested after Cromwell discovered he was in contact with Emperor Charles V, urging him take up arms against Henry VIII. Fisher refused to swear the Oath of Succession and was executed in June 1535.
- Thomas More followed Fisher to the block in July 1535 after he too refused to swear the oath. More was a much-loved figure and the crowd at his execution stood in shocked silence.

Source 11 Reginald Pole, writing to Henry VIII to explain why he would not return to England, 1537.

I wish for nothing more in life than to obey my king and serve God. Here is my concern. Every man who will not agree to give you the title of head of the church is made a traitor. A law has been passed which has put the best men of your realm both in virtue and in learning to death. They suffered the pain of traitors when all their deeds showed from the beginning of their lives to the end that they had always been your most faithful servants.

1 Read Source 11. What is Pole afraid of?
2 Who are the men he is referring to?
3 How do you think Henry VIII might have reacted to this letter?

Reginald Pole was a devout Catholic who watched in horror as the break with Rome unfolded. Fleeing to Padua, Italy, he launched a campaign to persuade the king not to go ahead with the divorce. Pole strongly criticised Henry for listening to men like Cromwell. Henry sent several representatives to Italy to meet with Pole and convince him to return to England, but Pole refused.

4 Why does Thomas More refuse to accept Anne Boleyn's children as future heirs to the throne?

> **Source 12** Thomas More, expressing his sentiments about the Oath of Succession.
>
> *But as for myself in good faith my conscience so moved me in the matter, that though I would not deny to swear to the succession, yet unto the oath that there was offered me I could not swear, without condemning my soul to perpetual damnation.*

In the monasteries

Elizabeth Barton (later known as the 'Nun of Kent') was one of the most outspoken critics of the annulment. Barton had developed a cult-like following in Kent as a prophet (someone given messages from God to pass on to people) after she had fallen ill, experienced trances and then been miraculously cured. She became a nun and continued to have visions. In one of these visions, an angel told her to go to the king and command him to amend his life. The angel said that if Henry married Anne Boleyn, God would seek vengeance. Barton even claimed to have seen the spot in Hell that was reserved for Henry unless he restored the pope's rights.

Barton told many monks and NUNS about her visions. John Fisher was said to have wept when he heard her revelations. She was arrested and put on trial for treason. Although she eventually confessed – under pressure – that she had made up the visions, she and five of her supporters were executed in 1534. Barton is the only woman in English history to have had her severed head displayed on London Bridge.

Others in religious orders who resisted the Act of Supremacy caused something of a dilemma for the king. The MONKS who were the most devout and widely respected were those who challenged Henry the most.

- There were six small Franciscan MONASTERIES (the largest at Greenwich, near London). All these refused to swear the oath and so they were shut down. The FRIARS were sent to the Tower.
- Three Charterhouse PRIORS who refused to acknowledge the royal supremacy were tried and executed for treason in May 1535. Three Charterhouse monks met the same fate in June.

After the execution of Thomas More, Archbishop Cranmer reached a compromise agreement with Stephen Gardiner and other conservative bishops about preaching. Preachers were to set forth the supremacy and DENOUNCE the power of the pope, but they could avoid taking sides in any of the other teachings (see Source 14).

5 Read Source 13. Why do you think Reginald Pole posed such a threat to the king?

6 Some people say that Cromwell was a devout Protestant, others say he was just ambitious and was seeking promotion for himself. Why do you think Cromwell was so angry with Throgmorton?

7 Read Source 14. What are priests not allowed to talk about? Which key Protestant beliefs are now allowed to be discussed?

8 Why do you think priests were banned from talking about so much?

9 How does this source demonstrate a change in Henry's religious beliefs?

> **Source 13** A scathing letter from Cromwell to Michael Throgmorton, who had shown some loyalty to Reginald Pole. Cromwell threatens both Throgmorton and his servant with death.
>
> *I thought that the singular goodness of the kings highness showed unto you, and the great and singular clemency showed to that detestable traitor your master, in promising him not only forgiveness but also forgetting of his most shameful ingratitude, unnaturalness, conspiracy against his honour, of whom he hath received no more.*

> **Source 14** Thomas Cranmer's orders for preaching, 1534.
>
> *Neither with nor against purgatory, honouring of saints, that priests may have wives; that faith only justified; to go on pilgrimages, to forge miracles … considering that thereupon no edification [improvement] can ensue in the people, but rather occasions of talk and rumour, to their great hurt and damage.*

KEY TERMS

Make sure you know what these terms mean and can use them confidently in your writing.

- annul
- anticlericalism
- chantry
- clergy
- humanism
- indulgences
- Lollards
- Lutheran
- Reformation
- relics

FOCUS TASK

Why did Henry break with Rome?

1 Review the cards you have been making (heir, conscience, power, money, individuals, reformist ideas). Arrange them on a large sheet of paper in order of importance. Then add lines and comments to show connections between the reasons for Henry's break with Rome.

Who drove the changes to the Church?

2 Historians including Christopher Haigh and A. G. Dickens disagree about who was driving the changes to the Church in England in the 1520s.

   a Dickens argues that the Reformation was driven from below – i.e. that there was popular call for change.

   b Haigh argues it was driven from above – by those in power.

   Which viewpoint is supported by the work you have done in this topic?

PRACTICE QUESTIONS

1 Explain why Henry VIII reformed the Church in the 1530s. (10)
2 Explain the role of Cromwell in reforming the Church in the 1530s. (10)
3 Study the sources in this topic. How far do they convince you that Henry VIII was manipulated into reforming the Church in England?

TOPIC SUMMARY

Henry VIII breaks with Rome

1 Henry VIII was a religious man who came to believe that he could not have a son because God was punishing him for marrying his brother's wife.
2 Henry petitioned the pope for an annulment, but the pope refused.
3 The king became so desperate that he looked at ancient texts to see if he had any powers to grant his own divorce.
4 When his lover Anne Boleyn fell pregnant, he married her secretly and urged his ministers to pursue the annulment as quickly as possible.
5 Henry VIII became Supreme Head of the Church of England and granted his own annulment.
6 Not everyone supported Henry's actions – some Catholics were willing to die rather than renounce the Catholic Church.

5.1 The suppression of the monasteries

FOCUS

In the last topic, you saw Henry VIII become Supreme Head of the Church of England, mainly so that he could marry Anne Boleyn. However, once Henry had this new power he began using it to introduce significant reforms. Probably the most devastating demonstration of his new authority was the dissolution of the monasteries. In this topic you will investigate:
- what monasteries were like in the 1520s and 1530s
- why Henry VIII destroyed the monasteries.

Source 1 The introductory paragraph of the Act for the Dissolution of the Lesser Monasteries, passed in 1536.

Sin, vicious, carnal and abominable living is daily seen and committed amongst the little and small abbeys, priories and other such religious houses of monks, canons and nuns. The governors of such houses consume and waste the ornaments of their churches and their goods and chattels to the great displeasure of Almighty God and to the great infamy of the King's Highness and the realm.

Source 1 suggests that the monasteries were dissolved because Henry VIII and his ministers wanted a purer Church in England. The words 'abominable living' suggest that monasteries were full of misbehaving monks who had long forgotten their promises to God. Suppressing the monasteries was therefore part of a wider set of reforms to the Church. You could also infer from this source that many people wanted the monasteries dissolved because they were wasteful and did not serve communities well.

In fact, evidence suggests that there were many other reasons that the monasteries were dissolved, including Henry VIII's need for money to fund his wars with France. There is also a wealth of evidence to suggest that many people did not want the monasteries to close at all. Monastic houses were beautiful buildings and a source of pride for local people. They also offered many vital services to communities, such as caring for the sick and poor.

FOCUS TASK

Why were the monasteries dissolved?

You need to understand the different reasons why Henry closed the monasteries. Copy the table below. As you read the topic, record any evidence you find that each reason influenced the actions of Henry VIII or his chancellor Thomas Cromwell. Sometimes the reason may be stated in a source. Sometimes you will need to infer it from a source. Sometimes it will be in the text. At the end of the topic, you will decide which you think was the most important reason.

Religious reasons (to help people get closer to God)	Financial reasons (to raise money for the king)	Anti-Rome sentiment (to reduce the influence of the pope)	Asserting Henry's power (to show he was in charge)

Source 2 Historian Geoffrey Moorhouse, writing in 2011.

A climate of legalised violence and terrifying penalties existed when the machinery of Dissolution was assembled, and it was frightening enough to subdue any other person with religious beliefs who might have been tempted to voice the opinions that had sent John Fisher, Thomas More and many others to their deaths. It was in this atmosphere that Thomas Cromwell carefully began to make his preparations with the utmost clarity. In the document that he produced just as the Act of Supremacy was being passed in 1534, which aimed to increase and augment his sovereign's finances, the most notable thing is the preciseness of the financial and other calculations he had made.

1 Study Source 2 carefully. How has the historian made use of the sources he has found?
2 Do you get the impression that Moorhouse has a personal opinion of the developments he describes? Explain your answer.

Henry VIII asserts his power

Henry VIII took his new role as Head of the Church of England very seriously. He believed it was his duty to reform the Church for religious reasons, so that it brought people closer to God. However, he also wanted to assert his own authority, to show that this really was 'his' Church of England, not the pope's.

Henry's key enforcer – the person who actually implemented his changes – was Thomas Cromwell. When the Act of Supremacy was passed, Cromwell was made vicegerent in spirituals (or vicar-general): the royal priest. It is difficult to know how far Cromwell shared Henry's religious objectives or beliefs because he barely wrote anything that revealed his inner thoughts. Most historians think that he probably embraced most of the new evangelical ideas, although he had political motives for wanting the break with Rome.

Enforcement of new religious policies

Cromwell had a strong legal and practical framework through which to enforce his and Henry's decisions:

- The Treasons Act of 1534 (strengthened in 1535) made it an act of treason even to speak badly of the king or Anne Boleyn, or against Henry's supremacy in the Church. This allowed the government to prosecute heretics more easily. The Nun of Kent and Thomas More (see page 149) were both executed under this law.
- Within the new Church hierarchy, the king and Cromwell would create a policy then order the bishops to carry it out. The bishops would pass this order down the line to the priests. Cromwell also had government agents called justices of the peace (JPs) to help him enforce his measures in towns and cities.

The oath of allegiance

In the past, monks, nuns and friars had sworn oaths of allegiance to the pope. After the break with Rome, however, monastic orders had to swear a new oath accepting Henry VIII as the Supreme Head of the Church and stating that the Bishop of Rome (the pope's official title) had no more authority than any other bishop. They were also told to remove the word 'pope' from all their service books and to urge ordinary people to commend to God the king, Anne Boleyn and Archbishop Cranmer in their prayers. There was enormous pressure to swear the new oath and monks were examined individually about their faith and obedience to the king.

FACTFILE

Monasteries

There were nearly 12,000 people living under monastic orders in England, in 900 religious houses of different sizes. These houses are collectively referred to as monasteries but they were actually made up of:
- 260 monasteries with 4,000 monks
- 300 monasteries with 3,000 CANONS
- 142 nunneries with 2,000 nuns
- 183 friaries with 3,000 friars.

Monks, nuns, friars

- Like monks and nuns, friars lived according to vows of poverty, chastity and obedience. However, friars worked out in the community whereas monks and nuns kept themselves separate so they could focus on personal devotion, such as regular prayer.

- Monks and nuns lived in a self-sufficient communities, growing their own food, while friars worked among ordinary people and relied on donations and other charitable support.
- Monks and nuns stayed in the same place, while friars committed to serve a region or province, so they moved around spending time in different houses.

Canons

- A canon was a priest who lived with other priests, but they were not strictly a religious order. They did not sign up to strict rules like monks. However, they did renounce private wealth.
- Any priest who wanted to keep his wealth became a secular canon – a canon living out in the community.

Source 3 Part of a sermon given by Robert Singleton, chaplain to Anne Boleyn in 1535. Cromwell ordered bishops and senior clergy to preach in favour of the religious changes in public places (such as town squares or crossroads) in all towns and cities.

God preserve his church universal
And this church of Englande special
And the supreme head of the
church our King
And grant us bliss without ending.
A M E N.

3 How can you tell that Cromwell had approved the sermon in Source 3?

4 It was very unusual for bishops to preach in public places. Do you think this would have had an impact?

5 Read Source 5. Beerly suggests that men of the Church are not promoting the king's cause. Why would this worry Cromwell?

6 Can we trust what Beerly says in this report?

Source 4 In a proclamation on 1 January 1536, Henry attacked the papacy and presented himself as a king who:

Daily studies to rid the realm of sin and increase virtue of the people, to the Glory of God. His loving subjects have been encouraged to commit sin and withdraw their devotion from God by the pope's corrupt and deceitful indulgences.

Source 5 Richard Beerly, a monk of Pershore, describing to Thomas Cromwell how members of religious orders really felt about Church reform.

Now I will tell your Grace about religious men, and how the king's commandment about telling the people of the pope's usurped power. ... Abbots, monks, priests are doing little or nothing to weaken the pope's power, and I myself know where they are still speaking of him as head of the Church.

Valor Ecclesiasticus

Cromwell's next task was to reform Church taxes, which would no longer be paid to Rome. He set up a commission to survey all the monasteries in England and gather details about the people, lands and rental incomes of each house. This commission was called Valor Ecclesiasticus (literally 'the wealth of the Church'). It began work on 30 January 1535.

Some historians have suggested that the Valor Ecclesiasticus was set up simply as a prelude to seizing the wealth of the monasteries. Others argue it was a necessary exercise to reform taxes. Both views are possible but it seems likely that the first was in both Cromwell's and Henry's minds:

- There is no doubt that Cromwell personally disliked monasticism and objected to the wealth of the Church. In the previous decade he had seen Wolsey close down some monasteries and use the income to establish schools and colleges. Cromwell knew that closing the monasteries could bring the king great wealth.
- Henry VIII also disliked the Church being so wealthy – Wolsey had been rich enough to build Hampton Court Palace, so large that it dwarfed some of the king's own palaces. In 1533, Henry had written that he wanted to 'reunite to the Crown the goods which churchmen held of it'. He liked the idea of confiscating some Church property to increase his own power and wealth.

Source 6 Valor Ecclesiasticus for St Werburgh's Abbey, Chester, 1535.

Income per year		Expenditure per year	
rents from land owned in the city of Chester and counties of Derby, Stafford and Lancashire	£720 12s 6d	to the abbey clerk and bailiffs	£27 0s 0d
tithes received	£352 12s 3d	payments to the Church	£12 19s 4d
		non-Church payments	£16 12s 4d
		alms	£14 0s 0d
Grand total	**£1,073 4s 9d**		**£70 11s 8d**

Source 7 Extracts from reports by two agents of Cromwell, Thomas Leigh and Richard Layton, who carried out visitations across the Midlands and North of England, 1535.

Lichfield: 'two of the nuns were with child'

Whitby: 'Abbot Hexham took a share of the proceeds from piracy'

Bradley: 'the prior has six children'

Abbotsbury: 'abbot wrongfully selling timber'

Pershore: 'monks drunk at mass'.

---

1 Historian Geoffrey Moorhouse describes Leigh and Layton like this:

'Leigh and Layton were not only inordinately zealous, extremely efficient and rather unpleasant men: they had each at different times made it clear to Cromwell that their activities in the service of the Crown were not in the least impartial and they hoped that the vicar-general would reward them for this.'

Does this affect your view of Source 7 or any other sources in this section?

The visitations

The Act of Supremacy gave Henry VIII the right to inspect all religious houses in England. As vicegerent, Cromwell could do the same. Such inspections, called VISITATIONS, had been part of Church practice for centuries. In the 1520s, Wolsey had closed down some monasteries because visitations had shown them to be ungodly.

Cromwell arranged a visitation of all the monasteries during the autumn of 1535. Officially, these visitations were to test the spiritual health of the monasteries, but the evidence suggests that Cromwell had another motive. He hand-picked six agents to conduct the visitations – all men he knew disliked the Catholic focus on relics and miracles and doubted the spiritual value of monastic life. His choice of commissioners, the speed with which they worked and the questions they asked all imply that Cromwell hoped the monasteries would be found to be failing and corrupt. The question remains whether his motives were religious or financial.

The commissioners' questions

At each monastery, the commissioners asked 86 questions. Some were factual (the number of monks or nuns, or their income). Others seem designed to expose serious failings:

- The commissioners asked whether the number of monks or nuns matched the number specified by the person who had founded the monastery. This suggests they were trying to catch out some of the smaller houses by claiming they were not fulfilling their obligations to the founder's will.
- Questions to abbots were designed to identify weak leadership. How had the master been chosen? Did the master ensure that the church and its buildings were kept in good repair? Was he charitable? Did anyone hold more than one office?
- Questions to monks and nuns focused on how sincerely devoted to God they were and how far they followed the rules of their order. Did they keep to the vows of poverty, chastity and obedience? Did the monks and nuns keep silence, fasting and abstinence? Did women come into the house? Did the brothers sleep together or in separate beds?

The commissioners' findings

The commissioners' findings were very critical of the monasteries. They reported ungodly behaviour – including sexual corruption – and lazy, unlearned monks. They found relics they believed were fake and described how these promoted superstitious practices. For example:

- St Ethelreda's wimple, 'through which they drew knotted strings or silken threads, which women thought good for sore throats' and 'St Audrey's wimple for sore breasts and comb for headaches'.
- At Bury St Edmund's: 'St Edmund's shirt, the blood of Christ, some parts of the holy cross, the stone with which St Stephen was stoned, the skull of St Petronilla, which simple folk put on their heads to prevent fever'.

The commissioners clearly felt that the focus on relics was unfit for religious houses. However, the number of relics they discovered suggests that these items were important to both monastic practice and people's beliefs.

Many historians believe that the visitors were looking to find fault. However, some monasteries, such as Durham, did receive favourable reports.

Source 8 Bishop Nicke's report on his visitation to Norwich Cathedral Priory, 1535.

3. The monks' friends have access to their chambers, and not to the room set aside for the purpose.

18. Women of bad character have access to the monastery.

16. Religion and chastity are not kept, through the fault of the sub-prior, who giveth an evil example.

30. The cell of Aldby is in great ruin and heavily burdened with debt.

34. The monks dance in the guesten-house.

2 Read Sources 7–9. What is the tone of these reports? Are they factual as you would expect?

Source 9 A report by the commissioner Richard Layton to Cromwell, about his visitation to the monastery of Maiden Bradley, August 1535.

I will also send you a bag of relics containing part of the Virgin Mary's dress, part of the Last Supper and some of the stone from the manger in which Jesus was born.

At Maiden Bradley the prior has six children and but one daughter married yet of the goods of the monastery, trusting shortly to marry the rest. His sons are tall men and wait upon him and be thanks God that he never meddled with married women, but only with fair unmarried maidens, for whom he has arranged good marriages.

Source 10 An image from a Book of Hours (a prayer book) from the early fourteenth century, depicting a friar and a nun enjoying music and dancing. ▼

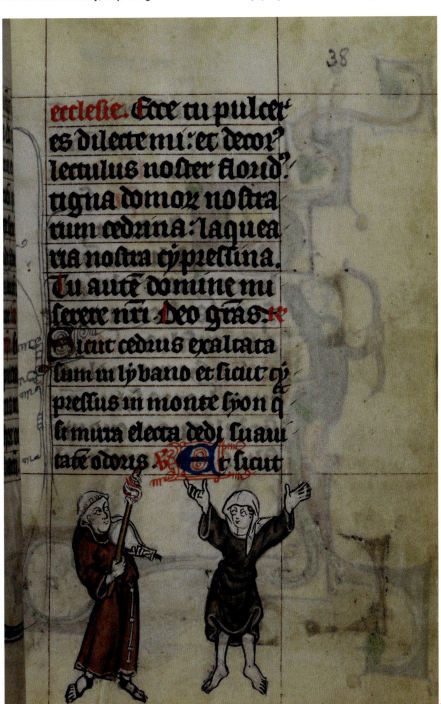

ACTIVITY

As far as we know, Source 10 and other similar sources were not used as evidence in the visitations. If they had been, what do you think one of Cromwell's agents would have done with Source 10? Write a short extract in the style of Sources 8 and 9 commenting on Source 10.

Source 11 On 12 May 1535, a group in Northamptonshire wrote on behalf of Catesby nunnery to correct some of the commissioners' findings. This group also wrote about St James's Abbey in Northampton as they believed it had been undervalued by the visitors.

They had found in perfect order, the prioress a sure, wise, discrete and very religious woman, with six nuns ... as religious and devout and with as good obedience as we have in time past seen or belikely to see. [The nuns do much] to the relief of the king's people, and his graces poor subjects they're likewise much relieved.

Source 12 A nineteenth-century copy of a sketch created in the thirteenth century by Matthew Paris. It shows monks transferring some relics to a new minster. ▼

1. Study Source 12. Why are the monks carrying the relic in this sort of procession?
2. What do you think the two disabled men are doing underneath the relic?
3. Why didn't Cromwell and some other reformers like the use of relics?
4. Study Source 13. Why is Sagar writing to Cromwell?
5. Why would Sagar invite Cromwell to the monastery?
6. Do Sources 11 and 13 prove that the monasteries were bad religious institutions?

Source 13 A letter from the abbot of Hailes, Stephen Sagar, to Cromwell, about his remarkable 'conversion experience'. He actually asked Cromwell to send commissioners to the monastery.

It is not unknown to your honour that there is in the monastery of Hailes, some blood which has been reported as a miracle. Now I tell your lordship that I am dreadfully worried that we are committing idolatry. ... I do most humbly beg your honour to come and investigate this matter to examine my truth and honesty, so that my conscience can be put at rest.

The process of dissolution

The visitations gave Cromwell the evidence he needed to proceed with the DISSOLUTION of the monasteries. However, the process that followed was complicated, and it emphasises how careful the king and Cromwell were to maintain the idea that what they were doing was legal and justified.

The dissolution of smaller monasteries

The Dissolution of the Lesser Monasteries Act (1536) gave the king power to close down religious houses with an annual income of less than £200, if they were failing to maintain a religious life. All property of the dissolved house would go to the Crown.

In practice, a new group of commissioners went to each of these small monasteries and carried out another inventory of its wealth and possessions, and assessed how well it was performing its religious duties. These commissioners were more generous than the first ones had been. If they reported that the monastery was still doing a good job, it was allowed to remain open as long as it paid a fine. As a result, 243 of 419 small houses were closed but the rest survived. Monks, nuns and friars were either given a pension and went to live in the community or they transferred to larger houses. Many smaller houses in the north of England remained open because there was no room for their monks to move to the larger monasteries.

Source 14 Instructions sent to abbots and heads of monasteries, 1535.

The king's power is by the laws of God most excellent of all under God on Earth and we ought to obey him before all other powers. The authority of the bishop of Rome is based not on holy scripture but on the craft and deceit of the Bishop of Rome and by princes tolerating the works of this bishop. By the king's supreme power and authority you are absolved from obedience and any oaths of loyalty sworn to the bishop of Rome. You are to allow the royal Visitors to inspect your houses and charters and any other documents. Any brother or sister in your house shall pray every day for the happiness and prosperity of our sovereign lord the king and his most noble and lawful wife Queen Anne.

7 How would you describe the tone of Source 14? Select words and phrases that support your answer.
8 Why is the pope referred to as the 'bishop of Rome'?
9 Is there anything significant about the way Anne Boleyn is referred to?

Source 15 The abbess of Little Marlow, writing to Cromwell after she agreed to the dissolution of her abbey, 1536.

Sir my request is to desire you to remember your promises made unto me and unto my friends, which I have always trusted. I beseech your goodness to inform me what kind of new post you intend that I shall have, or else to help me to some reasonable living on a pension. I have taken nothing from the abbey's wealth because your mastership commanded me that I should take nothing but leave the house as wealthy as I could, which commandment I followed: I hope all shall be for the best. I pray our Lord put in your heart to make provision for me according to His holy will and pleasure and wholly to rule your mastership by His spirit. Amen

Anne Boleyn suggested to the king that the money made from closing these monasteries should be used for religious purposes. However, by this time her influence over Henry was declining and the monastic wealth went straight to the Crown.

Unlike Henry's earlier Church reforms, the closure of the smaller monasteries was highly visible – and extremely unpopular among ordinary people. It helped fuel the rebellion known as the Pilgrimage of Grace (see page 163). Some monks, including some from smaller houses that had been spared dissolution in 1536, became involved in the rebellion.

'Voluntary dissolution' of the larger monasteries

The visitations continued. Henry and Cromwell maintained that their policy was one of reform, but by late 1537 it was clear that they intended to close all the monasteries. However, the process involved this time was very different from the first.

It began with Furness Abbey in Lancashire. The monks at Furness had been involved in the Pilgrimage of Grace and the abbot was afraid of being charged with treason. He asked to make a 'voluntary surrender' of his house, and Cromwell agreed. This set a pattern for other larger monasteries: if a religious house dissolved itself, its monks and nuns would be granted a generous pension. If they did not, they might be accused of treason and be closed anyway. After more than a year of harassment from Cromwell's men, forced oaths of allegiance, challenges to their loyalty and practices, and accusations of treason that had sometimes ended in priors being executed, it is not surprising that many monastic houses chose voluntary dissolution.

The LUTHERAN reformer and bishop of Worcester, Hugh Latimer, wrote to Cromwell in 1538. He begged that the priory at Great Malvern and several others be allowed to stay open. By then, however, the great priory at Lewes in Sussex had voluntarily dissolved and its property had passed to Cromwell himself. He would accept nothing less than total surrender from the rest.

The second Dissolution Act was passed in 1539, and within a year all the monasteries were gone. The Court of Augmentations, led by men such as Richard Rich, was set up to manage the income from the dissolution. In all, 563 houses were dissolved, 8,000 monks were pensioned off and the Crown's annual income more than doubled to £250,000. The resale of monastic land raised another £1.3 million.

Dissolution of the friaries

By early 1538, most people expected that the friaries would also be dissolved. In some houses all friars except the prior had already left and assets such as timber, chalices and vestments were being sold off. Cromwell put Richard Yngworth, bishop of Dover, in charge of ensuring the friaries were forced to close. To do this, Yngworth issued new instructions reinforcing the rules of each house and making friars resume a strict monastic life. The rules were so strict that friars were essentially forced to surrender their houses. If they did not, they faced homelessness and starvation for failing to comply.

Yngworth reported to Cromwell about the current tenant of the gardens, the general state of the friary buildings and whether the friary church had valuable lead on roofs and gutters. Mostly he said he had found little of worth because not many people left money to the friaries any more. Most friars were released from their vows and dismissed with around 40 shillings. Yngworth listed the friars remaining in each house at surrender so that Cromwell could provide them with legal permission to become SECULAR priests. Of all the friary churches in England and Wales, only St Andrew's Hall in Norwich and Greyfriars Church in Reading remain standing. Hardly a trace of the others remains.

The impact of the dissolution

Church buildings

Cromwell's men did not just take the keys to the monasteries and send away the monks and nuns. They also destroyed many buildings and stole hundreds of valuable items.

The surrender of Boxley Priory in Kent (January 1538) was particularly significant because it was one of the most important sites of pilgrimage in England. Pilgrimage and the relics that people came to see were among the 'superstitious' practices denounced by the commissioners. Few of the smaller monasteries contained pilgrimage sites, but when the bigger monasteries fell, some important shrines were lost.

The first goods to be seized were the lead roofs, gutters and plumbing. Buildings were burned down so it would be easy to get to this material. Cromwell's men sold building stone and slate roofs to the highest bidder. Many monastic outbuildings were turned into granaries, barns and stables. Ancient and precious items were melted down; the tombs of saints and kings were ransacked for whatever goods might be enclosed in them. Relics were destroyed or sold. Even the crypt of Alfred the Great at Winchester was not spared. Great abbeys and priories such as Glastonbury, Walsingham, Bury St Edmunds and Shaftesbury, which had flourished as pilgrimage sites for centuries, were reduced to ruins.

One of the greatest losses was that of the monastic libraries. For example, Worcester Priory had 600 books at the time of the dissolution; only six of them survived. Similarly, at the Augustinian abbey in York, a library of 646 volumes was destroyed; just three were saved.

Source 16 A photograph showing the defaced statue of a saint in Ely Cathedral. It was destroyed in 1536 when Cromwell's men shut down the abbey. ▼

> **Source 17** A description of the destruction of Roche Abbey in Yorkshire by Michael Sherbrook, writing in the 1560s.
>
> *It would have pitied any heart to see what tearing up of the lead there was and plucking up of boards and throwing down of spars. ... The persons that cast the lead into fodders, plucked up all the seats in the choir, wherein the monks sat when they said service – which were like to the seats in minsters – and burned them, and melted the lead therewithal, although there was wood plenty within a flight shot of them.*

1 Look at Source 16. Why might Cromwell's men have left most of the ornate carvings and only removed the face?
2 Read Source 17. Why did the commissioners destroy parts of the monastery? Why did they melt the lead?

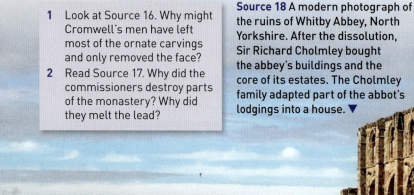

Source 18 A modern photograph of the ruins of Whitby Abbey, North Yorkshire. After the dissolution, Sir Richard Cholmley bought the abbey's buildings and the core of its estates. The Cholmley family adapted part of the abbot's lodgings into a house. ▼

> **Source 19** John Leland, writing about Malmesbury Abbey after the dissolution.
>
> *The whole lodgings of the abbey now belonging to one stump, an exceedingly rich clothier that bought them off the king. ... At this present time every corner of the vast houses of office that belonged to the Abbey be full of looms to weave cloth in, and this stump intends to make a street or two for clothiers in the back vacant ground of the abbey.*

> **Source 20** Accounts of the money received by the Crown after the dissolution of various monasteries.
>
> - *Monastery of Bindon in the county of Dorset £300.*
> - *Monastery of St James in the county of Northampton £333 6s 8d.*
> - *Monastery of De la Pre in the same county £266 13s 4d.*
> - *Monastery of nuns (St Mary's) in the city of Winchester £333 6s 8d.*
> - *Monastery of Shap in the county of Westmoreland £266 13s 8d.*
> - *Received on 14th day of August 1540 from Sir Richard Gresham, £11,137 11s 8d to the king for the site of the late monastery of Fountains in the county of Yorkshire.*
> - *Received the 22nd day of January 1541 from Sir Richard Cromwell, £4,963 owed to the king for the site of the late monastery of Ramsey in the county of Huntingdon.*

3 Do Sources 19 and 20 prove that rich people did not complain about the dissolution because they profited from it?

4 Does Source 20 prove that Henry VIII was only interested in the monasteries for their wealth?

The people

Many ordinary people felt that the monastic orders were there to pray on their behalf. Monks and nuns looked after the shrines at pilgrimage sites and the religious houses themselves were a fundamental part of life. The monks offered shelter to weary travellers, they were landlords upon whom large numbers of people relied for their houses, they employed servants, craftsmen and labourers. They grew crops and bred animals, they were important patrons of fisheries and butchers as they prepared feasts. When Henry VIII removed the monasteries, he deprived his subjects not just spiritually, but economically too.

Local commissioners were instructed to make sure that abbey churches used by local congregations were not destroyed. This saved more than 100 monastic buildings. A dozen or so wealthy families bought monastic buildings after the dissolution and donated them to the community. This perhaps demonstrates a desire to maintain these beautiful buildings for their religious purpose.

Many of the gentry profited from the dissolution of the monasteries, as they were able to buy monastic lands for less than market value. Some historians have suggested that this was one of the main reasons why the gentry did not strongly object to the dissolution. One example of a family that bought up monastic lands were the Giffards of Staffordshire, who bought a twelfth-century Augustinian priory and several nunneries. Despite this the Giffards were religious conservatives, and remained Catholic despite Henry's reforms. They turned Brewood priory into a safe house for nuns.

> **Source 21** Historian A. G. Dickens, writing in 1982.
>
> *With a few notable exceptions, monasticism was lukewarm and insular, commanding little veneration outside the cloister. Altogether, the English Church during the period 1500–30 stood poorly equipped to weather the storms of the new age.*

5 Read Source 21. Does Dickens convince you that people did not care about the dissolution of the monasteries?

FACTFILE

Timeline of the dissolution of the monasteries

1535 Valor Ecclesiasticus (a census of Church wealth) carried out, followed by visitations – a survey of the spiritual health of the monastic orders.

1536 First Act of Dissolution passed – all houses with an income of less than £200 dissolved. Some were exempted and many monks or nuns were transferred to larger houses or pensioned off. The Pilgrimage of Grace – a huge northern rebellion in reaction to the dissolution of the smaller houses – took place.

1537 Voluntary surrenders of larger houses began.

1538 Pressure increased for voluntary surrender. Within 16 months, 202 houses had dissolved.

1539 Second Act of Dissolution passed. This simply legitimised the 'voluntary' surrenders.

1540 The last of the religious houses to close, Waltham Abbey, surrendered in March 1540.

The impact of the dissolution

Monastic buildings: Most of the magnificent gothic church priories and abbeys were destroyed or left to ruin as timber, lead and other useful materials were stolen or sold off. Some of Henry's new wealth was spent on cathedral grammar schools such as Canterbury, Carlisle and Bristol. Christ Church College, Oxford and Trinity College, Cambridge were also established.

The poor: Monasteries had been a source of help for the poor and evidence suggests that the dissolution had a massive impact on poor relief.

Nuns: Nuns were not allowed to marry or become priests, so most faced extreme hardship.

Monks and friars: The majority (6,500) found alternative employment as secular priests and were given pensions. The rest faced poverty.

The gentry: Many people who would not otherwise have been able to buy land now could. Many lawyers, JPs and younger sons of landowning gentry were able to buy up relatively cheap land, creating a larger landowning class.

ACTIVITY

Create an information board for visitors to the ruin of Durham Priory. You will need to explain why it was destroyed and how and what impact it had on the surrounding area.

PRACTICE QUESTIONS

1 Explain why some people criticised monasteries in the 1520s and 1530s. (10)
2 Explain how the dissolution of the monasteries affected people in England. (10)

FOCUS TASK

Why were the monasteries dissolved?

You have been recording evidence for each of several reasons for the dissolution. Now use your completed table to decide how far you agree with this statement:

The monasteries were dissolved for two main reasons: for Henry VIII to ensure his supremacy over the Church in England and to fill the Crown's coffers.

TOPIC SUMMARY

The supression of the monasteries

1 In spring 1535, the Valor Ecclesiasticus surveyed the wealth of the Church, initially to reform Church taxes.
2 By autumn 1535, policy had shifted and visitations were carried out to survey the spiritual health of the monastic houses.
3 Cromwell's commissioners found ungodly behaviour, lazy, unlearned monks and many relics and superstitious practices.
4 The dissolution of the smaller monasteries started in 1536.
5 The popular uprising called the Pilgrimage of Grace broke out in response to the dissolution of smaller houses and fears about further reform.
6 Henry VIII began to associate monasteries with betrayal and forced larger monasteries to surrender for fear of being accused of treason.
7 The second Dissolution Act was passed in 1539, but by then most of the monasteries had voluntarily dissolved.

5.2 Responses to the dissolution of the monasteries

FOCUS

In this topic, you will learn about two major uprisings that took place mostly in response to the suppression of the monasteries. These were the most serious rebellions that Henry VIII faced in his entire reign and they involved men, women and children from all levels of society – from the nobility to humble peasant farmers. You will learn:

● how ordinary people felt about the dissolution of the monasteries
● why the Lincolnshire Rising took place
● how Henry VIII overcame the largest rebellion of his reign, known as the Pilgrimage of Grace.

FOCUS TASK

What was the real story of the Pilgrimage of Grace?

It is difficult for historians to discover the real story behind the Pilgrimage of Grace. The evidence either comes from people close to Henry VIII, who regarded the rebels as traitors, or from the rebels themselves, who felt they had good cause for their protest. Your task is to use the evidence in this topic to work out what *really* happened during the Pilgrimage of Grace. As you read the information, make notes under the headings below. At the end, you should be able to create a factfile to use for revision.

● Who took part?
● Where did it take place?
● How did it happen?
● Why did it happen?
● What were the consequences?

Source 1 Richard Morison was one of Cromwell's leading publicists. He wrote a book, *Remedy for Sedition*, within a few weeks of the Pilgrimage of Grace in 1536.

When EVERY man will rule, who shall obey? How can there be a common wealth, where he that is wealthiest is most likely to come to harm? No! Accept that wealth will come and go, lust is liked and law is refused, where up is down and down is up: an order must be found and those that rule do the best they can. This agreement is necessary so that those of the worser sort can be content that it is the wiser who rule and govern them.

You might infer from Source 1 that those involved in the rioting were all poor and that they were rebelling against the king because they were greedy for more wealth or unhappy with Henry's rule. In fact, the band of almost 40,000 rebels included men from the great noble families, such as Lord Darcy and Sir Robert Constable. They were rebelling against the king's advisers, who they thought were trying to change the Church they loved. This spontaneous outpouring of grief following the suppression of the smaller monasteries proved to be the most threatening rebellion Henry VIII faced in his entire 38-year reign.

Religious changes

Following the dissolution of the lesser monasteries, CONVOCATION (a group of leading bishops) met to agree what the fundamental beliefs of the Church of England should be. A group of RADICAL bishops led by Hugh Latimer wanted to abolish the cult of the saints, relics, pilgrimages, holy days, images and the use of lights in churches altogether. However, the older conservative bishops defended holy days and some other beliefs and practices. It took weeks for them to agree on anything.

Eventually Convocation issued the Ten Articles – the first official doctrine (prescribed teachings) of the Church of England. These specifically approved images, the cult of saints and chantries. However, the articles attacked the belief in purgatory and abolished all feast days that fell during harvest time (it was believed that taking time off work to celebrate the many feast days was one cause of poor harvests), as well as those that fell when courts were in session.

1 Study Source 2. Does this source suggest Henry was confident his changes would be followed or not? Explain your answer.

2 What does Source 3 reveal to historians about the origins of the protests in 1536?

3 Is it possible to say whether Source 3 or Source 4 is more useful to historians studying the Pilgrimage of Grace?

> **Source 2** An order from Henry VIII to his bishops, after he anticipated trouble if feast days were abolished, 1536.
>
> *Do not speak of the abolished feast days, because it will encourage the people to become unsettled or condemn the order ... pass over them with secret silence as these laws have already been abolished in convocation.*

The Lincolnshire Rising

Until the autumn of 1536, resistance to religious reform had largely come from individuals, such as Thomas More and the Nun of Kent. There were reports of women attacking the workmen sent to dismantle St Nicholas' priory in Exeter and trying to prevent the removal of lead from the abbey in Norfolk. However, there had been no strong, organised opposition. This changed in 1536, when over 40,000 men in northern England rebelled against the king to stop the suppression of the monasteries.

The rebellion began on 2 October 1536, when the Bishop of Lincoln's registrar arrived in the town of Louth to carry out a visitation. The people of Louth were immensely proud of their church spire, which had only been completed 20 years before. A man called Henry Thornbeck said the trouble began because people feared that 'church jewels should be taken; and after, that all cattle unmarked should be confiscated and christenings and burials taxed'. Rumours began to circulate in Lincoln that all the churches within five miles would be torn down.

The townspeople of Louth stood guard over the church all night. When the registrar arrived they seized him. The townspeople were led by a shoemaker named Nicholas Melton ('Captain Cobbler'), whose armed supporters were financed by church funds. Cobbler led 3,000 men to the nearby Legbourne nunnery and captured the royal commissioners who were at work there.

As the rebellion gathered pace, local gentry took over leadership. However, they could not control the crowds, and a man who worked for the bishop of Lincoln, Dr Raynes, was murdered. The people convinced 60 priests to swear to be true to God and them, and to ring bells throughout their parishes. At least 10,000 men marched to Lincoln. Lord Hussey, one of the county's great noblemen, feared for his life and fled despite feeling sympathy for the rebels. Monks from Barlings, Bardney and Kirkstead joined the rebel host, mounted and armed. At Lincoln, a new set of articles was drawn up and sent to London.

Henry VIII dispatched the Duke of Suffolk to suppress the rebels. Anyone who did not surrender would be charged with treason. When they heard this, the leaders of the Lincolnshire Rising backed down and pleaded for their lives. Unrest in the county continued, but the worst of the uprising came to a rather abrupt end.

> **Source 3** Extracts from the York Articles, drawn up at Lincoln and sent to the mayor of York on 9 October 1536.
>
> 1 *The suppression of so many religious houses ... whereby the service of God is not well [maintained] but also the [commons] of your realm be unrelieved, the which as we think is a great hurt to the common wealth. ...*
>
> 4 *Your grace takes of your counsel and being about you such persons as be of low birth and small reputation which hath procured the profits most especially for their own advantage, the which we suspect to be the lord Cromwell and Sir Richard Riche.*

The Pilgrimage of Grace

Just a few days after the Lincolnshire Rising, a much bigger rebellion started 160 km to the north. This became known as the Pilgrimage of Grace, and it spread across York, Durham, Northumberland, Westmorland and Cumberland and even to Lancashire and Cheshire.

4 What does Source 4 suggest was the main reason for the Pilgrimage of Grace?

Source 4 A photograph of a banner showing the Five Wounds of Christ. It was made by the people of Horncastle during the Pilgrimage of Grace. The Five Wounds referred to the wounds suffered by Christ in the Crucifixion. It was a well-known and powerful religious symbol so it is not surprising that this became one of the main emblems for the rebellion. ▼

Causes of the rebellion

Some rebels had economic concerns. Unemployment was increasing and closing the monasteries would make the problem worse, because many local people worked in the religious houses, helping to maintain them. Those who worked the land were also worried about changes such as the introduction of ENCLOSURES (changing land from public farmland to private land for grazing sheep). Interrogations carried out after the rebellion also mention the confiscation of unmarked cattle and taxes on marriages and christenings as key reasons for the rebellion.

However, the main cause of the rebellion was outrage about the changes to the Church. The people objected to the abbeys being torn down, the removal of precious items and the banning of holy days and prayers to the pope. Priests and monks supported the rebels with money and food. They also spread rumours about Henry's plans to increase taxes, confiscate the church cup (chalice) and plate (paten), and destroy churches. So far, only the smaller monasteries had been closed, but there were real fears that the larger ones would go the same way. This would be devastating for the people of the north, where the abbeys were a vital part of the community.

Source 5 The 'Pilgrim's Ballad' is thought to have been composed by the monks at Sawley Abbey in Lancashire. It had 16 verses in total. Crim, Crame and Riche are almost certainly Thomas Cromwell, Thomas Cranmer and Richard Rich.

Christ Crucified!
For thy wounds wide
Us commons guide!
Which pilgrims be,
Through God's grace,
For to purchase
Old wealth and peace
Of the spirituality
Great God's fame
Doth Church proclaim
Now to be lame
And fast in bounds,
Robbed, Spoiled and shorn
From cattle and corn
And clean forth born
Of houses and lands.
Crim, Crame and Riche
With their hell and the like
As sum men teach
God them amend!

1 Read Source 5. What does this ballad suggest the motives of the rebels were?

2 Study Source 6. What did the artist think of those involved in the Pilgrimage of Grace? What sort of people does he show leading the rebellion? Did he respect them?

3 Look at Source 7. Famously this banner was used to inspire parishioners against the Scots in times of war. Why do you think it was retrieved for this rebellion?

4 Does Source 8 show that the monasteries were the main concern of the rebels?

Source 6 An image showing the rebels marching towards York during the Pilgrimage of Grace. ▼

Leadership

A lawyer called Robert Aske emerged as one of the main leaders of the rebellion. He organised the people of Howdenshire into two companies and made them swear oaths to be true to God, the king and the commons. The oaths suggest the rebels did not believe that the religious reforms were true to God and they highlight the deeply felt religious concerns of those involved. Aske spoke of the rising as 'the Pilgrimage of Grace for the Common Wealth'. Other key leaders were Robert Bowes, Sir Christopher Danby and Lord Latimer.

Over 10,000 rebels marched to York. They entered the city on 16 October 1536, where Aske issued the mayor with a proclamation declaring their peaceful intentions. Hull fell to the rebels on 19 October and groups also gathered from Richmondshire, Mashamshire, Debergh and Nidderdale. They restored abbeys as they marched.

Source 7 St Cuthbert's Banner was retrieved from Durham Cathedral to lead the pilgrim army. ▼

Source 8 The Pontefract Articles, drawn up on 4 December 1536. Lady Mary was Henry's Catholic daughter by his first wife, Catherine of Aragon. Article 5 points to the tax 'First Fruits and Tenths', which were paid by the clergy and now went to the king rather than to Rome.

To have:

1 *the heresies ... within this realm annulled and destroyed*
2 *the supreme head of the church ... restored unto the see of Rome*
3 *the Lady Mary be made legitimate*
4 *the suppressed abbeys to be restored*
5 *the Tenth and First Fruits and Tenths clearly discharged.*
6 *the Observant Friars restored to their houses again.*
7 *the heretics ... [have] punishment by fire*
8 *the Lord Cromwell, the Lord Chancellor, and Sir Richard Riche ... [receive] punishment.*

FACTFILE

A map showing where the Pilgrimage of Grace took place.

Lincolnshire rebels
Yorkshire rebels
Cumberland rebels
Westmorland rebels
✗ Monasteries that took part

The Pontefract Articles

By late October the rebellion was made up of nine well-armed companies numbering over 30,000 men. The government was slow to act, and for three weeks the rising proceeded without interruption. Bowes was sent to meet Henry at Windsor, and the king offered a pardon to all but ten of the leaders. He also promised to listen to the pilgrims' grievances. Bowes reported back to the council of pilgrims. Together they drew up a list of concerns – the Pontefract Articles – that they intended to present to the king.

Crushing the uprising

The rebels managed to restore 16 of the 55 monasteries that had been dissolved in March 1536 and they may have gone on to greater success. However, Henry VIII had other plans. The king invited Aske to spend Christmas in London, promising that he would have the chance to air the pilgrims' grievances to parliament. Trusting that the king would be true to his word, Aske addressed a gathering of the 3,000 rebels, informing them that Henry had offered good terms for peace and encouraging them to disband.

> **Source 9** Robert Aske, in a speech about the Pilgrimage of Grace delivered in York, October 1536.
>
> *We have taken [this pilgrimage] for the preservation of Christ's church, of this realm of England, the king our sovereign lord, the nobility and commons of the same … the monasteries … in the north parts [they] gave great alms to poor men and laudably served God … and therefore the suppression of the monasteries diminishes the service of Almighty God.*

5 Read Source 9. According to Aske, why were the monasteries so important?

Henry's revenge

Henry VIII had lied to Aske – he was simply playing for time. Soon after making these promises, the king rounded up 216 people he believed were responsible for the rebellion, including Aske. Aske was found guilty of high treason and sentenced to be hanged, drawn and quartered. Henry insisted that the punishment should be carried out in York so that the local people could see what happened to traitors. On 12 July 1537, Aske was dragged through the streets of the city to the scaffold. Before his execution, he asked for forgiveness. He was then hanged almost to the point of death, revived, castrated, disembowelled, beheaded and his body was chopped into four pieces.

> **Source 10** A letter from Henry VIII to the earl of Derby, October 1536.
>
> *We lately commanded you to make ready your forces and go to the earl of Shrewsbury, our lieutenant to suppress the rebellion in the North; but having since heard of an insurrection attempted about the abbey of Salley in Lancashire, where the abbot and monks have been restored by the traitors, we now desire you immediately to repress it, to apprehend the captains and either have them immediately executed as traitors or sent up to us. We leave it, however, to your discretion to go elsewhere in case of greater emergency. You are to take the said abbot and monks forth with violence and have them hanged without delay in their monks' apparel, and see that no town or village begin to assemble.*

> **Source 11** The indictment of John Bulmer, April 1537.
>
> *John Bulmer … with other traitors, at Sherburn, Yorkshire, conspire to deprive the king of his title of Supreme Head of the English Church, and to compel him to hold a certain parliament and Convocation of the clergy of the realm, and did commit diverse insurrections … at Pontefract, diverse days and times before the said 10th of October.*

6 Look at Source 10. Why does Henry deal with the monks and abbots so ruthlessly? Why are they such a threat to him?

7 Does this source prove that the rebels were motivated by religious concerns?

8 Read Source 11. What is John Bulmer accused of?

Impact on monasticism

Some friars and priests encouraged the Pilgrimage of Grace by spreading rumours about Cromwell's intentions for the Church. After the rebellion, several monastery leaders were hanged for their part in it. Fear of being branded traitors meant the leaders of religious houses were more likely to give in to Cromwell's pressure for voluntary dissolution. In 1539, the abbots of Colchester, Glastonbury and Reading were hanged, drawn and quartered for treason for failing to surrender their priories. Their houses were dissolved and their monks given a basic pension of £4 per year.

Perhaps because of the harsh example Henry showed on this occasion, few other monks or nuns protested at all. The rest of the population was either too afraid or too busy trying to survive to launch any further rebellions. The Tudor propaganda machine saw to it that most were convinced that their parish churches would remain safe.

It is difficult to tell if ordinary people lamented the monasteries once they were gone. Many who could afford it scurried to claim the jewels, plate, timber and lead that was sold off. They may have been driven by a desire to preserve these religious objects, but it is more likely they wanted them for their monetary value.

ACTIVITY

This image was drawn many years after the dissolution of the monasteries and is therefore an interpretation of what happened. To work out if it is a faithful interpretation, answer the questions below.

1   What gave the artist the impression that greedy courtiers only cared about profits they could make (i.e. where did he get his evidence)? Can you name anyone who directly profited from the sale of monastic lands?
2   The monks in the picture look upset. Is there evidence that they cared about what happened?
3   Is this image useful for a historian researching the dissolution of the monasteries?

The original caption to the image reads: 'The Wonderful Story of Britain: King Henry and the Monasteries. Greedy courtiers' men carry away gold plate and jewels from a monastery. Original artwork from Treasure no. 87 (12 September 1964).

ACTIVITY

You are worried that Henry VIII's advisers are not telling him the full story about the impact of the dissolution of the monasteries on communities in England. Write a letter to the king, explaining what the impact has been.

PRACTICE QUESTIONS

1 Explain how the dissolution of the monasteries affected people in England. (10)
2 Study Sources 5, 8 and 11. How far do they convince you that the dissolution of the monasteries improved life for people in England? (10)

KEY TERMS

Make sure you know what these terms mean and can use them confidently in your writing.
- canons
- dissolution
- Lutheran
- visitations

Survival

Only three monastic orders survived the dissolution. Without their religious houses, and with no funding, most orders simply could not continue. The Dartford Priory in Kent attracted much support from the local community. The nuns were active in promoting learning, commissioning books and working within their community. This enabled them to continue living together in Sutton at Hone following the suppression. Only the Carthusian monks and the Bridgettine nuns of Syon Abbey survived as communities beyond Elizabeth I's succession in 1558, and this was because they chose exile rather than abandoning their vocation.

FOCUS TASK

What was the real story of the Pilgrimage of Grace?

Use your research for the Focus Task at the start of this topic to create a revision factfile about the Pilgrimage of Grace. You could use the headings you have been creating notes under. Try to only include *facts*. If there are some facts that you are not sure of, include them but make sure you say how certain you are about them.

1 Who took part?
2 Where did it take place?
3 What happened?
4 Why did it happen?
5 What were the consequences?

TOPIC SUMMARY

Responses to the dissolution of the monasteries

1 The dissolution of the smaller monasteries and fears about further Church reform provoked the largest rebellion Henry VIII faced in his 38-year reign.
2 The Lincolnshire Rising was violent. The rebels killed the Bishop of Lincoln's chancellor, suggesting a genuine spontaneous outpouring of feeling in October 1536.
3 The Pilgrimage of Grace, led by Robert Aske, began within days of the Lincolnshire Rising.
4 Aske referred to the rebellion as a 'pilgrimage' so that all rebels would understand his peaceful intentions. It also helped to unite everyone.
5 The rebels had many different grievances and were from different backgrounds, but they all shared a concern for the monasteries.
6 Henry VIII dealt with the rebels extremely harshly, executing 216 of the leaders.
7 There is little evidence of widespread discontent after these uprisings, probably because many of the gentry who might have led a rebellion actually benefited from the sale of monastic lands.

6.1 Reforming the churches

Although the causes of the English Reformation are still debated among historians, what is certain is that nobody could have escaped the transformation of religion between 1520 and 1550. By the end of the period, the Church of England had shifted away from using images to inspire and towards the teaching of biblical texts.

The once-ornate walls of churches were whitewashed. Candles were extinguished. However, the road to this reformed Church was not smooth. In fact, in many ways it was a confusing and contradictory time, as new people gained power at court and Henry changed his policies. In this topic, you will find out:

● the key pieces of legislation surrounding the Reformation
● who was driving each phase of religious change
● how the new religious policies were enforced
● the impact the Reformation had on the Church of England.

Source 1 An illustration from John Foxe's *Book of Martyrs*, published in 1563. This image shows iconoclasm at the top left corner with the banishment of papists from England. ▼

1   Look at Source 1. How does Foxe refer to Catholics?
2   Do you think he supports the destruction of images shown at the top?
3   He has drawn his ideal version of the Church in the bottom right-hand corner. Does this mean he was a Protestant or Catholic?
4   Why do you think Foxe made this image?

FOCUS TASK

How was the Reformation put in practice?

The table below summarises the changes you have studied so far. As you work through this topic, add more rows to it to summarise each change that takes place and to analyse its impact. This will be easier to do for some changes than others.

Date/main changes	Description of the change and its direction (more Catholic or more Protestant)	Impact of this change on church/clergy	Reason why the change took place
1530: clergy accused of *praemunire*	Henry wanted clergy to pledge their allegiance to him, not the pope.	Clergy had to pay a substantial fine to Henry and promise to support his divorce campaign.	It was a warning shot to the pope to convince him to grant the annulment.
1534: Act of Annates, First Act of Succession, Act of Supremacy	Gave Henry the right to collect taxes from the clergy instead of the pope. Made Henry head of the Church so he could grant his own annulment. Confirmed Anne Boleyn's children as legitimate heirs to the throne. Elizabeth Barton and several monks executed.	The clergy now took orders from the king about how they should preach.	Henry wanted to make a smooth succession for his children with Anne. The legislation was passed quickly in the end because she had fallen pregnant. Those who protested against the break with Rome were punished – Henry was asserting his authority over the Church.
1535: Coverdale Bible	The first English Bible was produced.	The clergy were used to being the source of authority in their churches. Giving people a Bible in their own language meant ordinary people could challenge what the clergy said if it conflicted with the Bible.	There were a number of reformers at court, brought in by the Boleyn family, who had persuaded Henry this was a good idea. Henry also agreed with the teachings of Erasmus.
1536: dissolution of the monasteries	The small monasteries were closed and their wealth went to the king.	Monks went to work in parishes or were pensioned off.	Henry wanted to exert his authority and to take wealth from the monasteries to fund his wars.

FACTFILE

Main measures of the English Reformation 1530–50
Phase 1: Henry VIII under the influence of the Boleyns

1530 Clergy accused of *praemunire*.

1533 Act in Restraint of Appeals.

1534 Act of Annates; First Act of Succession; Act of Supremacy; Elizabeth Barton and several monks executed.

1535 Publication of the Coverdale Bible (first English Bible).

1536 Act for Dissolution of Lesser Monasteries; Act of Ten Articles (removed sacraments); Anne Boleyn executed.

Phase 2: Henry VIII after the death of Anne Boleyn

1537 *The Institution of a Christian Man* replaced the Ten Articles.

1538 Execution of John Lambert for rejecting transubstantiation.

1539 Second Act of Dissolution; second English Bible produced – paid for by Cromwell himself; Act of Six Articles.

1540 Act for Dissolution of Greater Monasteries; Cromwell executed.

1543 *Necessary Doctrine of a Christian Man* written by Henry VIII; Act for Advancement of the True Religion.

1545 Chantries Act transfers ownership of the chantries to the king.

Phase 3: Reforms under Henry's son, Edward VI

1547 Royal Injunctions – preaching in English; chantries dissolved; Act of Six Articles repealed.

1548 Images removed from churches.

1549 First English prayer book.

1550 Act of Uniformity; destruction of images and altars.

How was the Reformation put into practice under Henry VIII?

The Act of Supremacy 1534

The Act of Supremacy in 1534 gave the king specific powers within the Church. He had rights of visitation (to survey the monasteries), the right to discipline and correct preachers, the right to supervise doctrine and the right to try heretics. The Treasons Act made it an offence even to speak against the king or his supremacy of the Church.

The English Bible

The reformers that the Boleyn family had introduced to court persuaded Henry to provide a Bible in English for every church. Erasmus (see page 136) believed that ordinary people should be able to study the Bible in order to build their faith, and Henry agreed with this. However, the clergy had always been the only authority in their churches. If the people could read the Bible for themselves, they might start to challenge the teachings of their priests.

Source 2 The title page of the Coverdale Bible – the first English Bible, printed in 1535. It was based on translations by Wycliffe and Tyndale. At the bottom is an image of Henry VIII on a large throne, surrounded by Church and political advisers. ▼

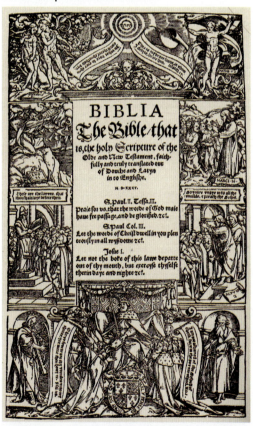

Source 3 Hugh Latimer, bishop of Worcester, strongly criticised the clergy to an assembly of priests and bishops in 1536.

They preach about souls being tormented in purgatory in most need of our help, and have no aid but us in this world. If this doctrine be not false, it is at least ambiguous, uncertain, doubtful and therefore rashly and arrogantly preached to the people. The other [doctrine of images] by all men's opinions, is manifestly false. I could speak of other such counterfeit doctrine.

Reforms slow down

Some historians argue that Henry might have continued on the road of Protestant reform if Anne Boleyn had not fallen from grace in 1536. Henry's second wife had been a strong influence on him in religious matters. The Boleyn family had introduced the king to the works of Simon Fish and William Tyndale, and had encouraged the promotion of reformers such as Cromwell, Cranmer and Latimer.

Henry allowed the Ten Articles to be published in 1536. These laws restricted holy days and the worship of saints and images. The following year *The Institution of the Christian Man* (also known as *The Bishops' Book*) was published. This book, written by a committee of 46 bishops headed by Cranmer, was meant to establish the key features of Henry VIII's Church of England. However, it did not go as far as reformers had hoped.

Despite Henry's anticlericalism, his dislike of the papacy and his disregard for the monasteries, he was deeply devoted to the traditions of the Catholic mass. Recently historians have suggested that Henry had no intention of establishing a Protestant Church in England. Instead he wanted to reform, renew and strengthen a Catholic Church led by him.

1   Study Source 2. Why do you think Henry wanted to include himself on the title page of the Bible with bishops and ministers surrounding him?
2   Read Source 3. What is Latimer so angry about?

Catholic principles restored

In his final years, Henry once again came under the influence of older, more conservative nobles at court. Catholic principles were re-established and traditional practices and beliefs defended. As evidence of this, John Lambert – a Protestant who did not believe in transubstantiation – was executed as a heretic.

In 1539, the Duke of Norfolk and Cuthbert Tunstall, the Bishop of Durham, wrote the Act of the Six Articles. These articles reaffirmed the importance of confession, the value of private masses and belief in transubstantiation. They also said that the clergy should be celibate. These were all things that the reformers had campaigned against. Hugh Latimer and another bishop, Nicholas Shaxton, resigned when the Six Articles were published.

Thomas Cromwell had been one of the most powerful reformers in Henry's court, but he too eventually fell out of favour with the king. A week after Cromwell's execution in July 1540, three leading reformers were burned for heresy. However, it seemed that Henry was trying to show some religious balance, as three Catholic supporters of his first wife, Catherine of Aragon, were burned at the same time.

The Necessary Doctrine and Erudition for Any Christian Man (or *The King's Book*) was published in 1543 to replace the 1537 *Bishops' Book*. Henry himself wrote this to lay out the revised teachings of the Church of England. He reasserted a belief in transubstantiation and rejected the reformist belief in justification by faith alone.

Bishop Stephen Gardiner pressed the king to withdraw the English Bible, claiming that it encouraged dissent. Instead, in 1543 Henry issued the Act for the Advancement of True Religion. This forbade members of the lower classes and all women below the gentry to read the Bible. In 1545, the first Chantries Acts marked the final stage of the dissolution of the monasteries. The act said that the wealth and land of the chantries had been wrongfully donated and would pass to the Crown.

All these measures seem like a turn back towards Catholicism. However, it is important to note that Henry was never going to give up his leadership of the Church. No monasteries or shrines were restored and reformers such as Cranmer kept their positions at court. The king's personal beliefs crucially defined how far Church reform would go.

Source 4 A letter from Henry VIII to Erasmus, c1527.

In the tender years of our youth when we knew you, our enthusiasm for you was intense; and that caused us to diligently study the books you have written, in which you make honourable mention of us. … Now you strenuously excel in promoting and explaining the Christian faith, we desire to assist and provide aid for your very pious and holy endeavours. … For we have for several years, and now feel that very thing; our breast, incited with doubt by the holy spirit, is kindled and inflamed with passion that we should restore the faith and religion of Christ to its pristine dignity … so that the corrupt and unreligious acts of the heretics are shattered, so that the word of God can run freely and purely.

3 Read Source 4. Why is this letter useful to historians studying Henry's motives for reforming the Church?

Source 5 A painting of Archbishop Cranmer by Gerlach Flicke, 1545–46. ▼

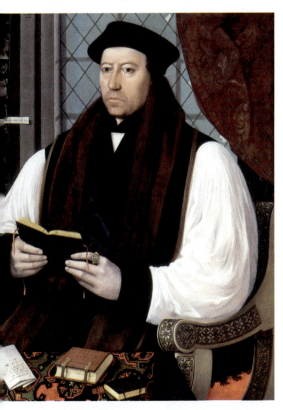

4 Look at Source 5. Why do you think Cranmer wanted books to be included in the painting?

PROFILE

Hugh Latimer (c1485–1555)
- Born c1485, the son of a yeoman.
- Studied at the University of Cambridge.
- Latimer was not influenced by Erasmus, but he did criticise the lack of quality preachers in England.
- He was a talented preacher and decided that there should be an English translation of the Bible to encourage better preaching.
- He criticised absentee bishops.
- He especially hated the amount of money spent on precious idols, feeling that this should be spent on the poor instead.
- Lost favour with Henry VIII because he refused to accept the Six Articles.
- Became a court priest again under Edward VI.
- Executed by Mary I, who wanted to restore Catholicism to England, in 1555.

How was the Reformation put into practice under Edward VI?

When Henry VIII died, his son Edward was only nine years old. Henry granted 12 men the role of adviser to Edward until he reached the age of 18. Somewhat surprisingly, most of these men were Protestant reformers, including their leader the Duke of Somerset, Edward's uncle. Two advisers who stood against any kind of changes to the Church were Bishop Stephen Gardiner and Cuthbert Tunstall, but they were in a minority on the council so their opinions were largely overruled. Somerset began a series of reforms that set the Church back on a more Protestant path. While there was some support for such changes in London, they had little backing elsewhere in England and this was a case of 'change from above' – that is, the government was driving it.

1 Study Source 6. Why is the pope slumped forward at the front?

2 What do you think the message of the painting is?

3 In what ways is this source similar to or different from Source 9 on page 147?

Source 6 An allegorical painting representing Edward VI being handed power by his father, Henry VIII. On the pope's vestment are written 'idolatry' and 'superstition'. The men with their backs to us are the protectors of the old religion. The men facing us towards the back of the painting are Protestant reformers. This was probably painted during Elizabeth I's reign. ▼

Reforms under Somerset

The Royal Injunctions 1547

In July 1547, a series of Royal Injunctions was issued, ordering all clergy to perform their spiritual duties. This was not a particularly radical move. The reformers in the council felt there would be less protest if they introduced changes gradually. In practice, the injunctions meant that the worship of images, the sprinkling of holy water and religious processions were banned. Priests had to read out the doctrine of justification by faith alone (a Lutheran belief) to their congregations. When bishops Stephen Gardiner and Edmund Bonner protested against these measures, they were imprisoned.

The Chantry Act 1547

In 1545, the land and wealth of the chantries had transferred to the king. In 1547, Somerset introduced another Chantry Act, which ordered them to be closed down. There were 2,374 chantries across the country, providing education and practical support for people as well as prayer services. Their closure was a logical extension of the dissolution of the monasteries. Although it was a religious measure – the reformers were against the idea of saying prayers for souls in purgatory – it was also a financial one. The closure of the chantries brought in £600,000. The Crown sold many chantries to private citizens. For example, in 1548 Thomas Bell purchased at least five chantries in Gloucester. The Chantry Act stated that the wealth of the chantries should be used for 'charitable' means and the 'public good'. Some of the dissolved chantries were converted into grammar schools, but most of the money went into the pockets of Edward VI's advisers.

Royal Proclamations 1548

Led by Thomas Cranmer, Edward VI's first parliament pushed the Protestant programme of reform further. Henry VIII's Act of Six Articles was repealed. The Royal Proclamations of 1548 ordered the removal of altars, sculptures and rood screens in all churches. This destruction of holy images and relics is known as ICONOCLASM and it was intended to rid England of its symbols of Catholicism. The proclamations also ended the popular festivals of Candlemas, Ash Wednesday, Palm Sunday and Good Friday. Despite opposition from the House of Lords, a law was passed allowing priests to marry.

Source 7 A letter from Archbishop Thomas Cranmer to all the bishops in England, c1549.

It has come to our knowledge that shrines and monuments remain in various places in our realm, much to the slander of our work and to the great displeasure of Almighty God. They are means to lure people to the old superstitions. We have written this letter expressly to command you, that upon receipt of it, you shall not only search in your cathedral for those things, and if any shrine, covering of shrine, table, monument of miracles or other pilgrimage is found, take it away so that there remains no memory of it … or you will answer for your actions.

4 Read Source 7. What is Cranmer asking the bishops to do?
5 What is the tone of the letter?
6 How is Cranmer enforcing religious reform in England?

The Book of Common Prayer 1549

The most controversial measure that took place under Edward VI was the introduction of the Book of Common Prayer in 1549. Cranmer led the committee that compiled the new book. It was written in English not Latin, but in many other ways it was quite conservative. Once again, Cranmer feared the reaction in parishes across the country if he went too far. It included a service of Holy Communion, but the wording over the sacrament could be interpreted in both Catholic and Protestant ways. The most significant aspect of the new prayer book was not what it included but what it left out. Eight bishops voted against it, but many reformers were equally unhappy, feeling it did not go far enough. Its introduction was widely unpopular, even provoking the Western Rebellion in 1549. Somerset was blamed for this and subsequently removed from power. He was executed in 1552.

Reforms under Northumberland

Somerset's replacement was the Duke of Northumberland, who began an even clearer drive towards Protestantism:

- Laws passed in January 1550 encouraged the defacing of images and abolished old service books, which had to be handed in so they could be destroyed.
- A Second Act of Uniformity required everybody in England to attend church on Sundays. This made it clear that the government was striving for Protestantism, not just reforming the abuses of Catholicism.
- A new, more radical prayer book was issued in 1552. It was deeply controversial but it was only opposed by two bishops and three peers in the House of Lords. By this time, traditionalists such as Bonner, Gardiner and Tunstall had been replaced by more radical thinkers.

Source 8 A painting by Hans Holbein showing Henry VIII as King Solomon – one of the most respected kings in the Bible. The story comes from I Kings 10: 1–13. ▼

Source 10 The front page of *Foxe's Book of Martyrs*, depicting the 'false' religion on the right against the 'true' religion on the left. ▼

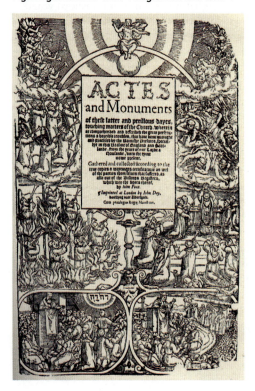

How were these reforms enforced?

Fear

Under Henry VIII: Firstly, the Treasons Act (see page 152) allowed the government to prosecute heretics more easily. Under Henry, Cromwell created policies and ensured that bishops and priests carried them out. His extensive power meant that he had many people working for him. These 'eyes and ears' all over the country created an atmosphere of fear. In addition, Henry VIII wrote to his bishops ordering them to hunt down any clergy who were preaching radical sermons of the 'evangelical' variety and to arrest those who presumed to marry.

Under Edward VI: The Act of Uniformity in 1552 replaced the First Book of Common Prayer with a second. It was an act of heresy not to use this prayer book. Judges were instructed to enforce the use of this prayer book, but this job really fell to the clergy. Although judges could issue punishments if necessary, in reality the government did not want hundreds of people in court on heresy charges, as this might have incited a rebellion. It was largely left up to the priests to persuade people to adopt the new religion. The government paid for a *Book of Homilies* – a series of sermons on key topics – to help clergy encourage the new beliefs. However, the historian Ronald Hutton found that out of the 91 parish churches across the country that he studied, only 19 bought a copy of the *Homilies*.

Source 9 In 1545, Stephen Gardiner heard about a play being performed at the University of Cambridge that mocked Henry VIII's religion. He wrote a letter to the vice-chancellor of the university.

I have heard that the play criticised Lent fasting, all ceremonies and the words of the Sacrament and Mass were not named, yet they were criticised. … if the king is not being obeyed here, how do you think we should punish this rudeness?

Propaganda

The government also used propaganda to convince people to accept religious reforms. Propaganda took a variety of forms. One historian has summarised it this way:

There were official declarations to startle the timid, translations to satisfy the historians, Latin works to influence the educated classes, legal treatises to satisfy the lawyers, tracts preaching the sinfulness of rebellion to keep the religious in line, pamphlets to attract the sensational-minded and even poems to win over the musically inclined.

Radical preachers also produced their own pamphlets and images to help build a 'more godly realm'. They tried to make their message clear and simple, so people who could not read would still understand. Much of the imagery produced at the time is in the form of ALLEGORY – telling a story through images. In fact, most of the sketches and woodcuts from this period that still survive today are anti-Catholic.

1 Study Source 8. Why do you think Henry VIII commissioned this painting?

2 What can Source 9 tell us about how Henry VIII enforced his religious policies?

3 Look at Source 10. What are the elements of the 'true' religion?

4 Compare Sources 1 and 10. According to Foxe, does Henry VIII or Edward VI do more to encourage the 'true religion'?

Impact on the fabric of the Church

Early impact

The first acts of Henry's Reformation, such as the Act of Supremacy, had little real impact on parish churches. The first great alterations came in 1538. Injunctions required every parish to purchase a Bible, extinguish all lights (candles) in the church except those on the altar and to remove any images that had been 'abused with offerings' (people would place candles or gifts in front of images of saints or their shrines). People could no longer worship saints, and relics were banned.

Snuffing out lights was perhaps the most dramatic of these injunctions. In most parish churches a candle had burned continuously for years before the image of a favourite saint. Some saints had as many as 13 constantly burning candles. These were paid for by parishioners and were a folk ritual more than a formal religious practice. The effect of the injunctions was that between 1538 and 1553 only one new image was added to any parish church. However, existing images of saints continued to be washed and repaired as they always had been.

Much more dramatic changes occurred in 1547, a few months after Edward VI became king. Statues, stained glass and church plate were removed, and the brass, pewter and iron was sold. It is said that within three years the 'campaign against saints' had triumphed across the country. In the same period, most church interiors were coated with white lime to cover wall paintings.

The order to remove images in 1550 caused widespread ICONOCLASM. However, many parishioners and clergy wanted to save the relics, statues and paintings of their favourite saints so many were hidden away. Sometimes the faces of the images were scrubbed off, but the rest was left in the church (see Source 11).

The religious changes ordered by Edward VI had to be paid for by local parishes. It was very expensive for a small parish to construct a pulpit and a communion table and to whitewash the walls. Many were forced to sell off chalices and other valuable items to pay for the new requirements.

5 Study Source 11. What has been changed on this painting?

6 Why do you think the people scrubbed out these details? Why did they leave the rest of the image?

7 Look at Source 12. Do you think this represents the destruction of the old religion or the implementation of new ideas?

Source 11 A defaced painting of the Virgin and Child on the fifteenth-century rood screen in Great Snoring, Norfolk. ▼

Source 12 At Binham Priory, Norfolk, the paintings on the rood screen of St Roche and St Mary Magdalen were painted over with text from the 1540 Bible. ▼

Enforcement

During the Reformation, churchwardens often had to meet with representatives of the king and bishops, who instructed and cross-examined them. The churchwardens of Yatton in north Somerset, for example, had to attend visitations in 1547, 1548, 1549 and then report twice to royal commissioners in 1550. The clergy were governed in a way they had never been before, partly because the reformers (rightly) suspected widespread concern about the changes. A study of churchwardens' accounts reveals that many traditional Catholic practices continued until the government forcibly stopped them. Six months after the 1538 injunctions, 80 per cent of churches in three Lincolnshire regions had still not bought an English Bible. However, the threat of a £2 fine encouraged their use and by 1545 most churches had several copies.

The Crown benefited financially from the removal of goods from the churches. The government was therefore even more keen to enforce the new rules. Commissioners were sent to seize linen, chalices, bells, plate, money and jewels. These representatives carried out their job with enthusiasm. For example, the vicar of Morebath in Devon was interrogated four times about the inventory of church goods he had submitted to the Crown.

Effects

The dissolution of the chantries had a devastating effect on the clergy. Many clerical staff lost their jobs. The law to ban the selling of church ales in 1547 also affected many clergy. This ban particularly affected clergy in the West Country, where the ales were an important source of income. The Crown now took the tithes and any profits from the sale of church goods. This meant that parishes lost many sources of revenue.

The majority of the clergy seem to have carried on as best they could, remaining in their posts as local vicars while adapting to the new laws. Few of them chose to confront or resist the government. One major effect, however, was a drop in the numbers of people who chose to join the clergy after the reforms began. In the 1540s no priests were ordained in the dioceses of Chester, Durham and Exeter and only a few in Lichfield, Lincoln and York. Even in the great religious centre of Canterbury there was a drop in the number of serving priests.

> **Source 13** Robert Parkyn was a Yorkshire priest who served through Henry VIII's to Elizabeth I's reign. He kept a chronicle charting the religious changes that were introduced throughout this period.
>
> *In many places of this realm (but especially in the South) neither bread nor water was made holy and spread amongst Christian people on Sundays, and was clearly avoided because it was idolatry. And also the crosses hanging over the altars (wherein was remaining Christ's blessed body) was spitefully cast away as an abominable thing, and were not used as part of the elevation of the host but they villainously despised them, speaking such words that Christian ears should not hear. Only that Christ's mercy is so much it saved them from the earth opening up and swallowing such villainous persons whole.*

1 Read Source 13. Which of the reforms during Edward VI's reign does Parkyn refer to?
2 Which of the reforms does he dislike the most?
3 Read Source 14. Why do you think the friars wrote this chronicle?
4 Do you think the Grey Friars supported the changes they are describing?

> **Source 14** An extract from the *Chronicle of the Grey Friars*.
>
> *Item the very day after in September [1547] began the king's visitation at Powlles, and all images pulled down ... and so all images pulled down throughout England at that time, and all churches new white-limed, with the commandments written on the walls ... the next 17th day of the same month [November] at night was pulled down the Rood in Powlls with Mary and John, with all the images of the Church ... also at the same time was pulled down throughout all the king's dominion in every church all Roods with images. Also this time was much speaking against the sacrament of the altar, that some called in Jack of the box, with diverse and other shameful names; and then was made a proclamation against it, and so continued.*

FOCUS TASK

Positive or negative?

Martin Bucer was a German Protestant reformer who was exiled to England. He said that the English Reformation was too negative. It removed signs of the old 'superstition' but little effort was made to substitute it with a new faith, particularly outside London.

Do you agree with Bucer? Copy the graph below and use it to chart the changes made to the Church of England. Remind yourself what happened in each year shown on the graph. Then decide how important each event was in bringing in new ideas or destroying old ones and write it in the relevant place on the graph.

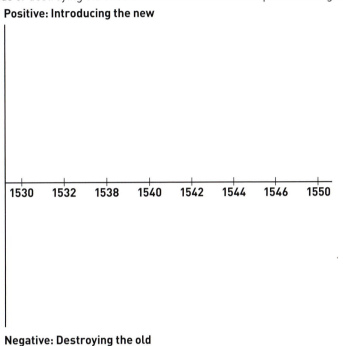

Positive: Introducing the new

1530 1532 1538 1540 1542 1544 1546 1550

Negative: Destroying the old

ACTIVITY

Imagine you work for a TV company that wants to make a 20-minute documentary about the main religious changes between 1534 and 1550. Plan what you would include in each section and decide how long each one will be. The sections are:

● changes to religious practice under Henry VIII, from 1534 onwards
● changes to religious practice under Edward VI
● enforcement of new religious practices
● impact on the fabric of churches.

PRACTICE QUESTIONS

1   Explain how religious reform changed the way people worshipped in the 1530s and 1540s. (10)
2   Explain why there were so many religious reforms between 1534 and 1550. (10)
3   Study Sources 2, 4 and 8. How far do they convince you that religious changes in the 1530s and 1540s were driven by the monarchs themselves?

TOPIC SUMMARY

How was the Reformation put in practice?

1   The Act of Supremacy made Henry head of the Church and gave him many powers to control it. He gradually made more use of these powers over the next 15 years.
2   Until 1536, his reforms were very Protestant (such as translating the Bible into English) but after Anne Boleyn died they became less so.
3   Henry remained emotionally attached to Catholicism and towards the end of his life he began reintroducing traditional ideas.
4   Henry's son had been brought up a Protestant. Despite being only nine years old when he succeeded to the throne, Edward VI had strong religious views and evidence suggests he drove many of the Protestant reforms that took place during his reign.
5   Images and statues were destroyed. Candles were removed from churches. Walls were painted white. A new English prayer book was introduced. It became compulsory to go to church. Chantries were closed.
6   These measures were enforced by a combination of propaganda and fear. Commissioners checked that the churches were doing what they were told.
7   Many churches faced financial crisis because they had lost several sources of income and had been forced to cover the cost of implementing the reforms.

6.2

The reaction of the people to the Reformation

FOCUS

FOCUS

In Topic 6.1, you examined the Reformation from the top down. You investigated what people in government did – how and why they tried to change the Church in England. Now you are going to look at the Reformation from the bottom up. You will consider how far the changes were really implemented and how people in England reacted to them.

This is a much harder task. One problem is evidence: it is difficult to know what ordinary people *did* let alone what they *felt* so many centuries ago. We also have to be careful about making generalisations. People reacted differently in different parts of the country. In some places there was considerable (even armed) resistance. In others there was willing (even enthusiastic) acceptance of the reforms. In most places the clergy and the LAITY simply did what they had to in order to keep their jobs. In this topic, you will examine:

- how ordinary people responded to the Reformation
- what form any resistance took
- why the Western Rebellion broke out in 1549.

FOCUS TASK

How did people in England react to the Reformation?

The historian A. G. Dickens, writing during the 1960s, said that Roman Catholicism was a failing religion by 1500 and therefore people welcomed the religious reforms under Henry VIII and Edward VI.

A more recent historian, Eamon Duffy, has conducted extensive research using local records. He has come to a different conclusion: medieval Catholic beliefs and practices were still strong in many parishes, despite the efforts of the Protestant reformers under Edward VI. Duffy argues that just because people followed the laws does not mean they agreed with them. He concludes that the religious beliefs of most ordinary people only really began to change in Elizabeth I's reign (1558–1603).

As you read through this topic, record evidence that supports each of these views. Use a table like the one below. The first one has been done for you.

Supports Dickens' view that people welcomed religious reform and there was a considerable number of Protestants in England	Supports Duffy's view that people resented religious reform and many tried to hold on to their traditions
Source 1: Edward Hoppaye is clearly a keen Protestant. He refers to justification by faith alone, which was a core belief of evangelicals. He also quotes from the Bible, suggesting he knew and studied it. These were beliefs and practices that the reformers wanted to develop in ordinary people. So this source might support the view that there was a growing population of evangelicals in England by 1548.	

Source 1 The will of Edward Hoppaye of Halifax, 1548.

I believe that my Redeemer liveth, and that the last day I shall arise out of the earth and in my flesh shall see my Saviour. This my hope is laid up in my bosom unto the last day that I and all other faithful shall appear before the majesty seat of God … and touching the wealth of my soul, the faith that I have taken and rehearsed is sufficient, as I believe without any other man's work or works. My belief is there is but one God and one mediator betwixt God and man, which is Jesus Christ … my merit is faith in Jesus Christ only, by which faith such works are good according to Christ words.

1 Read Source 2. What are the rebels concerned about? Write a headline for each of the numbered points.

Source 3 An allegory of the Catholic Church, by Stephen Bateman, in *A Christall Glasse of Christian Reformation*, published in 1569. Bateman was a Protestant preacher and the book that contained this picture was about the Seven Deadly Sins. It shows a remote monastery, with a cardinal riding on a dragon (a symbol of evil and corruption). A monk or priest sacrifices a lamb, which represents the Christian faith. ▼

2 What is the message of Source 3?
3 Does this image convince you that the Reformation worked and that most people supported the religious reforms?

'The Prayer Book Rebellion' 1549

The first demonstration of discontent with the religious reforms under Edward VI took place in Cornwall. It began in April 1548, when a group of men murdered Archdeacon William Body. Body had been carrying out a visitation to the area to make sure that church images had been destroyed. Ten of the ringleaders were hanged and for a while calm was restored.

However, when the Book of Common Prayer was issued in 1549, a full-scale rebellion broke out in Devon and Cornwall. Historians have identified other factors that contributed to the discontent in the region, notably the 'Sheep Tax', but there is no doubt that religious issues were central to the rebellion (see Source 2).

Source 2 Some of the 16 articles written up by the rebels outside Exeter, 1549.

2 *We will have the laws of our sovereign lord King Henry the VIII concerning the six articles, to be articles, to be in use again, as in his time they were.*

3 *We will have the mass in Latin, as was before, and celebrated by the priest without any man or woman communicating with him.*

7 *Images to be set up again in every church and all other ancient old ceremonies and heretofore, by our mother the holy church.*

8 *We will not receive the new service because it is but like a Christmas game, but we will have our old service of matins, mass, evensong and procession in Latin not in English, as it was before. And so we the Cornish men … utterly refuse this new English.*

The rebels demanded a return to the religious practices that had been accepted under Henry VIII. Humphrey Arundell, a major landowner, led the rebels in Cornwall. They marched under the banner of the Five Wounds of Christ, just as rebels had done during the Pilgrimage of Grace in 1536 (see page 163). By June 1549, a considerable force had gathered and the rising spread to Devon.

Sir Peter Carew, a committed reformer, tried to calm the rebels, but when one of his men set fire to the their defences, riots broke out. Around 2,000 rebels marched to Exeter on 10 July and besieged the city. Carew was replaced by Lord Russell, who eventually brought 8,000 men to save Exeter, which he had done by 14 August. He then marched westwards to suppress the rebellion in Cornwall. Around 4,000 people are believed to have died at the hands of the royal army during the fighting that followed.

Special punishment was reserved for the priests who the government believed had stirred up the rebellion. The vicar of St Thomas's Church in Exbridge, Robert Welshe, had refused to use the new Prayer Book and had been one of the leaders of the rebellion. However, he had prevented the rebels from setting fire to Exeter and even his enemies remarked on his honourable behaviour. This did not save him from a grotesque death. Lord Russell ordered that Welshe should be hung in chains from gallows on top of his church, dressed in his Mass vestments and with some Catholic artefacts. To prevent priests like Welshe influencing people in the future, it was ordered that the clergy had to have a licence issued by Archbishop Cranmer before they could preach outside their parish.

This rebellion – the Prayer Book Rebellion or Western Rebellion – was so brutally suppressed that it discouraged others from similar revolts. However, people found other ways of expressing their dissatisfaction, such as local landowners or judges refusing to enforce new laws.

National changes, local responses

The Prayer Book Rebellion underlines a key point about the Reformation. It was not the political aspects of the break from Rome that mattered to the majority of ordinary people. They were most concerned about the effects on their parish church, shrine or monastery and their local services. The rebellion also shows how the progress of the reformation differed from place to place. It might be fairly straightforward for the king and his officials to destroy signs of the old religion, but building a new, Protestant realm would be much more difficult.

London and the south-east

As the largest city in England, and the centre of commerce and government, London was very different from anywhere else in England. This was the place where reformers gathered and radical ideas spread. Southern and eastern parts of England that were close to London, as well as to the universities of Oxford and Cambridge, were more exposed to Protestant ideas. However, statistics suggest that even in London only 17 per cent of the population were 'evangelicals' during the 1540s. Essex came second with 14 per cent, and then Kent with 12 per cent. These figures may not be completely accurate, but they illustrate how the majority of the population remained traditionalists throughout the period of reform. Catholic beliefs seem to have survived among the gentry in Sussex and Norfolk well into the 1570s.

Preachers

One factor determining how people responded to the Reformation was the evangelistic efforts of preachers. For example, Hugh Latimer launched a preaching campaign in Bristol and Matthew Price spread Protestant ideas within the Severn Valley. Powerful and persuasive preaching was often a more effective way of changing people's beliefs than printed propaganda or visitations from government commissioners.

There are several examples of evidence to back this up. The churchwardens of Ramsey in Huntingdonshire (visited by radical preachers from Cambridge) sold their church plate and old painted cloth for 11 shillings. They used this money to pay for scripture to be written up from the new Prayer Book – and they did so before anyone told them to. The nearby parish of Alconbury also sold its chalice for £5 6d and used the money to whitewash the church walls and cover the church with scripture. However, it is worth noting that painting the church would not have cost this much, so someone in the church may well have profited from this action.

> **Source 4** Anne Askew, a Protestant poet, produced an account of her torture in the Tower of London in June 1546. It was smuggled out to her friends.
>
> *Then they did put me on the rack, because I confessed no ladies or gentlemen, to be of my opinion ... the Lord Chancellor and Master Rich took pains to rack me with their own hands, till I was nearly dead. I fainted ... and then they recovered me again. After that I sat two long hours arguing with the Lord Chancellor, upon the bare floor. ... With many flattering words, he tried to persuade me to leave my opinion. ... I said that I would rather die than break my faith.*

1 What can Anne Askew's confession in Source 4 reveal about attitudes towards faith during the 1540s?

◀ **Source 5** A sixteenth-century painting titled *Coronation of King Edward the Sixth, Popery banished True Religion Restored.*

2 Look at Source 5. Do you think the artist supports the religious reforms introduced under Edward VI?

Reaction to the destruction of the Chantries

The dissolution of the chantries after 1547 had a significant impact on ordinary people. At least a quarter of chantry priests had been making important contributions to the care of those in the local community. This was especially the case in the large parishes in northern England. Chantry priests also worked as teachers in both towns and rural areas, so education suffered when the chantries closed.

Some chantries were saved by selling them back to their congregations. At Blackrod and Eccleston in Lancashire, chantry priests refused to surrender their land and the tenants continued to pay rent to the priests. Rent-strikes took place across Lancashire and there are numerous examples of parishioners attempting to conceal chantry lands or equipment from commissioners. By 1560, there were 17 on-going investigations in Lancashire alone, to track down land that was unaccounted for. In Godmanchester in Huntingdonshire, the deeds of two chantries were burned to conceal them from the commissioners. People began to leave money to the poor instead of to chantries.

> 3 Study Source 6. What is the message of this painting?
> 4 Does this convince you that most people were becoming Protestants at this time?

Source 7 Birde Chantry Chapel at Bath Abbey, built in 1515. Prior Holloway surrendered Bath Priory to the Crown in January 1539. It was sold to Humphry Colles of Taunton. The church was stripped of lead, iron and glass and left to decay. Colles sold it to Matthew Colthurst of Wardour Castle in 1543. His son Edmund Colthurst gave the roofless remains of the building to the corporation of Bath in 1572 and it was later restored. ▼

Source 6 An anti-Catholic allegory dating from 1556, depicting Stephen Gardiner, Bishop of Winchester, along with bishops Bonner and Tunstall. They are shown as wolves dressed as sheep to entice Christ's flock – the ordinary people. ▼

Source 8 By the Chantries Act, the Crown had to guarantee a pension to all former chantry priests; however, it drastically reduced the number of people working in many churches. Here a priest writes about how chantry priests were missed.

There was in time past, four Chantry priests daily serving at the said Church of Eccles, which now live abroad at their pleasure, upon their pensions ... over and beside one priest which served at a certain chapel called Ellenbrooke within the said parish of Eccles, which lived upon the devotion of such as used to repair thither, to hear divine service, and there was also at the parish Church of Dean, three stipendary priest that daily served over there ... there is now but two priests to serve the said cure of all the said parish, that is to say one priest commonly called the Vicar of Eccles and the other commonly called the vicar of Deane.

> 5 Look at the information given in Source 7. What can the short history of this chapel reveal about why so few people resisted the dissolution of the chantries?
> 6 Why do you think the people of Bath paid for this chantry's restoration during the 1570s?

> 7 Read Source 8. Do you think the person who wrote this was upset about the dissolution of chantries? What makes you think this?

The fate of church treasures

In March 1551, commissioners ordered all remaining church plate to be taken away and destroyed. Many parishes dutifully sold this off, as well as other treasures, setting aside the money for parish use. By the time they made their visitations, the commissioners found little left to confiscate. Was this evidence that the people accepted the reforms? Historian Eamon Duffy suggests that the reason the clergy and parishioners were so quick to sell the church treasures was actually a 'panic-stricken stampede to avoid theft by the Crown' rather than a sign that they approved of the reforms. The loss of income from parish feasts, masses for the dead and the worship of saints also meant that churches were short of money. They probably needed the income from the sale of these church goods.

However, there are many examples of people simply hiding these treasures. In parishes such as Morebath in Devon, vestments and plate were concealed by parishioners to stop them being confiscated. In Maldon in Essex, parishioners hid the best chalice and saved it from the king's men. In 1550, a gentlemen named William Harris borrowed this chalice and promised to pay the church for it. Yet when Harris died in 1556 he listed the chalice in his will, so he clearly kept it for himself.

Church attendance and giving

The Second Act of Uniformity (1552) openly acknowledged that many people were refusing to attend church services. ABSENTEEISM (non-attendance) was by no means a new practice, but it was now taking place on a much larger scale. There is evidence of some people visiting churches outside their own parishes where they used the old prayer book. Such behaviour represented a statement of rebellion against government policy.

Another measure of how people felt about their church is what they did with their money. Evidence from the north of England shows that before the Reformation, 70 per cent of those who made a will left some money to their parish church. By Edward VI's reign this had fallen to 32 per cent. People did not trust or value the new religion as they had the old. People started leaving money for poor relief instead. Parishioners also seem to have resented the efforts to bring the Eucharist into the service on a weekly basis, because it meant they would have to provide bread and wine much more often.

1 Look at Source 9. Cranmer's commissioners are clearly criticising the parish of Northgate. What do they dislike about the parishioners' religious practices?
2 Does this source prove that most people ignored the changes bought in by Henry VIII?
3 Read Source 10. Why does the clergyman say he robbed the monastery?
4 Does this clergyman's response prove that people did not care about what was happening to the churches?

Source 9 Cranmer's commissioners found that William Kempe, the priest of Northgate, neglected to read the Royal Injunctions of 1547 to his parish, discouraged Bible reading and ignored the command of the Ten Articles to declare the 'right use' of holy water, holy bread and candles.

For lack whereof the most part of the parish be as ignorant in such things as they ever were, and many of them do abuse holy water, insomuch that against tempests of thunder and lightning many run to the church for holy water to cast about their houses to drive away ill spirits and devil, notwithstanding his Majesty's proclamations in the same.

Source 10 Yorkshire clergyman Michael Sherbrook, explaining why he took part in plundering one of the dissolved monasteries.

Might I not as well as others have some profit of the spoil of the abbey? For I did see all would away; and therefore I did as others did.

Reaction of the nobility

The gentry were responsible for keeping peace in the towns and villages. This meant that the king needed their support for religious reforms. Throughout the Reformation, most of the gentry remained loyal to the Crown. If they disagreed, they found a way to practise their own beliefs privately without causing confrontation. However, a few risked their positions (and their lives) to maintain the old religion, including John Scudamore and the Throckmorton family.

John Scudamore

Scudamore rose to prominence under Cromwell. He became MP for Hereford in 1529 but by 1536 he was working for the Court of Augmentations, which oversaw the dissolution of the monasteries. Like many Catholics, Scudamore profited from the dissolution, buying Dore Abbey in 1547 for £379. He continued to work for the government in Wales until his death in 1571. Despite his work for the reformers, though, Scudamore's will reveals that he remained unrepentantly Catholic. He donated much of his wealth to Jesuit priests, who were trying to being Catholicism back to England. He also left many books to students at Oxford University who were known Catholics.

Source 11 *The Ambassadors* by Hans Holbein, the greatest painter of the time. This picture shows Jean de Dinterville and Georges de Selve. The two men seem to be proud and wealthy. The objects on display show the achievements of the modern age. However, once decoded this image becomes a deep criticism of Henry VIII's Reformation. The men asked Holbein to paint them in this way to highlight the dangers of religious divisions. ▼

A hidden silver cross.

The navigational and astronomical instruments are misaligned, to give a sense of impending chaos.

A skull is drawn so that if you stand to the side of the painting, it becomes 3D. This represents the deaths that the artist believes will result from the break with Rome.

The book is open at the 'Veni Sanctus Spiritus', a hymn that was traditionally used to call for the unification of the Church.

5   Study Source 11 closely. What do you think the hidden silver cross represents?
6   Does this source prove that most people were unhappy with Henry's break with Rome?

The Throckmortons

Sir George Throckmorton's (see page 146) estates were in Warwickshire. He grew up in a conventional Catholic family and was a pious man. He went on pilgrimages and paid for masses for his soul from the monks of Evesham, Studley and Warwick, Oxford and Cambridge. He also paid for a chantry to be established in Coughton and funded the education of his tenants' children. He stood up in parliament and spoke against Henry VIII's annulment of his marriage to Catherine of Aragon and met regularly with other known Catholics.

Despite his opposition to the break with Rome and the dissolution of the monasteries, George Throckmorton always demonstrated loyalty to the king. In 1536, during the Pilgrimage of Grace, he mustered 300 men to help defeat the rebels. He was imprisoned several times for meeting with papists, but he never plotted against the king. Throckmorton kept his position as a Justice of the Peace. Edward VI trusted Throckmorton and asked him to carry out inventories of Church assets in Warwickshire and Worcestershire.

Yet Throckmorton's will reveals that despite his loyalty to the Crown, he remained a devout Catholic. He bequeathed his soul to 'Almighty God my maker and redeemer' and hoped to dwell among saints' company in Heaven.

KEY TERMS

Make sure you know what these terms mean and can use them confidently in your writing.
- absenteeism
- allegory
- iconoclasm
- laity

ACTIVITY

Create a spider diagram to record the changes that took place during the 1540s. Use the following headers as starting points:
- The way people worshipped
- The look of churches
- The rituals and feast days.

PRACTICE QUESTIONS

1 Explain the effects of religious change on English parishes in the 1530s and 1540s. (10)
2 Explain why some people resisted religious change in the 1530s and 1540s. (10)
3 Study Sources 5, 10 and 11. How far do they convince you that protests against religious reform were organised by devout Catholics? (20)
4 Study Sources 1, 2 and 9. How far do they convince you that the Reformation was deeply unpopular? (20)

TOPIC SUMMARY

Reactions to the Reformation in English churches

1 Historians have debated the effects of the religious reforms on ordinary people. Most have concluded that the reformers' ideas were slow to take hold, particularly outside London.
2 The closer people were to London the more Protestant they tended to be, but even in these areas support was quite low.
3 The Prayer Book Rebellion of 1549 in Cornwall and Devon was caused by Cranmer's new Book of Common Prayer, which introduced new evangelical ideas.
4 The ruthless treatment of the rebels prevented further outbreaks of resistance but there were more passive ways of resisting the changes, such as hiding church treasures, not going to church or not leaving money to a local church.
5 Many nobles managed to keep hold of their Catholic faith in private while loyally serving the king in public.

ASSESSMENT FOCUS

How the depth study will be assessed

The depth study on the Reformation will be examined in Paper 3, along with the historic environment study on castles. The depth study is worth 40 marks, which is 20 per cent of your total GCSE. You should spend about 45 minutes on this part of the paper. The questions could be on any part of the content so you need to revise it all.

Question 1 will test the first two assessment objectives:
- AO1: knowledge and understanding
- AO2: explanation and analysis.

Question 2 will test AO1 and AO2, but will also test:
- AO3: analyse, evaluate and make use of sources from the time.

Above all, the questions are assessing your ability to think and work like a historian. In the introduction, you looked at how historians work (page 4). There we set out some steps that historians take:

1 focus
2 ask questions
3 select
4 organise
5 fine tune.

The exam questions have already chosen a focus (stage 1) and they have asked questions (stage 2). What the examiner wants from you is stages 3, 4 and 5.

Question 1

Question 1 will ask you to explain an important aspect of the period you have studied. This may involve explaining the range of reasons for an event or development, or explaining the scale of the impact of an event or development. For example:

> ***Explain why the Church was wealthy in the early 1530s. (10 marks)***

Aim of the question
The key word here is 'why'. Examiners are looking for an explanation of *why* the Church was wealthy. It would be easy to miss this point and simply describe *how* the Church was wealthy.

The Question 1 medal ceremony

 Bronze (up to 25% of marks): You describe one or more examples of the role of the Church (e.g. the clergy prayed for the dead or helped the sick).

 Silver (up to 60% of marks): You explain how the Church became wealthy (e.g. people leaving money in their wills).

 Gold (up to 100% of marks): You build on the Silver level to make it clear why the Church became wealthy (e.g. why people left money to the Church in their wills). This will probably involve several reasons.

Even a Gold answer can be improved by ensuring you have:
- a clear conclusion that rounds off your argument
- provided a range of examples as supporting evidence and have included relevant and detailed knowledge in your supporting examples
- a balanced answer that shows you understand that there might be more than one view about the question, or that explains how the different factors are connected.

Advice

Select: Focus on the reasons for the Church's wealth. Select at least two causes.

Organise: The important thing is to organise your knowledge in a relevant way to answer the question. Have a clear sense of what you are trying to say. In this question, a good way to organise your answer might be:

> There were many reasons why the Church was so wealthy in the 1530s. The most important was that the Church was the centre of people's lives and so they gave it money. Another reason was that the Church was very effective in making money.

Fine tune: Do all the usual checking but make sure you say which of your reasons you think is more important.

Example answer

Comments

There is no need to improve this answer – it is a Gold response. It has a clear opening and it then sticks to the line that the opening suggests it will follow. The final sentence is not necessary, but it is a nice ending to the answer.

There is a good analysis of two separate causes. In each case the answer explains how the factor made the Church wealthy. It would be an easy mistake to simply list wills, pilgrimages, etc. without explaining why they made the Church wealthy.

There were many reasons why the Church was so wealthy in the 1530s. The most important was that the Church was the centre of people's lives and so they gave it money. Another reason was that the Church was very effective in making money.

The Church was extremely important in people's lives. Religion was central to everyone's life. One of the main reasons for the wealth of the Church was bequests. Many people, especially wealthy nobles, gave land to the Church during their lifetimes or in their wills when they died, to show their faith and possibly to gain favour with God. Many ordinary people gave donations to the Church to pray for their souls, which would mean that they would go to Heaven more quickly when they died and not have to suffer as long in purgatory. Many people also gave money to the Church because they were grateful. The Church took care of the old and the sick, for example.

The Church was also very wealthy because it was good at making money. One source of wealth was the tithe. This was a tax that all people had to pay and was one-tenth of their annual income, and this went to the Church. The Church also made money out of the sale of indulgences and from pilgrimages. People would travel many miles to shrines like Walsingham or holy places like Canterbury. The Church made money providing accommodation or selling religious artefacts like crosses.

Factors like these made the Church so rich that by around 1530 the Church's income was around 10 times greater than the Crown's.

Practice

There are plenty of practice questions at the end of every topic. Go back and try a couple of the 10-mark 'Explain...' questions. Then read over your answer and see which medal you might award yourself.

Question 2

Question 2 is a challenging question that requires effective use of knowledge and evaluation of sources. There will always be three sources and the question will ask you to explain how far the sources support a particular view. For example:

Study Sources A–C.

'The dissolution of the monasteries was a popular measure.' How far do Sources A–C convince you that this statement is correct? Use the sources and your knowledge to explain your answer. (20 marks)

Note: this question carries an additional 5 marks for effective use of spelling, punctuation and grammar and the use of specialist terminology.

Source A From a report on monastic houses published in 1535. The report was commissioned by King Henry VIII and supervised by the king's chief minister, Thomas Cromwell.

Lichfield: Two of the nuns were with child.

Whitby: Abbot Hexham took a share of the proceeds from piracy.

Bradley: The prior has six children.

Abbotsbury: Abbot wrongfully selling timber.

Pershore: Monks drunk at mass.

Source B From the Act to Suppress the Lesser Houses (the smaller monasteries and convents), 1535.

So much sin and disgusting living is seen daily in the small abbeys, priories, and other religious houses of monks, canons and nuns. This is upsetting to Almighty God and the king. Therefore these small houses will be utterly suppressed. The monks and nuns in them will be moved to the great and honourable monasteries in this realm, where they may be required to improve their lives. The possessions of these houses shall be put to better uses. They will be given to the king and his heirs to honour God and for the good of the realm.

Source C From a letter by Robert Aske, one of the leaders of the Pilgrimage of Grace, 1536.

The closing of the monasteries means that religious services will not be carried out, and the poor will not be looked after. The monasteries are much loved by the people.

Question 2 specialist advice

If you are not careful things could go badly wrong with this question. It asks: 'How far do Sources A–C convince you ...?' It does *not* ask: 'How far do you personally agree with ...?' So you must focus your answer on the sources and relate them to the viewpoint.

Show that you understand what each source is saying. This means comprehension *and* inference. An example of comprehension would be: 'Source A is saying that two nuns were pregnant.' An example of inference would be: 'Source A is saying the monasteries are immoral places.' This is an inference because the source does not say this anywhere. The candidate has inferred what the source's author is really trying to say – similar to working out the message of a propaganda poster or a cartoon.

Relate what the sources say to the view in the question – for example, whether each source convinces you that the statement is right or not.

Examiners often use the 'so what?' test when reading what candidates have written. If you only write 'Source A is saying that two nuns were pregnant' then the examiner will ask, 'So what? What's your point?' You may have thought that it was obvious that the writer disapproves and that this shows how people supported the dissolution, so you did not need to spell it out for the examiner. But you *do* need to spell it out! For example:

> Source A suggests that the statement is right. The author clearly disapproves of what is happening in the monasteries and convents. That is why he mentions the nuns being pregnant and other bad things. This writer would want the dissolution.

Remember – examiners cannot give marks for what you were probably thinking. They can only reward what you actually write.

Evaluate the sources in terms of whether they provide convincing support for the statement. This is partly about judging the reliability of the sources (but remember sources can never be reliable or unreliable in themselves; they can only be reliable or unreliable *about something*) but it is also much more. So in answering this question it is much better to use the words 'convincing' and 'unconvincing' and using a range of tools to help you.

The table below outlines some reasons why a source might be convincing or unconvincing about whether the dissolution was popular.

The Question 2 medal ceremony

 Bronze (up to 25% of marks): You says 'yes' or 'no' and pick out a few details from the sources.

 Silver (up to 60% of marks): You put together a clear argument and support it using the content of the sources.

 Gold (up to 100% of marks): You put together a clear argument and support it using the content of the sources, but you also evaluate the sources in a way that is valid and relevant to your answer.

Evaluation tools	Convincing because ...	Not convincing because ...
knowledge	It is supported by your own knowledge.	It is contradicted by your own knowledge.
author	You know something about the author which makes it convincing.	You know something about the author which makes it unconvincing.
purpose	It has a purpose which you think makes it convincing.	It has a purpose which you think makes it unconvincing.

Advice

Before you start, be sure to read the statement carefully. In the stress of an exam it can be easy to misinterpret it. In this case the statement is that the dissolution was popular. Make sure you are also clear about what the sources say (comprehension and inference).

Select: You need to select facts, events and developments that support or challenge the views in the sources. This question is about whether people supported the dissolution, so select items from this part of your knowledge wardrobe.

Organise: A good way to start this question is to show you understand what the sources are saying at face value and then to go on to evaluate them. This is probably the easiest approach, but you could also organise your answer by setting out the arguments and evidence that the sources are convincing and then setting out the counter-argument.

Fine tune: Do all the usual checking, but here it is worth making sure you used at least two of the three evaluation methods (knowledge, author and purpose). You will get more credit for using knowledge and author than you will for purpose.

Example answer

Comments

This answer is very good – a Gold medal again! It would probably get 17–18 marks. For each source there is a good comprehension and inference working together and related to the statement in the question. Then we have a range of ways in which the sources are evaluated – in relation to the question.

Improvements: Probably the only thing missing from this answer is a conclusion. It would be interesting to see which side of the argument the candidate found more convincing and why.

Source A partly convinces me that the statement is correct. It describes all kinds of bad behaviour by monks and nuns and even an abbot taking a share in the proceeds of piracy. It would have angered people at the time to see monks and nuns behaving so badly, so when the king came along and closed down these bad monasteries it would have been popular. On the other hand, I am not totally convinced by this source because it was from a report produced by Thomas Cromwell. He wanted to reform the Church in England. So it is possible that these reports were untrue or exaggerated to give Henry VIII an excuse to close down the monasteries.

Source B also partly convinces me that the statement is true. It also talks about the bad behaviour of the monks and nuns, so that means that Sources A and B support each other that people were angry about the monasteries. However, many of the MPs who passed this law and the other acts that suppressed the monasteries agreed with Cromwell and Cranmer (the Archbishop of Canterbury) that the English Church needed reforming and that monasteries stood in the way of this. Also, many of the MPs and other rich people in the country ended up owning the lands and wealth of these monasteries. So for them the dissolution would have been a positive measure.

Clearly Source C goes against the statement and convinces me that the dissolution was a very unpopular measure. Robert Aske says that the monasteries were much loved. He also talks about how losing the monasteries hurt the poor. This is an emotive source written by a rebel, but this makes it a reliable source about how some people reacted to the dissolution. Aske was one of the leaders of the Pilgrimage of Grace. This was a massive uprising protesting against the dissolution of the monasteries. Historians estimate that around 40,000 people marched in protest to Lincoln in October 1536, so we can say that Aske was not a one-off troublemaker.

In conclusion, I would say that it could be argued that the statement is true and untrue. The dissolution was popular with some people as we can see from Sources A and B, and from the views of the king and Cromwell and many MPs. On the other hand, Source C and the events of the Pilgrimage of Grace show it was very unpopular.

Practice

There are plenty of practice questions at the end of every topic. Go back and try a couple of the 20-mark source-based questions.

Keys to success

As long as you know the content and have learned how to think, this exam should not be too scary. The keys to success are:

1   Read the question carefully. Sometimes students answer the question they *wish* had been asked rather than the one that has *actually* been asked. So identify the skill focus (what they are asking you to do); do they want you to write a description, an explanation or a comparison? Identify the content focus (what it is about) and select from your knowledge accordingly.

2   Note the marks available. That helps you work out how much time to spend on answering each question. Time is precious – if you spend too long on low-mark questions you will run out of time for the high-mark ones.

3   Plan your answer before you start writing. For essays this is particularly important. The golden rule is: know what you are going to say, then say it clearly and logically.

4   Aim for quality not quantity: in the time limits of an exam you will not be able to write down everything you know. The marker would much rather read a short answer that really tackles the question than page after page of material that is not relevant.

5   Check your work. You will never have time in an exam to rewrite an answer but try to leave some time at the end to check for obvious spelling mistakes, missing words or other writing errors that might cost you marks.

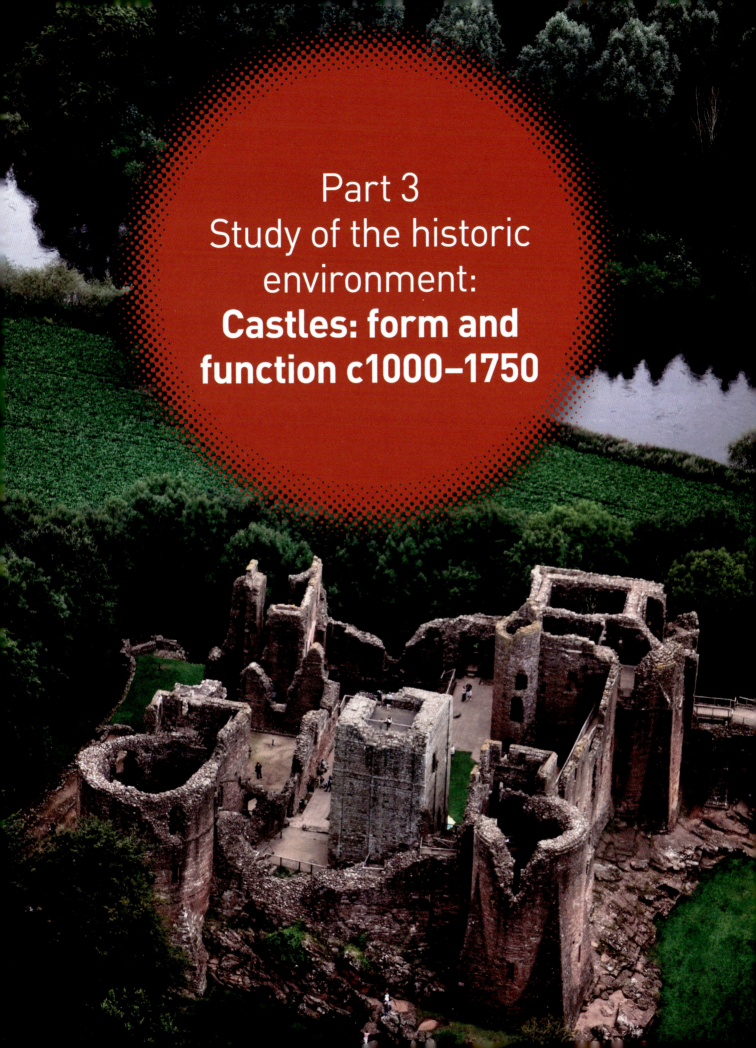

Part 3
Study of the historic environment:
Castles: form and function c1000–1750

Introduction to the study of the historic environment

You will be familiar with using historical sources from your history lessons. You have used many written sources – CHRONICLES, church records, official documents like *Domesday Book* or *Magna Carta*. You have used visual sources from the period you have been studying, and a few photographs and maps. In this study, the aim is to get you using another type of source – the historic environment.

Our focus is on castles, and how historians try to work out their story and that of the people who lived and worked in them. Experts can read castles and other buildings like you can read books or websites. When we put the evidence of buildings together with other evidence such as maps, photographs of the site, documents such as invoices and accounts, or letters to and from the people in the castle, it is possible to build up a detailed and interesting story.

You will be assessed on your knowledge of a key period of the castle – how and why it changed at particular times, for example. However, you will also be assessed on how historians use sources as evidence about the past. Remember – a source is *always* useful as evidence about something!

Countess Joan visits Goodrich Castle, 18 November 1296

Joan de Valence, the recently widowed Countess of Pembroke, spent the winter of 1296–97 at Goodrich Castle in Herefordshire, one of her main residences (see the photo on the previous page). She arrived on 18 November 1296, probably in a coach like the one pictured below. She had about 30 'upper servants' with her, who probably travelled with their families alongside them. Then there were about 15 'lower servants', plus carts (and carters) and pack animals for their luggage. This was a large group – perhaps 120 people.

Lords had their castles built in a particular spot for many reasons. They had to be convenient; they might need to defend an important place; and they needed to demonstrate the wealth and power of their owner (they were, in a way, propaganda in stone). Goodrich dominated an important crossing of the River Wye. The river itself, and the road that crossed it, were very important transport routes. As travellers entered the valley to cross the river, they would have been awed by the sight of the castle on top of the steep west side of the valley.

When Countess Joan's party settled into the castle, this sense of wealth and power probably increased. Four years of rebuilding had made Goodrich a state-of-the-art fortress palace. It had many comfortable rooms for the countess and her guests, as well as a new GREAT HALL and kitchens. Bright paint and tapestries decorated these rooms, which were heated by grand fireplaces. There was a series of large windows, most of which had seats so the countess and her guests could sit in comfort and look at the spectacular views. The first night's meal for this large party required 25 gallons of wine and three pigs.

How do we know all this detail from so long ago? This historic environment study shows you the range of skills and evidence you need to make statements like the ones you have just read.

7.1　How do we know about castles?

FOCUS

Source 1 shows two parts of Goodrich Castle. The keep is the tall, grey, rectangular building. In front of the keep there is another wall, built from a redder stone. Source 2 says the keep was built around 1150 and the outer wall was built around 1300. But how do we know? In this topic, you will learn the skills needed to make plans like Source 2. You will see it is a combination of:

● looking very carefully at what survives – **the stones**
● fitting this into what you know about different fashions in castle-building at different times – **the styles**
● using the surviving documents – **the story**.

There are castles all over England – indeed all over Britain, Europe and the Middle East. People built them, lived in them, changed them and sometimes fought over them for hundreds of years. You can probably look at Source 1 and say it is a castle without ever having seen it before or knowing anything about it. Castles were not simply defensive structures. They were homes, sometimes palaces, centres of administration and a way of displaying power and wealth. In this topic, you will concentrate on Goodrich Castle and the nominated castle (the one in your exam).

A landowner named Godric built the first castle at Goodrich before 1100. There were major changes in about 1150, 1300 and 1450. This is typical of a castle's history. Over a period of 400 years, the needs and ideas of the people who owned and lived in the castle changed. These changes are a big part of the puzzle in trying to work out how people used the castle and why it was built the way it was. For any particular part of the castle, the answer might be different at different times in its history.

The difference between the 1150 and the 1300 buildings at Goodrich is easy to spot. The stone used in 1150 is light grey and is cut in large, rectangular blocks. The 1300 stone is darker and the blocks are smaller. So, it is easy to tell them apart – but how do we know which came first? Styles help here: the KEEP is of the type built in the first hundred years after the Norman Conquest. The wall in front is a CURTAIN WALL, of the type built in the twelfth to fourteenth centuries. So style suggests a date of around 1300, and documents we have available offer a more specific date of 1293–96, when royal workers seem to have helped. The work may have been finished by late 1296, because when Countess Joan visited more than 200 people were living in the castle.

Source 1 Part of the keep and curtain wall at Goodrich Castle. ▼

keep (c1150)

curtain wall (c1300)

Source 2 A phased plan of the same part of Goodrich Castle, showing the approximate dates when parts were built. ▼

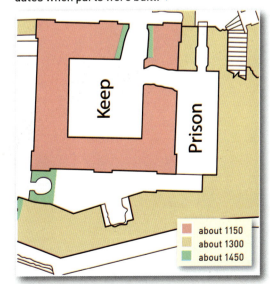

Keep

Prison

about 1150
about 1300
about 1450

Reading a wall

Once you know what to look for, you can read a wall just like you can read a page in this book. We will start by looking at the clues in the stone in Source 3, which show that at different times this area looked like Source 4 and Source 5.

Source 3 The East Range (looking north) of Goodrich Castle. ▼

FACTFILE

Corbels, beams and joists

JOISTS are long timbers that support walls or ceilings. Joists can be fixed to the walls or supported by beams, which are stronger timbers. Working out where the joists or beams joined the wall is the key to working out where the earlier floor levels were.

Corbels (stones that stick out from the wall), or neat holes or grooves to fit the joists into, or ledges to rest them on, are the things to look for.

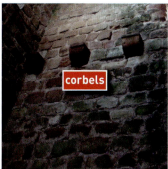
corbels

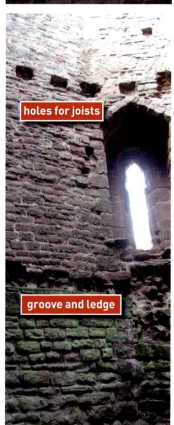
holes for joists

groove and ledge

Source 4 A single-storey hall from the late thirteenth century. ▼

Source 5 A later, three-storey building. ▼

The single-storey building

1 The scar of a roof-line runs diagonally between the two points marked 1 in Source 3. This is where the sloping roof joined the end wall of the (taller) gatehouse.
2 The stones in the outside wall have a gap where the door was.
3 The remains of the fireplace make sense with the floor level.

The three-storey building

4 This is a fireplace, with the chimney going up into the shadow. This means there must have been a floor at this level, and there cannot have been one in the single-storey building. The roof scar would cut through the fireplace.
5 This looks like a door that was cut in the tower after it was built – compare it with the original door (7). This could be an entrance to the same floor as the fireplace.
6 This looks like another door. This is the main evidence for this building having three floors.
8 This is a CORBEL (see Factfile), used to hold up a floor or a roof. It is a bit low to directly support the roof of this building, so the artist in Source 5 has suggested that a BEAM went up from the corbel to support the roof beams.
9 Two square holes have been cut in the wall, probably to fit two roof beams for the top of the ridged roof.
10 Another square hole, larger than the two at point 9. Again, these are probably for a roof beam, but one holding more weight.

An earlier version?

The windows marked 11 and 12, which originally provided light for the gatehouse behind this wall, do not really make sense with either of the buildings above. Window 12 was inside the roof of the single-storey building, which would be dark. The second floor of the three-storey building would cut across window 11 – a sure sign the window was from an earlier stage in the building. So originally, perhaps, there was no building here at all, or one with a lower roof.

FACTFILE

Fireplaces

Fireplaces give you different clues:
- A large fireplace probably means a large room.
- A fireplace with detailed carving probably means a grand room, or a private room for an important person.
- A fireplace is a good guide to where the floor was.

The best way to spot a fireplace is to look for a chimney. In early castles, the fire was often in the centre of the room, with no chimney. But for most of the period you are studying, fires were in fireplaces against the walls, and they had chimneys. In the top photo here, there was a stone hood over the fire and the smoke would have continued up through the top of the hood. In the smaller fireplace, you can see the remains of the start of the chimney going straight up.

Source 6 Inside the south-west tower, Goodrich Castle. ▼

FACTFILE

Doors and windows

Doors and windows are holes in the wall, and will always reveal a lot about the balance between defence and normal life in the part of a castle you are looking at.

For doors, look for evidence of hinges and slots for the locking bar (they confirm it was a door and tell you which side it might be locked from).

For windows, look for the balance between light and safety (see the contrast between pictures a and b). Also look to see how the window is finished internally (b has large windows with window seats – evidence that this was probably a grand room).

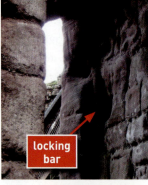
locking bar

Study Source 6.
1. Why is the bottom window so low? (Hint: either because medieval people were very strange or because the floor level has changed over time.)
2. What evidence can you find that there were changes to the tower at various times?

a

hinge

b

FACTFILE

Toilets

With over 200 people living in Goodrich, the castle needed a system for disposing of human waste. Toilets could just be a bucket with a seat, carried out and emptied when needed. But a better solution was to build permanent toilets (often called garderobes) and find a way of transporting the waste outside the castle. Building a toilet out from the top of an outside wall using corbelling was the simplest way (a). The seat was outside the base of the wall and waste simply dropped through. An alternative (b) was to build a toilet in the thickness of the wall, with a shaft running down inside the wall to a cesspit at the bottom. Look for:

● corbelled structures on an outside wall
● very small rooms, with evidence of a seat and a hole underneath it
● shafts through the thickness on the wall (c)
● holes on the outside wall (d) where waste could fall out, or where a child could be sent to climb in and empty the cesspit.

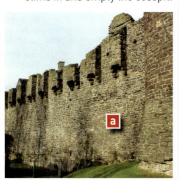

The big questions

When looking at any feature of a castle, there are several important questions you should always ask:

● Was it inside or outside the castle?
● Was it indoors or outdoors?
● What was its purpose – military, administrative, domestic or 'services'?
● Is there evidence that the answer to any of these questions changed during the life of the castle?

We will look at the military and administrative features later in this chapter.

Domestic features to look out for include the following:

● The great hall – a big room for feasts and day-to-day living and eating. Look for evidence of a high ceiling, large windows, a passage to the kitchen at one end, perhaps with two or three doors into the hall, a door and a passage or stairs to the private apartments of the lord and lady of the castle.
● Evidence that these private apartments may have included smaller rooms with high-quality features such as large windows (perhaps with a window seat), the remains of a well-carved fireplace and perhaps a private toilet. You may sometimes find the main private room, called a SOLAR, in plans.
● Castles usually had more than one set of private apartments. Most had a captain or governor who lived there all the time. They would need their own private apartments, as would important guests.

The service features might include a chapel, kitchens, storerooms, a BUTTERY (originally for keeping wine and beer, but later food as well), stables, toilets and a prison.

● Storerooms, the buttery and rooms used as a prison tend to be on the ground floor (or in cellars below). Look for evidence that a door was shut from the outside, and no or small windows.
● Stables would normally be away from the main living accommodation – they could be quite smelly!

Source 7 A part of the plan of Goodrich Castle. ▼

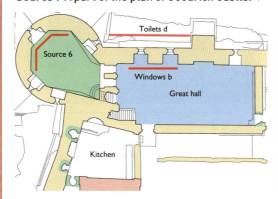

3 The areas shown in three photos showing parts of Goodrich are marked in red on Source 7 (the photos are Windows b, Toilets d and Source 6). What reasons can you find to support Source 7 that the blue not the green area was the great hall?

This photograph was taken looking down at what remains of the top of the north-west wall. Originally the wall was much higher. ▼

FACTFILE

Chapel

The castle community needed somewhere to worship, so castles usually had a church or large chapel. The lord's family might want a smaller private chapel – if so it was normally attached to their private apartments. Look for evidence of:

● a room that had an altar at the east end (sometimes the whole east end of a chapel might be raised a little)

● surviving features such as a sink for washing the vessels used in the mass, and a seat for the priest. The chapel in Goodrich has both, next to each other.

FACTFILE

Kitchens

A castle kitchen was big. It fed a large community. The kitchen was often in a detached building as they sometimes caught fire. Look for evidence of:

● at least one large fire (a) – meat would be roasted on a spit and pans could be held on hooks inside the fireplace.

● ovens for baking bread and pies (b). Medieval ovens were dome-shaped and heated by a fire of dry wood inside the oven.

● possibly a slightly sloping floor and a drain (c).

Source 8 The remains of the kitchen at Goodrich. ▼

1 Source 8 shows the left-hand wall of the kitchen on the plan in Source 9. In what ways do the plan and the photo support the conclusion that it was a kitchen?

Source 9 A plan showing the kitchen at Goodrich. ▼

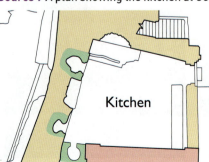

Kitchen

Different styles of castle building

One of the functions of a castle was to resist attack and to provide ways to kill attackers from a position of relative safety. Castle builders – and attackers – were in a 600-year arms race to get the advantage. New methods of attack led to new styles and new features in castle-building. Occasionally, new castles were built in the latest style, but normally it was a case of looking to adapt what was there already to make it stronger through elements in the latest style. Knowing the broad pattern of styles and when they were fashionable is therefore very useful in understanding the development of any castle.

Motte and bailey (c1000–c1150): Common in Normandy before the conquest, the Normans built hundreds of MOTTE and BAILEY castles in the 50 years after 1066. The motte was a large mound of earth with a wooden fence and tower on the top. The bailey was a large enclosure, made by digging a ditch and making a bank with the earth, with a wooden fence on top of the bank. These were cheaper than stone castles and fairly quick to build. They kept a small group of people safe. The problems were that wooden buildings could be attacked with fire, and that wood in earth rots, so eventually they would need rebuilding. In addition, the space on top of the motte was quite small, so living conditions could be cramped. Carisbrooke is a good example of a motte and bailey castle.

Stone keep castles (1066–c1225): From the Norman Conquest, some castles were built from stone, for example the Tower of London. These were much stronger and bigger (and so more convenient to live in), and they stood as symbols of Norman power. There were two main weaknesses. Firstly, they were still rather small for the size of the household and garrison that made use of them. Secondly, it was difficult to kill attackers from a keep. Defence was a passive strategy and these castles were often captured when the people were starved out after a long siege. There were three main types of stone keep castles:

- **Square keeps**' main defensive feature was their massive stone walls, often 5 m thick. The holes in these walls were a weakness. The door was usually on the first floor, reached by an external staircase, and the windows were very small on the lower floors. Square keeps were too heavy to be built on a motte. Good examples include Rochester and Dover.
- **Shell keeps** were built on the top of mottes. The outer wooden fence of a SHELL KEEP was replaced by a stone wall, with rooms built against the inside of this wall. Because it was on top of the motte, the walls were not as thick as in a square keep, but living on top of the motte was still cramped and inconvenient. Carisbrooke and Windsor are good examples.
- **Round keeps** were a later development of square keeps. Some castles were taken when attackers broke through the corners of square keeps, and a round keep avoided this weakness. However, building technology could not make a round keep anywhere near as big as a square one, so they were often too cramped. Pembroke and Conisbrough are good examples.

Curtain wall castles (c1125–c1350): Wooden bailey walls were replaced by stone walls, called curtain walls. A curtain wall castle did not just have a stone wall. It had several of them – with a number of defensive features – usually enclosing a considerable area, which might be divided into more than one bailey. Most castles that existed in this time became curtain wall castles. They could be very large (see the plans on pages 198–99). This solved the problem of not having enough space, and grand buildings could be built in the baileys. However, the size brought its own problem. Defenders needed a very large garrison to hold a wall running all round these large castles. If an attack came at just a couple of points, many of the defending soldiers would not be in a position to join the fighting.

ACTIVITY

1 Make and fill in a data sheet for each style of castle, giving each one a whole page:
   - Motte and bailey
   - Square keep
   - Shell keep
   - Round keep
   - Curtain wall
   - Concentric
   - Courtyard
   - Post-gunpowder
   Use the following sub-headings on each data sheet:
   - Date
   - Description
   - Problems
   - Evidence of style at Goodrich
   - Evidence of style at … [your nominated castle]
2 Create a table for the defensive features on pages 198–200, using the following headings:
   - Description
   - Problems
   - Example at Goodrich
   - Example at … [your nominated castle]
   Note that not every feature may have an entry in the last two columns.
3 Using the internet or resources from your teacher, find pictures or plans for each style and feature. Where possible, choose examples from your nominated castle.

Source 10 A plan of Carisbrooke Castle.

Source 11 A plan of Portchester Castle.

FACTFILE

Defensive features

Merlons and embrasures

MERLONS (a) and EMBRASURES (b) were cheap, but not much good. The defender was safe behind the merlon, but to look out or shoot, he would need to be in the embrasure, which would make him a good target. Embrasures could be fitted with shutters (c). Look for evidence of slots or holes for the axle.

Bratticing

Attackers were most dangerous at the foot of the wall – and to see that far down defenders had to lean a long way out – making them a good target. BRATTICING (d) was a wooden extension built out from the top of the wall. It offered much more protection. Look for evidence of a line of holes or corbels near the top of the wall for the beams to go through. Bratticing needed a lot of maintenance, and could be set on fire or smashed by large catapults.

Machicolations

Machicolations replaced bratticing with stone, corbelled out from the wall (e and f). They were expensive but stronger.

Source 12 A plan of Carlisle Castle.

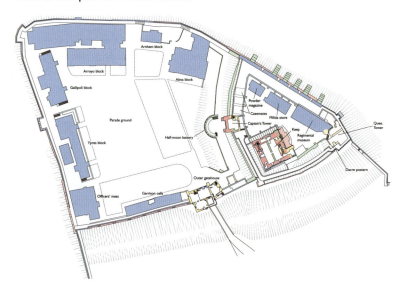

Source 13 A plan of Framlingham Castle.

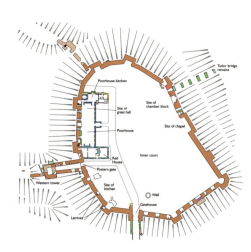

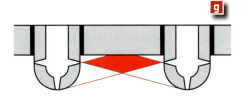

Towers and flanking fire

Fire from the side (FLANKING FIRE) was the best way to defend the base of the wall. Towers, sticking out from the wall, were the answer (g).

Barbicans

Castle designers created KILLING GROUNDS, crowding attackers together to make them an easy target. The entrance would always be a weak point because people needed to use it easily most of the time (when the castle was not being besieged), but they also needed to make it as safe as possible in case the castle was attacked. We call the defences of an entrance a BARBICAN. You can see them at all the castles except Stokesay on this page (Carlisle is hard to spot). At Goodrich, attackers were concentrated on two causeways then filed through a narrow tunnel (with 'murder holes' in the ceiling). Drawbridges, gates and portcullises slowed them down. It was a complex killing ground with well-protected firing places.

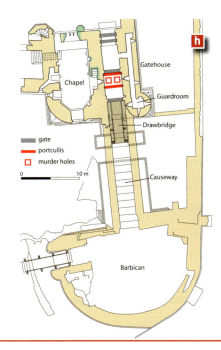

gate
portcullis
murder holes

0   10 m

Gatehouse
Chapel
Guardroom
Drawbridge
Causeway
Barbican

Source 14 A plan of Goodrich Castle.

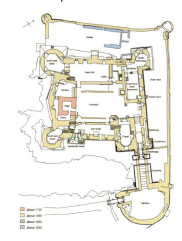

about 1150
about 1300
about 1450
about 1650

Source 15 A plan of Stokesay Castle.

1   All these castle plans are to the same scale. What questions about these seven castles do their different sizes make you want to ask?

2   Compare the plan of your nominated castle on this page with the phased plan on pages 220–29. When was each of the styles used in your specified castle?

Source 16 A plan of Kenilworth Castle.

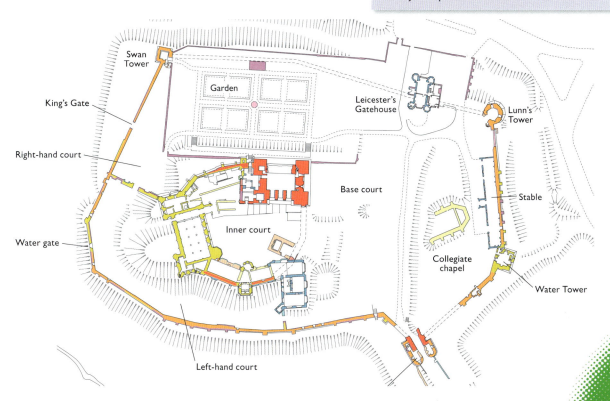

Swan Tower
King's Gate
Garden
Leicester's Gatehouse
Lunn's Tower
Right-hand court
Base court
Stable
Inner court
Water gate
Collegiate chapel
Water Tower
Left-hand court

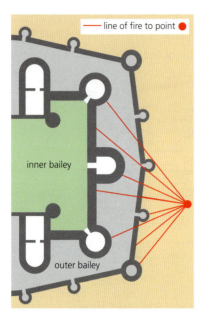

line of fire to point ●

inner bailey

outer bailey

How a concentric castle concentrates fire on any point.

Castles c1200–c1500

Concentric castles (c1200–c1350) had at least two curtain walls, one inside the other, with the inner wall much taller than the outer wall. The idea was to concentrate firepower – wherever the castle was attacked from, many defenders could shoot. Should attackers break though the outer wall, they would be concentrated together in the small space between the outer and inner baileys, which became a good killing ground. Beaumaris is a good example of a concentric castle built from scratch, but many castles developed a concentric element by building a shorter outer wall or a taller inner one. Dover and Goodrich show this development.

Gunpowder was first used in the fourteenth century, but to begin with it did not have much impact on castle design. It gave the defenders a new weapon and gun loops began to be added, especially to barbicans. Queenborough Castle (built 1361–77) was the first castle with cannon planned into its defences. In 1405, Henry IV captured three powerful castles – Berwick, Alnwick and Warkworth – using siege cannon. The balance of power was shifting, and by the middle of the century it had shifted decisively – using cannon, the French captured 60 English castles in France in one year.

Courtyard castles (c1370–1500): There were not many new castles in this period, but those there were tend to be smaller and to move the balance more towards comfort and convenience and away from defence. They were usually built around courtyards (smaller than the earlier baileys). The outside wall of the living space was also the outside wall of the castle. Such castles provided status and relative safety for less money, both in terms of building and running costs. Bolton and Raglan are good examples. In existing castles, this style can been seen in more lean-to buildings against the inside of the curtain walls.

Post-gunpowder castles c1500–c1650

Medieval castles had been tall and thin. Defences against gunpowder needed to be short and fat. Stone walls were shattered by the force of cannon balls. The answer was low walls (which were harder to hit) and then walls filled with earth (which absorbed the impact of the ball). To use cannon as part of the defence also required thick walls – cannon recoil and need space. In the 1530s, Henry VIII built a series of castles to use cannon to protect the south coast from possible invasion. Later, some castles were given new earth-wall defences, some as late as the Civil Wars (1642–51). Many castles were besieged during this time and, because they had shown some military value, some were 'slighted' (made indefensible) or completely destroyed afterwards.

No medieval castle could withstand developments in ARTILLERY after 1650, and castles that continued to have a military function relied on new defences. Most developed into grand homes or were abandoned. When the Duke of Marlborough won the Battle of Blenheim in 1704, his grateful nation built him not a castle, but a palace (Blenheim Palace, built 1705–33).

Source 17 A description of the wooden tower on top of the motte at Ardres, from a chronicle written about 1194. The motte was destroyed in 1855, so we do not know how big it was, but it was much larger than Abinger (Source 18).

On the ground floor were cellars and granaries, and great boxes, barrels, casks, and other domestic utensils. On the first floor were the living rooms, the rooms of the bakers and butlers, and the Great Chamber in which the Lord and his wife slept. Next to this was the dormitory of the waiting maids and children. In the inner part of the Great Chamber was a certain private room, where at early dawn, or in the evening, or during sickness, or for warming the maids and weaned children, they used to have a fire. On the upper floor were garret rooms in which, on the one side the sons (when they wished) and on the other side the daughters (because they were obliged) of the Lord of the House used to sleep. On this floor also the watchmen appointed to guard the house took their sleep. High up on the east side of the house was the chapel. There were stairs and passages from floor to floor, from the house into the kitchen, and from room to room.

1. Use Source 17 to make a possible plan for each of the three floors of the tower at Ardres. There is no right answer, because we do not know, but the best answers fit in everything the source tells you, use other knowledge about castles and interpret the source with common sense.
2. Using all three sources, explain what you would expect to find on top of the motte in a motte and bailey castle.
3. What are the strengths and weaknesses of each type of source?
4. Which source is most useful for answering the question of what was on top of a motte?

Using sources to tell the story of the castle

Historians use a range of sources to discover the story of a castle. Below are some of the different types of sources and the questions they can help us answer.

What was on the top of a motte?

Archaeology: Source 18 allows us to see what size and shape the buildings on the top of this motte were.

Chronicles: The history people wrote for themselves in medieval times sometimes includes descriptions (Source 17, which tells us things archaeology cannot).

Art: The art of the past can add to our picture. Source 19 shows a motte, with what is probably a wooden fence around the top (they are trying to set it on fire), and it shows a tower inside that fence.

Using the range of sources, we can see that sometimes they agree with each other – for example, Sources 17 and 19 on the fence around the top of the motte and the tower inside it. Each also brings something unique to help build our answer to the question.

Source 18 An archaeologist's plan of the top of the motte at Abinger. The marks show where wooden posts had been.

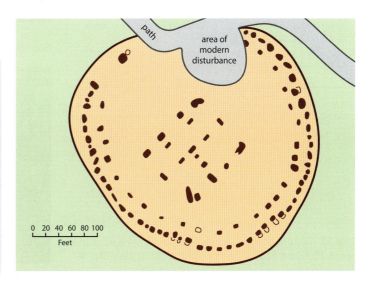

Source 19 A picture of an attack on a motte and bailey castle at Dinan, from the Bayeux Tapestry, made in the 1070s.

FACTFILE

Joan de Valence: 172 days at Goodrich Castle

Joan de Valence, who owned Goodrich, travelled between her different properties with a household of 50 or 60 people. During the visit to Goodrich:

● they drank about 25 gallons of wine and 60 gallons of beer a day; wine was bought in Bristol and beer in Monmouth as the castle's own brewery couldn't make enough

● they brought corn to bake bread from the surrounding area

● woodcutters on Joan's estates did 212 days' work cutting wood to heat the castle and cook the food, and 130 horses and a boat were used to bring the wood to the castle

● eleven important nobles visited Joan while she was at Goodrich – each would have brought their own household

● they ate 13,300 herrings during Lent (the six weeks before Easter)

● the Christmas Day feast involved 1½ beef cattle, 2 pigs, 12 ducks, 18 chickens, 2 peacocks, cheese, eggs and fish for those who would not eat meat for religious reasons

● she gave food for 20 poor people a day (and 61 on St Catherine's day)

● she sent a number of business letters, and employed a messenger to take them; London and her lands in Kent were a 12-day round trip for him

● a servant went to Bristol to buy new white robes for the entire household for Whitsun (six weeks after Easter).

1 What effect would a visit from Joan have on the castle?
2 What effect would a visit from Joan have on the surrounding area?
3 Make a sketch of the plan of the kitchen at Goodrich (see page 196). Mark on the fire and ovens.
4 How do these sources help you have a better answer than when you just had the plan and photo?

Source 22 The lord and his guests feasting, from a book made between 1320 and 1345 with many paintings of daily life. ▼

How did a lord live in a castle?

Private papers: These sometimes survive, like one small part of the papers of Joan de Valence. These enable us to find out about her time at Goodrich in 1296–97.

Art: This shows us, for example, a feast in the great hall, the fire cooks used, as well as what a baker's oven looked like in use.

Put this together with the plan and remains at Goodrich and it becomes clear that the archaeological evidence is actually the ghosts of a fireplace and an oven, which strongly suggests this is a kitchen.

Source 20 Cooks roasting fowl in front of the fire, from the same book as Source 22. ▼

Source 21 A medieval baker putting bread in the oven. ▼

Source 23 From the statutes of Dover Castle, made between 1265 and 1298.

I At sunset the bridge shall be drawn, and the gates shut; afterwards the guard shall be mounted by twenty warders on the castle walls.

II Any warder found outside the walls, or otherwise off his guard, shall be put in the Donjon prison, and punished besides in body and goods at the Constable's discretion.

IV It is established by ancient rule that if a chief guard discover a warder asleep, he shall take something from him as he lies ... or cut a piece out of part of his clothes, to witness against him in case the warder should deny having been asleep, and he shall lose his day's wage, viz 2d.

VI Either sergeant or warder using vile language shall be brought before the Constable, who shall have the matter considered. ... He who was in the wrong shall lose his day's pay – if the Constable so wills.

Source 24 Royal Orders for Carlisle Castle, 1316.

1 April: To John de Castre, constable of the castle of Carlisle. The king is sending John de Castre's messenger back with 200 marks to be used to govern the castle and town.

25 June: To John de Castre, he is to appoint lawful men to survey all the king's stores held by John de Bromleye, and give the stores and the list to Robert de Barton, whom the king has appointed keeper of his stores in the area. Bromleye has not handed over the stores as he was told, and may have disappeared.

28 September: To the sheriff of Cumberland, to spend 10 marks on repairing the houses and walls of Carlisle castle.

23 November: To the tax collectors of the North Riding of Yorkshire, to pay £82.54 to Andrew de Harkla as he is owed money for his ransom from the Scots and for wages for himself and his men for garrisoning the castle at Carlisle.

The same to the tax collectors of the East Riding for £300.

The same to the tax collectors of the West Riding for £200.

5 What does Source 23 suggest were the problems the constable of Dover Castle worried about?
6 List the things you can learn about Carlisle Castle from Source 24.
7 Does Source 25 prove more work was done on the Welsh castles in 1282 than in 1283?
8 Which of these sources is more useful for:
   a studying life in a castle?
   b understanding how royal castles were used?

Why do we know more about royal castles?

Just like the government today, the government in medieval times had lots of administrators – and they created a lot of records. The king's ministers sent orders to local government and to the constables of royal castles. Detailed accounts were kept showing how money was spent, and these accounts were sent back to London to be checked. Many of them survive today.

Legal documents: These were important at the time so they were kept carefully. They usually record the transfer of land, but Source 23 is unusual. It is a charter listing the statutes of Dover Castle – the rules for the garrison.

Orders: Orders issued from the government – copies of which were kept in London – tell us a lot about the day-to-day running of castles, for example when money was spent for repairs or how they were garrisoned. Source 24 just picks out the orders for Carlisle Castle for one year, but hundreds of years of these documents survive.

Accounts: These are the lifeblood of government. Edward I built a series of mighty castles in Wales during his wars of conquest. Source 25 summarises what we can discover from the accounts of the building of these castles. The king took skilled and unskilled workers from all over England to work on this massive castle-building programme.

Castles owned by Joan de Valence probably generated almost as many orders and accounts as a royal castle, but they have been lost. Government records are more likely to survive.

Source 25 A map summarising the data in the royal accounts about the workers used on the Welsh castles, 1282–83. ▼

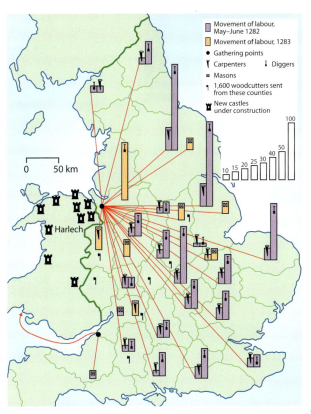

203

Source 26 The phased plan and remains of part of the kitchen at Goodrich Castle. ▼

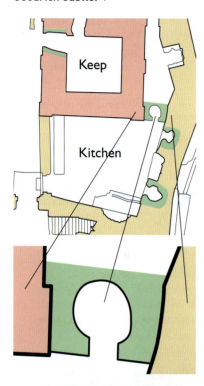

This topic has concentrated on what you can learn from the stones, the styles and the story. Your study of castles requires you to concentrate on your nominated castle as well as having a good general understanding of the subject.

You will need more information about your nominated castle. The castle factfiles on pages 220–29 give you the key information to start you off – a copy of the phased plan, a view of the site today, information about its major events and a photo with evidence from the site.

1   Using materials from your teacher or an internet search for images of your castle, find photographs of parts of the castle that the phased plan says were built in different times. Source 26 on this page is another example. The starting point is the phased plan of the kitchen next to the keep. One small section of this plan has been enlarged and placed next to a photograph that shows the remains at this point. The keep (peach on the plan) has large rectangular stones. The oven (green on the plan) has stones that are smaller, a different colour and irregular.
    Find and explain at least three examples like this for your nominated castle.
2   Using the factfile, make a timeline of the main events in the story of your castle.

TOPIC SUMMARY

How do we know about castles?

1   Historians have to work out a lot about the use and development of a castle from the remains as they are today.
2   Corbels, grooves, ledges and holes for beams are all evidence of where a floor or a roof might have been.
3   Fireplaces, doors and windows are all good clues about where floors were, and also about the social status of the people who used the room.
4   Toilets could just be a bucket with a seat, but later they were usually built-in and can be spotted by the remains of a seat over a shaft or a hole.
5   Most castles had chapels – they often had a small sink and/or a seat cut into a wall.
6   Kitchens were usually in a separate building because of the fire risk. Evidence includes very large fireplaces (a lot of cooking was over an open fire) and bread ovens.
7   Most castles started as motte and bailey castles, built from earth and wood.
8   Many castles had stone keeps added between c1070 and c1225.
9   Curtain wall castles (c1125–c1350) could be very large, with strong walls and additional defensive features.
10 Concentric castles (c1200–c1350) had higher walls and towers inside shorter outer walls to maximise firepower.
11 Siege cannon were first effective in about 1400 and by 1450 they could destroy any existing castle wall in time.
12 Courtyard castles (c1370–1500) were smaller and more comfortable. After siege cannon, it was hard for any castle to survive a determined siege.
13 Post–gunpowder castles (c1500–c1650) had low, thick walls, usually filled with earth.
14 Chronicles were history books written in medieval times, usually describing the recent past. They have stories of sieges and some descriptions of castles.
15 Private and state records, such as accounts, give us evidence of life in castles.

7.2 The functions of a castle

FACTFILE

The development of Goodrich

c1070–c1125 Motte and bailey castle built by Godric.

c1125–50 Goodrich was close to the Welsh border, and raids into England were common. The stone keep was built.

1138–1247 Goodrich owned by powerful nobles who did not live there. A constable controlled the castle, which was home to a small community and garrison.

1216 Goodrich was besieged by the Welsh, but quickly relieved by English troops.

1247–1327 Goodrich owned by the de Valence family – major landowners who moved between various castles. Major works included a new curtain wall and much grander domestic buildings.

1277–95 Wales was conquered by Edward I in a series of wars and the border was strategically important.

1327–1421 Goodrich was owned by another powerful family, which spent less time there but strengthened the barbican, rebuilt the chapel and added a prison.

FOCUS TASK

What were the functions of a castle?

The table below lists the functions of a castle that are covered in this topic. Fill in the information below the heading 'Type' for Goodrich Castle and your nominated castle. Return to this table and fill in the information as you read about each function.

The functions of a castle	
Goodrich Castle	**Nominated castle**
Type (royal or baronial)	
Goodrich was first built as a baronial castle, but in 1176 …	e.g. *First built by King William II in 1092, Carlisle was a royal castle …*
Site	
Protection	
Power base	
Living and working	
Defensive	
Later uses	

Royal and baronial castles

An easy distinction to make is between a ROYAL CASTLE, controlled by the monarch, and a BARONIAL CASTLE, controlled by one of their subjects. It is an important distinction, and more documentary evidence survives about royal castles. So, why were some castles royal? The main reason is that they guarded (or dominated) strategically important places. The Tower of London was always a royal castle, and it dominated London. Dover (guarding the most important channel crossing) and Carlisle (guarding the western end of the border with Scotland) were always royal castles. Others became royal castles for short periods. There were two main reasons for this:

- **Lack of an heir:** Goodrich was a royal castle between 1176 and 1204, because the owner died without an heir and it was only 28 years later that the king granted it to a new lord. Kenilworth also became a royal castle when the owner died in 1174. This was a time of civil war and the king, Henry II, decided it was strategically important so he garrisoned and strengthened it. Kenilworth remained a royal castle for 70 years and there was significant rebuilding in this time.
- **Confiscation:** Sometimes the monarch simply seized control of a castle, if its owner had been charged with treason, perhaps, or because it seemed strategically too important to leave in private hands. Henry II took Portchester in 1154 for strategic reasons. He ruled lands on both sides of the Channel and Portchester dominated a major cross–Channel harbour. It remained a royal castle.

FACTFILE

London's three castles

The castles built in London just after the Norman Conquest provide evidence that there was no great master plan for castle-building in England. As well as the Tower of London – the royal castle on the eastern edge of the city – there were two baronial castles, Baynard's Castle and Montfichet Tower. These were both in the west of the city and stood right next to each other!

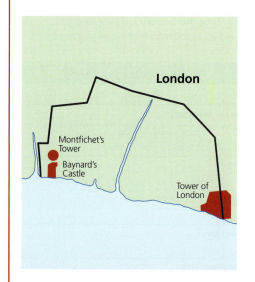

Montfichet's Tower was demolished in 1213. The original Castle Baynard was torn town before 1276 and a replacement built to the east of the site shown on the map. This castle was destroyed by fire in 1428 and rebuilt by the Duke of Gloucester as his London palace. The Great Fire of London (1666) destroyed this third Baynard's Castle.

Baynard's Castle in 1647.

Not all barons were equally rich and powerful, and not all baronial castles were the same. The plans on pages 198–99 show the difference in size of some of them. Stokesay, for example, was as much a fortified house as it was a castle. We would call Lawrence of Ludlow – who bought the manor in 1270 – a businessman. He was one of the richest men in the country and he wanted to keep both his family and his wealth safe. The years from 1250 to 1325 were a time of growing lawlessness and unrest. Taxes were high, harvests often poor and crime increasing. Stokesay was one of many new, smaller castles built in this period. They were not strong enough to hold out against a major siege, but they would keep the inhabitants safe from thieves or a peasant uprising.

At the other end of the scale, Framlingham and Kenilworth (from 1266 to 1399) were owned by powerful nobles who wanted large castles – part palace and part military stronghold. Just as the greatest nobles attended the king at his court, so the lesser nobles and knights would attend their lord in his castle. The castle therefore must be grand – reflecting the power and prestige of its owner. The great hall, where meals were taken and formal business often conducted, needed to be large and richly decorated. There must be accommodation for important guests and their followers. These castles also needed to be strong enough to withstand a major siege.

The site of the castle

There are nearly 2,000 castle sites in England and Wales. They were not built to any national master plan to make the country stronger. Some royal castles were built for strategic reasons immediately after the Norman Conquest, but individual lords built most castles wherever they wanted to on their lands.

Castle-building took place from the 1050s through to the 1540s, but there were some periods when many were built in a short time:

- in the first 40 years after the Norman Conquest (including Goodrich, Carlisle, Framlingham and Portchester)
- during the civil wars in the reigns of Stephen and Matilda (1135–54); the next king, Henry II, destroyed many of these when he restored order
- from the late thirteenth century and through the fourteenth century, when trade and the profits of war with France made wider groups of people wealthy (Stokesay is in this group).

In the first 40 years after the conquest, many castles were built in towns and, symbolically, existing houses were often torn down to make room. For example, in Lincoln 166 of the 970 houses in the town were torn down. Most of these town castles were royal castles. Later medieval towns often grew up around castles that had been built on rural sites. The castles provided security and a ready market of wealthy people.

The first builder of any castle had to answer two key questions:

- Where on my estate, roughly, do I want my castle?
- Once the area has been decided, which is the best exact spot to build on?

There were different criteria for each decision. After the conquest, Norman lords were given large tracts of land, often a day's ride across. This land included villages and perhaps even small towns. The most important factors in deciding where in this land the castle might go were:

- **Strategic:** Was there an important river crossing or harbour to protect?
- **Communications:** From the castle, it would ideally be possible to get to all the important parts of the lord's estate and back within a day. Also, it should be reasonably convenient for a lord to get from his lands to other parts of the country that he may need to travel to.
- **Administration:** The castle would be the base for governing the area, collecting taxes and administering justice.
- **Economic:** Whether the wealth came from towns and trade or from farming, it was useful to be able to protect the economically significant parts of the territory.

Once the castle builder had decided on the general site, he had to home in on the specific spot for his castle. It is a mistake to think that most castles were built on hills. People lived in the castle all year round so being positioned high on a hill was not the most convenient location. Castles were rarely (if ever) attacked, so defence was not always the most important consideration. Obviously, the castle had to have a good water supply, both in case of attack and for convenience. The castle was usually much the tallest building in the area. This was significant for two reasons. It gave the garrison a good field of view, so they could see any threats a long way off. It also meant the castle could be seen from a large area – underlining the importance of the lord. Castle builders took care over the views of the castle people had as they approached it, going as far as moving roads or creating artificial lakes to make the castle look more impressive at first sight.

Protection

The Normans believed that castles did not just protect the people inside them; they protected the whole country. The lack of castles in Saxon England was one of the reasons they believed their conquest succeeded. The diagram shows what they thought. When you invaded a country, it would be dangerous to ignore enemy castles. The reason for this is the garrisons could come out once your army had passed and disrupt your communications back home. They could capture messages and supplies. The alternative, then, was to either besiege and capture every castle on the way, or leave enough troops behind to besiege each castle to keep the garrison inside. If you did the first, you advanced very slowly, and your enemy had time to gather a larger army. If you did the second, your army got smaller each time you left troops besieging a castle. This is what is shown in the diagram – how an attacking army nearly twice the size of the defending army could be brought down to the same size by the time they gave battle because of the number of troops left to besiege castles.

ACTIVITY

Draw a grid like the one below and give each factor a mark out of 10 for each of the three suggested sites.

	A	B	C
strategic			
communications			
administration			
economic			
Total			

Legend:
- Possible castle site
- Town
- Hills
- Best farming land
- Main roads
- Major trade routes

How castles made a country safer from invasion.

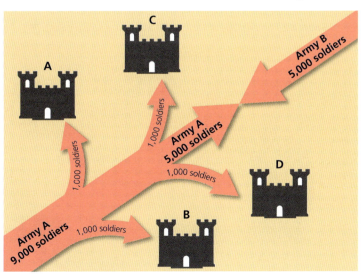

Henry VIII's coastal castles

Between 1539 and 1545, Henry VIII built a specialist group of castles. They were designed with one function in mind: to protect the country from invasion by installing cannon in castles positioned where a potential invasion fleet might land. These castles were built to be garrisoned by soldiers; there was no grand accommodation for a lord.

Source 1 A plan of Raglan Castle. All this was built after 1435. ▼

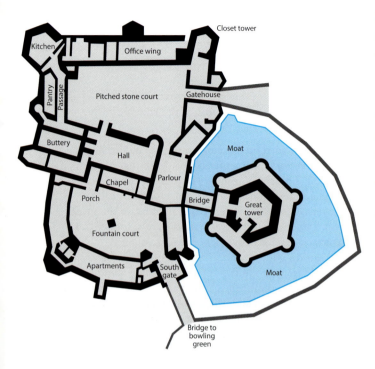

Protecting those inside the castle

Protecting those inside from those outside has been the most obvious function of a castle since the first motte and bailey castles. All the complicated defensive systems of curtain walls, flanking fire, MACHICOLATIONS and barbicans are just ways of keeping the people inside safe by making it easier to kill those outside.

Raglan Castle offers an interesting refinement in keeping people safe. The oldest part of the castle was built around 1435, yet it has a building that looks like a keep – and the mid-fifteenth century is too late for castle designers to build a keep. The Great Tower is a FINAL REFUGE, separated from the rest of the castle (and from the outside world) by a moat. It could be defended against the rest of the castle. There could be two reasons for this:

- It provided a final refuge for what remained of the garrison if the rest of the castle fell to the enemy.
- It provided a place for the lord's family and most trusted followers in the event that the garrison turned on the lord.

The idea of creating a final refuge was not new. Castle designers had been using it since motte and baileys. If attackers captured the bailey, the defenders could retreat to the motte. The fifteenth century was a dangerous time. It began with the overthrow and later murder of Richard II and in 1455–87 there was a series of civil wars. Perhaps these events influenced the designers of Raglan to make the final refuge just a little bit safer from the rest of the castle?

> 1 'Source 2 proves that Henry VIII thought invasion was a real threat in the years 1539–45.' Do you agree?
> 2 Look back at the plans of Goodrich and your nominated castle. Can you find a final refuge in each one?

Source 2 The castles of Henry VIII along the south coast. ▼

Power and symbolism

Castles provided a power base. In a castle, a lord (or constable) would have soldiers and the castle kept them relatively safe. Their power stretched at least half a day's ride or march. There was no police force and for most of the time, no army. The lord's soldiers enforced the law and kept the area safe. All but the most serious crimes were tried in the lord's court, inside the castle. The castle, therefore, was the centre of both actual and legal power.

The castle was symbolic too. After the Norman Conquest, many castles were built where the previous Anglo-Saxon lord had lived. This emphasised how new people and customs had replaced the old. However, it also gave a sense of continuity: people would pay their taxes and come for justice to the same place.

At a time when most people lived in simple houses made from wood with a thatched roof, the multi-storey castles – usually made from stone – underlined the wealth, the power and the separateness of the upper classes. One way of emphasising this was to paint the outside of the castle. For example, the keep of the Tower of London is known as the White Tower because the outside was painted white to make it look more magnificent. Instructions from Henry III survive to whitewash the outside of the keeps of Corfe and Rochester castles, and to mend the gutters of the White Tower to stop rainwater spoiling the whitewash.

Castle owners also wanted to show off to each other. Changing a castle by adding the latest features was a good way to show wealth and good taste. Men rising up the social scale, like Lawrence of Ludlow (who built Stokesay), built a castle as a way of demonstrating their new position and prestige.

Kings could use castles for symbolic and military reasons at the same time. When Edward I conquered northern Wales, he built a series of strong castles that both helped him control the land and demonstrated his new power (see the map on page 203). One of them, Conway, was built on the site of the grave of the Welsh national hero Llewellyn the Great.

Source 3 Historian Malcolm Hislop, writing in 2013.

Caernarfon Castle was intended to evoke Constantinople, capital of the Eastern Roman Empire. The princes, of Gwynedd traced their ancestry to Magnus Maximus, who established himself as Roman Emperor in 383 BCE. Tradition associated Maximus with the Roman town of Segontium, close to Caernarfon. With this castle Edward was portraying himself as the successor of the Emperor and his supposed descendants the Welsh princes.

3   Look at Sources 4 and 5. What similarities are there between the walls of Constantinople and Caernarfon?

4   Do you agree with the judgement of the historian in Source 3? Explain your answer.

Source 4 Part of the surviving Roman walls of Constantinople (modern Istanbul). They were famous for the bands of colour, made by using courses of tile. ▼

Source 5 Part of the walls of Caernarfon Castle, built by Edward I in the 1280s. ▼

Living and working

Castles were both the home and the workplace of a large community that was divided into strict social levels. At the top was the lord or lady and his or her family, then any noble guests they may have, then their most important followers such as the constable of the castle. There was also a hierarchy among the servants, from the head cook and the butler (who was in charge of the wine) down to the unskilled labourers and kitchen skivvies. Life and work were very different depending where people were in this hierarchy.

Some parts of castle life were very formal. The great hall was often the site for ceremonial events. In the great hall the lord or the constable would:

- meet and greet noble guests
- eat – the lord's family ate on a stage (the DAIS) at one end of the hall, raised up so they could be seen
- conduct business, such as receiving payments of rent from the tenants
- hold court sessions to conduct trials and legal business.

Many others ate in the great hall, but lower down. In the first castles many people slept in the hall too, but that changed as more sleeping accommodation was added later. Another change was an increasing desire for privacy for the most important people in the castle. The lord's family started to spend time in private rooms. These were often reached from a door off the dais in the great hall.

Source 6 The remains of the east side of the great hall at Kenilworth Castle. ▼

Source 7 Extracts from *Sir Gawain and the Green Knight*, a poem written 1375–1400. The poem is more than 2,500 lines long and is set in the time of King Arthur. In this section, Gawain visits a perfect castle.

Knights and squires came to bring him to the Great Hall, where a fine fire fiercely burned. Then the lord came down from his chamber with good manners to greet Gawain there. He said, 'You are welcome, treat my home as your home'.

The lord led him to a chamber, and chose a man to serve him, with several others to help. They took him to a bright bedroom with a beautiful bed, with a canopy of silk bordered with gold, and fur bedcovers, heavily embroidered. The curtains hung from golden curtain rings and ran on cords. The walls were hung with tapestries from Toulouse and Turkey, and, on the floor, were carpets too.

In the Great Hall, he sat in a fine chair, and warmed himself. Soon servants set a table on trestles, with a clean white tablecloth, a saltcellar, and silver spoons. He washed well and went to the table. Servants served him with sumptuous food well-seasoned with costly spices, double helpings, as was right, and all kinds of fish – some baked in pies, some grilled over hot coals, some slowly boiled, some in spicy stews, and all the sauces were made just to his taste.

---

1 Look at Source 7. List all the things you can learn about life in castles from this extract.

2 The castle described in Source 7 is fictional. Does this mean it is not a useful source for historians? Explain your answer.

Source 9 Instructions from Henry III to the constable of Dover Castle, about showing an important French nobleman round the castle, 1247.

When Gaucher de Châtillon shall come to Dover he shall take him into that castle and show the castle off to him in eloquent style, so that the magnificence of the castle shall be fully apparent to him, and that he shall see no defects in it.

3 Study Source 8 carefully. List all the things the artist has shown that are supported by evidence from this section.

4 Which of the sources in this section is most useful in helping you understand how a great hall was used? Explain your answer.

Source 8 An artist's reconstruction of the great hall at Kenilworth Castle in the fourteenth century. The cutaway in the lower right shows the cellars underneath. ▼

FACTFILE

Decoration

The walls of the main rooms would not have been left as bare stone in the way we see them today. Before c1250, the walls would normally be whitewashed, perhaps with the lines between the stones picked out in red. After c1250, walls were usually plastered and then painted, and some parts of the wall might be covered by wood panelling or tapestries. Colours could be very bright (see Source 10). Henry III's favourite colour scheme was gold stars on a green background. Floors were covered by rushes at first, and in the more public parts of the castle this continued. Increasingly, the private rooms of the lord, and certainly the dais in the great hall, would be floored with colourful glazed tiles.

Source 10 An illustration from a fifteenth-century manuscript showing a king, bishops and great nobles eating in state on the dais of a great hall, while musicians play in a gallery. ▼

Source 11 A description of dinner on a normal day at Raglan Castle in the 1640s.

At eleven o'clock the Castle Gates were shut, and the tables laid; two in the Dining-Room; three in the Hall; one in Mrs Watson's Apartment, where the Chaplains eat, two in the Housekeeper's Room, for women.

The Earl came into the Dining-Room, attended by his Gentlemen. At the first Table sat the noble Family, and such of the Nobility as come there. At the second Table sat Knights and honourable Gentlemen.

In the Hall, at the first table sat the Steward, the Comptroller, the Master of the Horse, the Master of the Fish-ponds with such Gentlemen as came there under the degree of a knight. At the second table sat the Sewer [responsible for serving food], with the Gentlemen Waiters, and pages, to the number of twenty-four. At the third table sat the Clerk of the Kitchen, with the Yeoman Officers of the House, two Grooms of the Chambers.

1   Sketch a plan of Raglan (see page 208), including the kitchen, buttery, great hall, dining room and the private apartments. Study Source 11. Mark on the tables, who ate where and the route the food would have taken.
2   'The dining room (above the parlour) at Raglan was for high-status people. It had large elaborate windows on to the courtyard and moat.' How far do Sources 12 and 13 support this statement?
3   Compare the impressions of castle life from the early twelfth century (Source 17 on page 201), the late fourteenth century (Source 7, page 210) and the mid-seventeenth century (Source 11, above). What changes, and what stays the same?

Castles were in use for hundreds of years and, during this time, the domestic accommodation of most castles changed more than the military features did. Two major trends in society show up in changes we can see in many castles:

● a move towards more **privacy**. You see it most in the accommodation for the high-status people in the castle, but also in things like adding towers with lots of toilets (which were for the soldiers and servants). At Raglan (Source 12) the grand private apartments were reached from a door off the dais in the great hall, and by the 1640s the owner (the Earl of Worcester) and his family normally ate in the private dining room. At Goodrich the GARDEROBE (toilet) tower was added about 1450.
● an **increase in the size of the household**. You see this in the increase in the accommodation, usually built against the inside of the curtain walls, from the late thirteenth century onwards. Households continued to get bigger in the fifteenth and sixteenth centuries, and you can often find more than one round of adding extra accommodation.

Look closely at the PHASED PLANS of your nominated castle. Can you see evidence of these two trends in society in its remains? If you can't, is there a reason? For example, later changes that obliterate evidence of earlier changes.

Source 12 A phased plan of the private apartments at Raglan Castle (shaded beige). See the whole plan on page 208 to understand how this fits in to the rest of the castle. ▼

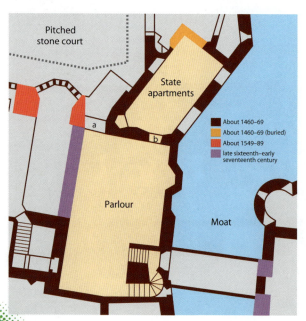

Pitched stone court

State apartments

About 1460–69
About 1460–69 (buried)
About 1549–89
late sixteenth–early seventeenth century

a
b

Parlour

Moat

Source 13 The remains of the wall of the dining room over the parlour at Raglan Castle, showing the area between a and b on Source 12. ▼

Sieges – the castle at war

There is some disagreement between historians as to whether castle builders were much interested in war and the possibility of sieges. Castle revisionists point out that many castles were built over a 600-year period, but not many sieges took place. They suggest that castles were built in a military style, as bases for an upper class that wanted to reflect traditional military functions and traditions in the style of their castles. These historians suggest that the symbolism of castles and their peacetime functions were more important. As we look at the military functions of castles, keep the arguments of the revisionists in mind.

Historians have identified at least 1,897 castles that existed between 1066 and 1660. Some of them only stood for 20–50 years, but others survived for most of the 600 years we are studying. In all, we know of 1,022 sieges. Both these numbers are probably too small, because not all castles have left a written record or traces in the ground, and not all sieges were recorded either. Even so, the revisionists have a point – there were almost two castles to every one siege, and most sieges lasted a few weeks or months, not 600 years.

Besieging a castle – choices and tactics

The first choice for an attacking commander was whether to starve the garrison out or to STORM THE CASTLE (fight your way in). Starving could take a long time, and you probably did not know how much food and drink they had. But storming could cost you a lot of troops, and you might not even win. Luckily, there was a third option – CONDITIONAL RESPITE. Here you met with the commander of the castle and agreed that eventually you would win. The only thing that would save the castle would be a relief force – their side sending an army to rescue them. So, to avoid unnecessary bloodshed, you agreed a time (perhaps three months) and agreed that if a relief army did not arrive by then, the castle would surrender. During the period of conditional respite, the defenders were not supposed to do anything to strengthen the castle. In one famous siege, at Newbury in 1152, the castle commander, fitz Gilbert, agreed a period of respite and handed over his son as hostage. He then cheated and got in more stores. King Stephen had the son put in a catapult and threatened to fire him back into the castle unless fitz Gilbert handed over the stores. Fitz Gilbert shouted back from the battlements that he had the equipment to make another son, so Stephen could do what he liked. Stephen let the boy live.

Until about 1400, the range of tactics for smashing a hole in the wall and storming the castle were simple (see Factfile). After 1400, however, the availability of large siege cannon changed the balance of power. Cannon had much more force than stone-throwing engines, and they could breach the strongest walls with time, the right cannon and experienced gunners.

Figure 14 A graph showing the total number of sieges known to historians, 1060–1660. ▼

Rochester 1215: a medieval siege

In 1215, after his barons had forced him to sign *Magna Carta*, King John raised an army to fight them and win back the power he had lost. Rochester Castle was held by the barons and John's army was in Kent. He wanted to attack the barons in London, but felt he could not leave Rochester Castle behind him: it protected a fortified bridge over the River Medway, which was the main route to London. With a strong stone curtain wall and a square keep inside it, the castle had a garrison of about 100 knights plus their soldiers. The siege began on 11 October. John himself arrived on 13 October and had stone-throwing engines set up on a hill overlooking the castle.

> **Source 15** An extract from the account of Roger of Wendover, a monk and historian, writing between 1220 and 1231.
>
> *The king did not allow the besieged any rest day or night. For, amidst the stones hurled from the engines, and the missiles of the crossbows and archers, frequent assaults were made by the knights and their followers, so that when some were tired, other fresh ones succeeded them in the assault; and with these changes the besieged had no rest.*
>
> *The besieged, too, tried to delay their own destruction. They were in great dread of the cruelty of the king. Therefore, that they might not die unavenged, they made no small slaughter amongst the attackers. The siege was prolonged many days owing to the great bravery and boldness of the besieged, who hurled stone for stone, weapon for weapon, from the walls on the enemy.*
>
> *At last, after great numbers of royal troops had been slain, the king, seeing his engines had little effect, employed miners, who soon threw down a great part of the walls. The provisions of the besieged failed them, and they were obliged to eat their horses. The soldiers of the king now rushed to the breaches in the walls, and by constant fierce assaults they forced the besieged to abandon the castle, though not without great loss on their own side. The besieged then entered the keep.*

If you read Source 15 carefully, you may think Roger's language shows some sympathy for the barons and a dislike of John ('dread of the cruelty of the king'; 'great bravery and boldness of the besieged'). Where we can check the facts of his account, this idea is supported although his time scheme might be slightly wrong. John sent orders on 14 October to the mayor of nearby Canterbury to make ('by day and night') and send to the king's army as many picks as they could. So mining was on his mind from the start of the siege. Once a breach was made, his troops stormed it and drove the defenders back into the keep, which became a last refuge.

> **Source 16** An extract describing the siege from the *Barnwell Chronicle*, another medieval history, written close to the time.
>
> *King John put expert miners to work. They cut their way underground until at last they were under one of the great corner towers. As they moved soil and rock out, they put wooden beams in, with pits props underneath them, to hold up the roof above their heads. They worried every time the beams creaked from the great weight above them. The defenders worried too. Every night they heard tapping sounds under the ground but could do nothing about it. After two months, when the miners came out, brushwood and branches were carried into the tunnels and fat from 40 pigs. Then a fire was started. The fire crackled and sizzled as all the timbers caught fire and blazed until they collapsed. With a great roar the tower fell down.*
>
> *The defenders fell back behind a strong wall, for such was the structure of the keep that a very strong wall separated the half that had fallen from the other. The defenders did not give in until they had nothing but horseflesh and water to sustain them, which they found hard, having been brought up in luxury.*

At least one part of this story checks out. John sent an order from the siege to his chief supporter saying: 'Send us with all speed by day and night forty of the fattest pigs of the least good sort for eating, to bring fire beneath the tower.' The defenders surrendered on 30 November 1215.

Source 17 Phased plans of the first three floors of the keep of Rochester Castle. ▼

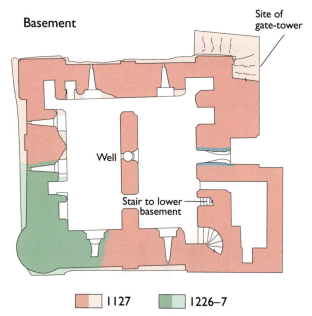

Basement

Site of gate-tower

Well

Stair to lower basement

▭ 1127   ▭ 1226–7

Source 18 The remains of the keep and curtain wall for Rochester Castle, taken from the south-east. ▼

Chris John

First floor

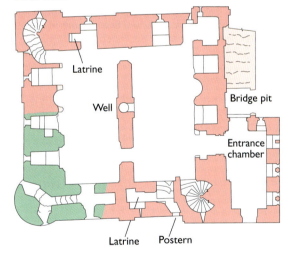

Latrine

Well

Bridge pit

Entrance chamber

Latrine   Postern

Second (principal) floor

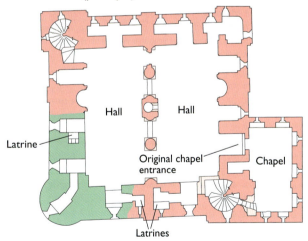

Latrine

Hall   Hall

Original chapel entrance   Chapel

Latrines

1 Does the language of Source 16 give you any reason to think the writer supported King John?

2 Study Source 17. Do the remains of the castle support the *Barnwell Chronicle*'s account of the capture of the keep? Explain your answer.

3 Rochester is one of the best surviving examples of a square keep. Study Source 17 carefully and explain how people entered the keep in 1127.

Source 19 The remains of Wardour Castle from the air. ▼

Wardour: a siege in the Civil War

When the English Civil War broke out in 1642, the country did not have many professional soldiers. Most of those involved in the fighting had to learn as they went. In the first years of the war, castles proved difficult to capture. By the 1640s, stone walls should not have been able to withstand siege with modern artillery, but there were not many siege cannon or officers trained to use them. The siege of Wardour Castle is typical. The only cannon available were far too small to do serious damage to the walls. Instead, the attackers used the traditional tactics of starving out the garrison, UNDERMINING and storming.

Strategically, castles helped each side control land – and controlling land meant being able to collect taxes. The garrison of a castle like Wardour could also raid enemy supply CONVOYS and disrupt communications. Wardour was a very small castle, but it tied up Royalist forces for over three months until the siege was over.

By 1645, parliament had a well-equipped and professional army that was better able to attack castles. Increasingly, castles were unable to hold out against a proper siege unless they had low, earth-filled walls. Make sure you know what happened to your nominated castle during the Civil Wars of the 1640s.

Source 20 From an account of the siege of Wardour Castle, written by Edmund Ludlow, who commanded the parliamentary garrison defending the castle against the Royalist siege. The siege began in December 1643, and ended on 18 March 1644. These are extracts from a much longer account, and a gap of days (or weeks) is marked '…'.

The besiegers were commanded by Captain Bowyer, who offered us terms to leave the castle, which we declined. He threatened that great numbers of horse and foot, and several cannon, were on their way. He boasted of the right of his cause and spoke of our danger and inevitable ruin. Captain Bean, our cannoneer, told him we were sure of the right of our cause too, and would stay. He fired at Bowyer, and caught him in the heel. He fell to the ground. No one dared fetch him all day. By nightfall his wound had gangrene and he died. …

We now had no beer, only water in the well. Our corn was low and so we rationed it. There were now a hundred men. When our meat ran out we killed and ate one of the horses. The enemy then had a lucky shot, which broke the chain of our portcullis, so we could no longer use the gate. We barricaded it up on the inside; now we had no way out but through a window, for we had walled up our other doors earlier. …

The enemy now decided to dig a hole in the castle wall to blow the wall up, or to tunnel under it, supporting the tunnel with timber, then light a fire in the tunnel to bring the wall down. They brought up thick oak planks to the walls one dark night, on either side of the castle. Our men found them on one side and beat them off, forcing them to leave the planks behind. They had more luck on the other side, and got the planks set up to form a shelter. In the morning we heard them digging. We could not trace where the noise of digging was coming from. Then we found them and tried to shift them by pouring down hot water and melted lead, to little effect. We then threw hand grenadoes, and they were forced to go, leaving their tools and provisions. …

[About the middle of January, 1644] Now the King sent Sir Francis Doddington with more men to the castle, and among them an engineer to undermine the castle. As soon as we heard them beginning to dig, we began to try to undermine them, but the floor was too hard to break through. …

On the Thursday morning I lay down to sleep in my room. At some time between ten and eleven of the clock, the mine exploded. I was flung up as it exploded, amid clouds of dust.

As soon as the dust cleared I found my window towards the enemy blown open, with so big a hole as you could have driven a cart through it. They now made haste to storm the castle – the rubble from my window had made them a path to it. I could not get my pistols to fire. I had to trust to my sword to keep back the enemy. I was, at first, alone in holding them off. There was no way into my room but through the courtyard window. I called through this window to the men that were there requiring them to help at once. [Men] came to my assistance who I ordered to fill up the breach and the doors with the bed, chairs, tables and all else to hand. My room being made safe, I went to see what other breaches had been made. I found one breach, in the room under me, which was well defended, but there was one in the gun room that was not defended at all. I put a guard there, and ran to the upper rooms, which had many doors and windows blown open, at every one of which I placed a guard in some way proportional to the danger. …

We lost three of our men in the blast from the mine, but the rest were safe. But our corn supplies were blown up, as was much of our ammunition. We had some meat left, about enough for four days, so I thought it was best to hold out for as long as we could, hoping to get the best possible terms of surrender from the enemy. No one had been shot during the storm, though some had been slightly wounded, and I had an enemy bullet pierce my hat close to my head. The besiegers had lost ten of their men, killed by shot. …

The castle was now in such a poor state, as were we, that I said I would surrender on conditions. Firstly, no one was to be put to the sword. Secondly, none of my party was to be ill treated. Lastly, we would soon be exchanged for prisoners on their side. Sir Francis Doddington said they would agree to my terms, so I returned to the castle and ordered my soldiers to lay down their arms.

Source 21 A plan of the ground floor of Wardour Castle today. ▼

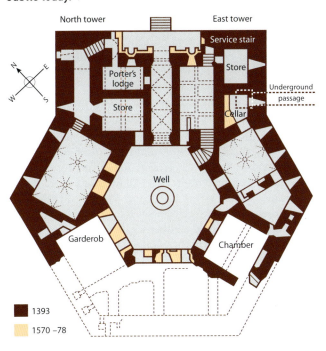

1393

1570–78

1 Study Source 19.
  a Was Wardour Castle built on high ground or lower ground?
  b Why might the original builder have made this decision?
2 Source 20 gives you seven incidents from the siege of Wardour, Make a table with three columns:
  a What the attackers did.
  b What the defenders did.
  c Were these tactics traditional or modern in 1643–44?
  Fill in the table for each incident.
3 How useful is Ludlow's account as a source for this siege?
4 Which of the other sources on this page is the most useful in addition to Ludlow's account?
5 Why were old-fashioned castles so significant in the Civil War?
6 Is the evidence of the sieges of Rochester and Wardour enough to prove wrong the revisionists' argument that castles were not mainly military?

Source 22 The remains of Wardour Castle from the south-west. ▼

The later history of the nominated castles

- **Carlisle** surrendered to the Jacobites without a fight in 1745 and was recaptured the same year by a royal army after a short siege. It became an army base, arsenal and – from 1819 until 1959 – a barracks.
- **Framlingham** was sold to a rich lawyer in 1635. He died childless, leaving the castle to his old Oxford college on condition that they pulled down parts of it and built a poorhouse. After a period of bad management, a new poorhouse was built in 1729, which lasted until a change in the national system caused its closure in 1839. The former poorhouse was used as a parish hall and the castle became popular with tourists. Ownership transferred to the state in 1913.
- **Kenilworth** was slighted in 1649–50, and the castle lands were converted into farmland, with the gatehouse as the farmhouse. From the 1780s it became popular with tourists, especially after Sir Walter Scott's novel *Kenilworth*, about Queen Elizabeth I, was published in 1821. It remains a tourist destination.
- **Portchester** was sold by Charles I in 1632 to a local landowner, who rented it back to the government to use as a prisoner-of-war camp in 1665. It was used for this purpose on and off until 1814. The army left in 1819 and it stood empty until the state took it over in 1926, caring for the site and opening it to the public.
- **Stokesay** was slighted but remained inhabited until the early eighteenth century. Until the early nineteenth century it was rented out as workshops, including a barrel-maker (in the hall) and a blacksmith (in the south tower, which caused a fire in 1830). It became popular with early tourists from the 1840s, and survived until it was bought and restored by a rich businessman in 1869.

Later uses

The end of the Civil War saw many castles slighted. This theoretically meant they were no longer defensible, but the living accommodation of many castles was badly damaged too. From the 1650s onwards, castles were much less likely to be inhabited. They were used in many different ways:

- **Prisons:** Buildings with strong walls to keep people out could easily be used to keep people in. Some bigger castles were prisons until very recently – Oxford Castle until 1996 and Lancaster until 2011.
- **Quarries:** Stone is expensive and difficult to quarry and all over the country were buildings nobody was using that had lots of fine stone. Many castles lost a lot of their walls between the seventeenth and nineteenth centuries as people – either legally or illegally – took the stones to use in their houses and farms.
- **Industrial uses:** Castle sites included large and strong buildings. Some of these were leased or bought for use in different industries. The keep of Canterbury Castle was used as a coke store for the gasworks (which were built in its bailey) until the 1920s.
- **Tourism:** Medieval ruins became fashionable in the late-eighteenth century. People liked to visit them and enjoy these picturesque sites. Having ivy growing all over the walls added to the effect.

Goodrich Castle was abandoned after it was slighted in 1648. The ditch was used as a cattle enclosure, but the buildings seem to have been ignored until the 1780s, when it became a tourist site.

Source 23 The entrance to Goodrich Castle, from the barbican, in the nineteenth century. ▼

1. Compare the photo of Goodrich in Source 23 with the modern photos of the site in this chapter. How has the castle changed since 1872?
2. Why do you think these changes have happened?
3. How has tourism affected the later history of Goodrich and the five nominated castles?
4. Is tourism a better use for castles than using them as prisons, quarries and industry?
5. How typical is the later history of your nominated castle (see Factfile)?

Explain why Goodrich Castle was largely rebuilt just before 1300.

TOPIC SUMMARY

What were the functions of a castle?

1 Royal castles were controlled by the monarch, baronial castles were owned by lords. Royal castles normally guarded somewhere strategically important, or the monarch controlled them for a short time before passing them on to a noble as a reward.
2 Castles were not always built on the highest ground – they had to be convenient to live and work in.
3 Castles could make a whole country harder to attack, because it was dangerous to ignore them and besieging them cost time or soldiers – or both.
4 Henry VIII built a series of castles on the south coast to use cannon to stop enemy ships landing an invasion force.
5 Many castles had a place of final refuge, which could be defended if the rest of the castle was captured.
6 Castles were important symbols of the power and prestige of a king or a lord.
7 A castle was a hierarchical community, and there was a lot of ceremony in castle life – the great hall was important as a ceremonial space.
8 In most castles the domestic accommodation was changed more than the military features: larger households (so more accommodation) and more privacy (so private apartments for important people).
9 Sieges were very unusual.

Bringing it all together: remains, context and function

You have built up a lot of knowledge about castles – and about two castles in particular. A question like the one on the left requires you to pull all this knowledge together. Consider what you know:

- A phased plan gives you the best understanding of when different parts of the castle were built (the Goodrich plan is on page 199).
- The different styles of castle building, and roughly the times when they were fashionable (for Goodrich stone keeps and curtain walls).
- The range of sources historians use to find out about individual castles (for Goodrich the importance of the surviving manuscripts of Joan de Valence, page 202).
- The importance of the main events in the story of a particular castle (for Goodrich, page 205).
- The main functions of a castle and how some of them changed through time.

Which of these things really helps to answer the question? Looking at the plan reveals that the big rebuilding around 1300 was in the curtain wall style. You should be able to explain some of the military and other factors that lay behind the decision to make these changes:

- The need for more living space in the castle, especially more space for the high-status people than the keep could provide.
- The need to replace earlier wooden structures.
- The desire to strengthen the defences of the bailey by building a strong wall with defensive features such as towers for flanking fire and a barbican.

The visit of Joan de Valence illustrates this and adds to the factors:

- Joan visited with a large household – which needed accommodation – and she was visited by other nobles who brought members of their households with them. So the need for accommodation was great.

From the story of Goodrich you could add:

- It had been owned by families that did not spend time there, then it came to the de Valence family, which did spend time there.
- This work was done around the end of Edward I's conquest of Wales, so perhaps it would be safe to improve the domestic features.

Then, from your understanding of the function of a castle, you might add:

- Goodrich was a baronial castle, owned at the time by a powerful noble family, which would have wanted to show off its power with a building appropriate to its importance and to administer its estates in the area.
- Goodrich had been besieged, so its owners might not want to ignore the need to make the castle safe – hence the strong towers and the barbican.

There is more here than you would be expected to remember in an exam, but it is a useful example of how you can bring together knowledge from each of the different ways of looking at castles covered in this chapter. Now you need to use the knowledge to support a good answer to the question. Remember: a list of facts and ideas is not an answer to a question. Plan out an argument, then use the facts and ideas to support your argument.

7.3 Castle factfiles

Portchester Castle

Source 1 Extracts from the phased plans of Portchester Castle. ▼

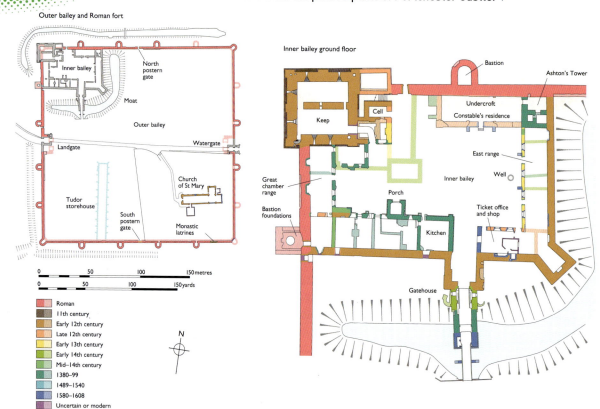

Outer bailey and Roman fort

Inner bailey
North postern gate
Moat
Outer bailey
Watergate
Landgate
Church of St Mary
Tudor storehouse
South postern gate
Monastic latrines

0   50   100   150 metres
0   50   100   150 yards

Roman
11th century
Early 12th century
Late 12th century
Early 13th century
Early 14th century
Mid–14th century
1380–99
1489–1540
1580–1608
Uncertain or modern

N

Inner bailey ground floor

Bastion
Ashton's Tower
Undercroft
Constable's residence
Keep
Cell
East range
Well
Great chamber range
Inner bailey
Porch
Bastion foundations
Ticket office and shop
Kitchen
Gatehouse

1. Explain where the area shown in Source 3 is in the plan (Source 1).
2. The plan shows different periods of building in this area. What evidence of this can you see in Source 3?

Portchester Castle is very unusual, in that it was built inside the walls of a Roman fort, which was already almost 800 years old and probably quite ruined. Inside the walls, the Roman buildings had been destroyed and a Saxon community lived and worked. Portchester became a royal castle because it guarded a great natural harbour, and remained important until Henry VIII's new castles defending the south coast superseded it. It continued to be valuable as a safe place for stores and then prisoners of war.

Source 2 A painting showing the remains of Portchester Castle as they are today. ▼

1	Inner bailey	6	Moat	11	Watergate
2	Keep	7	Gatehouse	12	Parish church of St Mary
3	Richard II's palace	8	North postern gate	13	Outline of Tudor stonehouse
4	Exit ranges	9	Outer bailey		
5	Ashton's Tower	10	Landgate		

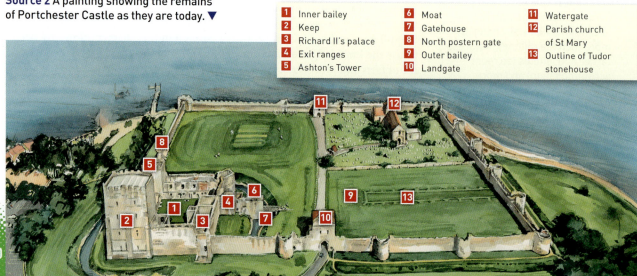

Source 3 A section of the remains today. The tall building is the keep. ▼

FACTFILE

Portchester Castle

285–290 Roman fort built at Portchester.

c1066–86 First Norman castle on the site, built by William Maudit. He probably had the moat to protect the inner bailey dug and built a wooden wall inside it.

c1120–48 William Pont de l'Arche rebuilt the keep and the inner bailey walls in stone.

1143 Priory founded inside the walls; its church later became St Mary's, the parish church.

c1154 Henry II took Portchester as a royal castle. He often visited, as it was a convenient port for France.

1173–74 Pipe rolls (royal accounts) show the gates, keep, walls and bridge were repaired. This included bratticing and catapults for defence. Garrisoned 10 (later 20) knights.

1183 Repairs to a royal residence in the inner bailey that was not the keep. This building was later replaced. [Pipe rolls]

1216 The castle was besieged and captured by Louis of France, who was fighting with the English barons against King John.

1217 Castle recaptured by Henry III, John's son and successor. The new king ordered that the castle be destroyed, but this did not happen. Instead repairs were made.

1256 Major repairs. [Pipe rolls]

1274 A survey reported the castle was in need of repair.

1289–96 Major repairs, including a new inner gate, a new drawbridge, bratticing and a tower on the sea wall.

1320–26 Over £1,100 spent on works – a massive sum. Work included repairs to the keep, the king's house, land gate and water gate, strengthening the gate of the inner bailey and building a new hall with floor tiles and painted walls.

1335–44 Significant repairs, including making some of the Roman walls useable and building a new wall to stop galleys entering from the sea.

1369 Repairs to some towers and to the wall walks and gates due to a threat of invasion from France.

1385 Ashton's tower finished, barbican extended.

1390 Part of the west wall fell down.

1396–99 Richard II built new and better domestic accommodation, including the great hall and great chamber, kitchens and changes to the keep, plus decorated glass for the windows. Costs included candles to allow the builders to work at night.

1415 Portchester was Henry V's base for the invasion of France that led to the Battle of Agincourt.

1441 A royal surveyor described the castle as 'right ruinous and feeble'. Some repairs were started.

1450 The constable of the castle, Robert Fiennes, wrote to the king complaining: 'The gates have been broken, both within and without, the drawbridge fallen down, the towers, turrets and barbicans fallen down, and other houses of office [buildings] fail both in their roofs and floors.'

1489–1501 Repairs made.

1512 A gunpowder mill was established inside the walls.

1527 A large military storehouse was built, 73 m long by 9 m wide. Portchester was now mainly a military depot.

1535 Henry VIII visited the castle and agreed some repairs.

1583 With danger of invasion growing, £250 was allocated to the repair of Portchester. Some stone was taken from the castle for use in the new defences of Portsmouth.

c1605 The eastern range was rebuilt.

1609 A surveyor reported that most of the buildings, apart from the eastern range, were ruinous because the lead covering the roof had been stolen and rain had rotted the roof timbers. No repairs were made.

1628 Used as a stores depot for the navy.

1632 Sold by Charles I to Sir William Uvedale.

1644 Garrisoned for a while in the Civil War, but not attacked.

1665–1763 Used as a prisoner-of-war camp.

1763–94 Abandoned.

1794–1814 Used as a prisoner-of-war camp.

1819 Returned to the private owners.

1926 Passed back to the care of the government.

Carlisle Castle

Source 1 Extracts from the phased plans of Carlisle Castle.

▨	12th century
▨	13th–15th century
▨	16th–early 19th century
▨	Mid-19th–20th century

1 Explain where the area shown in Source 3 is in the plan (Source 1).
2 The plan shows different periods of building in this area. What evidence of this can you see in Source 3?

Carlisle Castle is unusual in that it was built as, and has always been, a royal castle. Built on the border between England and Scotland, it has been besieged much more often than is usual. It was last besieged and captured as recently as 1745. Over hundreds of years it was ignored by the government when relations with Scotland were good, and strengthened when they were bad. It is a medieval castle that was modernised to use cannon in its defence. It became a barracks and army depot in the early nineteenth century, when the government was worried about social unrest during the Industrial Revolution.

Source 2 A painting showing the remains of Carlisle Castle as they are today. ▼

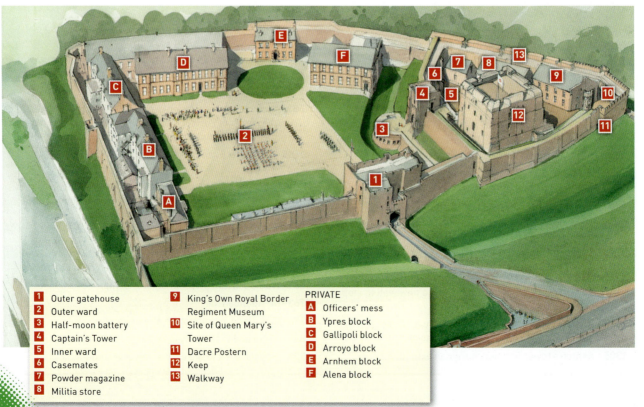

				PRIVATE	
1	Outer gatehouse	9	King's Own Royal Border Regiment Museum	A	Officers' mess
2	Outer ward	10	Site of Queen Mary's Tower	B	Ypres block
3	Half-moon battery			C	Gallipoli block
4	Captain's Tower	11	Dacre Postern	D	Arroyo block
5	Inner ward	12	Keep	E	Arnhem block
6	Casemates	13	Walkway	F	Alena block
7	Powder magazine				
8	Militia store				

FACTFILE

Carlisle Castle

1092 William II captured Carlisle from the Scots and built a castle there. This castle may just have been an earth bailey topped with a wooden wall. No remains survive.

1122 Henry I ordered new stone castle and city walls be built.

1136 Carlisle was taken by the Scots. Civil war in England meant no attempt to recapture it.

1136–57 Scottish king David I controlled the castle. The keep was probably begun in Henry I's time and finished during David's rule. David died in the castle in 1153.

1157 The Scots withdrew and Henry II of England took control. He strengthened the defences. Henry probably had the gatehouse of the inner ward built.

1174 William I of Scotland besieged the castle for three months. After some hard fighting, the constable of the castle and William agreed a period of conditional respite, during which Henry II defeated and captured William.

1186 Henry II visited the castle and ordered a new royal palace to be built against the north wall.

1186–88 Parts of the palace built – a chamber for the king, a small tower and a chapel.

1201 Worried by the possibility of war with Scotland, King John spent £214 strengthening the defences of the castle. War did not break out.

1216 King Alexander of Scotland besieged the castle. The south curtain wall was undermined, and the outer and inner gatehouses badly damaged by catapults. The castle was captured.

1217 The Scots returned the castle. The siege did so much damage it took years to make the castle strong again.

1226–27 Repairs to the keep after the damage of the siege.

1232–33 Repairs to the curtain wall.

1237 Scotland abandoned all claim to Carlisle.

1256 A survey: guttering, doors and windows of the keep missing; many of the floors rotten; outer and inner gates still unrepaired after the siege; the wood (doors, windows and bratticing) had been stolen or burned.

1264–69/1285–90 Some repairs were made, but not enough to return the castle to its pre-siege state.

1296 Edward I began his wars to conquer Scotland. This meant Carlisle was a key base for his operations.

1297–1303 The moats were cleared, new bratticing made and improvements to the great hall.

1307–12 New east gatehouse built, defences strengthened and a bath was installed in the palace for the queen.

1315 The Scots besieged the castle: well-organised, with a large catapult, attempts to undermine and fill in the moat for a siege tower to storm the walls. The castle had a strong garrison of almost 500 soldiers. The mines flooded, there was so much rain the Scots could not fill in the moat and the siege tower sank in the mud.

1321 & 1335 Surveys reported severe problems including (1321) two sections of the outer bailey wall had collapsed and (1335) the outer gatehouse 'ruinous'.

1363/1367–71 Some repairs to the keep and walls.

1378–83 New outer gatehouse built.

1380/1384 Five cannon added, two on the roof of the keep.

1430 The castle had six (more powerful) iron cannon.

1483 The tile tower built.

1488 Henry VII's master gunner modernised the defences.

1522/1523/1526 Surveys: partly ruinous, not enough cannon.

1532–33 Some money spent strengthening the defences.

1538 Survey: £1,000 needed for repairs; £53 was spent.

1541–42 Major work: cannon platform on keep roof, curtain walls strengthened for cannon, half-moon battery built.

1577–78 Significant repairs, including to the keep.

1603 James VI of Scotland became James I of England: no possibility of war between England and Scotland.

1617 James I visited the castle, saw it was badly decayed and did nothing to repair it.

1633 Most of the cannon removed.

1642 Castle refortified as a Royalist stronghold in the Civil War.

1644–45 City and castle besieged by Scots and parliamentary troops, a long siege until the garrison was starved out.

c1700 Garrison withdrawn.

1716 Used as a prison after the Jacobite rebellion failed.

1745 Surrendered to the Jacobites without fighting, the Jacobite garrison of 400 surrendered after the castle was attacked by powerful artillery in December.

1746 The castle used as a prison and storehouse.

1819 Worried by the possibility of revolution, the government built a barracks at the castle.

1945 Anti-aircraft gun installed on top of the keep.

1959 Carlisle barracks closed.

Source 3 A section of the remains of Carlisle Castle today. ▼

Framlingham Castle

Source 1 Extracts from the phased plans of Framlingham Castle.

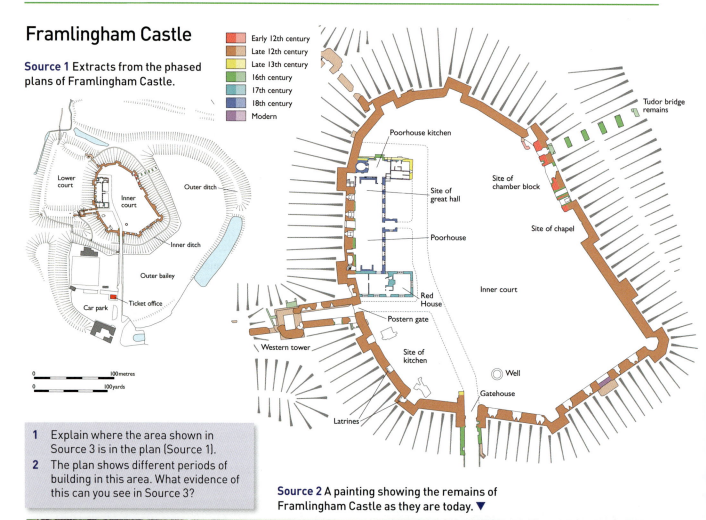

▮	Early 12th century
▮	Late 12th century
▮	Late 13th century
▮	16th century
▮	17th century
▮	18th century
▮	Modern

1 Explain where the area shown in Source 3 is in the plan (Source 1).
2 The plan shows different periods of building in this area. What evidence of this can you see in Source 3?

Source 2 A painting showing the remains of Framlingham Castle as they are today. ▼

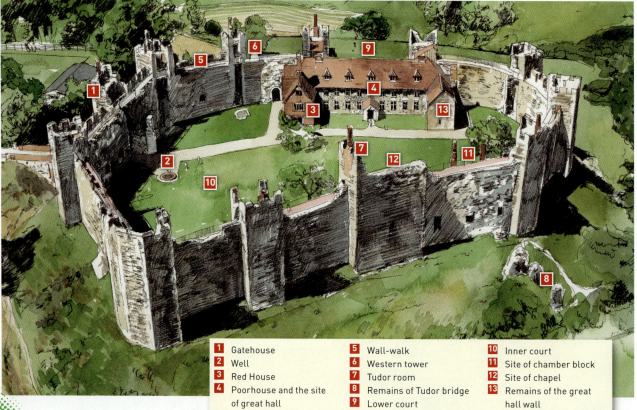

1	Gatehouse	**5**	Wall-walk	**10**	Inner court
2	Well	**6**	Western tower	**11**	Site of chamber block
3	Red House	**7**	Tudor room	**12**	Site of chapel
4	Poorhouse and the site of great hall	**8**	Remains of Tudor bridge	**13**	Remains of the great hall wall
		9	Lower court		

FACTFILE

Framlingham Castle

1066–1107 Roger Bigod built the first castle, made from wood.

1140 Hugh Bigod was made Earl of Norfolk.

1145–48 During the civil wars of Stephen's reign, Framlingham was big enough for the Archbishop of Canterbury and his court to live there.

c1150–57 First stone buildings, a chamber block and a chapel (later part of the eastern curtain wall) built.

1157–65 Henry II confiscated Framlingham from Hugh Bigod. Garrisoned by royal troops until given back to Hugh in 1165.

1173 Hugh Bigod rebelled against Henry II but was defeated and exiled. Walls of Framlingham destroyed.

1189 Hugh's son, Roger Bigod II, was given his title and castle back by Richard I. He started to build the stone curtain wall.

1216 Roger Bigod II was a leader of the barons who forced King John to sign *Magna Carta*. In the civil war that followed, John besieged Framlingham. Bigod was not there – the garrison was 26 knights, 20 sergeants-at-arms, seven crossbowmen, one chaplain and three others. The castle surrendered after two days. In the peace that followed Bigod got the castle back.

1248 Roger Bigod III became one of the richest barons in the country when he inherited lands and titles from his mother's father.

1270–1306 Roger Bigod IV made many improvements, including building new lodgings, re-roofing the knights' lodgings, adding some towers and the 'great dairy and cowshed'.

1306–12 Roger IV owed a huge debt of taxes and was virtually bankrupt. He made the king his heir and when he died in 1306 the castle passed to the Crown. In 1312, the king gave it to his half-brother, Thomas Brotherton.

1383 Framlingham was inherited by Margaret Brotherton, who became Duchess of Norfolk.

1483–89 Framlingham was inherited by John Howard, Duke of Norfolk, who started major repairs and rebuilding, but was killed (on the losing side) at the Battle of Bosworth in 1485. Framlingham was confiscated and then passed to Thomas Howard in 1489.

1489–1524 Framlingham was Thomas Howard's main residence and he had much work done in the castle. When he died in 1524 his body lay in state in the castle chapel for four weeks, and the chapel and gatehouse were wrapped in 400 metres of black cloth.

1524 The new Duke of Norfolk did not live at Framlingham but at a grand house at Kenninghall, Norfolk.

1547 Thomas Howard was imprisoned for treason and Framlingham was confiscated by the king and passed to his sister Mary. The castle was in a poor state, a survey noted: 'Many houses of the same castle is in great decay, and [many] of them is like to fall down unless they be shortly repaired.'

1553 Edward VI died; a plan to replace him with Lady Jane Grey failed when Mary raised an army at Framlingham and Lady Jane's supporters deserted. Thomas Howard was released and given back his lands.

1572 Thomas Howard was executed for treason. The castle was confiscated by Elizabeth I and used as a prison.

1589 A survey of the castle reported: 'The castle of Framlingham is in great ruin and decay in divers places.'

1603 James I returned Framlingham to the Howard family, but they did not live there.

1635 Framlingham sold to Sir Robert Hitcham.

1636 Hitcham died, leaving Framlingham to Pembroke College, Cambridge, on condition it was used to benefit the poor of Framlingham and two other towns. This included setting up almshouses and a school for '30 or 40 of the poorest and neediest' children.

1654–66 The Red House was built, perhaps for the schoolmaster, then turned into a poorhouse. The castle was used for plague victims.

1669–99 The Red House was used as a pub, perhaps with some poor from the three towns living there.

1699–1729 The Red House used as a poorhouse for children.

1729–1839 A new poorhouse was built on the site of the great hall.

1839–1913 Local uses including as a parish hall and a local prison, increasing the number of tourists after the railway reached Framlingham in 1859.

1913 Given to the forerunner of English Heritage to run.

Source 3 A section of the remains of Framlingham Castle today. ▼

No evidence survives that there was a motte and bailey castle at Framlingham, but there probably was one. The first Norman lord may have used this site for his first castle and some of the existing earthworks could have been part of that castle.

What remains today is a very unusual castle. It was one of the great castle-palaces of the Middle Ages, with (presumably) grand accommodation within the existing curtain wall. However, all that has been demolished and some of it would have been under the Red House. It was certainly a castle designed to impress people when they saw it in the distance, with the castle reflected in the mere.

Kenilworth Castle

Source 1 Extracts from the phased plans of Kenilworth Castle.

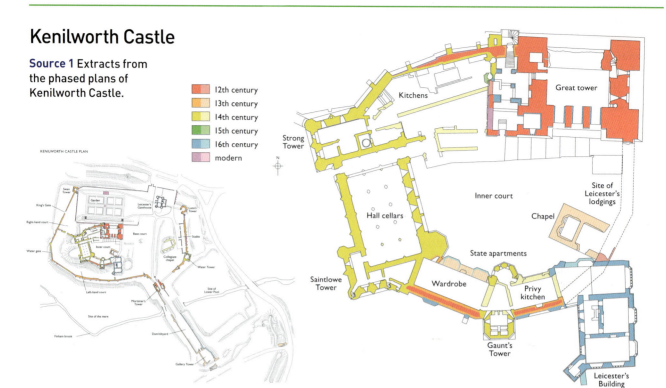

1 Explain where the area shown in Source 3 is in the plan (Source 1).

2 The plan shows different periods of building in this area. What evidence of this can you see in Source 3?

Kenilworth was one of the great castle palaces of medieval England. It was so powerful, and in such an important strategic position in the Midlands, that Henry II took it as a royal castle (although it was given back to great lords three times). Twice it was the headquarters of rebels, first Simon de Montfort and then the House of Lancaster in the Wars of the Roses. The Lancastrian John of Gaunt deliberately made it like a royal palace. The Earl of Leicester upgraded it again, trying to show himself a fit husband for Elizabeth I.

Source 2 A painting showing the remains of Kenilworth Castle as they are today. ▼

1	Outlying features	**7**	Great hall	**14**	Collegiate chapel
2	Mortimer's Tower	**8**	Saintlowe Tower	**15**	Lunn's Tower
3	Base court	**9**	State apartments	**16**	Water Tower
4	Inner court	**10**	Leicester's Building	**17**	Outer curtain wall
5	Great tower and forebuilding	**11**	Outer court	**18**	Elizabethan garden
6	Kitchens	**12**	Leicester's Gatehouse	**19**	Path to the Peasance
		13	Stable		

FACTFILE

Kenilworth Castle

1120s Geoffrey de Clinton built the first castle at Kenilworth. It is likely that the keep was built at this time because of the similarities between it and the keep of another castle owned by the de Clintons nearby at Brandon.

1173/4 The castle was so powerful and strategically important that Henry II took it as a royal castle.

1210–15 King John built domestic accommodation and parts of the outer curtain wall and gatehouse.

1241 Henry III ordered repairs and improvements to the king's chapel, the king's chamber, the queen's chamber, the keep, the gates and the southern curtain wall.

1244–65 Henry gave the castle to Simon de Montfort, who was killed leading a rebellion against Henry. His followers fled to Kenilworth.

1266 De Montfort's followers were besieged in Kenilworth. Archaeologists have found 140-kg stone balls fired by the besiegers' trebuchets over 320 m from where they could have been set up. It was not possible to undermine the walls because of the water defences. An attempt to storm the castle failed. Starving, the garrison finally surrendered.

1267 Henry granted the castle to his son, Edmund of Lancaster.

1296–1322 Thomas of Lancaster, with about 500 retainers at the castle, entertained on a scale to rival the king. He probably had the water tower built to make more accommodation.

1314–22 A new chapel was built in the outer bailey.

1347 The great hall was improved and repaired.

1361 Kenilworth passed to John of Gaunt, a son of Edward III, who became Duke of Lancaster.

1371–83 Gaunt spent regularly on repairs and improvements.

1389–93 Gaunt built new accommodation, the state apartments, on the south and west sides of the Inner Court.

1399 Gaunt's son became king and Kenilworth a royal castle.

1414 Henry V ordered the building of the pleasance – pleasure gardens and royal apartments half a mile from the castle at the other end of the mere. It was probably a copy of the garden palaces of Islamic Spain.

1424/1461 New kitchens built in the castle.

1492–93 Henry VII, who often stayed at the castle, had a tennis court built and some other improvements made.

1524 Henry VIII picked Kenilworth as one of the four royal castles he wanted kept in good repair for his visits.

1524–26 The pleasance was abandoned and its timber-framed banqueting house re-erected in the base court.

1530–32 New royal accommodation was built (timber-framed) on the east side of the inner court.

1553 New stables built.

1563 Queen Elizabeth gave the castle to her favourite, Robert Dudley, Earl of Leicester.

1568–75 Leicester made extensive alterations to the keep, built a new gatehouse and a grand new domestic accommodation (Leicester's Building).

1575 Queen Elizabeth visited Kenilworth, staying for 17 days, with great pageants and entertainments.

1588–1642 Leicester died without an heir and the castle eventually returned to royal ownership. Both James I and Charles I visited it, and it remained an impressive palace.

1642–47 Kenilworth was abandoned by the royalists early in 1642 and garrisoned by parliament for the rest of the war.

1649–50 Parliament ordered the slighting of the castle – part of the keep and sections of the curtain wall were destroyed.

1650s Parliament granted the castle to officers in lieu of their arrears of pay – the gatehouse became a farmhouse and the domestic buildings were plundered for building material for other farms. Most was left as a roofless ruin.

1660–1860s The castle was a farm. Visiting the ruins became fashionable, especially after the publication of Sir Walter Scott's historical novel *Kenilworth* in 1821.

1860s–1958 The castle was cared for as a tourist attraction. In 1958, it was given to the Kenilworth town council.

Source 3 A section of the remains of Kenilworth Castle today. ▼

Stokesay Castle

Source 1 Extracts from the phased plans of Stokesay Castle.

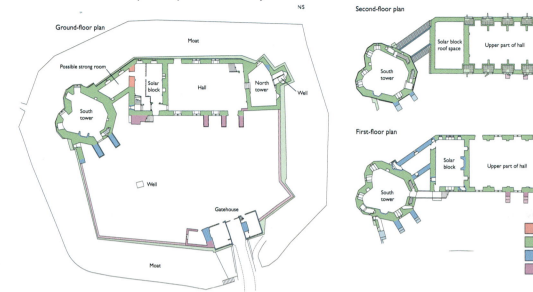

	Early 13th century
	1285–1305
	1639–64
	19th century and later

1 Explain where the area shown in Source 3 is in the plan (Source 1).
2 The plan shows different periods of building in this area. What evidence of this can you see in Source 3?

There was probably a fortified manor house at Stokesay before the castle was built in around 1285–91, but we have no evidence about it. Lawrence of Ludlow, a wool merchant and one of the richest men in England, built the current castle. He died soon after, commanding a trading fleet for the king that ran into a storm. For most of its history Stokesay was lived in by tenants of the owners and the tenants quietly got on with their lives. The castle was captured in the Civil War, but without any fighting. So much of it has survived relatively unchanged because the tenants were not rich enough to make major alterations.

Source 2 A painting showing the remains of Stokesay Castle as they are today. ▼

1	Gatehouse	6	North tower
2	Courtyard	7	Solar block
3	Curtain wall	8	Stairway
4	Well	9	South tower
5	Hall	10	Moat

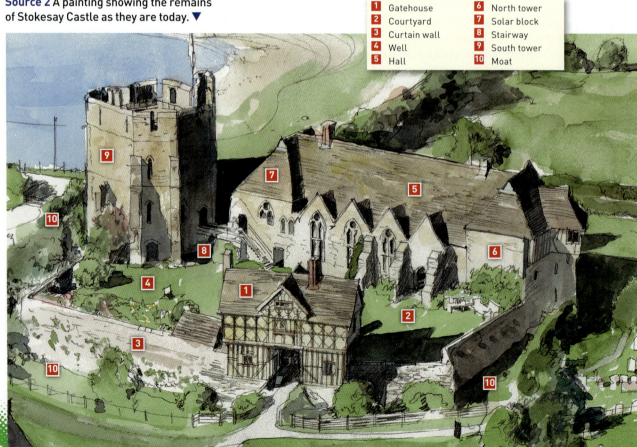

FACTFILE

Stokesay Castle

1086 Stokesay, called 'Stoches', held by the Norman Lacy family.

1100–35 Stoches had been split into North and South Stoke. South Stoke was held by the Say family, known as Stokesay.

1241 Walter de Lacy died and Stokesay passed to John de Verdon, his daughter's husband. There was probably a castle at Stokesay at this point, but no trace of it remains.

1261–63 Wood cut in these years is used in the current solar block. It is likely this wood was used in the earlier castle, and reused when the new castle was built in 1285–91.

1264–81 Verdon was captured in the civil war between Henry III and Simon de Montfort. When freed he went on crusade, leaving a tenant in Stokesay.

1281 Lawrence of Ludlow bought Stokesay.

c1285 Work started on building the new castle. Lawrence probably lived in Shrewsbury until the castle was finished.

1291 Lawrence was granted a 'licence to crenellate' – this was official royal permission to build a castle and a sign of Lawrence's new social standing as a lord. He probably moved to the castle about this time.

1294 Lawrence drowned when a royal fleet he commanded taking wool to sell in the Netherlands was caught in a storm.

1294–1498 The Ludlow family – members of the local ruling class – continued to live in the castle.

1498 Sir Richard Ludlow died and his granddaughter Anne, who married Thomas Vernon, inherited Stokesay Castle.

c1577 Henry Vernon repaired the top floor of the tower.

1598 Henry Vernon, badly in debt, sold Stokesay Castle to Sir Richard Mainwaring for £6,000.

1620 Mainwaring sold Stokesay and other property in Shropshire to Dame Elizabeth Craven, widow of a former Lord Mayor of London.

1624 Dame Elizabeth died; the castle passed to her son William Craven (later the Earl of Craven), one of the richest men in the kingdom. He owned estates all over England and spent very little time at Stokesay.

1633 Craven is known to have visited Stokesay.

1640–41 Craven's accounts show he spent just over £500 on work on the castle. Tree-ring dating of the timbers used in the gatehouse shows that the wood used was cut in 1639–41, so we can be sure this was the new gatehouse.

1642 Royalists garrisoned the castle during the Civil War.

1645 In June, parliament's forces captured the castle. They outnumbered the garrison and summoned it to surrender. The garrison refused and the Parliamentarians prepared to storm the castle (which meant they could kill all the garrison according to the 'Laws of War'). Offered another chance to surrender, the garrison did – probably without a shot being fired. Parliamentarians garrisoned the castle.

1646–47 The castle was slighted – the curtain walls considerably reduced in height.

1647 The Baldwyn family had the tenancy of the castle.

1709–1830 The Baldwyns moved away and sub-let the castle.

1813 A visitor, John Britton, described the castle as 'abandoned to neglect, and rapidly advancing to ruin: the glass is destroyed, the ceilings and floors are falling, and the rain streams through the opening roof on the damp and mouldering walls.' The hall was being used as a barrel-making workshop and the solar as a grain store.

1830 The basement of the South Tower was a blacksmith's workshop. A fire destroyed all the floors of the tower.

1853 Lord Craven, whose family still owned the freehold of the castle, made repairs to stop it decaying any further.

1869 The castle was bought by John Allcroft, who built a grand house to live in nearby and also restored the castle.

Source 3 A section of the remains of Stokesay Castle today. ▼

7.4 The development of a castle

FOCUS TASK

What is the story of *your* castle?

English Heritage plans to commission a series of websites about major castles. Each castle's site will follow the same structure (see Figure 1). You have been invited to pitch for the job of creating the content for the site for your nominated castle. To pitch well, you need to plan the following:

- **The main castle landing page:** This must hook people's interest and make them want to know more. It should include: a single image to sum up the castle, with an explanation of why this was chosen; introductory text (maximum 100 words); navigation text.
- **History pages:** Three sample pages:
  - The site, where it is, why it was built there.
  - Main changes landing page: an overview of the main changes to the castle, with block text and image for each change discussed on a linked page. Maximum 70 words per block. Linked pages are not needed at this stage.
  - Main functions landing page: an overview of the main functions of the castle, with block text and image for each function to be shown discussed on a linked page. Maximum 70 words per block. Linked pages are not needed at this stage.
- **The tour:** Four sample pages:
  - Landing page: this should be a plan with the areas highlighted that will hyperlink to a page on a particular feature.
  - Three sample feature pages.
- **The argument:** English Heritage wants visitors to know there is a disagreement between historians about why castles were built. You must use the standard introductory text (Source 1) and then explain how far the evidence of your castle supports either argument.

To keep costs under control, English Heritage has developed three wireframes of different page designs that the website will use (see Figure 2). For each page apart from the tour landing page, you must work with one of these three page designs.

You should use the material on your nominated castle in this book and any other material about the castle you have been given. Wherever you can, explain on web pages *how* you know what you are describing. Historians do two different types of work: researching and communicating. When they have finished their research and know what they think, the job is not over. It is just as hard to work out the best way of explaining something – and that is what this task requires you to do.

Source 1 The revisionist's view.

Originally historians thought that castles were mainly military buildings, and that changes in the way castles were designed and built were as a result of an 'arms race' between new methods of attacking castles, and defences to nullify those new measures.

More recently, some historians, called revisionists, have seen castles as symbols of the power of the castle owner, with this symbolism, domestic comfort, and administrative convenience the main reasons for changes in castle design.

Figure 1

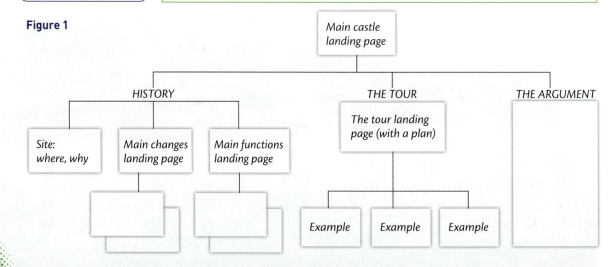

Figure 2

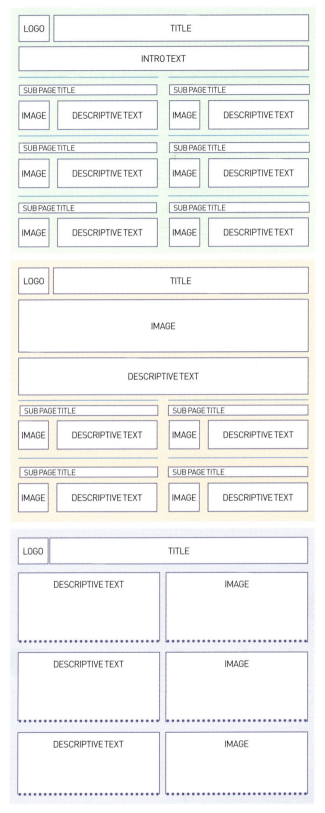

The functions of the castle

The best way to do this task, and to prepare for your examination, is to relate the nominated castle to what you have learned about castles in this chapter. The place to start is with the functions of the castle – be clear about them and this will give you a good base from which to work. You looked at the different functions of a castle in Topic 7.2.

Royal or baronial: This is the first thing to be sure about. When was the castle first built, and who by? If it started life as a baronial castle, was it taken over by the Crown at any point? If it was, be clear whether this was because of its strategic importance, as a punishment or because the owner's family died out with no heirs. If it ever was a royal castle, how long did it stay one? Topic 7.3 is a good place to check if you are unsure of any of the answers to these questions.

Site: Does the castle guard something of clear strategic value, like a harbour or a bridge? Was it built on a major transport route? Did it protect a town or did a town grow up because there was a castle? Was it built on the highest ground available or was the site a compromise between convenience and safety?

Symbolism: What effect would the castle have had on the people who lived near it? Is there any evidence to suggest it was built with any thought as to how it looked from nearby roads and rivers? Did it replace something? Can you explain any of the changes made to the castle because they make its owner look richer and more powerful?

Administration: Is there any evidence of how the castle was used as a centre from which to run the lord's estates? Is it possible to work out what parts of the castle would be used for a court or formal meetings?

Accommodation: To what extent was it a barracks for soldiers, and to what extent was it a palace for the rich and the powerful? Were there special parts of the castle for the rich and powerful, and if so when were they built or changed? How did the castle change as a living space over hundreds of years?

Castle life: What do you know about life in the castle? Was there a great hall? If so, did it change? Did the provision of toilets change? Where were the kitchens? How big were they?

Defensive features: How would the castle have been defended? Did these defensive features change over time?

The phased plan you can find in Topic 7.3 is a key source for starting to answer most of these questions. Also, if you can, you should explain how evidence for what you say can still be found in the remains of the castle.

Source 2 A list of the servants of Joan de Valence at Goodrich Castle who were given money for new shoes at Easter 1297.

The chapel clerk,

Humphrey [of the mistress's chamber],

John of the Wardrobe,

Richard the usher,

the mistress's laundress,

Waiter the farrier [who shoed horses],

John Bendogeda,

John Cely,

Richard the Sauserer [a specialist chef],

John the Baker,

the mistress's herald,

Isaac [of the kitchen],

Richard of Stanes,

John the mistress's palfreyman [groom],

Hec the coachman,

Burgeys,

Adam the carter,

the groom of Edward Burnel,

Davy the coachman

John the carter,

a half-rate to Henry Pendyn.

Fitting the castle into its contexts

Notice the plural in the title. A castle does not have just one context – it has several.

It has **historical contexts** – the things that were happening when the castle was built and when major changes were made to it. The top half of the timeline below gives you some starting points, but some specific research about the castle at different times will probably help, too. And it does not just have one historical context, there will be one for each major change.

It also has a **developmental context** – what were the up-to-date styles and fashions in castle-building when the changes were made? Do the changes fit neatly into this pattern or not? What about some of the trends in society? Do the changes give more privacy to the most powerful? Is there evidence that the castle needed to house more people as the typical size of noble households grew?

Again, you will find that the castle factfile and the phased plan are good places to start. It is worth looking at the main events and building periods in the castle's history against the timeline. Do not expect everything to fit neatly. The timeline needs to have a lot of generalisations. Sometimes when something does not fit, the reasons may be very interesting!

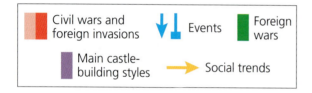

Civil wars and foreign invasions

Events

Foreign wars

Main castle-building styles

Social trends

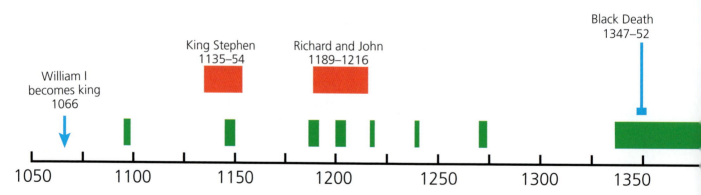

Black Death 1347–52

King Stephen 1135–54

Richard and John 1189–1216

William I becomes king 1066

1050 1100 1150 1200 1250 1300 1350

REVIEW TASKS

1   Study Source 2 (opposite) and Source 3 (on page 234). Which of these sources
    is more useful to a historian studying the domestic accommodation at Goodrich
    Castle?

The best way to answer this type of question is:
- focus on the subject, in this case *domestic accommodation*
- consider what you can learn from each source; write a paragraph with
  examples about each source
- consider possible limitations or problems with the source; again, write a
  paragraph about the limitations of each source
- make sure you have a conclusion; you have been asked a question, so answer
  it. Sometimes it can help to start with the conclusion: 'A historian would find
  Source 2 more useful because …'

There are two historical skills you should remember and use:
- **Inference:** This requires making a deduction. If you simply said 'There was a
  coachman called Hec and another called Davy', that would be comprehension.
  A deduction would be: 'There was a farrier, a groom, two carters and two
  coachmen, *so horses were an important part of the life of Joan's household, and the
  accommodation would have needed to include stables.*'
- **Distinguish between information and evidence:** This is very important (and
  making an inference usually means you are using the source as evidence not
  for information). You use a source as *evidence* when you make a statement
  about the past, and back it up by using the source. '*So horses were important*' is
  a *statement*, and the farrier, groom, two carters and two coachmen are *evidence*
  from the source to support it.

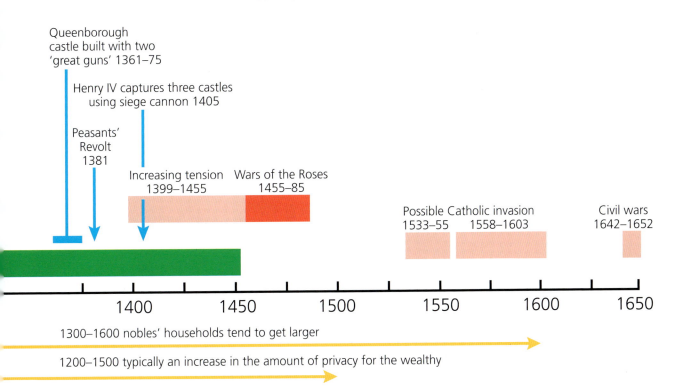

Queenborough
castle built with two
'great guns' 1361–75

Henry IV captures three castles
using siege cannon 1405

Peasants'
Revolt
1381

Increasing tension   Wars of the Roses
1399–1455   1455–85

Possible Catholic invasion   Civil wars
1533–55   1558–1603   1642–1652

1400   1450   1500   1550   1600   1650

1300–1600 nobles' households tend to get larger

1200–1500 typically an increase in the amount of privacy for the wealthy

The final exam

You know what to expect: two sources and two questions. But do not make the mistake of thinking this means you know what to do and you should just get started. You need to study the two sources closely. The examiner has picked these exact two sources for a reason – for the particular things you can learn from them. So look, read, and think!

Source 3 An aerial photograph of the remains of Goodrich Castle, near the English border with Wales. ▼

KEY TERMS

Make sure you know what these terms mean and are able to use them confidently in your writing.

- bailey
- baronial castle
- beam
- bratticing
- breach (in a wall)
- buttery
- chronicle
- conditional respite
- corbel
- curtain wall
- dais
- embrasure
- final refuge
- flanking fire
- garderobe
- garderobe tower
- great hall
- joist
- machicolations
- merlon
- motte
- oilet
- phased plan
- royal castle
- shell keep
- solar
- storm a castle
- undermining

Source 4 Extracts from the accounts of Joan de Valence on 18 November 1296, the day she arrived at Goodrich Castle for a long stay.

Item 10 shillings 6 pence in procuring 3 carts to transport the mistress's property by road.

Item 6 pence for a horse to carry the mistress's money by road.

Item 2 shillings, 5 pence for 8 horses and 4 carters, loaned by the abbot of Gloucester and the abbot of Nutley for transporting the mistress's property by road, staying a night across the river Wye, unable to get across.

Item 16 pence to John the baker for 8 days travelling from Exning to Goodrich Castle to bake bread there before the mistress's arrival, and 16 pence to Isaac [of the kitchen] travelling to Goodrich Castle to prepare the larder there.

Source 3 will not have been the only photograph the examiner had to choose from – so what is there in this one you should notice? What exactly can you see?

- the barbican
- how large the gatehouse is
- the curtain walls with flanking towers
- the GARDEROBE TOWER
- the keep – which shows up as a different colour stone
- the inner courtyard.

Question 1 asks you about the *keep*, so that will be part of it. Question 2 focuses you on *rebuilding*, so what does the photograph tell you about that?

It is the same with Source 4. Do not just think about what you learn with reading – that they used candles, ate fish, the coachman's name was Hamo. What can you *infer* – Joan took a lot of possessions with her (five carts and a horse for the money); her arrival was carefully planned (sending ahead the baker and Isaac of the kitchen). The examiner thinks you should be able to use some of this in your answer to Question 2 – so do not disappoint them!

ASSESSMENT FOCUS

How the study of the historic environment will be assessed

The historic environment study on castles will be examined in Paper 3, along with the British depth study on the Reformation. The historic environment part is worth 20 marks – 10 per cent of your total GCSE. You should spend about 30 minutes on this part of the paper. Each year the exam is on a different site – and you will have studied it in depth.

Question 1 will test the first two assessment objectives:
- AO1: knowledge and understanding
- AO2: explanation and analysis.

Question 2 will test AO1 and AO2, but it will also test:
- AO3: analyse, evaluate and make use of sources from the time.

Above all, the paper is assessing your ability to think and work like a historian. In the introduction, you looked at how historians work (page 4). There we set out some steps that historians take:
1. focus
2. ask questions
3. select
4. organise
5. fine tune.

The exam questions have already chosen a focus (stage 1) and they have asked questions (stage 2). What the examiner wants from you is stages 3, 4 and 5.

Question 1

Question 1 will ask you to explain an important aspect of the history of the castle you have studied. This will cover a period in the history of the castle but not its whole history. For example:

> **Explain why Conwy Castle fell into disrepair in the period 1400–1600. (10 marks)**

 Bronze (up to 25% of the marks): You describe a few events relating to the castle (e.g. no money was spent on the castle after 1400 and in 1406 there were only 12 archers).

 Silver (up to 60% of the marks): You explain how the castle fell into disrepair (e.g. after 1400 no money was spent on the castle; by the early 1500s it was used for storage but mostly unmanned; local people started to steal the stone).

 Gold (up to 100% of the marks): You build on the Silver level to make it really clear why the castle fell into disrepair (e.g. Wales was no longer a war zone). This will probably involve several reasons.

Even a Gold answer can be improved by ensuring you have:
- a clear conclusion that rounds off your argument
- used a range of examples as supporting evidence and included relevant and detailed knowledge in your supporting examples
- a balanced answer which shows you understand that there might be more than one view about the question or explains how the different factors are connected.

Aim of the question
The key word here is 'why'. Examiners are looking for an explanation of why the castle fell into disrepair. It would be easy to miss this point and simply describe what happened to the castle.

Advice

Select: Focus on the reasons why the castle fell into disrepair. Select at least two causes.

Organise: The important thing is to organise your knowledge in a relevant way to answer the question. Have a clear sense of what you are trying to say. In this question a good way to organise your answer might be:

> There were several reasons why Conwy Castle fell into disrepair in this period.
> First of all ...
> Another reason why Conwy declined was ...

Fine tune: Do all the usual checking but make sure you say which of your reasons you think is more important.

Example answer

Comments
There is no need to improve this answer – it is a Gold medal response. It has a clear opening and then sticks to the line that the opening suggests it will follow. The final sentence is not necessary but it is a nice ending to the answer. There is a good analysis of two separate reasons. In each case the answer explains how the factor sent Conwy into decline.

> By 1400, English rulers believed that their control of Wales was relatively secure. For most of that time England was torn by the Wars of the Roses and the battles in this war were not fought in Wales.
>
> Another reason why Conwy declined was that English rulers no longer needed a military outpost there. By the 1520s, Conwy was being used again but not really as a military building. Henry VIII did carry out repair work on the castle but not on a big scale. The castle was used as a prison and as a place for storing goods and as a place where official visitors could stay. Henry was fighting wars in Ireland, and Conwy was a useful staging post for armies and officials on their way to Ireland but it did not have an important military role.
>
> So the combination of location and changing political situation meant that English rulers did not need or want to spend money on Conwy Castle in the period 1400–1600. This view is supported by the fact that when the English Civil War began in the 1640s and troops from Ireland were brought into England through North Wales Conwy was repaired and played an important military role again.

Practice

We gave this answer a Gold medal. You can use the same idea to assess your own answers on your nominated castle. Afterwards, read over your answer and see which medal you might award yourself.

Question 2

Question 2 is a challenging question that requires effective use of knowledge and an understanding of how historians use sources. There will always be two sources. One will usually be a document and the other a visual source such as a map, a photograph or a plan. For example:

> ***Study Sources A and B. Which of these sources is more useful to a historian studying the first hundred years of Conwy Castle (from the 1280s to the 1380s)? (10 marks)***

 Bronze (up to 25% of the marks): You summarise the sources or pick out a few details from the sources.

 Silver (up to 60% of the marks): You make an inference to explain how the content of each source is useful about the history of the castle (e.g. A is useful as it shows the size and scale of Conwy Castle).

 Gold (up to 100% of the marks): You make an inference to explain how the content of each source is useful about the history of the castle and the role of the castle at particular times (e.g. A is useful as it shows the size and scale of Conwy Castle. The fact that it was so big tells us ...).

Source A An aerial photograph of the remains of Conwy Castle in North Wales.

Source B Extracts from accounts showing spending on Conwy Castle in the period 1283–1330.

March 1283 to November 1284 £5819

December 1284 to December 1292 £7870

February 1296 to February 1301 £500

December 1304 to December 1330 £88

Question 2 specialist advice

This question asks you to compare two sources and explain whether you think one source is more useful than the other. There are a few essential points to bear in mind.

All sources are useful for investigating some aspect of the past. Do not try to argue that one source is useful and the other one is *not*.

Examiners want you to show how each source is useful. They are not interested in how it is not useful. You will get no credit for this. Candidates often argue that a source is biased so it is not useful. But actually if a source is biased then that makes it useful – it tells us about the author of the source. It is a good idea to think 'How is it useful ...?' rather than 'How useful is it ...?'

Comparing the sources is quite difficult so examiners will give you a bit of leeway. It is acceptable to explain how each source is useful about different things. You will not be penalised if you do not argue that one is more useful.

Even a Gold medal answer can be improved by ensuring you have:
● a valid conclusion that rounds off your argument
● evaluated several sources in your answer
● clearly explained why historians hold particular views.

Advice

Before you start, make sure you are clear about what the sources say (comprehension and inference).

Select: You need to select facts, events and developments that support or challenge the views in the sources. So select items from this part of your knowledge wardrobe.

Organise: A good way to start this question is to show you understand what the sources are saying at face value and then go on to explain why historians find this information useful.

Fine tune: Do all the usual checks, but above all make sure that you have made inferences, and that your inferences are supported.

Example answer

> Both sources can be useful to historians studying Conwy Castle in this period. Source A is extremely useful because it can tell us many things about why Conwy Castle was built and why it was built in that particular place. We can see from the photograph that Conwy was built at the mouth of the River Conwy. This was so that the castle could be supplied effectively, even if it was under attack from the land. It was also so that the castle could control trade going up and down the river.

Comments

This answer is very good – a Gold medal again! It would probably get 10 marks. For each source comprehension and inference work together well and relate to the question. As well as pointing out how the source is useful about the castle, the candidate has used knowledge effectively to show how the castle was important in the events of the time.

Probably the only thing you could criticise about this answer is that it is too long. It is probably worth about 17 out of 10! This is not as good as it sounds. When you over-answer, you usually run short of time for other questions.

When Edward I chose this site he went against the usual policy of putting castles on high ground so that the Castle could control the river. Source A is also useful in showing how determined Edward I was to conquer Wales and hold on to it. The massive fortifications and towers we can see were designed to intimidate and oppress the Welsh as well as to provide English forces with a secure base. Source A has its limitations of course. As it is a modern photograph it shows the road layout and the railway bridge next to the castle. This modern development obscures features and details which might have been visible in earlier maps or plans. And obviously the castle is now a ruin and so the photograph cannot show us what it was like in the period 1280–1380 when it was a thriving and important site with many troops and officials. On the other hand Source A does show us the basic layout of the castle and so we know that this is what it looked like then and now.

Source B is also useful to historians. Obviously it shows how much was spent on the castle at different times. From this we can tell that the castle must have been important to Edward I. The first two figures show the main cost of the castle when it was being built. This would be hundreds of millions of pounds today. This shows how serious Edward I was about conquering Wales and how important Conwy was in his plans to do that. The other figures are also useful. The £500 shows us what the running costs were for the castle once it had been built. This was actually relatively cheap because castles this size could cost a lot more. The figures from 1304 to 1330 suggest that the castle was not really being used much and that there were few soldiers or servants running it. We know that in the 1300s the conquest of Wales was fairly successful and this source is useful evidence to support that view. As with Source A, the source does have its limitations. The most obvious one is that it covers a limited time period. Also we need to use other sources such as chronicles to check some of the points we make, such as Wales being more peaceful in the early 1300s.

On balance I think that Source A is the more useful source because it provides evidence that does not need to be checked and it covers a longer time span than Source B. Source B is very useful but for different purposes and overall Source A is better.

Practice

Once again we gave this answer a Gold medal. You can use the same idea to assess your own answers on your nominated castle. Afterwards, read over your answer and see which medal you might award yourself.

Keys to success

As long as you know the content and have learned how to think, this exam should not be too scary. The keys to success are:

1   Read the question carefully. This may sound obvious, but there is a skill to it. Sometimes students answer the question they *wish* had been asked rather than the one that has *actually* been asked. So identify the skill focus (what they are asking you to do). Do they want you to write a description, an explanation or a comparison? Identify the content focus (what it is about) and select from your knowledge accordingly.

2   Note the marks available. That helps you work out how much time to spend on answering each question. Time is precious – if you spend too long on low-mark questions you will run out of time for the high-mark ones.

3   Plan your answer before you start writing. For essays this is particularly important. The golden rule is: know what you are going to say, then say it clearly and logically.

4   Aim for quality not quantity: in the time limits of an exam you will not be able to write down everything you know and can think of – even if it is relevant. The marker would much rather read a short answer that really tackles the question than page after page of material that is not relevant.

5   Check your work. You will never have time in an exam to rewrite an answer but try to leave some time at the end to check for obvious spelling mistakes, missing words or other writing errors that might cost you marks.

Glossary

abdicated gave up the throne or other position of power

absenteeism failing or refusing to go to church services on Sunday

Act of Supremacy law passed by Henry VIII making himself head of the church in England in 1534

allegory a story designed to make a point through representations (e.g. representing ordinary people as a flock of sheep or an enemy as a demon)

altar the table in a church where the priest says most of the service

anarchy the breakdown of law and order

Anglo-Saxon Chronicle a history of Anglo-Saxon England written by a series of authors (probably monks) from the mid-ninth century to 1154

annates a type of tax paid by churches to the pope, usually when a bishop was ordained

annul to end a marriage by saying that it had never been legal in the first place; people talk about Henry VIII seeking a divorce, but actually he sought an annulment – the concept of divorce did not exist in Tudor times

anticlericalism hostility towards priests and other members of the Church

archbishop a senior churchman, who answered only to a cardinal or the pope

artillery heavy missile weapons; it usually refers to cannon but could include catapults

atheling a prince of the royal family in Anglo-Saxon England

authority the right to command or rule

bailey an area of open ground in a Norman castle, usually surrounded by a defensive wall

Bank of England a bank set up in 1694 to take care of the finances of the country and to help governments pay for wars or other important activities

barbican a fortified gatehouse

baronial castle a castle belonging to a baron rather than the monarch (barons usually had to get permission to build or develop their own castles)

baron a nobleman from the medieval period; barons usually owned land from the monarch and in return served in government or provided troops in times of war

Bayeux Tapestry a visual representation of the events of 1066, probably commissioned by Odo, the bishop of Bayeux

beam a strong strip of wood designed to hold up floors or other parts of buildings

Bill of Rights A law passed after the Glorious Revolution in 1688, which said that Catholics could not inherit the British throne

bishop a senior churchman, usually in charge of a cathedral

bishopric the area under the control of a bishop (also known as a diocese)

borough a village or a hamlet, depending on what it had been in medieval times

bratticing a protective wooden extension built out from the top of a castle wall

breach a hole made in a defensive wall, usually by artillery

buttery a food store

canon a type of priest

celibacy being unmarried and not having relations with the opposite sex

chalice the ornamental cup that held wine in the mass, representing the blood of Christ

chancellor a senior position in government, usually chief minister or, in later periods, the minister in charge of finance

chantry religious services for a particular cause, usually to remember someone who had died and often paid for by the will of the dead person; the term chantry is sometimes used to describe chantry chapels

charter a document issued by a monarch, usually giving authority to an individual (such as a royal official) or group to act in a certain way or collect a tax

chivalry a set of rules and code of behaviour that knights were supposed to follow, including mercy to defeated enemies and respect for women

Christendom countries where the main faith was Christianity, mostly in western Europe

chronicle a history, usually of royal families or the history of countries; chronicles could be completed by more than one author

chronicler a person who writes a chronicle, usually a monk

churchmen officials of the church, including the pope, cardinals, archbishops, bishops, priests, curates, monks and many others

clergy any officials of the church (priests, monks, etc.)

conditional respite an agreement between forces attacking and defending a castle that the castle would be surrendered after a certain period of time if the defenders were not helped by other forces

conscription compulsory service in armed forces or related work

constituencies areas represented by MPs in parliament

constitution the laws that decide how a country is governed

convocation a gathering, usually of important people in the Church

convoy a group of ships or land vehicles gathered together for protection

corbel a bracket on a building, usually supporting a floor above

crusade a religious war

curates assistants to the parish priests

curtain wall the outer defensive wall in a castle

dais a raised platform

Danegeld money paid by Anglo-Saxon rulers to stop attacks by Viking forces

Danelaw an area in eastern England with a substantial population of Danes and other Vikings

denounce publicly condemn

deposed removed from power

devolution the process of passing power to others

dispensation exemption from a requirement, or permission to do something

dissolution abolishing or closing something down

doctrine a set of beliefs

Domesday Book a collection of information about landholding in England, created in 1086

Domesday survey the survey that created the information in the *Domesday Book*

earl a senior member of the nobility

earldom land ruled by an earl

embrasure the space between battlements on a castle (for firing at attackers)

enclosures fencing off fields for private animal farming that were once available for public use

Eucharist a holy ritual in which bread and wine is believed to be transformed into the body and blood of Christ

evangelical a radical believer who wanted to spread their faith

excommunicate ban from the Church

exile being forced to live outside your own country against your will

feudalism a system of land ownership and duties in medieval times (not a term used at the time)

final refuge the most secure part of a castle

flanking fire attacking an opponent from the side

friar a monk, usually belonging to one of four orders (Carmelite, Dominican, Franciscan or Augustinian), who often travelled and preached rather than being based in a monastery

fyrd the militia force of Anglo-Saxon England – part-time fighters who were called up when needed

garderobe the toilet in a castle

garderobe tower the tower containing the garderobe

gentry the lesser nobles, lower in rank than barons, earls or dukes – mostly knights

Glorious Revolution the name given to the overthrow of King James II in 1688, when William III and Mary II were invited to take the throne of England

great hall the main hall of a castle, usually the main space for eating and entertaining

Harrying of the North a series of attacks on northern England by William the Conqueror in 1069–70

Heaven and Hell belief about the afterlife in Catholic England

heresy contradicting the teachings of the Church

host the bread that represents the body of Christ in the mass

House of Commons initially described the lesser nobles and other members of parliament, but by the twentieth century the term was also used for the building where they met

House of Lords initially described the greater nobles and senior churchmen, but by the twentieth century the term was also used for the building where they met

housecarl professional soldiers of Anglo-Saxon rulers

humanism an intellectual movement that took a scientific approach to the Bible and other issues

hundred a division of land in Anglo-Saxon England, usually with enough people and resources to provide the king with 100 troops

iconoclasm the practice of challenging accepted beliefs

idolatry worshipping an image or a statue

indulgences payments collected by the Catholic Church in return for the promise of spending less time in purgatory after death

infer to reach a judgement about an issue from a historical document or image

interdict a ban

joist a wooden beam, usually supporting a floor

justice system the elements of the legal system including royal or government officials, judges, courts

justification by faith alone the idea that people could only reach Heaven through faith and that giving money to the Church or going on pilgrimages made no difference

keep the major fortification inside most castles

killing grounds areas around or in castles designed to trap attackers

knight an important landowner, usually given lands by a more senior noble (e.g. an earl) and who then owed the earl a certain number of days of military service per year

laity ordinary members of society, not officials of the Church

laymen members of the laity

legislation laws

legitimate legal (although sometimes the term was used to mean reasonable)

lesser nobles noblemen who were below barons in rank and importance, usually knights

Lollards a religious group which argued that priests and the Church were less important than reading the Bible

looting stealing food or property, often in times of war

Lutheran inspired by the teachings of the Protestant reformer Martin Luther

machicolation an opening in the floor of a castle which allowed defenders to drop stones or liquids or other missiles on attackers

Magna Carta a charter issued in 1215 by King John under pressure from rebel barons, which granted some important rights and agreed to other changes to the power structure in England

mason a stone-worker

mass the main ceremony of the Catholic Church

member of parliament someone chosen to represent an area (constituency) and help make laws

merlon the solid section of a battlement in a castle

middle classes professional people in jobs such as finance, insurance and administration, as well as shopkeepers and those in practical professions such as architects and engineers

migrants people who move to work and sometimes settle in a different country or area

minster an important church or cathedral (e.g. York Minster)

monasteries communities of religious men (or women) who live away from the world and combine work and prayer in their lives

monk a male member of a religious order (e.g. Cistercians); monks usually lived in a monastery

motte a large man-made mound used as the foundation of a castle, with a tower usually placed on top

National Debt the amount of money owed by the government; the National Debt is usually larger in times of war

nobles important members of society, usually landowners

nun a female member of a religious order (e.g. Carmelites); nuns usually lived in a convent or abbey

oilet a specially shaped opening in a castle wall to allow defenders to fire crossbows

ordination the act of making a man a priest (usually in a ceremony)

papacy the office of the pope, the head of the Catholic Church

parliament a group of people commanded by the monarch to advise them; parliament developed from the medieval period to become the main power in Britain in the nineteenth century

patronage giving money, land, jobs or other favours in return for loyal service or support

persecute to attack people (through the law or actual violence), usually on the basis of race or nationality or religion

phased plan a map or diagram that shows the different stages of building and rebuilding of a castle or other structure

pilgrimage a journey to a site of religious importance

pious holy or having deep faith

pluralism holding Church positions in more than one parish

Political Nation the people who have some say in how the country is run; the Political Nation changes over time

pope the head of the Roman Catholic Church, based in Rome, Italy

praemunire a law passed by Henry VIII which said that the pope had no authority in England

prior a senior monk in a monastery

Privy Council a group of high-ranking officials or nobles who advise the monarch

propaganda a particular set of ideas or information that is spread for a political purpose; propaganda can come in many different forms

Protestant the term given to Christians in Europe who protested against some aspects of the Catholic Church in the fifteenth century

Provisions of Oxford an agreement made in 1285 which set out the roles and rights of monarchs and their subjects; often described as England's first constitution

purgatory a place where the souls of the dead suffered for their sins before they were allowed to go to Heaven

Puritans radical Christians who believed in simple church services and studying the Bible rather than following the Catholic Church, priests or bishops

radicals political groups in the nineteenth century which campaigned for political reform

recusancy refusing to attend Church of England services

Reformation the term used to describe Henry VIII's break from the Roman Catholic Church to create the Church of England

relics remains that were said to be holy; relics were often claimed to be the bones of a saint or part of a holy object

Renaissance a movement in fifteenth- and sixteenth-century Europe that emphasised the importance of learning and scientific approaches as well as faith

retainers the followers of an important noble; in many cases retainers functioned as a private army

rood screen a wooden screen in a church, which kept the ordinary people away from the priest and the altar

royal castle a castle owned by the monarch

saboteurs spies or agents who attempt to undermine a war effort by actions such as damaging property or machinery or spreading false rumours

sacrament a religious ceremony, particularly in the Catholic Church (e.g. Holy Communion, baptism)

secular non-religious

serf a low-ranking member of society

shell keep a type of castle, essentially a stone tower on top of a motte

sheriff a key royal official, responsible for justice, taxes and many other roles within a local area

shire an area under the control of an earl in Anglo-Saxon England

solar a lord's private room in a castle

spiritual religious

storm (a castle) to attack a castle

suffrage the right to vote

taxes money or goods paid by the population to a monarch or government

tenant farmer a farmer who does not own the land he farms but rents it from a landlord

thegn a noble in Anglo-Saxon society

theologians scholars who study religion

tithes a tax of one-tenth of a person's income, which went to the Church

Tory a political party that emerged in the eighteenth and nineteenth centuries

transubstantiation the Catholic belief that the bread and wine in the mass actually become the body and blood of Christ

treason to speak or take action against the ruler of a country

treaty a document agreed between two groups (usually countries) to end a conflict

trebuchet a type of artillery used against castles

undermining tunnelling underneath the walls of a castle to make them collapse

vestments robes worn by a priest

veto to block a proposal or action

Vikings people from northern Europe who raided and settled in England from the eighth to the eleventh centuries

villein a low-ranking member of medieval society

visitations inspections made by officials of Thomas Cromwell to monasteries in the 1530s

Wessex a southern Anglo-Saxon kingdom

Whig a political party that emerged in the seventeenth century

Witan the council of senior nobles in Anglo-Saxon England

writ an instruction sent by the monarch to one of his officials, usually a sheriff

Index

Acknowledgements

The Publishers would like to thank the following for permission to reproduce copyright material.

Photo credits
p.4 Illustration by David Parkins for *The Economist*; **p.7** © Active Museum/Alamy Stock Photo; **p.12** © Tim W; **p.13** © 2004 TopFoto; **p.14** *t* © The Fitzwilliam Museum, Cambridge, *b* © The British Library Board; **p.16** Wikimedia; **p.17** Mary Evans Picture Library; **p.21** © World History Archive/TopFoto; **p.22** © Interfoto/Alamy Stock Photo; **p.25** © Historic England Archive; **p.27** *t* © Fine Art Images/HIP/TopFoto, *b* © Skyscan.co.uk; **p.32** © The British Library Board; **p.35** © The British Library Board; **p.38** © The British Library Board; **p.40** *l* © The British Library Board, *r* © travelibUK/Alamy Stock Photo; **p.41** © Adrian Bradbury www.bfdc.co.uk; **p.44** © 1 Collection/Alamy Stock Photo; **p.45** © The British Library Board; p.52 © DEA Picture Library; **p.53** © Pictorial Press Ltd/Alamy Stock Photo; **p.54** *l* © Granger, NYC./Alamy Stock Photo, *r* Active Museum/Alamy Stock Photo; **p.56** © Hulton Archive/Stringer; **p.57** *tl* © Painting/Alamy Stock Photo, *tr* © Archivart/Alamy Stock Photo, *b* © Active Museum/Alamy Stock Photo; **p.60** © The British Library Board; **p.64** © Historic Royal Palaces; **p.65** © Universal History Archive/Contributor/Getty Images; **p.67** © Hulton Archive/Handout; **p.68** © The British Library Board; **p.70** © The British Library Board; **p.71** © The British Library Board; **p.72** *l, r* © The British Library Board; **p.73** © Wikimedia/Edmund Goldsmid; **p.75** © The British Library Board; **p.76** © The British Library Board; **p.79** © Print Collector/Getty Images; **p.80** © The British Library Board; **p.82** Image courtesy of the Bank of England Archive M6/48; **p.83** © Granger, NYC./Alamy Stock Photo; **p.88** © Historic England Archive; **p.89** © Heritage Images/Getty Images; **p.90** *t* Wikimedia, *b* Wikimedia/John Leather; **p.92** *t The Reformers' Attack on the Old Rotten Tree, or the Foul Nests of the Cormorants in Danger*, satirical cartoon, pub. by E. King, c.1831/British Library, London, UK/© British Library Board. All Rights Reserved/Bridgeman Images, *b* © The British Library Board; **p.94** Royal Collection Trust/© Her Majesty Queen Elizabeth II 2016; **p.95** *t,b* © World History Archive/Alamy Stock Photo; **p.97** *t* © The Conservative Party Archive/Getty Images, *b* Image Courtesy of The Advertising Archives; **p.98** © The British Library Board; **p.99** © Museum of London/Heritage-Images; **p.100** Front cover of 'Votes for Women', 26th November 1915 (litho) (b/w photo), English School, (20th century)/© Museum of London, UK/Bridgeman Images; **p.103** *t* © The National Army Museum/Mary Evans Picture Library, *b* © Wikimedia/National Archives; **p.105** © Robert Opie Collection; **p.107** © George W. Hales/Stringer/Getty Images; **p. 108** *l* © The Scout Association/ Mary Evans Picture Library, *m* © The National Archives/ Getty Images, *r* © World History Archive/Alamy Stock Photo; **p.109** Reproduced by permission of The Labour Party; **p.112** The Conservative Party Archive/Getty Images; **p.113** © Peter Brookes/News UK; **p.114** © Imagestate Media Partners Limited – Impact Photos/Alamy Stock Photo; **p.115** © Raymond Jackson/Associated Newspapers Ltd/Solo Syndication; **p.116** © Greenpeace/David Sims; **p.117** © Bill McArthur; **p.127** © Leemage/Getty Images; **p.130** © Pictorial Press Ltd/Alamy Stock Photo; **p.131** *l* © Tim Gainey/Alamy Stock Photo, *r* © Robin Weaver/Alamy Stock Photo; **p.132** © geogphotos/Alamy Stock Photo; **p.137** © akg-images; **p.139** © The British Library Board; **p.143** Henry VIII (1491-1547), Cleve, Joos van (c.1485-1541)/Burghley House Collection, Lincolnshire, UK/ Bridgeman Images; **p.144** © UniversalImagesGroup/Getty Images; **p.147** © The Art Archive/Alamy Stock Photo; **p.155** © The British Library Board; **p.156** © Lebrecht Music and Arts Photo Library/Alamy Stock Photo; **p. 158** *t* © CBW/Alamy Stock Photo, *b* Kristine Aleksina/123RF; p.163 Badge of the Five Wounds of Christ (embroidered textile), English School, (16th century)/His Grace The Duke of Norfolk, Arundel Castle/Bridgeman Images; **p.164** © Hulton Archive/Stringer/Getty Images; **p.166** *The Wonderful Story of Britain: King Henry and the Monasteries*, Jackson, Peter (1922-2003)/Private Collection/© Look and Learn/Bridgeman Images; **p.168** © UniversalImagesGroup/ Getty Images; **p.170** © Culture Club/Getty Images; **p.171** © Pictorial Press Ltd/Alamy Stock Photo; **p.172** King Edward VI (1537-53) and the Pope, c.1570 (oil on panel), English School, (16th century)/National Portrait Gallery, London, UK/Bridgeman Images; **p.174** *t* © Print Collector/ Getty Images, *b* © Culture Club/Getty Images; **p.175** *l, r* © Holmes Garden Photos/Alamy Stock Photo; **p.179** Folger STC 1581 Bd.w. STC 1585 Copy 2 Used by permission of the Folger Shakespeare Library under a Creative Commons Attribution-ShareAlike 4.0 International License; **p.180** *The Coronation of King Edward the Sixth, Popery banished true religion restored, The Duke of Somerset Lord Protector beheaded* (litho) (b/w photo), English School, (16th century)/Private Collection/Bridgeman Images; **p.181** *t* Anti-catholic allegory depicting Stephen Gardiner, Bishop of Winchester, 1556 (tempera on panel), English School, (16th century)/ Private Collection/Photo © Christie's Images/Bridgeman Images, *b* © Angelo Hornak/Alamy Stock Photo; **p.183** © Fine Art Images/Heritage Images/Getty Images; **p.189** © Adrian Sherratt/Alamy Stock Photo; p.190 © The British Library Board; **p.191** *l* © Paul Shuter, *r* © Historic England Archive; **p.192** © Paul Shuter; p.193 *l* © Paul Shuter, *r* ©